PLAYS ON THE PASSIONS

PLAYS ON THE PASSIONS

(1798 edition)

Joanna Baillie

edited by *Peter Duthie*

broadview literary texts

Canadian Cataloguing in Publication Data

Baillie, Joanna, 1762-1851
    Plays on the Passions
(Broadview literary texts)
Also known as A Series of plays

ISBN 1-55111-185-3
I. Duthie, Peter, 1950- .   II. Title.   III. Title: Series of plays.   IV. Series.
PR4056.P52 2000 822'.7 C00-932507-7

Broadview Press Ltd., is an independent, international publishing house, incorporated in 1985.

North America:
P.O. Box 1243, Peterborough, Ontario, Canada K9J 7H5
3576 California Road, Orchard Park, NY 14127
TEL: (705) 743-8990; FAX: (705) 743-8353;
E-MAIL: customerservice@broadviewpress.com

United Kingdom:
Turpin Distribution Services Ltd.,
Blackhorse Rd., Letchworth, Hertfordshire SG6 1HN
TEL: (1462) 672555; FAX (1462) 480947; E-MAIL: turpin@rsc.org

Australia:
St. Clair Press, P.O. Box 287, Rozelle, NSW 2039
TEL: (02) 818-1942; FAX: (02) 418-1923

www.broadviewpress.com

Broadview Press gratefully acknowledges the financial support of the Book Publishing Industry Development Program, Ministry of Canadian Heritage, Government of Canada.

Broadview Press is grateful to Professor Eugene Benson for advice on editorial matters for the Broadview Literary Texts series and to Professor L. W. Conolly for editorial advice on this volume.

Text design and composition by George Kirkpatrick

PRINTED IN CANADA

Portrait of Joanna Baillie by John James Masquerier. Courtesy of the
Hunterian Art Gallery, University of Glasgow.

Contents

Appendix E: Contemporary Reviews

Acknowledgements

Boswell recollected Johnson saying that a "man will turn over half a library to make one book" (*Life of Johnson* 613). I admit I have not come close to exhausting the contents of any library during this project. However, those who graciously and generously offer their sometimes unsolicited help with the turning and shuffling and searching of such a task prove themselves invaluable.

A warm thank you to the following librarians and resource people from afar who received telephone calls, faxes, and e-mails from a stranger yet enthusiastically invested their time and energy in the project as if it were their own. Thank you to Alice Schreyer, Curator of Special Collections, The University of Chicago Library; Denise Pulford at the Hunterian Art Gallery, Glasgow, Scotland; Ms. Gayle Barkley, Library Assistant in the Manuscript department at the Huntington and Olga Tsapina, Curator of American Historical Manuscripts; Dr. Iain G. Brown, Assistant Keeper, Manuscripts Division, National Library of Scotland; Matthew Derrick at The Royal College of Surgeons of England; Dr. Barry A. Meyers-Rice, University of California (Davis) [barry@carnivorousplants.org]; Rob Gibson at the Scottish Bureau; and the many voices I spoke with at the Yale Drama Library.

I would especially like to thank the following for permission to quote passages in the appendices found within: the Clarendon Press of Oxford University for John Locke's *An Essay Concerning Human Understanding* (Appendix A.1), edited by Peter H. Nidditch; Dolphin Books of Doubleday & Co. for David Hume's *Enquiry concerning Human Understanding* (Appendix A.2); Oxford University Press for Edmund Burke's *A Philosophical Enquiry into the Origin of our Ideas of the Sublime and Beautiful* (Appendix A.3), edited by Adam Phillips; Liberty Fund for Adam Smith's *The Theory of Moral Sentiments* (Appendix A.4), edited by D.D. Raphael and A.L. Macfie; the Henry E. Huntington Library and Art Gallery for the Larpent text of the prologue and epilogue to *De Monfort* (Appendix C); and Methuen

& Co. for William Wordsworth's "Preface" to *Lyrical Ballads* (Appendix D.1 and 2).

Closer to home, thank you to all the librarians at the University of Calgary Library and the University of Alberta Library.

A special thanks to Dr. Pamela MacCallum, Dr. Anne McWhir, Dr. David Oakleaf, and Dr. Vivienne Rundle at the University of Calgary who, over the last three years, have provided indispensable intellectual support. Thank you to my colleagues at Mount Royal College – to Dr. Jerré Paquette and Dr. Kenneth Robson for their continued moral support and especially to Dr. Jill Andrews, Bill Bunn, and Dr. Diana Patterson for the many animated conversations in the hallway. Thank you to my friends Dr. Graham Hunter and Sheila Warren for sharing their medical and digital imaging expertise respectively. And thank you to Dr. Judith Bailey Slagle, for reading this manuscript and sharing some new information from her current research on Baillie.

Throughout the years I have been extremely fortunate to count Dr. Stephen Rowan of Seattle University as one of my closest friends. Many thanks are due to him. His good spirited encouragement has been invaluable; his joy of learning and passion for teaching infectious.

And to Dr. Lorne Macdonald, without whom this project would not have been realized, my deepest thanks. His quiet encouragement and acute academic insight have been my mainstay while studying at the University of Calgary.

Finally, to my dear wife, Beth, and my wonderful children, Allison and Christopher – thank you for accompanying me on this long walk through the eighteenth century. Without you it would have been a lonely one.

This book is dedicated with love to my mother and father, Joyce and Fred Duthie.

Or, if to touch such chord be thine,
Restore the ancient tragic line,
And emulate the notes that rung
From the wild harp, which silent hung
By silver Avon's holy shore,
Till twice an hundred years rolled o'er,
When she, the bold Enchantress, came,
With fearless hand and heart on flame!
From the pale willow snatched the treasure,
And swept it with a kindred measure,
Till Avon's swans, while rung the grove
With Montfort's hate and Basil's love,
Awakening at the inspired strain,
Deemed their own Shakspeare lived again.

Sir Walter Scott, *Marmion*, Introduction Canto 3

Joanna Baillie's life in Hampstead

Of Joanna Baillie's remarkably long life of eighty-nine years
(1762-1851), nearly sixty were spent a carriage ride from the
exploding metropolis of London, nearly thirty of them in
Hampstead. One of the many close friends and literary colleagues who enriched Baillie's life, novelist Maria Edgeworth
(1767-1849), affords us a rare and invaluable insight into
Hampstead in a letter (Edgeworth, *Letters* 112-16) she wrote to
her mother from Joanna and Agnes Baillie's home, near Red
Lion Hill,[1] on October 13, 1818.

---

1 By reading through fifty years of Camden tax records in London, Dr. Judith Bailey
Slagle has recently corrected much of the misinformation about Joanna Baillie's
whereabouts over her lifetime. From 1784 to 1791, Baillie, with her mother
Dorothea, and sister, Agnes, kept house in London for her brother, Matthew, at
Great Windmill Street. And from 1791 to 1798, after Matthew's marriage to Sophia
Denman, the Baillie women took up various residences in the country (Sunbury,
Hythe, and Maldon) until settling in Colchester. It was in 1798 that they moved to
Hampstead, first living near Red Lion Hill. In a Camden Local Studies letter dated

For 6 or 7 miles as we approached Hampstead the whole
country seemed to be what you might call a *citizens paradise* – not a *fools* paradise though a fastidious man of taste
or an intolerant philosopher might think them synony-
mous terms. No here are means of *comfort* and enjoyment
more substantial than ever were provided in any fools paradise. Then such *odd* prettinesses – Such a variety of little
snuggeries and such green trellices and bowers and
vinecovered fronts of houses that look as if they had been
built and painted in exact imitation of the cottages in the
front and side scenes of Drury-lane – the vines spreading
over squares like a paper-hangers vine paper – And all the
houses so slight – as if each proprietor had said to himself
"Now I'll run me up a box in the *country* and be rural and
happy!"

Carriages of all sorts running and rolling past – Lan-
daus – gigs – garden carts – ass carts – ass carriages – low
wheeled – very pretty – numbers of riding parties –
children especially on asses and ponies looking so happy!
– schoolboys rising in their little stirrups and lending their
little souls to the delight of the sunshine holiday. At one
house as we passed we saw a groupe a line of white robed
ladies mother aunts and sisters I am sure who on Hampstead Heath had just come out of their house without hat
or bonnet to see the first mounting and performance on
horseback of an urchin of 7 year old who was on horseback I suppose for the first time – he was in a blue jacket
and trowzers *the moral*[1] of Pakenham – on a little long
tailed poney – first walking then trotting manfully backwards and forwards to the delight of mother sister and
aunt, under a row of shady trees.

In the centre of this bucolic enclave of women and children,
Edgeworth describes Joanna Baillie and her older sister, Agnes

---

March 1813, Baillie directs Margaret Holford Hodson by informing her that "our
house is the 2d on the left hand as you enter the Village near the Red Lion Inn"
(Slagle, *Collected Letters* vol. 2). From 1820 to 1851, Baillie and Agnes lived in
Bolton House at Holly Bush Hill.

1   A symbolic figure.

(1760-1861), as the "most kind and cordial warm hearted creatures" who, on Edgeworth's arrival, run down their stone walkway to greet her, thanking her profusely for coming to stay for another four days. Their home is a haven of gracious hospitality and good conversation, and an elegant simplicity graces even the breakfast table, which is attended by a "tidy maid servant."

But more impressive is the conversation, free of social pretension and brimming with "feelings and opinions." The Baillies' conversation, Edgeworth notes, was new and novel, "not old trumpery literature over and over again and reviews &c but new anecdotes of people, and circumstance worth telling apropos to every subject that is touched upon and frank free observations on character without either ill nature or fear of committing themselves." In Edgeworth's estimation, Joanna and Agnes were "quite *safe* companions – no blue-stocking tittle-tattle or habits of worshipping or being worshipped – Domestic affectionate creatures – good to live with – without fussing, continually doing what is most obliging and whatever makes us feel most at *home.*"

Edgeworth's letter not only introduces us to this "sweet Spot," as William Wordsworth (1770-1850) described Hampstead (Wordsworth, *Letters* 8:97), Baillie's creative centre from which she wrote her lyric and narrative poems and her twenty-seven plays, but later also offers us an understanding of the greater world beyond, simmering and brooding in contrast to the tranquility of Hampstead. During Edgeworth's visit, the women visit the "forlorn-looking" home of Mrs. Anna Laetitia Barbauld (1743-1825), who had first moved to Hampstead with her husband in 1787 and had entered the Baillie circle through her connection to Dr. Denman, Joanna's older brother Matthew's (1761-1823) future father-in-law. Mrs. Barbauld's husband was a pastor of a dissenting church in the town, one of the attractions of Hampstead for the Baillie women. By the time of Edgeworth's visit, however, Barbauld was widowed and living in Stoke Newington, just a short carriage ride from the Baillies' home along the Old Kent Road, a "dismal place," according to Edgeworth, "with its rows of pointed poplars veiled in smoke and its swampy Dutch appearance with its ditchy-canal called the *new River*! – and such a smell of mixed coal-smoke, and brick-kiln...." Baillie's close friend, Sir Walter Scott (1771-1832), also relates in expansive detail in a letter to her his "dreadful fright" when, returning to London from Hampstead, he chanced upon some "thorough-paced London ruffians" (Scott, *Letters* 3:37). William Wordsworth, too, on one of his visits to London from Grasmere writes to his wife about the city's "ferocious and savage" temperament. He notes despairingly that the "national character ... has been changing for these thirty or 40 years during the growth of the manufacturing and trading system the Malady has been forming its self, and the eruption has now begun, but where it will end heaven knows" (Wordsworth, *Letters* 8:92). In closing, he promises his wife that he will "keep out of the way of riots...." And Baillie herself, on moving to Hampstead, writing from the removed perspective of a traveller, records this impression of London from what she calls "Hampstead's heathy height":

> "What hollow sound is that?" approaching near,
> The roar of many wheels breaks on his ear.
> It is the flood of human life in motion!
> It is the voice of a tempestuous ocean!
> With sad but pleasing awe his soul is fill'd,
> Scarce heaves his breast, and all within is still'd,
> As many thoughts and feelings cross his mind,
> Thoughts, mingled, melancholy, undefined,
> Of restless, reckless man, and years gone by,
> And Time fast wending to Eternity.
>
> ("London," *Works* 796)

Hampstead, indeed, was an island within a "tempestuous ocean" of dramatic, unprecedented industrial and social change. Consider that in the year of Baillie's birth the Seven Years' War (1755-63) – a war that consolidated what we might call today a new world order – was coming to an end. France, for instance, ceded Canada and Cape Breton Island (November 1762) as well as Grenada (March 12, 1762) in the West Indies and French possessions in Africa to Great Britain, and the Mississippi River was recognized as the boundary between Louisiana and the British colonies. Britain, at the time of this peace, was reaching the summit of its powers. George III was crowned in 1760 and moved in and out of insanity until being formally declared insane in 1811, dying in Baillie's fifty-eighth year (1820). The French Revolution was but a distant speck on the political horizon. Technologically, in 1762, John Roebuck (1718-94) devised a method for converting cast iron into malleable iron at his Carron ironworks in Stirlingshire, and John Harrison (1693-1776) received the Board of Longitude's prize for an accurate chronometer which determined the longitude at sea within eighteen minutes. By the year Baillie died, Louis Napoleon III (1808-73), nephew of Napoleon Bonaparte (1769-1821), dissolved the French constitution in a coup d'état. Queen Victoria (1819-1901) was in the fourteenth year of her reign. The American James Bogardus (1800-74) had constructed the first cast-iron frame building, and George Bond (1825-65) had photographed the moon at Cambridge, Massachusetts. In Great Britain, the Great Exhibition opened in Hyde Park in May, the first double-decker bus was introduced, and iron production had reached three million tons.

Into this time of dynamic change, Joanna Baillie was born in the manse of Bothwell, Lanarkshire, Scotland on September 11, 1762, the third child of the Reverend Mr. James Baillie (1722-78) and Dorothea Hunter Baillie (1721-1806). On a profound level she experienced the harsh realities of a hostile world and its inevitable propensity toward imperfection; Baillie's unnamed twin sister died only a few hours after her birth. Following the Reverend Baillie's clerical and academic career in the rural area south of Glasgow from the village of Bothwell and the parish of St. Brides to Hamilton, the Baillie family finally found themselves feeling momentarily secure in the larger centre of Glasgow, where James Baillie taught divinity at Glasgow University. But after Reverend Baillie's sudden death in 1778, they were moving again – Matthew to study medicine at Oxford and with his uncle Dr. William Hunter (1718-83), a famous anatomist and obstetrician in London, and the women to the Hunter family's rural seat at Long Calderwood, near East Killbride.

When Dr. William Hunter died, the Baillie women left Scotland as their residence forever and made their way south to join Matthew. Following in the Hunter family medical tradition – their other uncle, John (1728-93), was a physiologist and surgeon and the founder of scientific surgery – Matthew by now had practiced medicine for three years before inheriting William Hunter's Windmill Street School of Anatomy and house. William, a paternalistic older brother, had felt entitled to the benefits of John's research. This led to quarrels and an unfortunate separation. Matthew's return to John, the rightful heir, of the Long Calderwood home that William had misguidedly left to him was a posthumous resolution of the dispute. Starting his career in his uncles' lucrative practice, Matthew became a prominent London physician himself, later becoming "physician-extraordinary" to George III and earning more than sufficient funds to provide for his mother and sisters as well as his own family. Through medical circles, Matthew began courting Sophia, the daughter of Dr. Denman, a fashionable obstetrician at the time, and sister of "Tommy," later known as the Lord Chief Justice of the Queen's Bench. When he married Sophia in 1791, the Baillie women moved yet again.

Drifting on the currents of masculine endeavour, Joanna, Agnes, and their mother moved from the Great Windmill Street address and explored a country lifestyle, trying Colchester first, before finally settling on Hampstead in 1798 (see p.11, n.1). Just as Prospero's island was a vortex of his magical arts, Hampstead, in its relative isolation from London, became a powerful centre of female domesticity and artistic creativity. As early as April 21, 1791, dated in Samuel Rogers's (1763-1855) journals, the Baillie women were already moving on the periphery of London's literary circles, most likely introduced by Baillie's aunt, Ann Home Hunter (1742-1821), wife of John Hunter and author of "My Mother Bids Me Bind My Hair" and other songs set to music by Haydn. By 1798, Baillie had become more central to literary discussions organized by Mrs. Barbauld, both as participant and subject. Since Baillie's *Plays on the Passions* were published anonymously in January of that year, the other participants of the salon were not aware that the very author who was the object of their speculation[1] and praise sat within their midst. Later in life Baillie would, in a sense, hold literary court in Hampstead, bestowing upon a few friends and admirers what Wordsworth called a "very unusual mark of regard" (Wordsworth, *Letters* 8:113) – an invitation to dinner, usually preceded by a walk on the heath. Of the visitors to the Baillie household, Maria Edgeworth took particular note of the many men of quality who admired Baillie's work and who exhibited themselves a social consciousness. In just one conversation with the Baillies the names of Mr. Gurney[2] (1788-1847), Samuel Hoare (1778-1856), and Mr. Fowell Buxton[3] (1786-1845) arose (Edgeworth, *Letters* 118). Other distinguished men of the day who sought out Baillie were Sir Walter Scott (1771-1832), William Wordsworth, William Sotheby (1757-1833), and James Fenimore Cooper (1789-1851), and even her ferociously adversarial critic Francis Jeffrey (1773-1850), to name only a few.[4]

Too frequently biographers of Baillie have portrayed the author who chose to delineate the stronger passions as a woman in retirement. Of the world, writes Florence MacCunn, Baillie "knew little – as little of the world behind the footlights as of the larger world which it is supposed to portray" (291). In the most thorough biography of Baillie to date, written in 1923 and reprinted by Yale University as late as 1970, author Margaret Carhart unfortunately perpetuates this

---

1 London literary circles hummed with rumours and speculation after the anonymous publication of *Plays on the Passions*. The names of Sir Walter Scott, John Philip Kemble and even Matthew Baillie were circulated, because of what many thought to be the masculine style of the introductory discourse and plays. But some strongly suspected Ann Radcliffe to be the author. This rumour began in a letter by a Mrs. Jackson on May 21, 1799 and led to Mrs. Piozzi declaring that, indeed, Radcliffe had admitted to the authorship (Carhart 15-16). Rictor Norton explores at some length the trauma this rumour caused Radcliffe in his *Mistress of Udolpho: The Life of Ann Radcliffe*. By 1800 suspicion had shifted to Anne Hunter because of hints of a Scottish flavour throughout the text.

2 John Joseph Gurney was a Quaker banker and philanthropist. He was the brother of Mrs. Elizabeth Fry (1780-1845), a prison reformer, also described in Edgeworth's letter as an intimate friend of Baillie.

3 Later Sir Thomas Fowell Buxton, 1st Bart. Buxton was an English brewer and social reformer.

4 See note to *Introductory Discourse* on Aloma E. Noble's thesis (110).

image, writing that Baillie's "life was sheltered from all harsh contact from the world; she herself was never shaken by any of the passions that stir the soul of a man to the depths" (190). There is no doubt that the letters and anecdotes available to us reveal a reserve typical of Baillie's birth and her times. We must, though, be very careful not to impose our late twentieth-century notions of the *private* and the *public* on our predecessors since, as Leo Braudy points out, "private life in our sense is a concept that slowly emerges in the course of the eighteenth century" (392).

To continue a myth of Baillie as blissfully removed from or immune to the impact of the broader social dynamics of her times is a terrible injustice. For instance, we know Baillie revealed to Mary Berry in a letter in 1802 that she acutely felt the frustrating pressures and isolation of being a woman of her class, especially one drawn to the world of theatre. Writes Baillie, "We have got a company of strollers at present who act in the Flask Tavern, and even after them I have a very great hankering, but how to get this gratified with all due regard to propriety, having neither man nor woman that will go with me, I have not wit enough to devise" (qtd. MacCunn 292). She also recoiled at social deceit and subscribed throughout her life to a brutal, terse honesty that occasionally complicated her social relationships with women such as Mrs. Damer.[1] Though Baillie was guided by the stoic adage "Let well alone" (qtd. Edgeworth, *Letters* 317), she was obviously hurt bitterly enough by Francis Jeffrey's scathing review[2] of her project on the passions that she refused to meet with him on her visit to Edinburgh in 1808. The prominent reviewer's regular and harsh attacks on Baillie as a playwright no doubt had some impact on her career, not to mention an even more significant one on her psyche. Though it does speak to Baillie's powers of forgiveness that she and Jeffrey became cordial friends after he retired from the *Edinburgh Review* around 1828, Margaret Carhart

---

1 Anne Seymour Damer (1749-1828) was an English sculptor and friend of Horace Walpole. See MacCunn 299.

2 See Francis Jeffrey, *The Edinburgh Review* (Appendix E.2).

sensed[1] that Baillie's "bitterness towards him seems to have made her doubt the sincerity of his later praise" (49). Yet, for the most part, a sense of connection to the broader world was a source of great joy to Baillie. Her friend William Sotheby witnessed such a moment one day during a visit to her home. Up to her elbows in flour, she called Sotheby into the kitchen and eagerly urged him to pull a piece of paper from the pocket of her apron. Recounted Sotheby, "it was a play-bill sent to her by some friend in the country, setting forth that some obscure provincial company was about to perform Miss Joanna Baillie's celebrated tragedy of *De Monfort*." "There Sotheby," exclaimed Baillie "I am so happy! You see my plays can be acted somewhere!" (Frances Kemble's *Recollections of a Girlhood* 350, qtd. *Carhart* 41-42).

Modern scholars such as Catherine Burroughs (*Closet Stages* 32) are working at reversing the perception of Baillie as a retiring soul.[2] Indeed, Burroughs suggests that Baillie is one of a number of contemporary women writers instrumental in politicizing, rather than retiring to, the domestic space. An endearing story related by Maria Edgeworth to her sister about some earlier family history confirms the pulse of scientific experimentation and social reform that beat at the very heart of Hampstead. The story features a scientist and a young, activist "hero," Matthew Baillie's son, William, who, despite the good intentions of science, took pity on a poor, distressed cat. Writes Edgeworth:

> You may, perhaps, have heard the name of a celebrated Mr. Brodie,[3] who wrote on poisons, and whose papers on this subject are to be found in the Transactions of the Royal Society, and reviewed in the Edinburgh Review, in 1811. He brought some of the Woorara poison,[4] with

---

1 Margaret Carhart described Jeffrey's regular critical attacks as the "sole shadow" on Baillie's "delightful intercourse between many of the brightest men and women of the day" (*Life* 47).

2 See also Anne Mellor *Romanticism and Gender* 3.

3 Sir Benjamin Collins Brodie (1783-1862) was a surgeon who advocated a milder treatment than amputation for the treatment of the diseases of the joints.

4 Curare is a strong poison extracted from the bark of certain South American trees.

which the natives poison their arrows and destroy their victims. It was his theory that this poison destroys by affecting the nervous system only, and that after a certain time its effects on the nerves would cease as the effects of intoxicating liquors cease, and that the patient might recover, if the lungs could be kept in play, if respiration were not suspended during the trance or partial death in which the patient lies. To prove the truth of this by experiment he fell to work upon a cat; he pricked the cat with the point of a lancet dipped in woorara. It was some minutes before the animal became convulsed, and then it lay, to all appearance, dead. Mr. Brodie applied a tube to its mouth, and blew air into it from time to time; after lying some hours apparently lifeless, it recovered, shook itself, and went about its own affairs as usual. This was tried several times, much to the satisfaction of the philosophical spectators, but not quite to the satisfaction of poor puss, who grew very thin and looked so wretched that Doctor Baillie's son, then a boy, took compassion on this poor subject of experiment, and begged Mr. Brodie would let him carry off the cat. With or without consent, he did carry her off, and brought her to his aunts, Joanna and Agnes Baillie. Then puss's prosperous days began. Agnes made a soft bed for her in her own room, and by night and day she was the happiest of cats; she was called Woorara, which in time shortened to Woory. (Edgeworth, *Letters* 316-17).

Edgeworth's delightful anecdote isolates two very powerful urges in Baillie's life – the urge to experiment and the urge to reform. Growing up around medical luminaries, whose young profession had been founded on inventive empiricism, must surely have inspired Baillie to examine the intricate living and thinking processes of the world (see Appendix A). In fact, as a young girl Baillie first explored mathematics before she developed her reading and writing skills. But as the daughter of a country minister, she also honed her charitable instincts at the kitchen door of the manse, where she administered to many a "way-worn traveller" (*Works* vi). The editor of the 1851 edition even suggests it was here as well that Baillie began to gather an "early store of incident and the knowledge of human nature" that fuelled her literary career. She carried on the Hunter family tradition of doing "good by stealth" (MacCunn 296), donating half of her earnings[1] from her writing to charity and helping others. Ellen Donkin especially recognizes Baillie's efforts to provide for young women writers "a quiet sense of community, confidence and direction" (182). Baillie also regularly helped writers and friends in all walks of life. In an 1808 letter, Scott advises Baillie on how to manage the publishing affairs of her "protégé" John Struthers (1776-1853), a cowherd, shoemaker, and author of *The Poor Man's Sabbath*, whom Baillie had met on her visit to Glasgow and the Western Highlands the same year (Scott, *Letters* 2:56-57). Another letter from Baillie to Scott in 1822 describes an old friend and "Schoolfellow" of hers "whose husband is insolvent and dying," Baillie believed, of a broken heart (Scott, *Letter-books* 262). Baillie explains to Scott that she has "offered to edit for [her friend's] benefit a volume of collected poems, to be published by subscription; and being anxious to have as much good MS. poetry in the book as may be, I am soliciting my literary friends to contribute." Even within her family circle, Baillie's concerns for equality and general human improvement are tinged with the imagery of Mary Wollstonecraft (1759-97) (see Appendix B). In another of the many letters to Sir Walter Scott, she shares her worries about the imminent marriage of her niece to a young soldier named Milligan, assigned to the Dragoons at Waterloo. In Baillie's estimation, her niece is "a very clever woman, fond of books, and with a mind and taste well culti- vated," while her fiancé is "a plain, honest soldier, whose education had been quite neglected and who, dogs and horses and military matters excepted, has little information on any subject" (Baillie, Slagle 1:353).

---

1 In 1820 Baillie consulted with Sir Walter Scott about asking Longman for one thousand guineas for the outright purchase of her three legends of Wallace, Colum- bus, and Lady Gisel and four Ballads, an amount which Scott termed a "moderate sum."

As Baillie reached her thirty-sixth year, in 1798, these urges for experimentation and social and aesthetic reform united to forge the bold scope of her literary project,[1] *A Series of Plays: in which it is attempted to delineate the stronger passions of the mind* Vol 1. Baillie's intellect was one keen on "abstract theorizing, problem solving, and philosophizing" (*Dictionary of Literary Biography* 5), notes Marlon Ross, so it seems fitting that after an early anonymous publication of her *Poems* in 1790 and three months of expended effort on a now lost play entitled *Arnold*, Baillie should have found her literary voice in a theoretical system. In her *Introductory Discourse*, written a few months after *Count Basil*, *The Tryal*, and *De Monfort*, Baillie outlines a plan based upon a universal curiosity in human nature described by the moral writers[2] of her time. Every individual to some degree possesses, in Baillie's words, a "sympathetick curiosity" and therefore "is more or less occupied in tracing, amongst the individuals he converses with, the varieties of understanding and temper which constitute the characters of men; and receives great pleasure from every stroke of nature that points out to him those varieties" (67-68). However, "those who reflect and reason upon what human nature holds out to their observation, are comparatively but few" (75), for most of life's events "stand single and unconnected in their minds," though they can be "induced" by good drama to make those connections. Baillie theorizes that at "the beginning of its career the Drama was employed to mislead and excite" (104), yet it has the potential to be a school for moral instruction. Intrigued by the "actual

---

1   We may always wonder just how original to Baillie this project was. Perhaps works as early as Ben Jonson's *Every Man in his Humour* (1598) and *Every Man out of his Humour* (1599) played a role. Margaret Carhart cites two possible sources of Baillie's inspiration. Alexander Pope lists the passions in *Essay on Man*. 2. 117-20, and in 1781 the Haymarket Theatre presented *The School of Shakespeare, or Humours and Passions* which, in five acts, represented five passions in Shakespearean motifs (190-91). Also, Mary Hays wrote in the first line of the preface to her novel *Memoirs of Emma Courtney* that "the most interesting, and the most useful, fictions, are, perhaps, such, as delineating the progress, and tracing the consequences, of one strong, indulged, passion, or prejudice ... by which the philosopher may calculate the powers of the human mind." See also the introduction and John Locke (Appendix A.1).

2   See Appendix A.

operation" (107) of the passions, those "great disturbers of the human breast" Baillie feels drama, both tragedy and comedy, had become too obsessed with the events of the play and the trappings of fashion and intrigue to be instructive in any moral way. Many plays, to her mind, imperfectly represented the passions in a "transient, loose, unconnected manner" (91) at the height of their "fury." Passions "encrease and nourish themselves on very slender aliment; it is from within that they are chiefly supplied with what they feed on" (92). To represent a passion in only one stage of its development is a misrepresentation of that passion. But by tracing the passions in "their rise and progress in the heart" (91), drama can have a more profound moral effect because the passions can be more naturally represented. Thus "the Drama improves us by the knowledge we acquire of our own minds, from the natural desire we have to look into the thoughts, and observe the behaviour of others" (90).

At the core of Baillie's theories is her abiding belief that the "love of nature dwells within us" and that an audience subjected to a play filled with the "marvellous and unnatural" will be delighted when it is offered, even accidentally, a "genuine stroke of nature." Baillie's philosophy is one based on a sense of natural goodness. We can be distracted from our natural inclination, from "our native and favourite aliment," by a rich diet of the "marvellous." "Yet we can never so far forget it, but that we will cling to, and acknowledge it again." In her introduction, Baillie therefore calls for a return to a natural aesthetic and to a more natural depiction[1] of dramatic characters in both action and voice. Surveying and discarding the recent offerings in comedy, she coins a new name for a more naturalistic theatre which "represents to us this motley world of men and women in which we live." In Baillie's view, many of her contemporaries were producing an exaggerated drama that became a "quest of the ludicrous" and stretched believability "beyond the bounds of nature," destroying every effect they wished to achieve. If dramatic characters are to "speak for themselves," the dramatist

---

1 See William Wordsworth "Preface" to *Lyrical Ballads* (Appendix D.1).

must emphasize nature in her writing and "not situation." As well, Baillie warns that poetry, rich in "simile, metaphor, allegory and description," can often tempt us "to forget what we really are, and what kind of being we belong to," both with the images and events it represents and in the language it uses. Dramatists have revelled in the "embellishments of poetry,"[1] representing "men and women speaking and acting as men and women never did speak or act," rather than subscribing to simple observations of human nature.

Baillie's original plan for the *Plays on the Passions* was to delineate the passions of love, hate, ambition, fear, hope, remorse, jealousy, pride, envy, revenge, anger, joy, and grief. By 1812, however, in her preface to the third volume, she justifies her decision to make alterations to this original plan. She explains:

> Joy, Grief, and Anger, as I have already said, are generally of too transient a nature, and are too frequently the attendants of all our other passions to be made the subjects of an entire play. And though this objection cannot be urged in regard to Pride and Envy, two powerful passions which I have not yet named, Pride would make, I should think, a dull subject, unless it were merely taken as the groundwork of more turbulent passions; and Envy, being that state of mind, which, of all others meets with least sympathy, could only be endured in Comedy or Farce, and would become altogether disgusting in Tragedy. I have besides, in some degree, introduced this latter passion into the work already by making it a companion or rather a component of Hatred. (*Works* 231)

With these alterations to her plan and the publication of her 1802 and 1812 volumes, only the passions of remorse, jealousy, and revenge remained. By the publication of her *Miscellaneous Plays* in 1836, Baillie deleted revenge, a "frequently exposed"

---

1   See *Introductory Discourse,* note to Thomas Gray (86).

passion (*Works* 312), from the list and declared her project complete (see Chronology).

The 1798 edition, then, launched Baillie's ambitious project by focusing on the first two passions on her list: love and hate.[1] The first play, *Count Basil: A Tragedy*, explores the powerful love of a young officer for Victoria, the daughter of the politically ambitious Duke of Mantua. The infatuated Basil is easily manipulated by Victoria, herself the unwitting pawn of her father, who is plotting with the King of France, and his unscrupulous advisor, Gauriecio. Caught up in his obsession with Victoria, Basil mindlessly shirks his duty to his men and to Charles V, who awaits his support at the battle of Pavia. Count Rosinberg, a man of depth though tainted with the libertine social trappings of a military officer, unsuccessfully attempts to influence Basil to march his troops from Mantua. The Countess of Albini, Victoria's life-long governess and a feminine ideal of morality and education,[2] works at tempering Victoria's seductive urges, but the maze of sensual and political deception delays Basil long enough that the battle comes to a conclusion, and the Emperor wins without Basil's support. Alienated and disgraced, Basil takes his own life.

Baillie intended to accompany each of the tragedies with a comedy exploring the same passion. The second play in this edition, *The Tryal: A Comedy*, is the comic companion to *Count Basil*. The heiress Agnes, an obvious dramatic tribute to Baillie's sister, spins a madcap web around the ridiculous men of fashion who gravitate to Bath in search of a wealthy heiress. Hoping to find a man of value, Agnes assumes the identity of her less-privileged cousin, Mariane. While the recently engaged Mariane proceeds on her own defiant project to expose and discredit two fops, Sir Loftus Prettyman and Mr. Opal, Agnes, feigning churlishness, rebuffs the affections of a young lawyer, Harwood, hoping to prove that he loves her only for herself and not her social position. At the peak of the play's slapstick absurdity, Agnes puts Harwood to the ultimate

---

1   See John Locke (Appendix A.1.i).
2   See Mary Wollstonecraft, *Vindication* (Appendix B).

test, uniting Mariane, Withrington, and a caricature of the eighteenth-century businessman, Mr. Royston, in a Hamlet-esque play-within-a-play. Presented with a letter forged by Agnes that would dangerously compromise the character of Lady Fade, a woman of social stature yet of tenuous means, Harwood renounces all his amorous ambitions for Agnes. With Harwood's worth proven, he and Agnes are engaged, Withrington bestows a lucrative dowry on Mariane, Withrington's house is restored to order, and the play concludes with the laughter and conviviality of a television sit-com.

De Monfort: A Tragedy, the last play, represents the only delineation of hatred in this volume. Its comic companion, The Election, did not appear until the second volume. De Monfort traces the Marquis De Monfort's hatred for an early rival, Rezenvelt, a curious, somewhat mysterious figure, who now shares the same rank with De Monfort yet who was clearly once "low in fortune" (2.2.122). Childhood memories of a young, defiant Rezenvelt haunt De Monfort. Tortured by his complex hatred, De Monfort retreats to Amberg, a small German town away from the conventional society that might expose him to Rezenvelt. Just as the creature in Mary Shelley's[1] (1797-1851) science fiction classic Frankenstein, or, The Modern Prometheus (1818) haunts the young Dr. Frankenstein; Rezenvelt coincidentally appears in Amberg and once again disturbs De Monfort's tenuous grip on his passions. Despite the moderating effects of De Monfort's loving sister, Jane De Monfort, even the well-meaning but socially frivolous behaviour of Count Freberg, a long-time friend of quality, drives De Monfort into irrational fits. Finally, suspicious of Rezenvelt's attentiveness to Jane and driven by rumour, De Monfort murders him in the dark recesses of the forest. With a gothic flourish, the play draws to a close in the dimly lit chapel of a nearby convent, where De Monfort is confronted with the corpse of Rezenvelt and dies alongside his adversary from remorse.

Despite Baillie's life-long dedication to her work – she continued to publish individual and collected dramas and poems,

---

1   In her journal Mary Shelley records having read A Series of Plays; in which it is Attempted to Delineate the Stronger Passions (1798, 1802, 1812), Ethwald (1802), De Montfort [sic] (1798), and Orra (1812) in late 1814.

including a religious treatise entitled *A View of the General Tenor of the New Testament Regarding the Nature and Dignity of Jesus Christ* (1831) – early biographers such as Donald Carswell have claimed that the 1812 volume marked the end to Baillie's literary career. He writes, "Already her star was beginning to pale. It had looked brilliant enough while it had been solitary, but now the great romantic planets had swum into the firmament" (180-81). Whether right or wrong in his assessment, there is a tone to Carswell and other early biographers of Baillie that we must note with suspicion. As Margaret Carhart notes, between 1800 and 1826, "the leading theatres of England, Scotland, Ireland, and the United States" (*Life and Work* 109) produced one or more of seven plays[1] written by Baillie – *De Monfort* and *Count Basil* amongst them – featuring some of the greatest actors of her age. She met the challenges of London society with grace and determination and, despite the prejudices of the day, succeeded at what she had set out to accomplish – to write dramas for the stage. In re-evaluating the work of Joanna Baillie, we must ultimately reconsider our cultural definitions of success. We must also examine the impact of our culture's notions of class, gender, and creative expression in a competitive, consumer-based economy, the very issues that may very well have left Baillie weary. For on Saturday, February 22, 1851, the day before she died, Joanna Baillie expressed a "strong desire to be released from life" (*Works* xviii).

The moral writers and the Scottish Enlightenment

Considering eighteenth-century London society's infatuation with fame,[2] Baillie's *De Monfort* may offer a small clue as to why she grew as weary with the world as she did. Early in the play (1.2.14-19) De Monfort alerts his servant Manuel to the existence of social serpents, those, in his estimation, "who in the path of social life/Do bask their spotted skins in Fortune's sun,/And sting the soul." As it is now, falling out of fashion was a decidedly poor career move in Baillie's day, leaving one open

---

1   For a fuller discussion of Baillie's performance record see Carhart Chapter 4.
2   See Leo Braudy's *The Frenzy of Renown: Fame and Its History.*

to sentiments such as those conveyed by Sara Coleridge in a letter written from Hampstead to Miss E. Trevenen in 1833. Though describing Baillie as the "sensible, amiable old lady that *was* a great poetess thirty years ago," she declares her "flame of genius" extinguished. Willing to concede that some of her poetry was "far above that of any other woman," she then claims that Baillie "*never* possessed" learning and that her "surprisingly narrow and jejune" criticism was proof of Baillie's "so slight an acquaintance with fine literature in general." The most cursory study of this volume, however, would refute Coleridge's uncharitably harsh assessment.

Turning to *De Monfort* again, we can no doubt hear Baillie's rebuttal to Coleridge in the voice of Jane De Monfort when she offers to join with her brother in "the study of some art,/Or nobler science, that compels the mind/To steady thought progressive, driving forth/All floating, wild, unhappy fantasies" (2.2.42-45). Margaret Carhart relates a story recorded in Samuel Rogers' journal for April 21, 1791 of a conversation at the house of Miss Williams in Hampstead. When the conversation focused on Scotland, Henry Mackenzie (1745-1831) attacked its men of genius, and Baillie parried with the name of Adam Smith (1723-90). Though Mackenzie, the author of *Man of Feeling*, did not allow her to make her point, Baillie had the last word in her *Introductory Discourse*. Reading through it, we can detect the thought and style of Smith (see Appendix A.4) and can perhaps even locate the passage in Smith's *The Theory of Moral Sentiments* (1759) that inspired Baillie to coin the phrase "sympathetick curiosity." Smith writes, "General lamentations, which express nothing but the anguish of the sufferer, create rather a curiosity to inquire into his situation, along with some disposition to sympathize with him, than any actual sympathy that is very sensible" (see Appendix A.4.i). As well, in her later preface to her play *The Martyr*, first published alone in 1826 and, in 1836, included in her three volumes of twelve plays simply entitled *Dramas*, Baillie reveals her familiarity with the work of Dugald Stewart (1753-1828), a student of Thomas Reid's (1720-96). She refers to Stewart as a "great philosophical writer" (see Appendix A.5), citing his discussion on superstition in *Elements of the Philosophy of the Human Mind* (1792)(1.368).

Critics of Baillie, both contemporary and modern, have been reluctant to place Baillie and the overall architecture of her 1798 edition within the philosophical and psychological context of her day. Just as David Hume (1711-76), a great eighteenth century philosopher, was recognized in his own time more as a writer, Baillie, a writer, creatively explored early psychology. Taking a long historical view of Baillie's project, we must not ignore the obvious scientific sources that fuelled her creative intellect. Popular convention has led generations of both casual and serious students of literature to associate the eighteenth century with reason and not passion. The entire century, however, embraced a dynamic re-examination of reason. Like lava pouring up from the subterranean caverns of the earth, the streams of moral thought at this time formed a new psychological landscape within the social sciences. Writers and thinkers of all types grappled to reconcile the head with the heart.

Psychology as we know it today did not exist in 1798. Philosophers, scientists, medical men, and writers, free from modern professional discrimination, worked together to understand the sources of human knowledge. In doing so, they were freeing human experience from predetermined theological scripts, finding motive within the nervous system of the individual, and laying the foundations for modern psychological inquiry. The late seventeenth century and entire eighteenth century was a gradual rejection and a secularization of the seventeenth-century Cartesian model of knowledge and reality. René Descartes (1596-1650), entertaining a system of innate ideas as a model for all knowledge, extended the precision of mathematical ideas to all of human thought,[1] giving preference to the head over the heart. In Cartesian terms, we could know the world only through an extension of our intellect and not our senses. The physical processes of the nerves and the brain were merely events of God, and intellectual

---

1 See *Discours de la méthode* (1637) and *Les Passions de l'âme* (1649).

inquiry was seen as our only connection with God and the human soul.[1]

John Locke (1632-1704), the founder of Liberalism and English Empiricism, supported Cartesian rationalism yet refuted Descartes's notion of "innate ideas." He seemed to find some abstract inspiration in Thomas Hobbes's (1588-1679) theories of material motion, but he could not abide Hobbes's pessimistic interpretation of reality. Preceding Jean-Jacques Rousseau (1712-78) by more than half a century, Locke not only believed in an Edenic notion of nature regulated by unalterable laws which expressed the will of God but also gave validity to the sensations in the acquisition of knowledge and an understanding of the passions (see Appendix A.1.i). Contrary to Descartes, Locke visualizes the mind as a "white Paper, void of all Characters, without any Ideas" (*Essay* 2.1.2) that becomes a vast storehouse filled by the operation of the senses. Explaining his theory of sensationalism, Locke writes: "Let any one examine his own Thoughts, and thoroughly[2] search into his Understanding, and then let him tell me, Whether all the original *Ideas* he has there, are any other than of the Objects of his *Senses*; or of the Operations of his Mind, considered as Objects of his *Reflection*: and how great a mass of Knowledge soever he imagines to be lodged there, he will, upon taking a strict view, see, that he has *not any* Idea *in his Mind, but what one of these two have imprinted* ..." (*Essay* 2.1.5). Ideas, including the "*Ideas* of our *Passions*," could be simple or complex – they were ideas that were copies of nature and ideas "of the Mind's own making" (*Essay* 4.4.5). Locke's world could confidently account for the "Certainty" of moral knowledge as easily as it could for the physical sciences and mathematics. Thanks to Locke, the sense of an inner being – a human psychology – was taking shape.[3]

This was the tradition of thought upon which the eighteenth century's interest in the passions and moral inquiry was

---

1 See Nicolas Malebranche's (1638-1715) *De la recherche de la vérité* (1674), and *Traité de morale* (1684).

2 Fully or completely.

3 John Dussinger notes that Locke's inquiry into multiple selves was an "implicit recognition of unconscious involuntary forces in the dynamics of the mind" (*Discourse of the Mind* 33).

founded. Englishman David Hartley (1705-57), who believed in the Lockean model of infinitesimal vibrating particles, developed associational psychology (see Appendix A.5.i). In his *Observations on Man, His Frame, His Duty, And His Expectations* (1749), he describes ideas as stemming from sensation, not reflection. Pain and pleasure drive hatred and love, pushing us to a variety of actions. Hartley's theories, which enjoyed considerable influence until 1824, gave some sense of empirical grounding to Wordsworth and Coleridge's ideas of mental experience. Other British thinkers such as Edmund Burke (1729-97), who anonymously published his *A Philosophical Enquiry into the Origin of our Ideas of the Sublime and Beautiful* (1756), also believed that feeling, and not reason, was the power that moved him (see Appendix A.3). Following in the tradition of Locke and Hume, political writer and novelist William Godwin (1756-1836) accepted Hartley's theories of association yet rejected his more concrete theories of vibrations, arguing from a sensationalist psychological perspective that our environment and culture shape us.

Perhaps Baillie's awareness of the moralist thinkers naturally developed from the contact the men in her life had with them. It is very likely that her uncle William Hunter,[1] who studied and practised medicine in both Glasgow and Edinburgh before moving to London, came in contact with some of the luminaries who were the foundations of the Scottish School. Francis Hutcheson (1694-1746), professor of Moral Philosophy at Glasgow from 1729 until his death, became recognized as the pioneer of the *common-sense* school of philosophy, known since the 1960s as the Scottish Enlightenment. From 1740 to 1746, Adam Smith was Snell Exhibitioner at Balliol College, Oxford, where Matthew Baillie completed some of his studies more than thirty years later, but during James Baillie's brief tenure as Professor of Divinity at the University of Glasgow between 1776 and 1778, he must have come in contact with Thomas

---

1 According to Judith Slagle (personal communication), Baillie never met Dr. William Hunter, but Dr. John Hunter and Matthew Baillie did. Baillie maintained close relationships with both, and perhaps the spirit of some of this thought took that route to Baillie's meditations.

Reid (1710-96), who moved to the University of Glasgow from Aberdeen in 1764 to accept the Chair in Moral Philosophy previously held by Smith.

Francis Hutcheson turned the liberal thought of John Locke and his early protégé Anthony Ashley Cooper, 3rd Earl of Shaftesbury (1621-83) into a cohesive philosophy of practice. In *An Essay on the Nature and Conduct of the Passions and Affections* (1728), Hutcheson confronts the dualism of human motivation, attempting to show that, contrary to Hobbes's claims, there is no difference between benevolent affection and self-love. Benevolence, or fellow-feeling,[1] is in our self-interest; from this fellow-feeling all our happiness flows. Proposing that "the Nature of human Actions cannot be sufficiently understood without considering the *Affections* and *Passions*" (*Essay* 1.1), not reason, Hutcheson gave birth to a psychology of emotions.

David Hume is an exception to this line of academic philosophers. He never held a university professorship, but in 1752 became the keeper of the Advocates' Library in Edinburgh. In his *Treatise of Human Nature*, published first between 1739-40, and then again, in 1748, in *Enquiry concerning Human Understanding*, Hume declares that he seeks his reputation in "contributing to the instruction of mankind" (*Treatise* 1.4.7). He situates the "science of man" as the support to all the other sciences and lays beneath them all "experience and observation" (*Treatise* Introduction). Hume makes the boldest statement yet regarding the passions: reason, he declares "is, and ought only to be, the slave of the passions" (*Treatise* 2.3.3). His trust shifts from reason to the imagination. Our understanding of the world stems more from belief than 'real' knowledge; thus, it is an act of sensitivity rather than cognition. The self is "nothing but a bundle or collection of different perceptions" (*Treatise* 1.4.6), a self in "perpetual flux and movement." In an analogy vivid enough to have sparked the keen imagination of a young future playwright such as Baillie, Hume likens the mind to a "kind of theatre, where several perceptions succes-

---

1 A linguistic precursor to "empathy" which would gain usage much later in the early twentieth century.

sively make their appearance; pass, repass, glide away, and mingle in an infinite variety of postures and situations." So dependent is our thought upon the organs of sensation that "our eyes cannot turn in their sockets without varying our perceptions." Skeptical of a reality not founded on fact and observation, Hume constructs a psychological and moral reality on immediate feeling and confirms for himself Hutcheson's notion of a moral instinct.

Adam Smith assumed Francis Hutcheson's chair in Moral Philosophy at Glasgow in 1752. Though he is known today chiefly as an economist, in his time he was noted more as a moralist and a theorist in aesthetics. His *Theory of Moral Sentiments* (1759) was vital to the Scottish Enlightenment, emphasizing a human capacity and drive for sympathy that leads to the formation of social bonds with others. Sympathy, to Smith, "does not arise so much from the view of the passion, as from that of the situation which excites it" (*Moral Sentiments* 1.1; see Appendix A.4 and Baillie's *Introductory Discourse*, below, p. 91). Thomas Reid, author of *Inquiry into the Human Mind* (1764), vowed to rescue the thinking of Hume from skepticism and deliver it up to the intuitive, and he thought of himself in the empiricist tradition as an anatomist of the mind (*Inquiry*, Introduction). Reid succeeded Smith at Glasgow University, while his student Dugald Stewart succeeded Adam Ferguson (1723-1816) to the chair in Moral Philosophy in Edinburgh. All gave practical shape to the ideas of Francis Hutcheson and the Scottish School, with wide-ranging effects as far as Europe and the United States.

Whether or not Baillie actually read Hume or Hutcheson, we cannot absolutely be certain. But we can see in her work the philosophical moral tradition that they helped shape. Hume's interest in his *Treatise* to track the "whole bent or tendency" of a passion "from the beginning to the end" (*Treatise* 2.2.9; see Appendix A.2) and his treatise's themes of love and hatred point to the germination of the 1798 edition's overall plan. And reading Hutcheson's *Essay* and *A System of Moral Philosophy* (1755), we can discern Baillie's sense of the moral utility of theatre in his notion that "publickly useful" actions are also "privately useful" (*Essay* 2.1). We can also sense here

Basil's struggle between public honour and private desire (*Essay* 1.1), Albini's concern for education as moral nourishment (*System* 1.5.4), and De Monfort's lawlessness from overpowering passions (*Essay* 1.2 and 2.4). Baillie's "Diable boîteux" (see *Introductory Discourse*, below, p. 70) becomes a literary likeness of an eighteenth-century surgical theatre in which she makes the passions palpable and subject to physical inquiry. Baillie constructed for herself in the psychological realm a literary model of what the men who surrounded and supported her did in the physical realm. Intelligent and blessed with a stimulating intellectual environment, yet excluded from the world of scientific inquiry because of her gender, she launched her own examination of the psyche. In her own way, Baillie not only encouraged the application of theory to diverse areas of human endeavour, she made critical steps toward developing a process of understanding the subconscious long before Freud. By more firmly merging literature and psychology, she demonstrated an important unified and not compartmentalized approach to learning.

Joanna Baillie and the theatre of her day

Quite by chance, Joanna Baillie's career came to fruition during what could be seen as a more than fifty-year hiatus[1] of serious drama in Britain. Writing on the public taste at this time, Michael Booth notes[2] that the period between 1747 and 1776 was "one of the most stable and prosperous periods of eighteenth century theatre." It wasn't until 1842 that figures such as William Charles Macready (1793-1873), as the new manager of Drury Lane, took concrete steps to attract "the fashionable, the educated and the respectable back into the legitimate theatre" (13), just as Samuel Phelps (1804-78) converted Sadler's Wells, a once unruly melodrama house, into a respectable home for Shakespeare and legitimate drama during his tenure there between 1844 and 1862. Independent of any particular concern for Joanna Baillie's work, Booth isolates 1850 as a critical date in London stage history. In that year, Charles Kean began his

---

1 For a fuller debate of this issue, see Allardyce Nicoll, *The English Theatre* and Paul Kuritz, *The Making of Theatre History*.
2 See *The Revels History of Drama in English* 29.

nine-year tenure as manager at the Princess's Theatre, "a management that really marked the beginning of the end of a drama based upon the support of the popular audiences, without significant participation from the fashionable, the socially respectable and the intellectually cultured segments of the population" (14).

The interest in Baillie throughout the twentieth century has been sporadic but regular, from Margaret Carhart's biography and Donald Carswell's chapter on Baillie in his study of Scott's circle in 1930, to Bertrand Evans's more expansive call for a critical "re-evaluation"[1] of Baillie in 1947. As a result, the question has continually arisen – if Baillie was the talk of London and the topic of salons and important literary dinners,[2] why is her historical shadow on English theatre so faint? Donald Carswell's explanation is the most blunt. "Joanna Baillie's vogue," he writes, "was never popular: it was confined to literary people, and it is the amiable weakness of literary people that they are apt, if they are impressed by an author's aim, to overpraise his actual accomplishment" (285). More recently Ellen Donkin has asked the same question[3] within the more specific context of Baillie's contemporary female playwrights[4] who wrote for the London stage between 1775 and 1800. Donkin's "operating assumption" is that there were "gender complications" in the eighteenth century that affected the public contact with directors and actors necessary in the preparation of a play. Specifically to Baillie, Donkin extends her thesis to a conclusion of almost conspiratorial proportions. Since writing had become

---

1 See *Gothic Drama From Walpole to Shelley* 200.
2 Samuel Rogers writes about one such dinner at Thomas Moore's house (1779-1852) at which Rogers, Moore, and Byron spoke of Walter Scott, who had published *The Lady of the Lake* in 1810 and *The Vision of Don Roderick* in 1811, and of Joanna Baillie, whose latest tragedy, *The Family Legend*, was playing in Edinburgh.
3 There does seem to have been some tension between Baillie and John Kemble. Baillie wrote to Sir Walter Scott on April 2, 1823 that "I would have contrived to weave in a line to [Kemble's] honour in that little poem, tho' during his life I always considered him as being rather unfriendly to me. Perhaps it was my own fault: he was proud and I may have done something to offend him – I think I once unwittingly did so" (Slagle 418). Also see *Getting into the Act: 1776-1829*.
4 They include Frances Brooke (1724-89), Frances Burney (1752-1840), Hannah Cowley (1743-1809), Elizabeth Inchbald (1753-1821), Sophia Lee (1750-1824) and Hannah More (1745-1833).

an avenue for women to enter the establishment independently – Hannah Cowley and Elizabeth Inchbald were two who thrived under an earlier tacit, benevolent system of mentoring established by David Garrick (1717-79) – in Donkin's view, the male-dominated profession retrenched and actively thwarted the creative efforts of female playwrights. Even though Baillie held a secure position in London's privileged upper-middle class, Donkin suggests that Richard Sheridan single-handedly "took care of making sure Baillie did not get a foothold" (176) in a lucrative career in the theatre, and that Sheridan's actions as manager were symptomatic of a larger trend of "the job of ideological containment" dispersing into the critical community at large.

As we continue this re-evaluation of Baillie, though, we cannot completely ignore what Donkin calls the "quaint" (2) historical realities of public theatre understood within the context of a developing mercantile culture. Baillie's was a time of unprecedented dramatic commercial expansion. Familiar social issues to us today were then yet fully described. For instance, Samuel Johnson was one of the first to contemplate the impact of excessive advertising on his culture, raising the same modern concerns one might raise about television.[1] But more specific to drama, art is not immune to market forces. Though British patent laws since the Licensing Act of 1737 attempted to restrict performances to only two patent theatres, Drury Lane and Covent Garden, ironically, this monopoly may well have accelerated an already significant shift in public taste from classical tragedy and Augustan comedy to farce and burlesque. As the publication date of the *Plays on the Passions* approached, further laws attempted to maintain the tight monopoly on conventional London theatre, but the Act of 1752 had made it possible for a succession of new theatres, including other places of public amusement, to conduct business within London and its environs by twenty miles. The inevitable compromise of all this legislation led to a flood of sensational theatrical diversions to the public. By the end of the century, one of the major threats

---

1   See *The Idler* No. 40, Saturday, 20 January 1759 (*The Broadview Reader*, 3rd ed. 17). Both William Wordsworth (1770-1850) and Joanna Baillie also shared a concern for the dissatisfaction disseminated by the press (see Carhart 37).

to the well-being of a patent theatre such as Drury Lane, the vehicle through which Baillie sought public exposure, was itself.

No doubt, the finances of serious dramatic productions were, to say the least, precarious. Drama in Britain had enjoyed predictable support from the aristocracy in the previous century. In an attempt to stabilize the business of theatre, small, intimate Augustan theatres were replaced with architectural monoliths that would seat as many as three thousand spectators.[1] The unfortunate irony here, however, was that eighteenth-century theatrical theory focused the audience's attention on the actors' faces. In the brief critique of David Garrick (1717-1779) in his *A Treatise on the Passions* (1747), Samuel Foote isolates the face as "more essentially concerned in acting, than all the other Parts of the Body" because it is the "index of the Mind" (15). The voice, Foote believed, was the mind's "Interpreter."[2] It is understandable, then, that any audiences seeking the rewards of serious drama would struggle with the physical conditions of the contemporary stage. Lamenting the impact of these larger theatres on the art of theatre, one disgruntled critic writes in the *Critical Review* (February 1803: 37, 200-12), "While our theatres are of their present preposterous size, the success of a good play is physically impossible: rant only can be heard, and grimace alone be seen: we must be content with farce and foolery, and pantomime and *Pizarro*"[3] (206). In the preface to her third volume of *Plays on the Passions* (1812), Baillie subtly reveals her own frustration with contemporary theatre in her recounting of the fate of *De Monfort: A Tragedy*. In modest tones perhaps tinged with some bitterness, she writes that *De Monfort*, "notwithstanding the great support it received from excellent acting and magnificent decoration"

---

1 In 1794 Drury Lane increased its seating from 2,500 to 3,611.

2 Baillie was especially concerned about the voices of the actresses. See the preface to the third volume of *Plays on the Passions*, *Works* 233. Also cf. the early work of Johann Kaspar Lavater (1741-1801) who, in his *Physiognomische Fragmente* (1775-78; translated into English by Holcroft in 1793), tried to create a science of the face (see Braudy 402).

3 A play written by August Friedrich von Kotzebue (1761-1819) and adapted by Richard Brinsley Sheridan (1799), which enjoyed 60 years of popularity on the British stage.

failed, during its eight performances,[1] "to produce houses sufficiently good to induce the managers to revive it afterwards. But
it ought to be acknowledged, that that piece had defects in it as
an acting play, which served to counterbalance those advantages; and likewise that, if any supposed merit in the writing
ought to have redeemed those defects, in a theatre, so large and
so ill calculated to convey sound as the one in which it was
performed, it was impossible this could be felt or comprehended by even a third part of the audience" (*Works* 232). With their
anxious eyes on public taste and the "bottom line," theatre
managers were shifting popular theatre into the non-verbal.

As one might expect of an explosive consumer economy –
an economy Baillie herself called "this commercial hurricane"
(Baillie, *Scott's Letter-books* 357) – this was not a time in which
one particular dramatic aesthetic reigned, and those who
attended the theatre were less interested in tragedy than in plays
that would make them laugh or bend their heart strings. As the
wealth and the pressures of urban society multiplied, demand
for entertainment rather than stimulation and intellectual reflection grew. London's potential audience was burdened with
an unpredictable economy, unprecedented population growth
(from 900,000 in the late eighteenth century to three million
at the middle of the nineteenth century), the increase of dis-
enfranchised workers living in squalor, the high probability of
disease and infant morality (not to mention the terrors of
a medical profession in its infancy), the filth of a rapidly
developing industrial city, conservative religious beliefs, the
growing internal pressures within a collapsing class system,
and the ever-widening ramifications of international revolu-

---

1   The editor of Baillie's 1851 collected works perpetuated a myth that has survived to
this day that *De Monfort* was performed at Drury Lane Theatre for 11 nights. In
fact, it was performed eight times (see *Dramatic Censor*; Appendix 4). After over 18
months as the anonymous author of *Plays on the Passions*, Joanna Baillie made her
appearance at the Drury Lane on April 29, 1800 to witness the first performance of
De Monfort, featuring the stage luminaries Mrs. Sarah Siddons as Jane De Monfort
and her brother, John Philip Kemble, as De Monfort. The production was a modified success, running until May 9, 1800. Though *De Monfort* enjoyed more successful runs elsewhere (Slagle 256), see Appendix E.4 for an interesting account of the
play's early struggles in London.

tion.[1] It is not surprising that the rising middle class was not particularly disposed to a theatre of serious inquiry.[2]

A new attitude was dawning. Indeed, Frances Burney (1752-1840) gives us a taste of this theatrical sea-change in her novel *Evelina* (1778). Burney takes us inside the Pantheon, a popular, short-lived location for balls and masquerades which opened in 1772. Accompanying Mrs. Mirvan and her daughter on a visit to London to meet Captain Mirvan, Evelina, a country girl, is at first taken by the beauty of the building. Though it has "more the appearance of a chapel, than of a place of diversion" (*Evelina*, 104), she soon discovers that the "awe and solemnity" (105) inspired by the building is neutralized by the behaviour of the audience. During one of the customary musical interludes, she is "astonished to find how little music is attended to in silence; for though every body seems to admire, hardly any body listens." Many of the young men attend merely to admire the "animated charms" (107) of the young women. In her description, Burney brings to life a cultural trend in eighteenth-century British theatre that became more prevalent as the nineteenth century developed. Many of London's genteel flatly rejected the theatre, and as in Burney's description, were more inclined to attend opera. Not only did music move them more profoundly than drama, it offered a more congenial audience.

Audiences, in any time, reflect social turmoil and shifting boundaries of acceptable behaviour – and the audience for Baillie's plays was no exception. She noted this problem first hand after an 1817 performance at the Lyceum of one of her later plays, *The Election*, during which the din of the audience – including a "madman" howling at the Duke of Wellington

---

1 Modern political scientists have estimated that homicide rates in early nineteenth-century London were double those of the 1970s. (See Francis Fukuyama's *The Great Disruption* [1999].)

2 Matthew Lewis (1775-1818), author of the novel *The Monk* (1796) and the play *The Castle Spectre* (1798) amongst many others, wondering why modern tragedies such as *De Monfort* have not enjoyed longer runs, comments in his prologue to his play *Alfonso* (1802) that the public is not inclined to favour theatrical tragedy when greater tragedies such as Britain's war with France are taking place in the theatre of the world. See Jeffrey Cox's *Seven Gothic Dramas: 1789-1825* 49.

from a side box – over-powered the efforts of the actors on stage (Donkin 32). Not only were members of the audience themselves bordering on intolerable, but the saloons and lobbies of even the patent theatres were also frequented by representatives of the thousands of prostitutes plying their trade (*Revels History* 12-13). Behaviour which was generally acceptable "especially in the years preceding the opening of the new Drury Lane and the greatly enlarged Covent Garden in the 1790's" (*Revels* 21) had declined into coarseness, vulgarity and tumult – "one long riot" – which did not improve until after 1850.

Reason, too, was becoming suspect, and any entertainment that captured the imminent Romantic sense of "spirit" caught the attention of a growing middle-class audience. By the late eighteenth century, the "cult" of sentimentalism had taken firm hold.[1] In France, Jean-Jacques Rousseau's *La Nouvelle Héloïse*, a moralistic tale of young fallen women saved through the institution of marriage, was an instantaneous success in February 1761, and by April of the same year was translated into English. In 1771, *The Man of Feeling* appeared, Henry Mackenzie's story about the good-hearted Harley, who discovers the harsh realities of the world while seeking his fortune. And in 1774, *The Sorrows of Young Werther*, Johann Wolfgang von Goethe's (1749-1832) novel about impossible and tragic young love, became the rage. These novels were in the minds of the middle-class reading public, their sensibilities spilling over into popular tastes in entertainment. Tragedy on the stage became comic-tragedy. Rationalism had become tagged as aristocratic; sentimentalism was the mark of the new, powerful middle class. This new middle class "wished to see its interests reflected on the stage," yet it found itself alienated. "What it sought, and what the sentimental dramatists gave, was an intermediate kind of play where occasional comic scenes alternated with others that made seri-

---

1 Allardyce Nicholl suspects that the sentimental trend in England began as early as the 1680s (*British Drama* 142). The political disturbances of the times of Charles II and James II and the Rebellion focused concern on governmental and religious problems and, ultimately, on social problems in general. Thomas D'Urfey (1653-1723) and Aphra Behn (1640-89) were early writers of this new sensibility.

ous, if facile, comments on the contemporary world" (Nicoll, *British Drama* 142). What began as no more than the introduction of a moral note – as in, for instance, Colley Cibber's *Love's Last Shift* (1696) – became a dramatic series of emotional crises happily ending with a moral lesson, a trend that lingered well into the nineteenth century in the form of the Gothic melodrama.[1]

In its thirst for variety, this middle-class audience began to seek out more and more non-verbal performance. Along with opera, pantomime performances – "dumb show" – a direct descendant of the Italian touring *commedia dell'arte*, and spectacle were the order of the day. Only one "mainpiece," John Gay's (1685-1732) *The Beggar's Opera* (1728), played more than the most popular pantomines. Audiences could gorge on a smorgasbord of quickly-crafted tragedy, comedy, or a ballad opera intermixed with farce or pantomime, "entr'acte songs, dances and other specialty numbers, processions and pageants, orchestral music before, during and between the individual pieces, and an ingenious variety of prologues and epilogues" (*Revels* 30). At both the minor and the patent theatres, audiences were likely to witness dancing bears or equestrianized versions of *Blue-Beard* (1811), reenactments of naval battles, or a dog named Carlo, in *The Caravan or the Driver and his dog* (1803) by Frederic Reynolds (1764-1841), leaping into the water to save a child.[2] Theatre managers exploited the popular and lucrative spectacle, spending enormous sums on their productions and keeping them in performance for considerable periods. In doing so, they inadvertently established "the rule of the modern 'run'" (Nicoll, *The English Theatre* 125). Spectacle was becoming big business. How modern its sensibility sounds when one considers the words of Frederic Reynolds, who

---

1   The sentimental tradition in British drama conjures up names and titles such as: Susannah Centlivre's (1669-1723) *The Gamester* (1705), William Taverner's (died 1731) *The Artful Husband* (1716-17) and *The Artful Wife* (1718), Sir Richard Steele's (1672-1729) *The Conscious Lovers* (1722), Richard Cumberland's (1732-1811) *The West Indian* (1771) and *The Jew* (1794), and Thomas Holcroft's (1745-1809) *The Road to Ruin* (1792).

2   For descriptions of actual performances, see Allardyce Nicoll, *The English Theatre* 121-22.

sneered at his detractors of his work by asking them, "What would they have called me, had they known, that I cleared three hundred and fifty pounds simply by a dog jumping into a small tank of water!" (qtd. in *Revels* 31).

Perhaps it is folly to attempt to isolate single impediments to Baillie's career within the history of British drama. But the playwright herself gave us some insight into how she and others were beginning to become trapped in a new collision of the word and the image, a collision that now virtually defines our Western consumer culture. Baillie's initial concern in her 1812 preface was directed towards the technical failings of contemporary theatre, not to the "prevailing taste for dramatic amusements" (*Works* 231) or the "want of inclination in managers to bring forward new pieces" (*Works* 232). Since Aristotle, drama had been a complex balance of the image and the word, and it would be unrepresentative of Baillie's craft to say that she disliked the spectacle of the stage. Florence MacCunn points out that even when Baillie was "quite an old lady she rejoiced that she could still heartily enjoy a farce or a pantomime" (292). Indeed, her readers may even sense in plays such as *Basil* Baillie's early "cinematic" eye, her ability to visualize grand processions and distant action.[1] Perhaps this is why Baillie persisted with writing plays and did not turn to the novel. To improve the illusion of theatre, she suggested better lighting technology, blocking procedures, and improvements to the depth of the stage (*Works* 233-34). Though she argued for intimate, well-lit theatres, so that even non-verbal spectacle could be more successful, she emphasized the very source of her dramatic project in the word, seeing the soliloquy as the "gradual unfolding of the passions" (*Works* 232). Baillie's sensibilities lay within the poetic word, yet she wrote for a diversion-seeking audience that was powerfully drawn to the image. Making a clear delineation between the word as a source of serious reflection and the entertaining qualities of the image, Baillie writes:

> The Public have now to choose between what we shall suppose are well-written and well-acted plays, the words

---

1   See Baillie's *The Beacon: A Serious Musical Drama, in Two Acts* (1812).

of which are not heard, or heard but imperfectly by two thirds of the audience, while the finer and more pleasing traits of the acting are by a still greater proportion lost altogether; and splendid pantomime, or pieces whose chief object is to produce striking scenic effect, which can be seen and comprehended by the whole. So situated, it would argue, methinks, a very pedantic love indeed for what is called legitimate drama, were we to prefer the former. A love for active, varied movement, in the objects before us; for striking contrasts of light and shadow; for splendid decorations and magnificent scenery; is as inherent in us as the interest we take in the representation of the natural passions and characters of men: and the most cultivated minds may relish such exhibitions, if they do not, when both are fairly offered to their choice, prefer them. (*Works* 231-32)

Baillie here shuns contemporary criticism that is disparaging of a theatregoing audience lacking in taste, rejecting its implicit classism in those kinds of criticism. Rather, she recognizes that her industrial-consumer culture is rapidly becoming a culture more cognizant of the image than the word. Certainly Baillie would never have been able to anticipate with what power her culture would embrace the image, keeping in mind that only twenty-seven years after the 1812 volume of plays was published, William Henry Fox Talbot (1800-77) was credited with the discovery of photography.[1]

Today, writers such as Neil Postman[2] theorize about our

---

1 As early as the 1930s Allardyce Nicoll touched momentarily on this notion when he wrote that "maybe we shall not be far wrong in likening the development of pantomimic spectacle and the minor theatres to that of the film and the 'picture house' of to-day" (*The English Theatre* 121). Leo Braudy also notes that "in our own time, of course, the acute awareness of how we appear to others is so obviously indebted to the innumerable forms of visual representation that we may miss the revolution in self-awareness marked by the career of Brummell, with its intriguing analogues in those of Byron, Napoleon, and others. It crystallizes as well a growing fascination with the visible nature of public people that helps engender the growth of caricature, vaudeville, and variety theatre; seizes ravenously on the new invention of photography; and later battens on movies, radio, and television" (405).

2 See *Amusing Ourselves To Death* (1986).

fascination for images over words in modern culture and our insatiable appetite for them. Just as Baillie did in her time, Postman embraces the potential of the modern media, yet fears the visual offers "fascination in place of complexity and coherence" (*Amusing Ourselves* 77). Similarly, for Baillie, valuable theatre is one in which the word reigns and there exists a "natural connection" (*Works* 230) of ideas, and in which the visual component supports those ideas and what they say about life as we experience it. It is not a theatre of disconnected visuals torn from sense. So dedicated is she to this theatrical ideal and to the value of public performance, that by 1812 she chooses to withhold further publication of her work, fearing that she may "run the risk of entirely frustrating [her] original design" (*Works* 231). Connecting the "logo-centrism," if we may call it that, of Postman and Baillie might seem tenuous. But it is important not only to consider further how Baillie's dream of a more naturalistic theatre did come to fruition in the nineteenth century with the appearance of the problem plays of Jones, Pinero, Wilde and Shaw, depicting middle- and upper-class settings, but also to ask, when we reach back to Baillie's life-work, what such a study reveals about ourselves. Baillie was challenged by a consumer-based, image-driven world, very much as we are today.

The 1798 edition as a text of social reform

Elizabeth Barrett Browning passionately declared Joanna Baillie to be "the first female poet in all senses in England."[1] Catherine Burroughs, a modern critic, though not as expansive in her praise, honours Baillie as Romantic drama's "mother" (*Closet Stages* 14). On the surface, Baillie's work certainly encapsulated the new Romantic spirit. The passions are foremost in her work, not as ornament but as her central source of creativity and explorations of aberrant psychology. We see her unwavering dedication to nature and a more natural use of language. Though it was contrary to the contemporary bourgeois optimism of the happy ending, we also see her steadfast adherence

---

1 Quoted in Kerry McSweeney's introduction to *Aurora Leigh* (Oxford: Oxford University Press, 1993) xvii.

to a tragic vision. Her frequent introduction of exotic, gothic elements into the settings and action of her plays moved toward the absolute darkness of suicide and suggestive relationships bordering on incest. And we see her intense interest in Shakespeare's creative genius and in improving the sense of three-dimensional realism in the theatre. So strong are the trappings of Romanticism in Baillie's work that modern proponents of her literary contributions to early nineteenth-century and Victorian literature (Brewer 44) have explored potential connections between the 1798 "Introductory Discourse" and Wordsworth's 1800 "Preface" to the *Lyrical Ballads* (see Appendix D).[1] At issue here, though, is both Baillie and Wordsworth's powerful debt to the eighteenth-century moralist thinkers. For instance, Wordsworth's famous definition of good poetry as "the spontaneous overflow of powerful feelings" (see Appendix D.1.i) is really a poetic meditation on the idea of the association of feelings (see Appendix A.5.i). As we have seen, Baillie's debt is no lighter.

Productive comparisons of Baillie's work to the Romantic movement and nineteenth-century Gothic drama, however, such as Jeffrey Cox's introduction to *Seven Gothic Dramas: 1789-1825*, focus not on the superficial, but rather on Baillie's connections to clandestine reform. Cox writes:

> Gothic drama is the most subtle theatrical attempt of the 1790's to resolve the ideological, generic, and institutional problems facing playwrights of the day. At least for a moment, the Gothic drama offered a way to overcome the strains placed upon theatrical representation − essentially through a new aesthetic of sensationalism. It seemed to resolve the tensions within the hierarchy of genres − essentially by discovering a new ground of high tragedy in the tactics of popular drama. And the Gothic provided the means to represent the ideological struggles of the day in a way that would not arouse the wrath and thus the censorship of the Lord Chamberlain's Examiner of Plays,

---

1 See Donald Reiman "Introduction" and Marlon B. Ross *The Contours of Masculine Desire.* (See also Appendix D.)

John Larpent.[1] The Gothic is *the* theatrical form in the 1790's because it could contain all of pressures placed upon the drama (12).

As Ellen Donkin notes, "playwriting, as a profession for women, was an overt violation of all the rules of social conduct. It conferred on women a public voice. It gave them some control over how women were presented on stage" (Donkin 18). As we have seen, Baillie wrote from a domestic centre with strong political impulses. This pattern is repeated throughout the plays in this edition. Central to each play is a woman who withdraws into the privacy of the "closet" in search of solutions to the problems of the world at large. This is the very arena in which we have previously failed to appreciate Baillie. Daniel Watkins writes in his "Class, Gender, and Social Motion in Joanna Baillie's *De Monfort*" that the fate of Joanna Baillie specifically and eighteenth-century drama more generally is "attributable to the inability − or unwillingness − of scholarship to probe the deeper structures of a work whose significance is barely glimpsed on its surface" (116). Watkins, though writing exclusively about *De Monfort*, describes the entire contents of Baillie's 1798 volume when he explains that:

... despite [Baillie's] awareness of the limitations of theater in her day, she chooses drama to reveal, in ways that lyric poetry cannot, the ideological conflicts disturbing and shaping the passions that constitute her primary thematic and psychological interest. As a genre in decline, drama in the Romantic age is at once weighted with nostalgia and desire for the once-powerful and stable social world that had brought it to prominence, and, at the same time, pressured by the confidence, individualism and sheer defiance of the social energies struggling to assert ... their new-found power and authority. (109)

The source of the thinking behind this statement is Fredric

---

1   John Larpent (1741-1824) was Examiner of Plays from 1737 to 1824.

Jameson, author of *The Political Unconscious* (1981), who believes any text is a "utopian moment" (55), a point at which the contradictions of the real world are symbolically resolved. Since history has a nasty habit of preserving only one voice from any confrontation, it behooves us as readers and critics to read for the other voices which were "stifled and reduced to silence" (85).

Using Jameson's model, the reader's role becomes one of mediation, "to demonstrate what is not evident in the appearance of things, but rather in their underlying reality" (39). This mediation must embrace the inherent structural contradictions and oppositions in the text; it must, in Jameson's words, "register its capacity for differentiation and for revealing structural oppositions and contradictions" (42) in order to bridge these ideological gaps to reach moments of symbolic unification. Through Jameson's method we are finding transhistorical vehicles "for our experience of the real" (48) which, when employed, will direct our attention to the "informing power of forces or contradictions which the text seeks in vain wholly to control or master ..." (49). Examining Baillie's work in this way, across social contradictions of class and gender, we can begin to see that she has compiled in the 1798 edition alone what appears to be a more cohesive collection than originally thought, one that develops a utopian solution to the social situation facing women at the end of the eighteenth century in England.

The anxiety that marks all three plays is expressed by a pervasive confusion in male-dominated social settings. The all-consuming love portrayed in *Count Basil* marks the struggle between a growing individualism and a sense of duty to the social collective. Though Basil can admit his status as part of the military collective – he tells the Duke "Were I indeed free master of myself,/Strong inclination would detain me here ..." (2.1.30-31) – yet in the next scene countering his friend Count Rosinberg's accusations that he is "weaker than a child" (2.2.101), he declares that he feels "a new-born pow'r" within himself that will make him "twenty-fold" the man he was "before this fated day." *The Tryal*, by contrast, seeks more a resolution to the insecurity between the genders in a declining aristocratic society. Amidst the superficiality of one soirée after the next and the social posturing, deceit and invasion of the values of commerce, Agnes conducts a test of Harwood's masculine integrity. Harwood's values are challenged by men of the establishment like Colonel Hardy who, on hearing that Agnes – at least to his understanding – is not an heiress, gives Harwood some equivocal advice: "That is a great mistake, to be sure" he tells Harwood, "yet many a man has not advanced the less rapidly in his profession, for having had a portionless wife to begin the world with. It is a spur to industry." And finally, *De Monfort* examines a threatened and decaying aristocracy in a world now driven by a robust yet rough, rising middle class. The traditional social hierarchy, upon which his identity relied, is being turned on its head; the old definitions of class and nobility no longer apply. De Monfort's deep-seated hatred for Rezenvelt seems to come from the relative ease with which his unwelcome peer rises from compromised beginnings to full status with De Monfort. Rezenvelt's impressive ascent through his class must certainly suggest to a disoriented De Monfort a corresponding fall. De Monfort's social position is now tenuous, and Rezenvelt exemplifies the new energy and brash confidence of a middle class that threatens to depose him.

Faced with these contradictions, Baillie constructs three utopian resolutions, restoring the woman's voice to each. In *Count Basil*, posed at the point of imminent battle between clashing male forces and caught within Victoria's gaze, Basil neglects his masculine duties. In an act of male solidarity, Rosinberg struggles to help Basil maintain his sense of himself, while Geoffry stands as a haunting, battle-worn, yet noble emblem of service to the state. On the other hand, the Duke and his minister, Gauriecio, are men, in Geoffrey's words, of "narrow policy" (3.1.98) who, in their Machiavellian ways, know how to turn the nobility of others' service into gain for themselves. Gauriecio particularly, who pretends to be the "tool and servant" (2.3.170) of the Duke, understands how to manipulate a social collective aroused with "warm heroic feelings" (3.2.15). Ironically, in manipulating a collaborator to incite dissension amongst Basil's troops, he provokes him to smash the collective of the army by inducing the troops to think. "And he who teaches men to think, though nobly," counsels Gauriecio, "Doth raise within their minds a busy judge/To scan [Basil's] actions" (3.2.25).

Amid this confusion is the Countess of Albini, who functions here as a momentary fantasy of how this male-dominated ideological struggle might be resolved. Magically, the link between the play's debate and its feminist resolution is the long-deceased mother of Victoria, a woman whom both Geoffry and Albini knew and admired. Her memory carries vestiges of a less confusing morality, but Geoffry can only "trace some semblance of her mother" (1.1.51) in Victoria. We become particularly aware of Albini in the second act, when she is seen attending to her young female charges, they playing chess and she "sitting by them reading to herself" (2.4.1sd). Though there is no concrete evidence of any connection between Baillie and Mary Wollstonecraft (1759-97), author of *A Vindication of the Rights of Woman* (1792) – indeed, middle-class women were not particularly disposed to liking Wollstonecraft (Donkin 28) – *Count Basil* can be seen as a skilful blending of Baillie's interests in human psychology with Wollstonecraft's political notions of tyranny (see Appendix B). Baillie's descriptive and ideological connections to Wollstonecraft are extensive and meticulously patterned. Of primary importance, however, is how Albini, living in a society in which women enslave themselves through their tyranny of sensuality over men, comes to stand as a voice of educated reason amid this social degeneration. She argues, as does Wollstonecraft, that the debate between collective responsibilities and the urges of an independent self is empty; in fact, the two poles find synthesis in the union of educated, aware women and men. After a discussion between Albini and her young charges, who have been extolling the virtues of "the triumphs of all-powerful beauty" (2.4.27), Albini questions their argument: "And is, indeed, a plain domestic dame,/Who fills the duties of an useful state,/A being of less dignity than she,/Who vainly on her transient beauty builds/A little poor ideal tyranny?" (2.4.33-37). Strong collectives are constructed on strong individuals. To reinforce the complexity and importance of the figure of Albini, Baillie links her ideologically with Rosinberg, who regards her with "profound respect" (3.3.128). He is, to Baillie's mind, the closest one might find to an ideal man – should we choose to accept this possibility – because of his intelligence, his inner respectability, his capacity for compromise and change, and his inclination to meet women on common ground.

With the typical bombast of an eighteenth-century comedy, *The Tryal* presents its case in its first lines. Just as Mr. Withrington's house stands as a monument to a confusing blend of conservative aristocratic and progressive bourgeois social conduct in Bath, then known for its frivolous, vacationing, aristocratic clientele, so does Withrington. To Withrington's opening line to Agnes and Mariane: "Pooh, pooh, get along, young gipsies, and don't tease me any more" (1.1.1), Agnes, immediately seizing her function in the play with language replete with legal connotations, replies: "So we will, my good sir, when you have granted our suit." Agnes becomes a comic fusion of Jane De Monfort in *De Monfort* and Countess of Albini in *Count Basil*. Though she seeks marriage, as young women of that time were expected to do, she reverses the roles of marital control. Her early catalogue of aristocratic men, and those who aspire to be so, and her critique of the accepted social mechanisms of marriage align her philosophically with Albini. Protesting to Withrington, Agnes does not speak like a compliant female of the eighteenth century (see 1.1.28-41). And Withrington does not chastise or correct her, as men of his station in other contemporary forms of sentimental fiction most certainly would have. Instead, he complies with his niece's wishes, partly in respect of her rationality but mainly from the pressure of Agnes's powerful sense of self. Baillie constructs Agnes from male Shakespearean roles; she is more of a Benedick than a Beatrice. With the will and manipulative powers of a female Petrucio, she taunts Harwood with a ruse of ill-tempered behaviour (3.2.83-124).

And so Agnes pushes him to the brink with her contrary behaviour, but it is in her transformation as a Hamlet, determined to prove Harwood's ultimate worth, that she engineers a final trial – a play, of sorts, within a play. Using some of the same devices that might be employed by contemporary writers of courtroom fiction, she strips away Harwood's conventional social trappings of to prove that he is, indeed, one of those distant men of sense. But when Harwood in effect collapses on the stand, he reveals his worth, not his guilt. Baillie has constructed, in comic form, a woman metaphorically seizing control of a male-dominated justice system and elevating it to an institution that discerns moral innocence from guilt. As well, in a resounding vote of support and a full test and transformation of the traditional use of the feminine pronoun, Withrington taunts the conniving Mr. Opal, a man of little substance, in his own pantomime of outrage over Opal's empty vows to Mariane, "I will not see my niece wronged. The law shall do *her* [my italics] justice, whatever expense it may cost me" (5.2.304-05).

De Monfort clearly represents the most dramatic display of masculine angst the 1798 edition has to offer, driven by elemental class rivalry. Daniel Watkins suggests that Jane De Monfort has "changed through the course of the drama in ways that keep a bourgeois sensibility alive" (115). After the deaths of Rezenvelt and De Monfort, "Jane's character gradually begins to represent, in idealized form, an individualism and subjectivity over against aristocratic and religious structures of value – to display, that is, bourgeois sensibilities shorn of the ugliness associated with Rezenvelt's character." Watkins views Jane De Montfort in her final entrance – a true Gothic scene set in the gloom of a convent chapel – as a "Roman matron" (114). Indeed, some of her speeches reflect this image; however, though Jane initially weeps in grief for her dead brother – as a reader of sentimental fiction might expect – she quickly "shakes off the weakness of grief, and ... steps forward with dignity" (5.4.113sd). This scene of Jane, surrounded by friends, servants, and clerics, becomes reminiscent of an early painting of Christ before the crucifixion. Baillie fuses the "Roman matron" with the image of a "feminized Christ," a figure beyond the fallible laws of the world. In her stage directions, Baillie writes: "*Here they all hang about her.* FREBURG *supporting her tenderly,* MANUEL *embracing her knees, and old* JEROME *catching hold of her robe affectionately.* BERNARD, *abbess, monks, and nuns likewise gather her, with looks of sympathy*" (5.4.104sd). When two officers of the law enter to determine De Monfort's cause of death, one "simple word" from Jane ends their investigation.

Baillie's women in the 1798 edition form a female triumvirate that infiltrates the key foundations of their culture. The Countess of Albini is a woman with a unified vision. For her, education is the powerful altering force in society, offering future solutions for a stronger social collective, a collective built on the strengths of both independent men and women. Agnes seeks control in legal models, forcing broader, more ideal notions of justice down into the social realm. And Jane De Monfort's speeches of final religious blessings shine as a spiritual and moral beacon above them all. It is no wonder that Mrs. Sarah Siddons reportedly demanded of Baillie, "Make me some more Jane De Monforts" (*Works* xi).

Contemporary Criticism of the 1798 edition

Some insight into the difficulties Baillie faced in the literary community is provided by a brief survey of the contemporary reviews (Appendix E) in response to the publishing phenomenon of the *Plays on the Passions*. She must have been greatly encouraged by the early reviews supportive of her design. The *Analytical Review* (May 1798) wrote approvingly of the plays as a "task of such extremely difficult execution" and of Baillie as a talented playwright who had a "complete ... knowledge of the springs of human action" and a "familiarity with every emotion of the heart ..." (524). While the reviewer of the *Critical Review* (September 1798) was at first "inclined to smile at a plan so methodical and so arduous" (13), he later appraised the preface as a product of "good sense and modesty" and the edition as a whole as a "work which ... will not only be honourable to the writer, but to the literature of our country." His sense of the 1798 edition was that though it was a "small part of the projected plan," the plays were enough to determine not only that the design was "excellent" but also that the author was "equal to the task of properly executing it" (21).

These reviewers also sensed great promise in the individual

plays. The *Monthly Review* (September 1798), written by a friend of Baillie's[1] who was unaware of the identity of the author, sensed a "rugged and inharmonious" quality to the verse and an "antientry of phrase which often savours of affectation." But he felt Baillie's characters were "in general strongly discriminated" and the scenes filled with "beautiful passages" (66). The *Critical Review* (September 1798) declared *Count Basil* an "admirable tragedy" (17) written by someone who had "studied nature deeply" and evocative of England's "old and excellent dramatic writers." Though *The Tryal* was seen as inferior to the tragedies, *De Monfort* was felt to reveal the "same genius, and the same knowledge of the human heart" (19) as *Count Basil*. The *Eclectic Review* (August 1813), in response to Longman and Co.'s three-volume edition, declares Baillie's work unlike other drama of the day. Her "personages are not always ranting or whining, in the extasies of love, or the agonies of despair, or the madness of rage: they really do talk ... like men and women of this world, – men and women who have some other bond of connection with the reader besides speaking the same language, and acknowledging the same rules of prosody" (168). Her characters are "strongly marked, and yet highly poetical, frail and infirm, and yet very interesting" (170). De Monfort, to this reviewer, is "brave and generous and manly, struggling with an infernal passion, bearing up and making head against it, and at length finally borne down by it, and brought to the perpetration of a deed cowardly, ungenerous, and unmanly," but it is the character of Rezenvelt he most admires. "There is a carelessness in the delineation of this character, a flowing freedom in the outline" which he feels is "seldom to be met with in Miss Baillie, and which puts us more in mind of Shakespeare than any thing in the volumes." The complex mix of "hatred" and "gibing gaiety" of Rezenvelt's character, exposed with a "carelessness that seems to mock the uneasiness it occasions," prompts the reviewer not to hesitate "in pronouncing De Monfort the most original tragedy of the present

---

1 Samuel B. Rogers (1763-1855), author of *The Pleasures of Memory* (1792), wrote this review (see *Works* x and Carhart 42-43).

age, and Rezenvelt a character the most her own of any she has produced" (171).

But as early as January 1799, reviewers, perhaps not as vociferously, voiced Francis Jeffrey's concern that Baillie's plan was a problematic vehicle to advance her dramatic theories (Appendix E.2). Even though in 1811 he included Baillie amongst the greatest poets of the age, including Robert Southey, William Wordsworth, and Samuel Taylor Coleridge, eight years earlier, in *Edinburgh Review* (July 1803), Jeffrey bluntly attacked not only the plan of Baillie's dramatic project but also her key purpose as a playwright – to write plays of moral import (see *Introductory Discourse*, below, p. 90). The *New London Review* declared the plan "more philosophical than dramatic" (72) and felt it capable of producing interesting plays, though neither a "practicable method" nor a "desireable one." This reviewer viewed Baillie's system of delineation as "too tedious and circumstantial for a species of composition of which the effect, whatever regard it may be necessary to pay to character and to passion, depends, in an equal degree, upon ACTION...." Baillie's delineations of character were too "languid and uninteresting in representation." Audiences, in this reviewer's estimation, do not have the "time, inclination, or capacity to enter minutely into discriminations of character." For this reason most "dramatists ... have generally hurried into the heart of a passion" (72-73). The *British Critic* (March 1799) expressed concerns that seldom will "one passion be found unconnected with others" (285). Conceding that though he felt Baillie capable of executing her plan, as Jeffrey had, this reviewer expressed his aesthetic and moral concerns that "To separate and individualize the passions, therefore, is to leave the path of Nature; and to make the possessor of one bad propensity in all other respects virtuous, is to apologize for vice, and to make us pity rather than abhor it" (185). The *Imperial Review* (March 1804) concurs that the passions mingle "promiscuously" (226) rather than adhere to botanical classifications (Appendix E.3). And the *Edinburgh Magazine* (June 1818) reviewer is concerned that the characters and the incidents in Baillie's plays are "merely a mirror in which to contemplate the passions, or rather a microscope, by means of which she seems to think that she has brought within the sphere of our vision things too minute for the naked intellectual eye" (517). This he feels is the "radical defect of her plays, and casts an air of restraint and formality over the whole of her performances," and it is because of her persistence in "fettering herself by a false system" (519) that her plays are not "added to the stock of the English Stage" (517).

In reading these reviewers, we must remain aware of their confirmed gender and cultural biases that challenged Baillie's belief in a "corresponding spirit" (*Introductory Discourse*, below, p. 86) between men and women. Francis Jeffrey predicted that Baillie just might well produce some unforgettable work in the future with the "proper management" (277). Contemplating the existence of "a sex in soul" (517), the *Edinburgh Magazine* (June 1818), in what was meant as a compliment,[1] discovered in Baillie's plays the merging of masculine "energy" and feminine "purity." These assumptions about gender spilled over into the reviewers' comments on the plays themselves. One finds it preposterous that Harwood, "a young man bred up in London, and on a companionable footing with fops of fashion," is able to fall in love instantaneously "with a girl, whose appearance is by no means seducing" (340). In the same vein, another, the *Imperial Review* (March 1804; Appendix E.3), struggles with Rezenvelt's interest in Jane De Monfort who, in its words, is represented as "verging into autumnal virginity" (343). Though conceding the potential for error here, the reviewer ventures that "we are not quite convinced that we should have been so industriously prohibited from imaging Jane of a more lovely age; which would have added probability to the suspicion her brother conceives of an attachment between her and Rezenvell [sic]." This reviewer comments, as well, on a pronoun agreement problem in *The Tryal*, a "grammatical inaccuracy" he

---

1 Byron is famous for two sexist compliments to Baillie. The first, he wrote in a letter (1815): that "Women (saving Joanna Baillie) cannot write tragedy. They haven't experienced the life for it." The second (1817) more boldly professed that "Voltaire was asked why no woman has ever written even a tolerable tragedy, 'Ah (Said the Patriarch) the composition of a tragedy requires testicles.' If this be true, Lord knows what Joanna Baillie does – I suppose she borrows them" (qtd. in Donkin 78).

notes, "not unfrequent in female conversation" (340).[1]

Just as their sexist perspective prevented them from hearing the voices of Baillie's heroines, the cultural myopia of these reviewers makes it impossible for them to see the social implications of her work. For instance, the critic of *Imperial Review* (March 1804; Appendix E.3) also struggled to reconcile the "different parts" (342) of *De Monfort*. Blind to the potential hatred between established and emerging classes, he guesses a "puerile lust after universal estimation, and a spiteful envy of his antagonist" as the cause of De Monfort's emotional distemper. Later the *Edinburgh Magazine* isolates the source of this inability to comprehend De Monfort's character. This reviewer accepts Othello's jealousy, for instance, as an accurate delineation of passion nurtured in the hot and passionate lands of the Moors. Of De Monfort's festering hatred, "it is the want of a proper soil in which to plant such a passion, and the culture necessary to its growth" (517) that he finds inconceivable.

Baillie bore the criticism and the resistance to her project bravely. In the preface to the second volume of *Plays on the Passions* (1802) she stoically describes the earlier response to her work as the "best calculated to make a work go on well – praise mixed with a considerable portion of censure" (*Works* 104).

This new edition of *Plays on the Passions* is not intended to force a false sense of totality upon the 1798 edition; rather, the intent is to offer it to a new reading public as something more than simply a fragment of a larger project. As interest in Baillie's writing slowly but surely grows, the 1798 edition deserves to be explored as a text unto itself. Indeed, it was Baillie's wish not to publish her work in large volumes in which the plays would "crowd, and jostle, and tread upon one another's heel" (*Works* 288). Here in one volume is an opportunity to re-think the character of the eighteenth century in all its dynamic diversity, to reconsider the role women played in the artistic communities of those times, and to review our place at the end of over two hundred years of profound social change. Baillie offers us

---

1 See note to *The Tryal* 4.1.37 and Appendix E.3 on Baillie's education.

all of this and more, along with an enjoyable reading experience and an eternal reminder of the joys of a constructive life dedicated to simple, creative expression. As Baillie humbly writes in her "An Address to the Muses":

> But O, such sense of matter bring!
> As they who feel and never sing
> Wear on their heart; it will avail
> With simple words to tell my tale;
> And still contented will I be,
> Though greater inspirations never fall to me.
>
> (Lonsdale, *Women Poets* 441)

Joanna Baillie: A Brief Chronology

1760 Joanna Baillie's sister, Agnes, is born, the first child of Reverend Mr. James Baillie and Dorothea Hunter Baillie.

1761 Joanna Baillie's brother, Matthew, is born.

1762 (September 11) Joanna Baillie and a twin sister are born in the manse of Bothwell, Lanarkshire, Scotland. Her unnamed sister dies hours later.

1766 James Baillie is appointed minister of the collegiate church at Hamilton.

1772 Joanna and Agnes attend boarding school.

1776 James Baillie is appointed Professor of Divinity in the University of Glasgow.

1778 James Baillie dies.

1779 Matthew Baillie leaves for Balliol College, Oxford under the guardianship of uncle William Hunter to study medicine. Joanna, her mother and Agnes leave for Long Calderwood (now owned by William Hunter).

1783 William Hunter dies. Matthew inherits the Hunter School of Anatomy on Windmill Street, London.

1790 Joanna publishes her first book of poems, included in her later volume *Poems*.

1791 Matthew Baillie marries Sophia Denman, a sister of Lord Chief Justice Denman (moves to Grosvenor Street). Joanna, Agnes, and their mother move from Sunbury, Hythe, and Maldon before settling in Colchester.

1793 Matthew Baillie publishes *The Morbid Anatomy of some of the most important Parts of the Human Body*.

1798 Joanna Baillie *Plays on the Passions Vol. 1*
Maria Edgeworth *Practical Education*
Elizabeth Inchbald *Lovers' Vows*
Matthew Lewis *Ambrosio; or The Monk* (4th ed.)
Thomas Malthus *An Essay on the Principle of Population*
Mary Wollstonecraft *The Wrongs of Woman; or, Maria*

1800 (April 29) *De Monfort* is performed at the Drury Lane Theatre.

The third edition of *Plays on the Passions* is published.

1801 Prologue for Miss Berry's *Fashionable Friends* is performed on Horace Walpole's former estate Strawberry Hill in November.

1802 The fourth edition appears. (Many changes are made to the plays in third and fourth editions. Most important changes to *De Monfort* are made in the fourth edition.) The second volume of the *Plays on the Passions* appears, which includes *The Election* (a comedy on hatred), *Ethwald*, Part I and II (a tragedy on ambition), and *The Second Marriage* (a comedy on ambition).

1804 *Miscellaneous Plays* is published, containing *Constantine Paleologus*, *The Country Inn*, and *Rayner* (2nd ed. 1805).

1806 The fifth edition of *Plays on the Passions* appears.
Baillie meets Walter Scott in London through William Sotheby.
Dorothea Hunter Baillie dies.
Joanna and Agnes visit Western Highlands and Glasgow. They visit Scott in March and April, travelling further north in May. They visit Robert Southey.

1810 The single play *The Family Legend* is published.

1811 Francis Jeffrey, the *Edinburgh Review* critic who brutalized Baillie's work in July 1803, ranks Baillie with the greatest poets of the age – Southey, Wordsworth, and Coleridge.

1812 The third volume of *Plays on the Passions* is published: *Orra* (a tragedy on fear), *The Dream* (a tragedy on fear), *The Siege* (a comedy on fear) and *The Beacon* (a serious musical drama on hope).
(Spring) Baillie and William Wordsworth meet Sir Humphrey and Lady Davy.
According to Margaret Carhart, this is the height of Baillie's career.

1813 Baillie meets Madame de Staël at dinner at Miss Berry's home.

1815 Lord Byron, as a member of the management committee at Drury Lane Theatre, tries to renew interest in Baillie's plays.

1820 From this point, Francis Jeffrey seldom visits London without visiting Baillie.

1821 Baillie receives £1,000 for *Metrical Legends of Exalted Characters* from Longmans.

1823 *The Martyr* (a tragedy) and *The Bride* (a drama) are published several times before 1836.

As a charitable gesture to raise money for a friend who was in some business difficulties, Baillie edits *A Collection of Poems, chiefly manuscript, and from Living Authors*.

1831 *A view of the General Tenor of the New Testament regarding the Nature and Dignity of Jesus Christ*, Baillie's expression of her belief in the human nature of Christ, is published.

1836 *Miscellaneous Plays* are published in three volumes. The first volume contains the *Plays on the Passions*: *Romiero* (a tragedy on jealousy), *The Alienated Manor* (a comedy on jealousy) and *Henriquez* (a tragedy on remorse). *The Martyr* is also included in this volume. The second volume contains *The Separation* (a tragedy), *The Stripling* (a tragedy in prose), *The Phantom* (a musical drama), and *Enthusiasm* (a comedy). The third volume contains *Witchcraft* (a tragedy in prose), *The Homicide* (a tragedy in prose and occasional verse), *The Bride* (a drama), and *The Match* (a comedy).

1840 Baillie elected an honorary member of the Historical Society of Michigan with numerous Americans and Maria Edgeworth, Anna Jameson, Harriet Martineau, Mary Russell Mitford, Mary Shelley, Madame D'Arblay (Frances Burney), and Lucy Aikin.

1851 Baillie's complete works – her "great monster book" – is published by Longman, Brown, Green, and Longmans in London.

Baillie dies Sunday, February 23, and is buried in the parish churchyard at Hampstead.

A Note on the Text

Joanna Baillie's first volume of *A Series of Plays: in which it is attempted to delineate the stronger passions of the mind. Each passion being the subject of a Tragedy and a Comedy* (known widely as *Plays on the Passions*) was published in London in 1798 by T. Cadell, Junior and W. Davies. Within the next eight years, five editions of the first volume appeared: the second edition in 1799, the third in 1800, the fourth in 1802, and the fifth in 1806. Not all these editions are easily available to Baillie's modern readers. More readily available is Baillie's "monster book," *The Dramatic and Poetical Works of Joanna Baillie*, published in London by Longman, Brown, Green and Longmans just prior to her death in 1851.

Since the 1798 edition was Baillie's anonymous debut and the talk of London's late eighteenth-century literary community, it is the intention of this edition to represent it as faithfully as possible. I have worked directly from the Woodstock facsimile edition (1990) and collated it to the 1806 edition of the first volume and the 1851 complete works. The 1806 edition accounts for most of Baillie's changes to this text; however, Baillie wrote to Samuel Rogers in 1832 that she was still actively making changes and had just recently finished her new set of corrections. Though Baillie then felt that all her "literary tasks" were finished, the 1851 edition still offers us what is perhaps our only definitive evidence of the 1806 and later changes to the critical introduction and plays of the 1798 edition.

A text such as the 1798 edition provides its own set of editing concerns. Baillie wrote enthusiastically for the stage, yet published her work first for a reading audience. In fact, she stopped publishing her work for a time, troubled that prior publication of her plays might inhibit later performance possibilities. Baillie did alter the meeting of Basil and Victoria in *Count Basil* (2.2.78-106), and extensive changes were made to *De Monfort*, especially throughout the first three acts, though they probably speak more about the influence of John Philip Kemble at the time than of Baillie's personal vision for the play.

However, for the most part, Baillie made few substantive structural changes to her work after the initial publication. She equated revision with "correction." It was tedious and laborious work, removed from the world of "serious thought." Her earlier punctuation and diction choices reflected an obvious interest in the delivery of the spoken word for the stage, yet her later changes demonstrate more concern for the readability of the text. The issue is that Baillie had two audiences. Therefore, the question that continually challenges a modern editor is how to retain and, indeed, enhance the performance qualities of the text while subtly eliminating potential distractions for a reading audience?

The most obvious difference between the diction of the 1798 edition and the later editions is that religious propriety took precedence over impulsive curses.

Expressions such as "O! damn it" (*Count Basil* 2.1.150) were reduced to "I" by at least 1806. Any grammatical slips have been retained and noted. One such small, yet illustrative, substantive variant occurs in *De Monfort* when Jane De Montfort asks "Is this the pace of one who bears good tidings?" (5.1.22). Though the word "pace" was changed to "face" at least by 1806, the original diction has been retained and noted because of its poetic and interpretive potential. A distraught Jane, looking for subtle clues of the imminent news of her brother's welfare, might focus first on the messenger's manner of walking before attempting to read his face. Also, in my estimation, the change resulted in a somewhat cumbersome repetition of the word in the next line.

Any obvious oversights have been emended. For instance, Colonel Hardy has been added to the "Persons of the Drama" of *The Tryal* (234). And spelling irregularities such as "it's" for "its" have also been silently emended. To eliminate confusion, contractions have been regularized, and any obvious spelling errors such as "De Montfort" for "De Monfort" (*De Monfort* 1.1.97) "rights" for "rites" (*Count Basil* 5.3.111), "night" for "right" (*Count Basil* 3.3.238), "bad" for "bade" (*Count Basil* 3.1.219), or "pale" for "pule" (*Count Basil* 3.3.41), "dot" for "don't" (*The Tryal* 1.2.94), and "hehind" for "behind" (*De Monfort* 1.1.157) have been emended silently, but in more interesting cases, with footnotes.

To retain the original flavour of the 1798 edition, the original punctuation has for the most part been retained. Generally, the 1798 edition exhibits a looser style than that of the 1851 edition. In *De Monfort*, for instance, the earlier edition reads "Borne down with sudden and impetuous force..." (3.2.98), whereas Baillie controls the line in the 1851 edition with a comma between "down" and "with." The added punctuation in the later edition creates a stronger internal voice in the reader yet, for the actor, eliminates numerous possibilities of delivery. Also, the 1798 edition's use of the semi-colon may seem odd to a modern reader, particularly when it ends a speech. This could simply have been Baillie's signal to the following actor to interrupt the speaker, or it may have been a cue to the actors in general to accelerate the flow of the dialogue.

In *The Tryal* we can also see a good example of how Baillie uses loose punctuation in the dialogue to construct her characters. In the 1851 edition, Royston's speeches are carefully controlled, while in the 1798 edition Baillie runs his language in a breathless, busy delivery that is appropriate to the character's scattered, entrepreneurial nature. There are, however, instances of punctuation in the original edition that pose impediments to the reader. In these cases, the punctuation has been silently emended. For instance, as in one such case in *De Monfort* (2.2.63-7), I have bowed to the 1851 edition. In this passage Jane De Monfort implores her brother, "By the affection thou didst ever bear me;/By the dear mem'ry of our infant days;/By kindred living ties, ay, and by those/Who sleep i'the tomb, and cannot call to thee,/I do conjure thee speak." The 1798 edition initially blurs the parallel structure here with a comma after "me." Here a modern reading audience can benefit from the subtle reinforcing of this parallel structure found in the 1851 edition. Otherwise, a careful reader may not initially recognize, despite the repetition of the preposition, that each phrase requires equal weight commensurate with the power of Jane

De Monfort's character. Of course, where obvious misprints have occurred as a result of creased paper in the press or sloppy typesetting, silent emendations have been made.

As well, all inconsistencies or blatant mistakes in stage directions which led to confusion in assigning speeches to characters or in visualizing the addressee of a speech have been silently emended. I have also regularized the punctuation of speech headings and stage directions.

It is, then, my sincere intent that this text capture the original spirit of Baillie's inaugural collection of the *Plays on the Passions*. I hope that this edition not only provides an enjoyable reading experience but also an appreciation of its colourful performance possibilities. Indeed, as argued in the Introduction, this text has an integrity of its own and should not be seen as a mere fragment of a larger, imperfect work.

A

SERIES OF PLAYS:

IN WHICH

IT IS ATTEMPTED TO DELINEATE

THE STRONGER PASSIONS OF THE MIND.

EACH PASSION BEING THE SUBJECT

OF

A TRAGEDY AND A COMEDY.

———————

LONDON:

PRINTED FOR T. CADELL, JUN. AND W. DAVIES, IN THE STRAND.

———————

1798.

INTRODUCTORY DISCOURSE

It is natural for a writer, who is about to submit his works to the Publick, to feel a strong inclination, by some Preliminary Address, to conciliate the favour of his reader, and dispose him, if possible, to peruse them with a favourable eye. I am well aware, however, that his endeavours are generally fruitless: in his situation our hearts revolt from all appearance of confidence, and we consider his diffidence as hypocrisy. Our own word is frequently taken for what we say of ourselves, but very rarely for what we say of our works. Were these three plays, which this small volume contains, detached pieces only, and unconnected with others that do not yet appear, I should have suppressed this inclination altogether; and have allowed my reader to begin what is before him, and to form what opinion of it his taste or his humour might direct, without any previous trespass upon his time or his patience. But they are part of an extensive design: of one which, as far as my information goes, has nothing exactly similar to it in any language: of one which a whole life time will be limited enough to accomplish; and which has, therefore, a considerable chance of being cut short by that hand which nothing can resist.

Before I explain the plan of this work, I must make a demand upon the patience of my reader, whilst I endeavour to communicate to him those ideas regarding human nature, as they in some degree affect almost every species of moral writings, but particularly the Dramatic, that induced me to attempt it; and, as far as my judgment enabled me to apply them, has directed me in the execution of it.

From that strong sympathy which most creatures, but the human above all, feel for others of their kind, nothing has become so much an object of man's curiosity as man himself. We are all conscious of this within ourselves, and so constantly do we meet with it in others, that like every circumstance of continually repeated occurrence, it thereby escapes observation. Every person, who is not deficient in intellect, is more or less occupied in tracing, amongst the individuals he converses with, the varieties of understanding and temper which constitute the characters of men; and receives great pleasure from every stroke of nature that points out to him those varieties. This is, much more than we are aware of, the occupation of children, and of grown people also, whose penetration is but lightly esteemed; and that conversation which degenerates with them into trivial and mischievous tattling, takes its rise not unfrequently from the same source that supplies the rich vein of the satirist and the wit. That eagerness so universally shewn for the conversation of the latter, plainly enough indicates how many people have been occupied in the same way with themselves. Let any one, in a large company, do or say what is strongly expressive of his peculiar character, or of some passion or humour of the moment, and it will be detected by almost every person present. How often may we see a very stupid countenance animated with a smile, when the learned and the wise have betrayed some native feature of their own minds! and how often will this be the case when they have supposed it to be concealed under a very sufficient disguise! From this constant employment of their minds, most people, I believe, without being conscious of it, have stored up in idea the greater part of those strong marked varieties of human character, which may be said to divide it into classes; and in one of those classes they involuntarily place every new person they become acquainted with.

I will readily allow that the dress and the manners of men, rather than their characters and disposition are the subjects of our common conversation, and seem chiefly to occupy the multitude. But let it be remembered that it is much easier to express our observations upon these. It is easier to communicate to another how a man wears his wig and cane, what kind of house he inhabits, and what kind of table he keeps, than from what slight traits in his words and actions we have been led to conceive certain impressions of his character: traits that will often escape the memory, when the opinions that were founded upon them remain. Besides, in communicating our ideas of the characters of others, we are often called upon to support them with more expence of reasoning than we can well afford, but our observations on the dress and appearance of men, seldom involve us in such difficulties. For these, and other reasons too tedious to mention, the generality of people appear to us more trifling than they are: and I may venture to say that, but for this sympathetick curiosity towards others of our kind, which is so strongly implanted within us, the attention we pay to the dress and the manners of men would dwindle into an employment as insipid, as examining the varieties of plants and minerals, is to one who understands not natural history.

In our ordinary intercourse with society, this sympathetick propensity of our minds is exercised upon men, under the common occurrences of life, in which we have often observed them. Here vanity and weakness put themselves forward to view, more conspicuously than the virtues: here men encounter those smaller trials, from which they are not apt to come off victorious; and here, consequently, that which is marked with the whimsical and ludicrous will strike us most forcibly, and make the strongest impression on our memory. To this sympa-thetick propensity of our minds, so exercised, the genuine and pure comick of every composition, whether drama, fable, story, or satire is addressed.

If man is an object of so much attention to man, engaged in the ordinary occurrences of life, how much more does he excite his curiosity and interest when placed in extraordinary situations of difficulty and distress? It cannot be any pleasure we receive from the sufferings of a fellow-creature which attracts such multitudes of people to a publick execution,[1] though it is the horrour we conceive for such a spectacle that keeps so many more away. To see a human being bearing himself up under such circumstances, or struggling with the terrible apprehensions which such a situation impresses, must be the powerful incentive, which makes us press forward to behold what we shrink from, and wait with trembling expectation for what we dread.[2] For though few at such a spectacle can get

---

1 Cf. Burke, *A Philosophical Enquiry* 43-44; ch. 15 (Appendix A.3.iii).

2 [Baillie's note] In confirmation of this opinion I may venture to say, that of the great numbers who go to see a publick execution, there are but very few who would not run away from, and avoid it, if they happened to meet with it unexpect-edly. We find people stopping to look at a procession, or any other uncommon

near enough to distinguish the expression of face, or the minuter parts of a criminal's behaviour, yet from a considerable distance will they eagerly mark whether he steps firmly; whether the motions of his body denote agitation or calmness; and if the wind does but ruffle his garment, they will, even from that change upon the outline of his distant figure, read some expression connected with his dreadful situation. Though there is a greater proportion of people in whom this strong curiosity will be overcome by other dispositions and motives; though there are many more who will stay away from such a sight than will go to it; yet there are very few who will not be eager to converse with a person who has beheld it; and to learn, very minutely, every circumstance connected with it, except the very act itself of inflicting death. To lift up the roof of his dungeon, like the *Diable boiteux*,[1] and look upon a criminal the night before he suffers, in his still hours of privacy, when all that disguise, which respect for the opinion of others, the strong motive by which even the lowest and wickedest of men still continue to be moved, would present an object to the mind of every person, not withheld from it by great timidity of character, more powerfully attractive than almost any other.

Revenge, no doubt, first began amongst the savages[2] of America that dreadful custom of sacrificing their prisoners of war. But the perpetration of such hideous cruelty could never have become a permanent national custom, but for this universal desire in the human mind to behold man in every situation,

---

sight, they may have fallen in with accidentally, but almost never an execution. No one goes there who has not made up his mind for the occasion; which would not be the case, if any natural love of cruelty were the cause of such assemblies.

1   In Alain René Lesage's picaresque novel *Le Diable boiteux* (1707), Asmodée, the engaging little devil-companion of Don Cléofas, takes immense pleasure in revealing human ugliness and depravity to his companion by gaily lifting off the roofs of houses. Margaret Carhart claims that this is Baillie's "only use of material from French literature" (78).

2   See Adam Ferguson's (1723-1816) *A History of Civil Society* (1767). Ferguson, the "so-called 'father of sociology'" (John and Julia Keay, *Collins Encyclopaedia of Scotland* 366), explored what he felt to be features common to "Red Indian," ancient Greek, and traditional Gaelic society, inspired by travellers' reports at the time. He was appointed commissioner to the American colonies in 1778 then engaged in the War of Independence about which Ferguson had written a pamphlet.

putting forth his strength against the current of adversity, scorning all bodily anguish, or struggling with those feelings of nature, which, like a beating stream, will oft'times burst through the artificial barriers of pride. Before they begin those terrible rites they treat their prisoner kindly; and it cannot be supposed that men, alternately enemies and friends to so many neighbouring tribes, in manners and appearance like themselves, should so strongly be actuated by a spirit of publick revenge. This custom, therefore, must be considered as a grand and terrible game, which every tribe plays against another; where they try not the strength of the arm, the swiftness of the feet, nor the acuteness of the eye, but the fortitude of the soul. Considered in this light, the excess of cruelty exercised upon their miserable victim, in which every hand is described as ready to inflict its portion of pain, and every head ingenious in the contrivance of it, is no longer to be wondered at. To put into his measure of misery one agony less, would be, in some degree, betraying the honour of their nation: would be doing a species of injustice to every hero of their own tribe who had already sustained it, and to those who might be called upon to do so; amongst whom each of these savage tormentors has his chance of being one, and has prepared himself for it from his childhood. Nay, it would be a species of injustice to the haughty victim himself, who would scorn to purchase his place amongst the heroes of his nation, at an easier price than his undaunted predecessors.

Amongst the many trials to which the human mind is subjected, that of holding intercourse, real or imaginary, with the world of spirits: of finding itself alone with a being terrifick and awful, whose nature and power are unknown, has been justly considered as one of the most severe. The workings of nature in this situation, we all know, have ever been the object of our most eager enquiry. No man wishes to see the Ghost himself, which would certainly procure him the best information on the subject, but every man wishes to see one who believes that he sees it, in all the agitation and wildness of that species of terrour. To gratify this curiosity how many people have dressed up hideous apparitions to frighten the timid and superstitious! and have done it at the risk of destroying their happiness or understanding for ever. For the instances of intellect being destroyed by this kind of trial[1] are more numerous, perhaps, in proportion to the few who have undergone it than by any other.

How sensible are we of this strong propensity within us, when we behold any person under the pressure of great and uncommon calamity! Delicacy and respect for the afflicted will, indeed, make us turn ourselves aside from observing him, and cast down our eyes in his presence; but the first glance we direct to him will involuntarily be one of the keenest observation, how hastily soever it may be checked; and often will a returning look of enquiry mix itself by stealth with our sympathy and reserve.

But it is not in situations of difficulty and distress alone, that man becomes the object of this sympathetick curiosity;[2] he is no less so when the evil he contends with arises in his own breast, and no outward circumstance connected with him either awakens our attention or our pity. What human creature is there, who can behold a being like himself under the violent agitation of those passions which all have, in some degree, experienced, without feeling himself most powerfully excited by the sight? I say, all have experienced; for the bravest man on earth knows what fear is as well as the coward; and will not refuse to be interested for one under the dominion of this passion, provided there be nothing in the circumstances attending it to create contempt. Anger is a passion that attracts less sympathy than any other, yet the unpleasing and distorted features of an angry man will be more eagerly gazed upon, by those who are no wise concerned with his fury or the objects of it, than the most amiable placid countenance in the world. Every eye is directed to him; every voice hushed to silence in his pres-

---

1 Baillie later explored the passion of fear in *Plays on the Passions, Vol. 3* (1812). In *Orra*, Hughobert, Count of Aldenberg, plots to frighten the young heiress, Orra, into marrying his son, Glottenbal, by locking her away in a remote, allegedly haunted castle. The plot takes some unexpected twists, and in the end Orra is driven mad from superstitious fear.

2 Cf. Burke, *A Philosophical Enquiry* 13.41 and 14.42 (Appendix A.3.i and ii) and Smith, *The Theory of Moral Sentiments* 1.1.1.7-16 (Appendix A.4.i and ii).

ence; even children will leave off their gambols as he passes, and gaze after him more eagerly than the gaudiest equipage. The wild tossings of despair; the gnashing of hatred and revenge; the yearnings of affection, and the softened mien of love; all that language[1] of the agitated soul, which every age and nation understands, is never addressed to the dull nor inattentive.

It is not merely under the violent agitations of passion, that man so rouses and interests us; even the smallest indications of an unquiet mind, the restless eye, the muttering lip, the half-checked exclamation, and the hasty start, will set our attention as anxiously upon the watch, as the first distant flashes of a gathering storm. When some great explosion of passion bursts forth, and some consequent catastrophe happens, if we are at all acquainted with the unhappy perpetrator, how minutely will we endeavour to remember every circumstance of his past behaviour! and with what avidity will we seize upon every recollected word or gesture, that is in the smallest degree indicative of the supposed state of his mind, at the time when they took place. If we are not acquainted with him, how eagerly will we listen to similar recollections from another! Let us understand, from observation or report, that any person harbours in his breast, concealed from the world's eye, some powerful rankling passion of what kind soever it may be, we will observe every word, every motion, every look, even the distant gait of such a man, with a constancy and attention bestowed upon no other. Nay, should we meet him unexpectedly on our way, a feeling will pass across our minds as though we found ourselves in the neighbourhood of some secret and fearful thing. If invisible, would we not follow him into his lonely haunts, into his closet, into the midnight silence of his chamber? There is, perhaps, no employment which the human mind will with so much avidity pursue, as the discovery of concealed passion, as the tracing the varieties and progress of a perturbed soul.

It is to this sympathetick curiosity of our nature, exercised upon mankind in great and trying occasions, and under the influence of the stronger passions, when the grand, the gener-

---

1   See Francis Hutcheson's discussion on Cicero's Fourth Book of *Tusculan Questions* (*Essay*.1.3).

ous, the terrible attract our attention far more than the base and depraved, that the high and powerfully tragick, of every composition, is addressed.

This propensity is universal. Children begin to shew it very early; it enters into many of their amusements, and that part of them too, for which they shew the keenest relish. It tempts them many times, as well as the mature in years, to be guilty of tricks, vexations, and cruelty; yet God Almighty has implanted it within us, as well as all our other propensities and passions, for wise and good purposes. It is our best and most powerful instructor. From it we are taught the proprieties and decencies of ordinary life, and are prepared for distressing and difficult situations. In examining others we know ourselves.[1] With limbs untorn, with head unsmitten, with senses unimpaired by despair, we know what we ourselves might have been on the rack, on the scaffold, and in the most afflicting circumstances of distress. Unless when accompanied with passions of the dark and malevolent kind, we cannot well exercise this disposition without becoming more just, more merciful, more compassionate; and as the dark and malevolent passions are not the predominant inmates of the human breast, it hath produced more deeds—O many more! of kindness than of cruelty. It holds up for our example a standard of excellence, which, without its assistance, our inward consciousness of what is right and becoming might never have dictated. It teaches us, also, to respect ourselves, and our kind; for it is a poor mind, indeed, that from this employment of its faculties, learns not to dwell upon the noble view of human nature rather than the mean.

Universal, however, as this disposition undoubtedly is, with

---

1 Though Baillie states in the preface to her volume entitled *Miscellaneous Plays* (1805), that she "not only never read any German plays, but was even ignorant that such things as German plays of any reputation existed" (*Works* 289), this paraphrasing sounds very similar to one of the 414 polemic epigrams written collaboratively by Johann Christoph Friedrich von Schiller (1759-1805) and Johann Wolfgang von Goethe (1749-1832), collected under the title of *Votive Tablets* (1797). An 1851 translation by Edgar A. Bowring reads:

The Key
Wouldst thou know thyself, observe the actions of others.
Wouldst thou other men know, look thou within thine own heart.

the generality of mankind it occupies itself in a passing and superficial way. Though a native trait of character or of passion is obvious to them as well as to the sage, yet to their minds it is but the visitor of a moment; they look upon it singly and unconnected: and though this disposition, even so exercised, brings instruction as well as amusement, it is chiefly by storing up in their minds those ideas to which the instructions of others refer, that it can be eminently useful. Those who reflect and reason upon what human nature holds out to their observation, are comparatively but few. No stroke of nature which engages their attention stands insulated and alone. Each presents itself to them with many varied connections; and they comprehend not merely the immediate feeling which gave rise to it, but the relation of that feeling[1] to others which are concealed. We wonder at the changes and caprices of men; they see in them nothing but what is natural and accountable. We stare upon some dark catastrophe of passion, as the Indians did upon an eclipse of the moon; they, conceiving the track of ideas through which the impassioned mind has passed, regard it like the philosopher who foretold the phenomenon. Knowing what situation of life he is about to be thrown into, they perceive in the man, who, like Hazael,[2] says, "is thy servant a dog that he should do this thing?" the foul and ferocious murderer. A man of this contemplative character partakes, in some degree, of the entertainment of the Gods, who were supposed to look down upon this world and the inhabitants of it, as we do upon a theatrical exhibition; and if he is of a benevolent disposition, a good man struggling with, and triumphing over adversity, will be to him, also, the most delightful spectacle.[3] But though this eagerness to observe their fellow-creatures in

She doesn't expect audience to take each passion alone

1 Cf. Stewart, *Philosophy of the Human Mind* 5.1.1.274-85 (Appendix A.5) and Wordsworth, "Preface" (1800) 246 (Appendix D.1.i).
2 The biblical king of Syria (c.841-820 BC). As an officer of King Benhadad, Hazael was sent to hear Elisha's predictions of Benhadad's health. While consulting with Elisha, Hazael was told of the horrific evil he would perform on the children of Israel as King of Syria. See 2 Kings 8:13.
3 Cf. Samuel Johnson's scathing review in 1757 of Soame Jenyns' *Free Inquiry into the Nature and Origin of Evil* in the *Literary Magazine* (1757) 2.13.171-75, 2.14.251-53, 2.15.301-06.

every situation, leads not the generality of mankind to reason and reflect; and those strokes of nature which they are so ready to remark, stand single and unconnected in their minds, yet they may be easily induced to do both: and there is no mode of instruction which they will so eagerly pursue, as that which lays open before them, in a more enlarged and connected view, than their individual observations are capable of supplying, the varieties of the human mind. Above all, to be well exercised in this study will fit a man more particularly for the most important situations of life. He will prove for it the better Judge, the better Magistrate, the better Advocate; and as a ruler or conductor of other men, under every occurring circumstance, he will find himself the better enabled to fulfil his duty, and accomplish his designs. He will perceive the natural effect of every order that he issues upon the minds of his soldiers, his subjects, or his followers; and he will deal to others judgment tempered with mercy; that is to say truly just; for justice appears to us severe only when it is imperfect.

In proportion as moral writers[1] of every class have exercised within themselves this sympathetick propensity of our nature, and have attended to it in others, their works have been interesting and instructive. They have struck the imagination more forcibly, convinced the understanding more clearly, and more lastingly impressed the memory. If unseasoned with any reference to this, the fairy bowers of the poet, with all his gay images of delight, will be admired and forgotten; the important relations of the historian, and even the reasonings of the philosopher will make a less permanent impression.

The historian points back to the men of other ages, and from the gradually clearing mist in which they are first discovered, like the mountains of a far distant land, the generations of the world are displayed to our mind's eye in grand and regular procession. But the transactions of men become interesting to us only as we are made acquainted with men themselves. Great and bloody battles are to us battles fought in the moon, if it is

---

1 Eighteenth-century philosophy had freer range than philosophy does today. Baillie is specifically referring to those thinkers whose interests took their meditations and writings into the early scientific consideration of human psychology.

not impressed upon our minds, by some circumstances attending them, that men subject to like weaknesses and passions with ourselves, were the combatants.[1] The establishments of policy make little impression upon us, if we are left ignorant of the beings whom they affected. Even a very masterly drawn character will but slightly imprint upon our memory the great man it belongs to, if, in the account we receive of his life, those lesser circumstances are entirely neglected, which do best of all point out to us the dispositions and tempers of men. Some slight circumstance characteristick of the particular turn of a man's mind, which at first sight seems but little connected with the great events of his life, will often explain some of those events more clearly to our understanding, than the minute details of ostensible policy. A judicious selection of those circumstances which characterize the spirit of an associated mob, paltry and ludicrous as some of them may appear, will oftentimes convey to our minds a clearer idea why certain laws and privileges were demanded and agreed to, than a methodical explanation of their causes. A historian who has examined human nature himself, and likewise attends to the pleasure which developing and tracing it, does ever convey to others,

---

1 [Baillie's note] Let two great battles be described to us with all the force and clearness of the most able pen. In the first let the most admirable exertions of military skill in the General, and the most unshaken courage in the soldiers, gain over an equal or superior number of brave opponents a compleat and glorious victory. In the second let the General be less scientifick, and the soldiers less dauntless. Let them go into the field for a cause that is dear to them, and fight with the ardour which such motives inspire; till discouraged with the many deaths around them, and the renovated pressure of the foe, some unlooked-for circumstance, trifling in itself, strikes their imagination at once; they are visited with the terrours of nature; their national pride, the honour of soldiership is forgotten; they fly like a fearful flock. Let some beloved chief then step forth, and call upon them by the love of their country, by the memory of their valiant fathers, by every thing that kindles in the bosom of man the high and generous passions: they stop; they gather round him; and goaded by shame and indignation, returning again to the charge, with the fury of wild beasts rather than the courage of soldiers, bear down every thing before them. Which of these two battles will interest us the most? and which of them shall we remember the longest? The one will stand forth in the imagination of the reader like a rock of the desert, which points out to the far-removed traveller the country through which he has passed, when its lesser objects are obscured in the distance; whilst the other leaves no traces behind it, but in the minds of the scientifick in war.

will employ our understanding as well as our memory with his pages; and if this is not done, he will impose upon the latter a very difficult task, in retaining what she is concerned with alone.

In argumentative and philosophical writings, the effect which the author's reasoning produces on our minds depends not entirely on the justness of it. The images and examples that he calls to his aid, to explain and illustrate his meaning, will very much affect the attention we are able to bestow upon it, and consequently the quickness with which we shall apprehend, and the force with which it will impress us. These are selected from animated and unanimated nature, from the habits, manners, and characters of men; and though that image or example, whatever it may be in itself, which brings out his meaning most clearly, ought to be preferred before every other, yet of two equal in this respect, that which is drawn from the most interesting source will please us the most at the time, and most lastingly take hold of our minds. An argument supported with vivid and interesting illustration, will long be remembered when many equally important and clear are forgotten; and a work where many such occur will be held in higher estimation by the generality of men, than one its superior, perhaps, in acuteness, perspicuity, and good sense.

Our desire to know what men are in the closet as well as the field, by the blazing hearth, and at the social board,[1] as well as in the council and the throne, is very imperfectly gratified by real history; romance writers, therefore, stepped boldly forth to supply the deficiency; and tale writers, and novel writers, of many descriptions, followed after. If they have not been very skilful in their delineations of nature; if they have represented men and women speaking and acting as men and women never did speak or act; if they have caricatured both our virtues and our vices; if they have given us such pure and unmixed, or such heterogeneous combinations of character as real life never presented, and yet have pleased and interested us, let it not be imputed to the dulness of man in discerning what is genuinely natural in

---

1 Dinner table.

himself. There are many inclinations belonging to us, besides this great master-propensity of which I am treating. Our love of the grand, the beautiful, the novel, and above all of the marvellous, is very strong; and if we are richly fed with what we have a good relish for, we may be weaned to forget our native and favourite aliment. Yet we can never so far forget it, but that we will cling to, and acknowledge it again, whenever it is presented before us. In a work abounding with the marvellous and unnatural, if the author has any how stumbled upon an unsophisticated genuine stroke of nature, we will immediately perceive and be delighted with it, though we are foolish enough to admire at the same time, all the nonsense with which it is surrounded. After all the wonderful incidents, dark mysteries, and secrets revealed, which eventful novel so liberally presents to us; after the beautiful fairy ground, and even the grand and sublime scenes of nature with which descriptive novel so often enchants us; those works which most strongly characterize human nature in the middling and lower classes[1] of society, where it is to be discovered by stronger and more unequivocal marks, will ever be the most popular. For though great pains have been taken in our higher sentimental novels to interest us in the delicacies, embarrassments, and artificial distresses of the more refined part of society, they have never been able to cope in the publick opinion with these. The one is a dressed and beautiful pleasure-ground, in which we are enchanted for a while, amongst the delicate and unknown plants of artful cultivation; the other is a rough forest of our native land; the oak, the elm, the hazle, and the bramble are there; and amidst the endless varieties of its paths we can wander for ever. Into whatever scenes the novelist may conduct us, what objects soever he may present to our view, still is our attention most sensibly awake to every touch faithful to nature; still are we upon the watch for every thing that speaks to us of ourselves.

The fair field of what is properly called poetry, is enriched with so many beauties, that in it we are often tempted to forget

---

1 Cf. Wordsworth, "Preface" (1800) 254 (Appendix D.1.i).

what we really are, and what kind of beings we belong to. Who in the enchanted regions of simile,[1] metaphor, allegory and description, can remember the plain order of things in this every-day world? From heroes whose majestick forms rise like a lofty tower, whose eyes are lightening, whose arms are irresistible, whose course is like the storms of heaven, bold and exalted sentiments we will readily receive; and will not examine them very accurately by that rule of nature which our own breast prescribes to us. A shepherd whose sheep, with fleeces of the purest snow, browze the flowery herbage of the most beautiful vallies; whose flute is ever melodious, and whose shepherdess is ever crowned with roses; whose every care is love, will not be called very strictly to account for the loftiness and refinement of his thoughts. The fair Nymph, who sighs out her sorrows to the conscious and compassionate wilds; whose eyes gleam like the bright drops of heaven; whose loose tresses stream to the breeze, may say what she pleases with impunity. I will venture, however, to say, that amidst all this decoration and ornament, all this loftiness and refinement, let one simple trait of the human heart, one expression of passion genuine and true to nature, be introduced, and it will stand forth alone in the boldness of reality, whilst the false and unnatural around it, fades away upon every side, like the rising exhalations of the morning. With admiration, and often with enthusiasm we proceed on our way through the grand and the beautiful images, raised to our imagination by the lofty Epic muse; but what even here are those things that strike upon the heart; that we feel and remember? Neither the descriptions of war, the sound of the trumpet, the clanging of arms, the combat of heroes, nor the death of the mighty, will interest our minds like the fall of the feeble stranger, who simply expresses the anguish of his soul, at the thoughts of that far-distant home which he must never return to again, and closes his eyes, amongst the ignoble and forgotten; like the timid stripling goaded by the shame of reproach, who urges his trembling steps to the fight, and falls like a tender flower before the first

---

1 Cf. Wordsworth, "Preface" (1800) 250-54 (Appendix D.1.ii).

blast of winter. How often will some simple picture of this kind be all that remains upon our minds of the terrifick and magnificent battle, whose description we have read with admiration! How comes it that we relish so much the episodes of an heroick poem? It cannot merely be that we are pleased with a resting-place, where we enjoy the variety of contrast; for were the poem of the simple and familiar kind, and an episode after the heroick style introduced into it, ninety readers out of an hundred would pass over it altogether. Is it not that we meet such a story, so situated, with a kind of sympathetick good will, as in passing through a country of castles and of palaces, we should pop unawares upon some humble cottage, resembling the dwellings of our own native land, and gaze upon it with affection. The highest pleasures we receive from poetry, as well as from the real objects which surround us in the world, are derived from the sympathetick interest we all take in beings like ourselves; and I will even venture to say, that were the grandest scenes which can enter into the imagination of man, presented to our view, and all reference to man completely shut out from our thoughts, the objects that composed it would convey to our minds little better than dry ideas of magnitude, colour, and form; and the remembrance of them would rest upon our minds like the measurement and distances of the planets.

If the study of human nature then, is so useful to the poet, the novelist, the historian, and the philosopher, of how much greater importance must it be to the dramatick writer? To them it is a powerful auxiliary, to him it is the centre and strength of the battle. If characteristick views of human nature enliven not their pages, there are many excellencies with which they can, in some degree, make up for the deficiency, it is what we receive from them with pleasure rather than demand. But in his works no richness of invention, harmony of language, nor grandeur of sentiment will supply the place of faithfully delineated nature. The poet and the novelist may represent to you their great characters from the cradle to the tomb. They may represent them in any mood or temper, and under the influence of any passion which they see proper, without being obliged to put words into their mouths, those great betrayers of the feigned and adopted. They may relate every circumstance however trifling and minute, that serves to develope their tempers and dispositions. They tell us what kind of people they intend their men and women to be, and as such we receive them. If they are to move us with any scene of distress, every circumstance regarding the parties concerned in it, how they looked, how they moved, how they sighed, how the tears gushed from their eyes, how the very light and shadow fell upon them, is carefully described, and the few things that are given them to say along with all this assistance, must be very unnatural indeed if we refuse to sympathize with them. But the characters of the drama must speak directly for themselves. Under the influence of every passion, humour, and impression; in the artificial veilings of hypocrisy and ceremony, in the openness of freedom and confidence, and in the lonely hour of meditation they speak. He who made us hath placed within our breast a judge that judges instantaneously of every thing they say. We expect to find them creatures like ourselves; and if they are untrue to nature, we feel that we are imposed upon; as though the poet had introduced to us for brethren, creatures of a different race, beings of another world.

As in other works deficiency in characteristick truth may be compensated by excellencies of a different kind, in the drama characteristick truth will compensate every other defect. Nay, it will do what appears a contradiction; one strong genuine stroke of nature will cover a multitude of sins even against nature herself. When we meet in some scene of a good play a very fine stroke of this kind, we are apt to become so intoxicated with it, and so perfectly convinced of the author's great knowledge of the human heart, that we are unwilling to suppose that the whole of it has not been suggested by the same penetrating spirit. Many well-meaning enthusiastick criticks[1] have given themselves a great deal of trouble in this way; and have shut their eyes most ingeniously against the fair light of nature for the very love of it. They have converted, in their great zeal,

---

1 Cf. Wordsworth, "Preface" (1800) 251-52 (Appendix D.1.i).

sentiments palpably false, both in regard to the character and situation of the persons who utter them, sentiments which a child or a clown would detect, into the most skilful depictments of the heart. I can think of no stronger instance to shew how powerfully this love of nature dwells within us.[1]

Formed as we are with these sympathetick propensities in regard to our own species, it is not at all wonderful that theatrical exhibition has become the grand and favourite amusement of every nation into which it has been introduced. Savages will, in the wild contortions of a dance, shape out some rude story expressive of character or passion, and such a dance will give more delight to his companions than the most artful exertions of agility. Children in their gambols will make out a mimick representation of the manners, characters, and passions of grown men and women, and such a pastime will animate and delight them much more than a treat of the daintiest sweetmeats, or the handling of the gaudiest toys. Eagerly as it is enjoyed by the rude and the young, to the polished and the ripe in years it is still the most interesting amusement. Our taste for it is durable as it is universal. Independently of those circumstances which first introduced it, the world would not have long been without it. The progress of society would soon have brought it forth; and men in the whimsical decorations of fancy would have displayed the characters and actions of their heroes, the folly and absurdity of their fellow-citizens, had no Priests of Bacchus[2] ever existed.[3]

---

1 [Baillie's note] It appears to me a very strong testimony of the excellence of our great national Dramatist, that so many people have been employed in finding out obscure and refined beauties, in what appear to ordinary observation his very defects. Men, it may be said, do so merely to shew their own superior penetration and ingenuity. But granting this; what could make other men listen to them, and listen so greedily too, if it were not that they have received from the works of Shakspeare, pleasure far beyond what the most perfect poetical compositions of a different character can afford.

2 Bacchus is the Roman god of wine, the Dionysus of the Greeks, son of Zeus and Semele. Bacchus was honoured at the Bacchanalia, a triennial festival which is considered to be the source of our dramatic tradition.

3 [Baillie's note] Though the progress of society would have given us the Drama, independently of the particular cause of its first commencement, the peculiar circumstances connected with its origin, have had considerable influence upon its

In whatever age or country the Drama might have its rise, tragedy would have been the first-born of its children. For every nation has its great men, and its great events upon record; and to represent their own forefathers struggling with those difficulties, and braving those dangers, of which they have heard with admiration, and the effects of which they still, perhaps, experience,would certainly have been the most animating subject for the poet, and the most interesting for his audience, even independently of the natural inclination we all so universally shew for scenes of horrour and distress, of passion and heroick exertion. Tragedy would have been the first child of the Drama, for the same reasons that have made heroick ballad,

character and style, in the ages through which it has passed even to our days, and still will continue to affect it. Homer had long preceded the dramatick poets of Greece; poetry was in a high state of cultivation when they began to write; and their style, the construction of their pieces, and the characters of their heroes were different from what they would have been, had theatrical exhibitions been the invention of an earlier age or a ruder people. Their works were represented to an audience, already accustomed to hear long poems rehearsed at their publick games, and the feasts of their gods. A play, with the principal characters of which they were previously acquainted; in which their great men and heroes, in the most beautiful language, complained of their rigorous fate, but piously submitted to the will of the Gods; in which sympathy was chiefly excited by tender and affecting sentiments; in which strong bursts of passion were few; and in which whole scenes frequently passed, without giving the actors any thing to do but to speak, was not too insipid for them. Had the Drama been the invention of a less cultivated nation, more of action and of passion would have been introduced into it. It would have been more irregular, more imperfect, more varied, more interesting. From poor beginnings it would have advanced in a progressive state; and succeeding poets, not having those polished and admired originals to look back upon, would have presented their respective contemporaries with the produce of a free and unbridled imagination. A different class of poets would most likely have been called into existence. The latent powers of men are called forth by contemplating those works in which they find any thing congenial to their own peculiar talents; and if the field, wherein they could have worked, is already enriched with a produce unsuited to their cultivation, they think not of entering it at all. Men, therefore, whose natural turn of mind led them to labour, to reason, to refine and exalt, have caught their animation from the beauties of the Grecian Drama, and they who, perhaps, ought only to have been our Criticks have become our Poets. I mean not, however, in any degree to depreciate the works of the ancients; a great deal we have gained by those beautiful compositions; and what we have lost by them it is impossible to compute. Very strong genius will sometimes break through every disadvantage of circumstances: Shakspeare has arisen in this country, and we ought not to complain.

with all its battles, murders and disasters, the earliest poetical compositions of every country.

We behold heroes and great men at a distance, unmarked by those small but distinguishing features of the mind, which give a certain individuality to such an infinite variety of similar beings, in the near and familiar intercourse of life. They appear to us from this view like distant mountains, whose dark outlines we trace in the clear horizon, but the varieties of whose roughened sides, shaded with heath and brushwood, and seamed with many a cleft, we perceive not. When accidental anecdote reveals to us any weakness or peculiarity belonging to them, we start upon it like a discovery. They are made known to us in history only, by the great events they are connected with, and the part they have taken in extraordinary or important transactions. Even in poetry and romance, with the exception of some love story interwoven with the main events of their lives, they are seldom more intimately made known to us. To Tragedy it belongs to lead them forward to our nearer regard, in all the distinguishing varieties which nearer inspection discovers; with the passions, the humours, the weaknesses, the prejudices of men. It is for her to present to us the great and magnanimous hero, who appears to our distant view as a superior being, as a God, softened down with those smaller frailties and imperfections which enable us to glory in, and claim kindred to his virtues. It is for her to exhibit to us the daring and ambitious man, planning his dark designs, and executing his bloody purposes, mark'd with those appropriate characteristicks, which distinguish him as an individual of that class; and agitated with those varied passions, which disturb the mind of man when he is engaged in the commission of such deeds. It is for her to point out to us the brave and impetuous warrior struck with those visitations of nature, which, in certain situations, will unnerve the strongest arm, and make the boldest heart tremble. It is for her to shew the tender, gentle, and unassuming mind animated with that fire which, by the provocation of circumstances, will give to the kindest heart the ferocity and keenness of a tiger. It is for her to present to us the great and striking characters that are to be found amongst men, in a way which the poet, the novelist, and the historian can but imperfectly attempt. But above all, to her, and to her only it belongs to unveil to us the human mind under the dominion of those strong and fixed passions, which, seemingly unprovoked by outward circumstances, will from small beginnings brood within the breast, till all the better dispositions, all the fair gifts of nature are borne down before them. Those passions which conceal themselves from the observation of men; which cannot unbosom themselves even to the dearest friend; and can, often times, only give their fulness vent in the lonely desert, or in the darkness of midnight. For who hath followed the great man into his secret closet, or stood by the side of his nightly couch, and heard those exclamations of the soul which heaven alone may hear, that the historian should be able to inform us? and what form of story, what mode of rehearsed speech will communicate to us those feelings, whose irregular bursts, abrupt transitions, sudden pauses, and half-uttered suggestions, scorn all harmony of measured verse, all method and order of relation?

On the first part of this task her Bards have eagerly exerted their abilities: and some amongst them, taught by strong original genius to deal immediately with human nature and their own hearts, have laboured in it successfully. But in presenting to us those views of great characters, and of the human mind in difficult and trying situations which peculiarly belong to Tragedy, the far greater proportion, even of those who may be considered as respectable dramatick poets, have very much failed. From the beauty of those original dramas to which they have ever looked back with admiration, they have been tempted to prefer the embellishments of poetry[1] to faithfully delin-

---

1   Though Thomas Gray (1716-71) was a popular poet of his day – having introduced a sense of the violent, the intuitive, and the sentimental into what became a new poetry of romanticism – other poets, such as perhaps Baillie here, struggled with his treatment of language. Cf. Wordsworth, "Preface" (1800) (Appendix D.1.ii). Samuel Johnson (1709-84) as well felt Gray's language was "too luxuriant." Johnson, in the chapter on Gray (Ch.7) in his *Lives of the English Poets* (1781), writes that "An epithet or metaphor drawn from Nature ennobles Art; an epithet or metaphor drawn from Art degrades Nature. Gray is too fond of words arbitrarily compounded."

More concerned w/ literature than psychology or philosophy

eated nature. They have been more occupied in considering
the works of the great Dramatists who have gone before them,
and the effects produced by their writings, than the varieties of
human character which first furnished materials for those
works, or those principles in the mind of man by means of
which such effects were produced. Neglecting the boundless
variety of nature, certain strong outlines of character, certain
bold features of passion, certain grand vicissitudes and striking
dramatick situations have been repeated from one generation
to another; whilst a pompous and solemn gravity, which they
have supposed to be necessary for the dignity of tragedy, has
excluded almost entirely from their works those smaller touches of nature, which so well develope the mind; and by showing
men in their hours of state and exertion only, they have consequently shewn them imperfectly. Thus, great and magnanimous heroes, who bear with majestick equanimity every vicis-
situde of fortune; who in every temptation and trial stand forth
in unshaken virtue, like a rock buffeted by the waves; who
encompast with the most terrible evils, in calm possession of
their souls, reason upon the difficulties of their state; and, even
upon the brink of destruction, pronounce long eulogiums on
virtue, in the most eloquent and beautiful language, have been
held forth to our view as objects of imitation and interest; as
though they had entirely forgotten that it is only from creatures
like ourselves that we feel, and therefore, only from creatures
like ourselves that we receive the instruction of example.[1]
Thus, passionate and impetuous warriors, who are proud, irritable, and vindictive, but generous, daring, and disinterested;

[1] [Baillie's note] To a being perfectly free from all human infirmity our sympathy
refuses to extend. Our Saviour himself, whose character is so beautiful, and so har-
moniously consistent; in whom, with outward proofs of his mission less strong than
those that are offered to us, I should still be compelled to believe, from being utterly unable to conceive how the idea of such a character could enter into the imagination of man, never touches the heart more nearly than when he says, "Father, let
this cup pass from me" [Matt. 26:39,42]. Had he been represented to us in all the
unshaken strength of these tragick heroes, his disciples would have made fewer
converts, and his precepts would have been listened to coldly. Plays in which heroes
of this kind are held forth, and whose aim is, indeed, honourable and praise-worthy,
have been admired by the cultivated and refined, but the tears of the simple, the
applauses of the young and untaught have been wanting.

setting their lives at a pin's fee[1] for the good of others, but incapable of curbing their own humour of a moment to gain the whole world for themselves; who will pluck the orbs of heaven from their places, and crush the whole universe in one grasp, are called forth to kindle in our souls the generous contempt of every thing abject and base; but with an effect proportionably feeble, as the hero is made to exceed in courage and fire what the standard of humanity will agree to.[2] Thus, tender and pathetick lovers, full of the most gentle affections, the most

---

1   At the value of a pin. Cf. *Hamlet* 1.4.65: "I do not set my life at a pin's fee."

2   [Baillie's note] In all burlesque imitations of tragedy, those plays in which this hero is pre-eminent are always exposed to bear the great brunt of the ridicule; which proves how popular they have been, and how many poets, and good ones too, have been employed upon them. That they have been so popular, however, is not owing to the intrinsick merit of the characters they represent, but their opposition to those mean and contemptible qualities belonging to human nature, of which we are most ashamed. Besides, there is something in the human mind, independently of its love of applause, which inclines it to boast. This is ever the attendant of that elasticity of soul, which makes us bound up from the touch of oppression; and if there is nothing in the accompanying circumstances to create disgust, or suggest suspicions of their sincerity, (as in real life is commonly the case,) we are very apt to be carried along with the boasting of others. Let us in good earnest believe that a man is capable of achieving all that human courage can achieve, and we will suffer him to talk of impossibilities. Amidst all their pomp of words, therefore, our admiration of such heroes is readily excited, (for the understanding is more easily deceived than the heart,) but how stands our sympathy affected? As no caution nor foresight, on their own account, is ever suffered to occupy the thoughts of such bold disinterested beings, we are the more inclined to care for them, and take an interest in their fortune through the course of the play: yet, as their souls are unappalled by any thing; as pain and death are not at all regarded by them; and as we have seen them very ready to plunge their own swords into their own bosoms, on no very weighty occasion, perhaps, their death distresses us but little, and they commonly fall unwept. [Burlesque: from the Italian *burla* (ridicule, mockery), was a literary composition or dramatic representation aimed at provoking laughter by treating comically a serious subject or reducing the spirit of a serious work to a caricature. The burlesque was connected to amorous adventures and debauchery. Henry Fielding (1707-54) had great aspirations to write comedy in the tradition of William Congreve (1670-1729), yet he excelled in the lesser modes of farce and burlesque. His masterpiece of burlesque, *The Tragedy of Tragedies: or The Life and Death of Tom Thumb the Great* (1731), for instance, had a reputation of making even the sternest of men laugh. Richard Brinsley Sheridan (1751-1816), a later producer of burlesques, wrote *The Critic* (1779) based on *The Rehearsal* (1671) by George Villiers, 2nd Duke of Buckingham (1628-87). Cf. Alexander Pope's *Moral Essays* (1731-35), Epistle 3, in which he describes burlesque, and Sir Walter Scott's (1771-1832) *Peveril of the Peak* (1823).]

amiable dispositions, and the most exquisite feelings; who present their defenceless bosoms to the storms of this rude world in all the graceful weakness of sensibility, are made to sigh out their sorrows in one unvaried strain of studied pathos, whilst this constant demand upon our feelings makes us absolutely incapable of answering it.[1] Thus, also, tyrants are represented as monsters of cruelty, unmixed with any feelings of humanity; and villains as delighting in all manner of treachery and deceit, and acting upon many occasions for the very love of villainy itself; though the perfectly wicked are as ill fitted for the purposes of warning, as the perfectly virtuous are for those of example.[2] This spirit of imitation, and attention to effect, has

1 [Baillie's note] Were it not, that in tragedies where these heroes preside, the same soft tones of sorrow are so often repeated in our ears, till we are perfectly tired of it, they are more fitted to interest us than any other: both because in seeing them, we own the ties of kindred between ourselves and the frail mortals we lament; and sympathize with the weakness of mortality unmixed with any thing to degrade or disgust; and also, because the misfortunes, which form the story of the play, are frequently of the more familiar and domestick kind. A king driven from his throne, will not move our sympathy so strongly, as a private man torn from the bosom of his family. [Baillie may be alluding here to the well-known scene in Chapter 34 of Henry Mackenzie's (1745-1831) novel *The Man of Feeling* (1771), in which not only one but two fathers risk being torn from their families. On Christmas Eve, old Edwards saves his son, Jack, from a roguish press-gang, by purchasing his freedom with all his savings and enlisting himself. Margaret Carhart recounts a journal entry of Samuel Rogers' about a Hampstead gathering on April 21st, 1791, at which he met Henry Mackenzie. "When the conversation turned on Scotland, Mr. Mackenzie attacked its men of genius, and Joanna Baillie mentioned the name of Adam Smith. Mr. Mackenzie did not allow her to make her point, but interrupted, and was off on another long tirade" (13). Also cf. Wollstonecraft, *Vindication of the Rights of Men* 58, in which she describes the mentally infirm King George III as "A father torn from his children,—a husband from his affectionate wife,—a man from himself!"]

2 [Baillie's note] I have said nothing here in regard to female character, though in many tragedies it is brought forward as the principal one of the piece, because what I have said of the above characters is likewise applicable to it. I believe there is no man that ever lived, who has behaved in a certain manner, on a certain occasion, who has not had amongst women some corresponding spirit, who on the like occasion, and every way similarly circumstanced, would have behaved in the like manner. With some degree of softening and refinement, each class of the tragick heroes I have mentioned has its corresponding one amongst the heroines. The tender and pathetick no doubt has the most numerous, but the great and magnanimous is not without it, and the passionate and impetuous boasts of one by no means inconsiderable in numbers, and drawn sometimes to the full as passionate and impetuous as itself. [For Baillie's reference to "some corresponding spirit" cf.

likewise confined them very much in their choice of situations and events to bring their great characters into action; rebellions, conspiracies, contentions for empire, and rivalships in love have alone been thought worthy of trying those heroes; and palaces and dungeons the only places magnificent or solemn enough for them to appear in.

They have, indeed, from this regard to the works of preceding authors, and great attention to the beauties of composition, and to dignity of design, enriched their plays with much striking, and sometimes sublime imagery, lofty thoughts, and virtuous sentiments; but in striving so eagerly to excell in those things that belong to tragedy in common with many other compositions, they have very much neglected those that are peculiarly her own. As far as they have been led aside from the first labours of a tragick poet by a desire to communicate more perfect moral instruction, their motive has been respectable, and they merit our esteem. But this praise-worthy end has been injured instead of promoted by their mode of pursuing it. Every species of moral writing has its own way of conveying instruction, which it can never, but with disadvantage, exchange for any other. The Drama improves us by the knowledge we acquire of our own minds, from the natural desire we have to look into the thoughts, and observe the behaviour of others. Tragedy brings to our view men placed in those elevated situations, exposed to those great trials, and engaged in those extraordinary transactions, in which few of us are called upon to act. As examples applicable to ourselves, therefore, they can but feebly affect us; it is only from the enlargement of our ideas in regard to human nature, from that admiration of virtue, and abhorrence of vice which they excite, that we can expect to be improved by them. But if they are not represented to us as real and natural characters, the lessons[1] we are taught from their

---

Wollstonecraft, *Vindication of the Rights of Woman* 150: "... I will allow that bodily strength seems to give man a natural superiority over woman.... But I must insist, that not only the virtue, but the knowledge of the two sexes should be the same in nature, if not in degree...." Also cf. Appendix B.]

1 John Dennis (1657-1734) and Joseph Addison (1672-1719) debated earlier in the century the source of dramatic lessons. Dennis believed it was a rational issue and

conduct and their sentiments will be no more to us than those which we receive from the pages of the poet or the moralist.

But the last part of the task which I have mentioned as peculiarly belonging to tragedy, unveiling the human mind under the dominion of those strong and fixed passions, which seemingly unprovoked by outward circumstances, will from small beginnings brood within the breast, till all the better dispositions, all the fair gifts of nature are borne down before them, her poets in general have entirely neglected, and even her first and greatest have but imperfectly attempted. They have made use of the passions to mark their several characters, and animate their scenes, rather than to open to our view the nature and portraitures of those great disturbers of the human breast, with whom we are all, more or less, called upon to contend. With their strong and obvious features, therefore, they have been presented to us, stripped almost entirely of those less obtrusive, but not less discriminating traits, which mark them in their actual operation. To trace them in their rise and progress in the heart, seems but rarely to have been the object of any dramatist. We commonly find the characters of a tragedy affected by the passions in a transient, loose, unconnected manner; or if they are represented as under the permanent influence of the more powerful ones, they are generally introduced to our notice in the very height of their fury, when all that timidity, irresolution, distrust, and a thousand delicate traits, which make the infancy of every great passion more interesting, perhaps, than its full-blown strength, are fled. The impassioned character is generally brought into view under those irresistible attacks of their power, which it is impossible to repell; whilst those gradual steps that led him into this state, in some of which a stand might have been made against the foe, are left entirely in the shade. These passions that may be suddenly excited, and are of short duration, as anger, fear, and oftentimes jealousy, may in this manner be fully represented;

maintained that we learn "virtue by seeing its rewards." Addison, on the other hand, preferred the emotions and believed that "the spectacle of tragedy teaches, more obliquely, such things as humility, forbearance, and distrust of worldly success" (Carlson M. 128). Cf. Review in *Literary Leisure* (Appendix E.1).

but those great masters of the soul, ambition, hatred, love, every passion that is permanent in its nature, and varied in progress, if represented to us but in one stage of its course, is represented imperfectly. It is a characteristick of the more powerful passions that they will encrease and nourish themselves on very slender aliment; it is from within that they are chiefly supplied with what they feed on; and it is in contending with opposite passions and affections of the mind that we least discover their strength, not with events. But in tragedy it is events[1] more frequently than opposite affections which are opposed to them; and those often of such force and magnitude that the passions themselves are almost obscured by the splendour and importance of the transactions to which they are attached. But besides being thus confined and mutilated, the passions have been, in the greater part of our tragedies, deprived of the very power of making themselves known. Bold and figurative language belongs peculiarly to them. Poets, admiring those bold expressions which a mind, labouring with ideas too strong to be conveyed in the ordinary forms of speech, wildly throws out, taking earth, sea, and sky, every thing great and terrible in nature to image forth the violence of its feelings, borrowed them gladly, to adorn the calm sentiments of their premeditated song. It has therefore been thought that the less animated parts of tragedy might be so embellished and enriched. In doing this, however, the passions have been robbed of their native prerogative; and in adorning with their strong figures and lofty expressions the calm speeches of the unruffled, it is found that, when they are called upon to raise their voice, the power of distinguishing themselves has been taken away. This is an injury by no means compensated, but very greatly aggravated by embellishing, in return, the speeches of passion with the ingenious conceits, and compleat similies of premeditated thought.[2]

---

1 Cf. Wordsworth, "Preface": "it is proper that I should mention ... that the feeling ... gives importance to the action and situation and not the action and situation to the feeling" (Appendix D.i.8).

2 [Baillie's note] This, perhaps, more than any thing else has injured the higher scenes of tragedy. For having made such free use of bold hyperbolical language in the inferior parts, the poet when he arrives at the highly impassioned sinks into total inability: or if he will force himself to rise still higher on the wing, he flies beyond nature altogether, into the regions of bombast and nonsense.

There are many other things regarding the manner in which dramatick poets have generally brought forward the passions in tragedy, to the great prejudice of that effect they are naturally fitted to produce upon the mind, which I forbear to mention, *Thank God!* lest they should too much increase the length of this discourse, and leave an impression on the mind of my reader, that I write more on the spirit of criticism, than becomes one who is about to bring before the publick a work, with, doubtless, many faults and imperfections on its head.[1] *← conventional modesty*

From this general view, which I have endeavoured to communicate to my reader, of tragedy, and those principles in the human mind upon which the success of her efforts depends, I have been led to believe, that an attempt to write a series of tragedies, of simpler construction, less embellished with poetical decorations, less constrained by that lofty seriousness which has so generally been considered as necessary for the support of tragick dignity, and in which the chief object should be to delineate the progress of the higher passions in the human breast, each play exhibiting a particular passion, might not be unacceptable to the publick. And I have been the more readily induced to act upon this idea, because I am confident, that tragedy, written upon this plan, is fitted to produce stronger moral effect than upon any other. I have said that tragedy in representing to us great characters struggling with difficulties, and placed in situations of eminence and danger, in which few of us have any chance of being called upon to act, conveys its moral efficacy to our minds by the enlarged views which it gives to us of human nature, by the admiration of virtue, and execration of vice which it excites, and not by the examples[2] it holds up for our immediate application.[3] But in opening to us the heart of man under the influence of those passions to

---

1 Cf. *Hamlet* 1.5.81-86. Also see Burroughs about women's preface writing in the eighteenth century, Chapter 3.

2 Nahum Tate (1652-1715) created a new, immensely popular version of *King Lear* (1681) in which Cordelia is spared and betrothed to Edgar. Joseph Addison (1672-1719) believed that such an ending destroyed the beauty of the play, while Samuel Johnson (1709-84) was so disturbed by the tragic ending that he confessed that he could not endure re-reading it until 1765 (See Carson 136).

3 Cf. Dugald Stewart, *Elements of the Philosophy of the Human Mind* (Appendix A.5.ii).

which all are liable, this is not the case. Those strong passions that, with small assistance from outward circumstances, work their way in the heart, till they become the tyrannical masters of it, carry on a similar operation in the breast of the Monarch, and the man of low degree. It exhibits to us the mind of man in that state when we are most curious to look into it, and is equally interesting to all. Discrimination of character is a turn of mind, tho' more common than we are aware of, which every body does not possess; but to the expressions of passion, particularly strong passion, the dullest mind is awake; and its true unsophisticated language the dullest understanding will not misinterpret. To hold up for our example those peculiarities in disposition, and modes of thinking which nature has fixed upon us, or which long and early habit has incorporated with our original selves, is almost desiring us to remove the everlasting mountains, to take away the native land-marks of the soul; but representing the passions brings before us the operation of a tempest that rages out its time and passes away. We cannot, it is true, amidst its wild uproar, listen to the voice of reason, and save ourselves from destruction; but we can foresee its coming, we can mark its rising signs, we can know the situations that will most expose us to its rage, and we can shelter our heads from the coming blast. To change a certain disposition of mind which makes us view objects in a particular light, and thereby, oftentimes, unknown to ourselves, influences our conduct and manners, is almost impossible; but in checking and subduing those visitations of the soul, whose causes and effects we are aware of, every one may make considerable progress, if he proves not entirely successful. Above all, looking back to the first rise, and tracing the progress of passion, points out to us those stages in the approach of the enemy, when he might have been combated most successfully; and where the suffering him to pass may be considered as occasioning all the misery that ensues.

Comedy presents to us men as we find them in the ordinary intercourse of the world, with all the weaknesses, follies, caprice, prejudices, and absurdities which a near and familiar view of them discovers. It is her task to exhibit them engaged in the busy turmoil of ordinary life, harassing and perplexing themselves with the endless pursuits of avarice, vanity, and pleasure; and engaged with those smaller trials of the mind, by which men are most apt to be overcome, and from which he, who could have supported with honour the attack of greater occasions, will oftentimes come off most shamefully foiled. It belongs to her to shew the varied fashions and manners of the world, as, from the spirit of vanity, caprice, and imitation, they go on in swift and endless succession; and those disagreeable or absurd peculiarities attached to particular classes and conditions in society. It is for her also to represent men under the influence of the stronger passions; and to trace the rise and progress of them in the heart, in such situations, and attended with such circumstances as take off their sublimity, and the interest we naturally take in a perturbed mind. It is hers to exhibit those terrible tyrants of the soul, whose ungovernable rage has struck us so often with dismay, like wild beasts tied to a post, who growl and paw before us, for our derision and sport. In pourtraying the characters of men she has this advantage over tragedy, that the smallest traits of nature, with the smallest circumstances which serve to bring them forth, may by her be displayed, however ludicrous and trivial in themselves, without any ceremony. And in developing the passions she enjoys a similar advantage; for they often most strongly betray themselves when touched by those small and familiar occurrences which cannot, consistently with the effect it is intended to produce, be admitted into tragedy.

As tragedy has been very much cramped in her endeavours to exalt and improve the mind, by that spirit of imitation and confinement in her successive writers, which the beauty of her earliest poets first gave rise to, so comedy has been led aside from her best purposes by a different temptation. Those endless changes in fashions and in manners, which offer such obvious and ever-new subjects of ridicule; that infinite variety of tricks and manoeuvres by which the ludicrous may be produced, and curiosity and laughter excited: the admiration we so generally bestow upon satirical remark, pointed repartee, and whimsical combinations of ideas, have too often led her to forget the warmer interest we feel, and the more profitable lessons we receive from genuine representations of nature. The most interesting and instructive class of comedy, therefore, the real characteristick, has been very much neglected, whilst satirical, witty, sentimental, and, above all, busy or circumstantial comedy have usurped the exertions of the far greater proportion of Dramatick Writers.

In Satirical Comedy,[1] sarcastick and severe reflections on the actions and manners of men, introduced with neatness, force, and poignancy of expression into a lively and well supported dialogue, of whose gay surface they are the embossed ornaments, make the most important and studied part of the work: Character is a thing talked of rather than shewn. The persons of the drama are indebted for the discovery of their peculiarities to what is said to them, rather than to any thing they are made to say or do for themselves. Much incident being unfavourable for studied and elegant dialogue, the plot is commonly simple, and the few events that compose it neither interesting nor striking. It only affords us that kind of moral instruction which an essay or a poem could as well have conveyed, and, though amusing in the closet, is but feebly attractive in the Theatre.[2]

In what I have termed Witty Comedy, every thing is light,

---

1 Though the complex variety of comedy at this time thwarted any attempts to classify it, Baillie was not the first to take on the challenge. Isaac Bickerstaffe (1733-1808) conceived of two kinds: of "Character" or "Heart and Understanding" (sentimental comedy) and "Intrigue" (his own drama). Reverend Charles Jenner (1736-74) described three: comedy of "wit and character" and comedy of "nature and sentiment," both of which he borrowed from Diderot and "Comedy of Stage-trick and Decoration." Hannah Cowley (1743-1809), in her preface to *The Town Before You* (1797), could not see a distinction between farce and sentimental comedy and, dismayed by contemporary public taste, gave up writing plays altogether. Perhaps Baillie formed her classification on plays such as William Wycherley's (1640-1716) *The Country Wife* (1675) for satirical comedy, William Congreve's *The Way of the World* (1700) for witty comedy, Sir Richard Steele's (1672-1729) *The Conscious Lovers* (1722) for sentimental comedy, and any one of the many adaptations of Molière's plays by dramatists such as Hugh Kelly's (1739-77) *The School for Wives* (1773) and Charles Macklin's (1699-1797) *The School for Husbands* (1761) for busy comedy. See Bevis, *The Laughing Tradition* 84-88.

2 [Baillie's note] These plays are generally the work of men, whose judgement and acute observation, enable them admirably well to generalize, and apply to classes of

playful, and easy. Strong decided condemnation of vice is too weighty and material to dance upon the surface of that stream, whose shallow currents sparkle in perpetual sun-beams, and cast up their bubbles to the light. Two or three persons of quick thought, and whimsical fancy, who perceive instantaneously the various connections of every passing idea, and the significations, natural or artificial, which single expressions, or particular forms of speech can possibly convey, take the lead thro' the whole, and seem to communicate their own peculiar talent to every creature in the play. The plot is most commonly feeble rather than simple, the incidents being numerous enough, but seldom striking or varied. To amuse, and only to amuse, is its aim: it pretends not to interest nor instruct. It pleases when we read, more than when we see it represented; and pleases still more when we take it up by accident, and read but a scene at a time.

Sentimental Comedy treats of those embarrassments, difficulties, and scruples, which, though sufficiently distressing to the delicate minds who entertain them, are not powerful enough to gratify the sympathetick desire we all feel to look into the heart of man in difficult and trying situations, which is the sound basis of tragedy, and are destitute of that seasoning of the lively and ludicrous, which prevents the ordinary transactions of comedy from becoming insipid. In real life, those who, from the peculiar frame of their minds, feel most of this refined distress, are not generally communicative upon the subject; and those who do feel and talk about it at the same time, if any such there be, seldom find their friends much inclined to listen to them. It is not to be supposed, then, long conversations upon the stage about small sentimental niceties, can be generally interesting. I am afraid plays of this kind, as well as works of a similar nature, in other departments of literature, have only tended to encrease amongst us a set of sentimental hypocrites; who are the same persons of this age that would have been the religious ones of another; and are daily doing morality the same

men the remarks they have made upon individuals; yet know not how to dress up, with any natural congruity, an imaginary individual in the attributes they have assigned to those classes.

kind of injury, by substituting the particular excellence which they pretend to possess, for plain simple uprightness and rectitude.

In Busy or Circumstantial Comedy, all those ingenious contrivances of lovers, guardians, governantes and chamber-maids;[1] that ambushed bushfighting amongst closets, screens, chests, easychairs, and toilet-tables, form a gay varied game of dexterity and invention; which, to those who have played at hide-and-seek, who have crouched down, with beating heart, in a dark corner, whilst the enemy groped near the spot; who have joined their busy school-mates in many a deep-laid plan to deceive, perplex, and torment the unhappy mortals deputed to have the charge of them, cannot be seen with indifference. Like an old hunter, who pricks up his ears at the sound of the chace, and starts away from the path of his journey, so, leaving all wisdom and criticism behind us, we follow the varied changes of the plot, and stop not for reflection. The studious man who wants a cessation from thought, the indolent man who dislikes it, and all those who, from habit or circumstances, live in a state of divorce from their own minds, are pleased with an amusement in which they have nothing to do but to open their eyes and behold; the moral tendency of it, however, is very faulty. That mockery of age and domestick authority, so constantly held forth, has a very bad effect upon the younger part of an audience; and that continual lying and deceit in the first characters of the piece, which is necessary for conducting the plot, has a most pernicious one.

But Characteristick Comedy, which represents to us this motley world of men and women in which we live, under those circumstances of ordinary and familiar life most favourable for the discovery of the human heart, offers to us a wide field of instruction, adapted to general application. We find in its varied scenes an exercise of the mind analogous to that which we all, less or more, find out for ourselves, amidst the mixed groupes of people whom we meet with in society; and which I have already mentioned as an exercise universally

---

1 Governesses and chamber-maids, both types of female household servants that became stock theatrical characters.

pleasing to man. As the distinctions which it is its highest aim to discriminate, are those of nature and not situation, they are judged of by all ranks of men; for a peasant will very clearly perceive in the character of a peer, those native peculiarities which belong to him as a man, though he is entirely at a loss in all that regards his manners and address as a nobleman. It illustrates to us the general remarks we have made upon men; and in it we behold, spread before us, plans of those original groundworks, upon which the general ideas we have been taught to conceive of mankind, are founded. It stands but little in need of busy plot, extraordinary incidents, witty repartee, or studied sentiments. It naturally produces for itself all that it requires; characters who are to speak for themselves, who are to be known by their own words and actions, not by the accounts that are given of them by others, cannot well be developed without considerable variety of judicious incident; a smile that is raised by some trait of undisguised nature, and a laugh that is provoked by some ludicrous effect of passion, or clashing of opposite characters, will be more pleasing to the generality of men, than either the one or the other when occasioned by a play upon words, or a whimsical combination of ideas; and to behold the operation and effects of the different propensities and weaknesses of men, will naturally call up in the mind of the spectator moral reflections more applicable, and more impressive than all the high-sounding sentiments, with which the graver scenes of Satirical and Sentimental Comedy are so frequently interlarded. It is much to be regretted, however, that the eternal introduction of love as the grand business of the Drama, and the consequent necessity for making the chief persons in it such, in regard to age, appearance, manners, dispositions, and endowments, as are proper for interesting lovers, has occasioned so much insipid similarity in the higher characters. It is chiefly, therefore, on the second and inferiour characters, that the efforts, even of our best poets, have been exhausted; and thus we are called upon to be interested in the fortune of one man, whilst our chief attention is directed to the character of another, which produces a disunion of ideas in the mind, injurious to the general effect of the whole. From this cause, also, those characteristick varieties have been very much neglected, which men present to us in the middle stages of life; when they are too old for lovers or the confidents of lovers, and too young to be the fathers, uncles, and guardians, who are contrasted with them; but when they are still in full vigour of mind, eagerly engaged with the world, joining the activity of youth to the providence of age, and offer to our attention objects sufficiently interesting and instructive. It is to be regretted that strong contrasts of character are too often attempted, instead of those harmonious shades of it, which nature so beautifully varies, and which we so greatly delight in, whenever we clearly distinguish them. It is to be regretted that in place of those characters, which present themselves to the imagination of a writer from his general observations upon mankind, inferiour poets have so often pourtrayed with senseless minuteness the characters of particular individuals. We are pleased with the eccentricities of individuals in real life, and also in history or biography, but in fictitious writings, we regard them with suspicion; and no representation of nature, that corresponds not with some of our general ideas in regard to it, will either instruct or inform us. When the originals of such characters are known and remembered, the plays in which they are introduced are oftentimes popular; and their temporary success has induced a still inferiour class of poets to believe, that, by making men strange, and unlike the rest of the world, they have made great discoveries, and mightily enlarged the boundaries of dramatick character. They will, therefore, distinguish one man from another by some strange whim or imagination, which is ever uppermost in his thoughts, and influences every action of his life; by some singular opinion, perhaps, about politicks, fashions, or the position of the stars; by some strong unaccountable love for one thing or aversion from another; entirely forgetting, that such singularities, if they are to be found in nature, can no where be sought for, with such probability of success, as in Bedlam.[1] Above all it is to be regretted that those adventitious distinctions amongst men, of age, fortune, rank, profession, and

---

1 A contraction for St. Mary of Bethlehem in London, the first English asylum for the mentally insane.

country, are so often brought forward in preference to the great original distinctions of nature; and our scenes so often filled with courtiers, lawyers, citizens, Frenchmen, &c. &c. With all the characteristicks of their respective conditions, such as they have been represented from time immemorial. This has introduced a great sameness into many of our plays, which all the changes of new fashions burlesqued, and new customs turned into ridicule, cannot conceal.

In comedy, the stronger passions, love excepted, are seldom introduced but in a passing way. We have short bursts of anger, fits of jealousy and impatience; violent passion of any continuance we seldom find. When this is attempted, however, forgetting that mode of exposing the weakness of the human mind, which peculiarly belongs to her, it is too frequently done in the serious spirit of tragedy; and this has produced so many of those serious comick plays, which so much divide and distract our attention.[1] Yet we all know from our own experience in real life, that, in certain situations, and under certain circumstances, the stronger passions are fitted to produce scenes more exquisitely comick than any other; and one well-wrought

---

1 [Baillie's note] Such plays, however excellent the parts may be of which they are composed, can never produce the same strength and unity of effect upon our minds which we receive from plays of a simpler undivided construction. If the serious and distressing scenes make a deep impression, we do not find ourselves in a humour for the comick ones that succeed; and if the comick scenes enliven us greatly, we feel tardy and unalert in bringing back our minds to a proper tone for the serious. As in tragedy we smile at those native traits of character, or that occasional sprightliness of dialogue, which are sometimes introduced, to animate her less-interesting parts, so may we be moved by comedy; but our tears should be called forth by those gentle strokes of nature, which come at once with kindred kindness on the heart, and are quickly succeeded by smiles. Like a small summer-cloud, whose rain-drops sparkle in the sun, and which swiftly passes away, is the genuine pathetick of comedy: the gathering foreseen storm, that darkens the whole face of the sky, belongs to tragedy alone. It is often observed, I confess, that we are more apt to be affected by those scenes of distress which we meet with in comedy, than the high-wrought woes of tragedy; and I believe it is true. But this arises from the woes of tragedy being so often appropriated to high and mighty personages, and strained beyond the modesty of nature, in order to suit their great dignity; or from the softened griefs of more gentle and familiar characters being rendered feeble and tiresome with too much repetition and whining. It arises from the greater facility with which we enter into the distresses of people, more upon a level with ourselves; and whose sorrows are expressed in less studied and unnatural language.

scene of this kind, will have a more powerful effect in repressing similar intemperance in the mind of a spectator, than many moral cautions, or even, perhaps, than the terrifick examples of tragedy. There are to be found, no doubt, in the works of our best dramatick writers, comick scenes descriptive of the stronger passions, but it is generally the inferiour characters of the piece who are made the subjects of them, very rarely those in whom we are much interested; and consequently the useful effect of such scenes upon the mind is very much weakened. This general appropriation of them has tempted our less-skilful Dramatists to exaggerate, and step, in further quest of the ludicrous, so much beyond the bounds of nature, that the very effect they are so anxious to produce is thereby destroyed, and all useful application of it entirely cut off; for we never apply to ourselves a false representation of nature.

But a complete exhibition of passion, with its varieties and progress in the breast of man has, I believe, scarcely ever been attempted in comedy. Even love, though the chief subject of almost every play, has been pourtrayed in a loose, scattered, and imperfect manner. The story of the lovers is acted over before us, whilst the characteristicks of that passion by which they are actuated, and which is the great master-spring of the whole, are faintly to be discovered. We are generally introduced to a lover after he has long been acquainted with his mistress, and wants but the consent of some stubborn relation, relief from some embarrassment of situation, or the clearing up some mistake or love-quarrel occasioned by malice or accident, to make him completely happy. To overcome these difficulties, he is engaged in a busy train of contrivance and exertion, in which the spirit, activity and ingenuity of the man is held forth to view, whilst the lover, comparatively speaking, is kept out of sight. But even when this is not the case; when the lover is not so busied and involved, this stage of the passion is exactly the one that is least interesting, and least instructive: not to mention as I have done already, that one stage of any passion must shew it imperfectly.

From this view of the Comick Drama I have been induced to believe, that, as companions to the forementioned tragedies, a series of comedies on a similar plan, in which bustle of plot,

brilliancy of dialogue, and even the bold and striking in character, should, to the best of the authour's judgment, be kept in
due subordination to nature, might likewise be acceptable to
the publick. I am confident that comedy upon this plan is
capable of being made as interesting, as entertaining, and superiour in moral tendency to any other. For even in ordinary life,
with very slight cause to excite them, strong passions will foster
themselves within the breast; and what are all the evils which
vanity, folly, prejudice, or peculiarity of temper lead to, compared with those which such unquiet inmates produce? Were
they confined to the exalted and the mighty, to those engaged
in the great events of the world, to the inhabitants of palaces
and camps, how happy comparatively would this world be! But
many a miserable being, whom firm principle, timidity of character, or the fear of shame keeps back from the actual commission of crimes, is tormented in obscurity, under the dominion
of those passions which set the seducer in ambush, rouse the
bold spoiler to wrong, and strengthen the arm of the murderer.
Though to those with whom such dangerous enemies have
long found shelter, exposing them in an absurd and ridiculous
light, may be shooting a finely-pointed arrow against the hardened rock; yet to those with whom they are but new, and less
assured guests, this may prove a more successful mode of attack
than any other.

It was the saying of a sagacious Scotchman,[1] 'let who will
make the laws of a nation, if I have the writing of its ballads.'
Something similar to this may be said in regard to the Drama.
Its lessons reach not, indeed, to the lowest classes of the labouring people, who are the broad foundation of society, which can
never be generally moved without endangering every thing

---

1   We may never know exactly who this Scot was, if he ever existed at all, but he is
    quoted by Andrew Fletcher (1655-1716) of Saltoun, a Scottish patriot and oppo-
    nent of the Treaty of Union of 1707. Writing anonymously in *An Account of a Con-*
    versation Concerning a Right Regulation of Governments for the Common Good of
    Mankind (1704), Fletcher describes perhaps an imaginary conversation with the Earl
    of Cromarty, Sir Edward Seymour, and Sir Christopher Musgrave: "I knew a very
    wise man so much of Sir Chr——'s sentiment, that he believed if a man were per-
    mitted to make all the ballads, he need not care who should make the laws of a
    nation."

that is constructed upon it, and who are our potent and formidable ballad readers; but they reach to the classes next in order to them, and who will always have over them no inconsiderable influence. The impressions made by it are communicated, at the same instant of time, to a greater number of individuals, than those made by any other species of writing; and they are strengthened in every spectator, by observing their effects upon those who surround him. From this observation, the mind of my reader will suggest of itself, what it would be unnecessary, and, perhaps, improper in me here to enlarge upon. The theatre is a school[1] in which much good or evil may be learned. At the beginning of its career the Drama was employed to mislead and excite; and were I not unwilling to refer to transactions of the present times, I might abundantly confirm what I have said by recent examples. The authour, therefore, who aims in any degree to improve the mode of its instruction, and point to more useful lessons than it is generally employed to dispense, is certainly praiseworthy, though want of abilities may unhappily prevent him from being successful in his efforts.

This idea has prompted me to begin a work in which I am aware of many difficulties. In plays of this nature the passions must be depicted not only with their bold and prominent features, but also with those minute and delicate traits which distinguish them in an infant, growing, and repressed state; which are the most difficult of all to counterfeit, and one of which falsely imagined, will destroy the effect of a whole scene. The characters over whom they are made to usurp dominion, must be powerful and interesting, exercising them with their full measure of opposition and struggle; for the chief antagonists they contend with must be the other passions and propensities of the heart, not outward circumstances and events. Though belonging to such characters, they must still be held to view in their most baleful and unseductive light; and those qualities in the impassioned which are necessary to interest us in their fate,

---

1 Cf. Schiller. "The stage is an institution combining amusement with instruction, rest with exertion, where no faculty of the mind is overstrained, no pleasure enjoyed at the cost of the whole" (*Essays*, "The Stage as a Moral Institution" 345).

must not be allowed, by any lustre borrowed from them, to diminish our abhorrence of guilt. The second and even the inferiour persons of each play, as they must be kept perfectly distinct from the great impassioned one, should generally be represented in a calm unagitated state, and therefore more pains are necessary than in other dramatick works, to mark them by appropriate distinctions of character, lest they should appear altogether insipid and insignificant. As the great object here is to trace passion through all its varieties, and in every stage, many of which are marked by shades so delicate, that in much bustle of events they would be little attended to, or entirely overlooked, simplicity of plot is more necessary, than in those plays where only occasional bursts of passion are introduced, to distinguish a character, or animate a scene. But where simplicity of plot is necessary, there is very great danger of making a piece appear bare and unvaried, and nothing but great force and truth in the delineations of nature will prevent it from being tiresome.[1] Soliloquy, or those overflowings of the perturbed soul, in which it unburthens itself of those thoughts, which it cannot communicate to others, and which in certain situations is the only mode that a Dramatist can employ to open to us the mind he would display, must necessarily be often, and to considerable length, introduced. Here, indeed, as it naturally belongs to passion, it will not be so offensive as it generally is in other plays, when a calm unagitated person tells over to himself all that has befallen him, and all his future

---

1 [Baillie's note] To make up for this simplicity of plot, the shew and decorations of the theatre ought to be allowed, to plays written upon this plan, in their full extent. How fastidious soever some poets may be in regard to these matters, it is much better to relieve our tired-out attention with a battle, a banquet, or a procession, than an accumulation of incidents. In the latter case the mind is harassed and confused with those doubts, conjectures, and disappointments which multiplied events occasion, and in a great measure unfitted for attending to the worthier parts of the piece; but in the former it enjoys a rest, a pleasing pause in its more serious occupation, from which it can return again, without any incumbrance of foreign intruding ideas. The shew of a splendid procession will afford to a person of the best understanding, a pleasure in kind, though not in degree, with that which a child would receive from it. But when it is past he thinks no more of it; whereas some confusion of circumstances, some half-explained mistake, which gives him no pleasure at all when it takes place, may take off his attention afterwards from the refined beauties of a natural and characteristick dialogue.

schemes of intrigue or advancement; yet to make speeches of this kind sufficiently natural and impressive, to excite no degree of weariness nor distaste, will be found to be no easy task. There are, besides these, many other difficulties peculiarly belonging to this undertaking, too minute and tedious to mention. If, fully aware of them, I have not shrunk back from the attempt, it is not from any idea that my own powers of discernment will at all times enable me to overcome them; but I am emboldened by the confidence I feel in that candour and indulgence, with which the good and enlightened do ever regard the experimental efforts of those, who wish in any degree to enlarge the sources of pleasure and instruction amongst men.

It will now be proper to say something of the particular plays which compose this volume. But, in the first place I must observe, that as I pretend not to have overcome the difficulties attached to this design, so neither from the errours and defects, which, in these pages, I have thought it necessary to point out in the works of others, do I at all pretend to be blameless. To conceive the great moral object and outline of a story; to people it with various characters, under the influence of various passions; and to strike out circumstances and situations calculated to call them into action, is a very different employment of the mind from calmly considering those propensities of our nature, to which dramatick writings are most powerfully addressed, and taking a general view upon those principles of the works of preceding authours. They are employments which cannot well occupy it at the same time; and experience has taught us, that criticks do not unfrequently write in contradiction to their own rules. If I should, therefore, sometimes appear in the foregoing remarks to have provided a stick wherewith to break mine own pate,[1] I entreat that my reader will believe I am neither confident nor boastful, and use it with gentleness.

In the two first plays, where love is the passion under review, their relation to the general plan may not be very obvious.

---

1 Head or skull.

Love is the chief groundwork of almost all our tragedies and comedies, and so far they are not distinguished from others. But I have endeavoured in both to give an unbroken view of the passion from its beginning, and to mark it as I went along, with those peculiar traits which distinguish its different stages of progression. I have in both these pieces grafted this passion not on those open communicative impetuous characters, who have so long occupied the dramatick station of lovers, but on men of a firm, thoughtful, reserved turn of mind, and with whom it commonly makes the longest stay, and maintains the hardest struggle. I should be extremely sorry if, from any thing at the conclusion of the tragedy, it should be supposed that I mean to countenance suicide,[1] or condemn those customs whose object is the discouragement of it, by withholding from the body of the self-slain those sacred rites, and marks of respect commonly shewn to the dead. Let it be considered, that whatever I have inserted there, which can at all raise any suspicion of this kind, is put into the mouths of rude uncultivated soldiers, who are roused with the loss of a beloved leader and indignant at any idea of disgrace being attached to him. If it should seem inconsistent with the nature of this work, that in its companion the comedy, I have made strong moral principle triumph over love, let it be remembered, that without this the whole moral tendency of a play, which must end happily, would have been destroyed; and that it is not my intention to encourage the indulgence of this passion, amiable as it is, but to restrain it. The last play, the subject of which is hatred, will more clearly discover the nature and intention of my design. The rise and progress of this passion I have been obliged to give in retrospect, instead of representing it all along in its actual operation, as I could have wished to have done. But hatred is a passion of slow growth; and to have exhibited it from its beginnings would have included a longer period, than even

---

1 David Hume's (1711-76) essays on suicide and the immortality of the soul were completed and published around 1755. Controversy led to their physical removal from these publications. Clandestine French (1770) and English (1777) editions appeared, but it was not until 1783 that they were published with Hume's name attached, though not with his permission.

those who are least scrupulous about the limitation of dramatick time, would have thought allowable. I could not have introduced my chief characters upon the stage as boys, and then as
men. For this passion must be kept distinct from that dislike
which we conceive for another when he has greatly offended
us, and which is almost the constant companion of anger; and
also from that eager desire to crush, and inflict suffering on him
who has injured us, which constitutes revenge. This passion, as
I have conceived it, is that rooted and settled aversion, which
from opposition of character, aided by circumstances of little
importance, grows at last into such antipathy and personal disgust as makes him who entertains it, feel, in the presence of him
who is the object of it, a degree of torment and restlessness
which is insufferable. It is a passion, I believe less frequent than
any other of the stronger passions, but in the breast where it
does exist, it creates, perhaps, more misery than any other. To
endeavour to interest the mind for a man under the dominion
of a passion so baleful, so unamiable, may seem, perhaps, repre-
hensible. I therefore beg it may be considered that it is the passion and not the man which is held up to our execration; and
that this and every other bad passion does more strongly evince
its pernicious and dangerous nature, when we see it thus counteracting and destroying the good gifts of heaven, than when it
is represented as the suitable associate in the breast of inmates as
dark as itself. This remark will likewise be applicable to many
of the other plays belonging to my work, that are intended to
follow. A decidedly wicked character can never be interesting;
and to employ such for the display of any strong passion would
very much injure instead of improving the moral effect. In the
breast of a bad man passion has comparatively little to combat,
how then can it shew its strength? I shall say no more upon this
subject, but submit myself to the judgment of my reader.

It may, perhaps, be supposed from my publishing these plays,
that I have written them for the closet[1] rather than the stage. If
upon perusing them with attention, the reader is disposed to
think they are better calculated for the first than the last, let him

---

1   A place of private study; in this case, for the purposes of being read as opposed to
    being performed.

impute it to want of skill in the authour, and not to any previous design. A play, but of small poetical merit, that is suited to strike and interest the spectator, to catch the attention of him who will not, and of him who cannot read, is a more valuable and useful production than one whose elegant and harmonious pages are admired in the libraries of the tasteful and refined. To have received approbation from an audience of my countrymen, would have been more pleasing to me than any other praise. A few tears from the simple and young would have been, in my eyes, pearls of great price; and the spontaneous, untutored plaudits of the rude and uncultivated would have come to my heart as offerings of no mean value. I should, therefore, have been better pleased to have introduced them to the world from the stage than from the press. I possess, however, no likely channel to the former mode of publick introduction; and upon further reflection it appeared to me that by publishing them in this way, I have an opportunity afforded me of explaining the design of my work, and enabling the publick to judge, not only of each play by itself, but as making a part likewise of the whole; an advantage which, perhaps, does more than over-balance the splendour and effect of theatrical representation.

It may be thought that with this extensive plan before me, I should not have been in a hurry to publish, but have waited to give a larger portion of it to the publick, which would have enabled them to make a truer estimate of its merit. To bring forth only three plays of the whole, and the last without its intended companion,[1] may seem like the haste of those vain people, who as soon as they have written a few pages of a discourse, or a few couplets of a poem, cannot be easy till every body has seen them. I do protest, in honest simplicity! it is distrust and not confidence, that has led me at this early stage of the undertaking, to bring it before the publick. To labour in uncertainty is at all times unpleasant; but to proceed in a long and difficult work with any impression upon your mind that your labour may be in vain; that the opinion you have con-

---

1   *The Election*, Baillie's comedy on hatred, appeared in the second volume of *Plays on the Passions* in 1802.

ceived of your ability to perform it may be a delusion, a false suggestion of self-love, the fantasy of an aspiring temper, is most discouraging and cheerless. I have not proceeded so far, indeed, merely upon the strength of my own judgment; but the friends to whom I have shewn my manuscripts are partial to me, and their approbation which in the case of any indifferent person would be in my mind completely decisive, goes but a little way in relieving me from these apprehensions. To step beyond the circle of my own immediate friends[1] in quest of opinion, from the particular temper of my mind I feel an uncommon repugnance: I can with less pain to myself bring them before the publick at once, and submit to its decision.[2] It is to my countrymen at large that I call for assistance. If this work is fortunate enough to attract their attention, let their strictures as well as

---

1 Margaret Carhart describes some of them: "Among Joanna Baillie's thousand admirers, as [Sir Walter] Scott called them, were Wordsworth, Lord and Lady Byron, Southey, Maria Edgeworth, George Ellis, John Richardson, Mrs. Hemans, George Crabbe, Henry Reeve, William Sotheby, Lucy Aikin, Henry Crabb Robinson, Mrs. Grant of Laggan, Mrs. Jameson, Mrs. Siddons, George Ticknor, Harriet Martineau, Mary Berry, Mrs. Barbauld, William Erskine, Daniel Terry, and William Ellery Channing" (36). For a more complete description of Baillie's circle, see Aloma Noble's *Joanna Baillie as a Dramatic Artist*.

2 [Baillie's note] The first of these plays, indeed, has been shewn to two or three Gentlemen whom I have not the honour of reckoning amongst my friends. One of them, who is a man of distinguished talents, has honoured it with very flattering approbation; and, at his suggestion, one or two slight alterations in it have been made. [We will probably only ever be able to guess just who this might be. Men such as Mrs. Anna Laetitia Barbauld's husband, the dissenting minister in Hampstead from 1787 to 1802, or her brother Dr. John Aikin (1747-1822), who not only studied in Edinburgh, practised medicine in London, and wrote *Evenings at Home* (6 vols. 1799-1815) in conjunction with his sister, may have been too close to the inhabitants of Hampstead to keep the secret of Baillie's initial anonymity. Or, might Baillie also be referring to either Sir George Howland Beaumont (1753-1827), English landscape painter and art patron, or Charles James Fox (1749-1806) Liberal statesman and a later supporter (1783) of Lord Frederick North (1732-92)?. Florence MacCunn writes: "But Scott was not the only one among her contemporaries who hailed a new literary force in Joanna Baillie: Sir George Beaumont, that fastidious connoisseur of all the arts, declared that he had hardly dared to hope that such strains could be heard at the end of the eighteenth century, and Fox wrote five pages of eulogy in reply to Sir George's recommendation of the plays" (294). Further evidence to support this conjecture might be that the Hon. F. North wrote the prologue for the 1800 performance at Drury Lane, or that perhaps Baillie may have been making a silent nod to Beaumont by creating a character in *The Tryal* of the same name.]

their praise come to my aid: the one will encourage me in a long and arduous undertaking, the other will teach me to improve it as I advance. For there are many errours that may be detected, and improvements that may be suggested in the prosecution of this work, which from the observations of a great variety of readers are more likely to be pointed out to me, than from those of a small number of persons, even of the best judgment. I am not possessed of that confidence in mine own powers, which enables the concealed genius, under the pressure of present discouragement, to pursue his labours in security, looking firmly forward to other more enlightened times for his reward. If my own countrymen[1] with whom I live and converse, who look upon the same race of men, the same state of society, the same passing events with myself, receive not my offering, I presume not to look to posterity.

Before I close this discourse, let me crave the forbearance of my reader, if he has discovered in the course of it any unacknowledged use of the thoughts of other authours, which he thinks ought to have been noticed; and let me beg the same favour, if in reading the following plays, any similar neglect seems to occur. There are few writers who have sufficient originality of thought to strike out for themselves new ideas upon every occasion. When a thought presents itself to me, as suited to the purpose I am aiming at, I would neither be thought proud enough to reject it, on finding that another has used it before me, nor mean enough to make use of it without acknowledging the obligation, when I can at all guess to whom such acknowledgments are due. But I am situated where I have no library to consult; my reading through the whole of my life has been of a loose, scattered, unmethodical kind, with no determined direction, and I have not been blessed by nature

---

1   Samuel B. Rogers (1763-1855), author of *The Pleasures of Memory* (1792), reviewed this edition (*Monthly Review*, September 1798). Rogers became a close friend of Baillie's, and his positive review afforded her great encouragement. "Encouragement, received from the pen of a celebrated poet, did, in the words of Joanna, 'enable her to make head against criticism of a very different character'; and this expression from one of firm mind, tenacious of its convictions, showed how keenly she had felt strictures launched with all the poignancy consummate talent could employ" (*Works* x). See also Carhart 42-43 and introduction.

with the advantages of a retentive or accurate memory. Do not, however, imagine from this, I at all wish to insinuate that I ought to be acquitted of every obligation to preceding authours; and that when a palpable similarity of thought and expression is observable between us, it is a similarity produced by accident alone, and with perfect unconsciousness on my part. I am frequently sensible, from the manner in which an idea arises to my imagination, and the readiness with which words, also, present themselves to clothe it in, that I am only making use of some dormant part of that hoard of ideas which the most indifferent memories lay up, and not the native suggestions of mine own mind. Whenever I have suspected myself of doing so, in the course of this work, I have felt a strong inclination to mark that suspicion in a note. But, besides that it might have appeared like an affectation of scrupulousness which I would avoid, there being likewise, most assuredly, many other places in it where I have done the same thing without being conscious of it, a suspicion of wishing to slur them over, and claim all the rest as unreservedly my own, would unavoidably have attached to me. If this volume should appear, to any candid and liberal critick, to merit that he should take the trouble of pointing out to me in what parts of it I seem to have made that use of other authours' writings, which according to the fair laws[1] of literature ought to have been acknowledged, I shall think myself obliged to him. I shall examine the sources he points out as having supplied my own lack of ideas; and if this book should have the good fortune to go through a second edition, I shall not fail to own my obligations to him, and the authours from whom I may have borrowed.

How little credit soever, upon perusing these plays, the reader may think me entitled to in regard to the execution of the work, he will not, I flatter myself, deny me some credit in regard to the plan. I know of no series of plays, in any language, expressly descriptive of the different passions; and I believe there are few plays existing in which the display of one strong

---

1   Baillie's signature appeared on an "Address of certain authors of Great Britain to the Senate of the U.S." requesting the enactment of a copyright law, Feb. 2, 1837 (Huntington Museum 11234).

passion is the chief business of the drama, so written that they could properly make part of such a series. I do not think that we should, from the works of various authours, be able to make a collection which would give us any thing exactly of the nature of that which is here proposed. If the reader, in perusing it, perceives that the abilities of the authour are not proportioned to the task which is imposed upon them, he will wish in the spirit of kindness rather than of censure, as I most sincerely do, that they had been more adequate to it. However, if I perform it ill, I am still confident that this (pardon me if I call it, noble) design will not be suffered to fall to the ground; some one will arise after me who will do it justice; and there is no poet, possessing genius for such a work, who will not at the same time possess that spirit of justice and of candour, which will lead him to remember me with respect.

I have now only to thank my reader, whoever he may be, who has followed me through the pages of this discourse, for having had the patience to do so. May he, in going through what follows (a wish the sincerity of which he cannot doubt) find more to reward his trouble than I dare venture to promise him; and for the pains he has already taken, and that, which he intends to take for me, I request that he will accept of my grateful acknowledgments.[1]

---

1 [Baillie's note] Shakspeare, more than any of our poets, gives peculiar and appropriate distinction to the characters of his tragedies. The remarks I have made, in regard to the little variety of character to be met with in tragedy, apply not to him. Neither has he, as other Dramatists generally do, bestowed pains on the chief persons of his drama only, leaving the second and inferiour ones insignificant and spiritless. He never wears out our capacity to feel, by eternally pressing upon it. His tragedies are agreeably chequered with variety of scenes, enriched with good sense, nature, and vivacity, which relieve our minds from the fatigue of continued distress. If he sometimes carries this so far as to break in upon that serious tone of mind, which disposes us to listen with effect to the higher scenes of tragedy, he has done so chiefly in his historical plays, where the distresses set forth are commonly of that publick kind, which does not, at any rate, make much impression upon the feelings.

COUNT BASIL

A TRAGEDY

PERSONS OF THE DRAMA.

MEN.

COUNT BASIL, *a General in the Emperour's service.*
COUNT ROSINBERG, *his Friend.*
DUKE OF MANTUA.
GAURIECIO, *his Minister.*
VALTOMER.
FREDERICK, *Two Officers of* Basil's *Troops.*
GEOFFRY, *an old Soldier, very much maimed in the Wars.*
MIRANDO, *a little Boy, favourite to* Victoria.

WOMEN.

VICTORIA, *Daughter to the* Duke of Mantua.
COUNTESS OF ALBINI, *Friend and Governess to* Victoria.
ISABELLA, *a Lady attending upon* Victoria.
Officers, Soldiers, and Attendants, Masks,
Dancers, &c.

★ ★ *The Scene is in Mantua, and its environs.*

★ *Time supposed to be in the Sixteenth Century, when* CHARLES[1]
the Fifth *defeated* FRANCIS[2] the First, *at the Battle of Pavia.*[3]

---

1 Charles V (1500-58) was the Emperor of the Holy Roman Empire (1519-56) and
   the king of Spain (1516-56) as Charles I. Cold, austere, and proud, Charles stood for
   chivalric ideals and religious piety.

2 Francis I (1494-1547) as king of France engaged in battle with Charles V for most
   of his reign in repeated attempts to conquer parts of Italy and Burgundy. Throughout his life, Francis was notably influenced by women, especially his mother, his sister – Margaret of Navarre – and his mistresses.

3 A decisive military engagement between Charles V and Francis I on February 24,
   1525 to liberate the city of Pavia in the region of Abruzzi, Italy. The French
   infantry of over 28,000 men was virtually annihilated, and Francis I was taken prisoner, actions all leading to the Peace Treaty of Madrid. Coincidently, the times of
   Charles of Austria form the historical background for William Godwin's (1756-
   1836) second novel, *St. Leon* (1798), a story of true love tragically cut short, in
   which St. Leon at the age of 19 takes part in the siege of Pavia. See also notes to
   2.3.61 and 5.3.184.

COUNT BASIL.

ACT I.—SCENE I.

An Open Street, crouded with People, who seem to be waiting in expectation of some Show.

Enter a CITIZEN.

FIRST MAN. Well friend, what tidings of the grand procession?
CIT. I left it passing by the northern gate.
SECOND MAN. I've waited long, I'm glad it comes at last.
YOUNG MAN. And does the Princess look so wondrous fair
As fame reports?
CIT. She is the fairest lady of the train,
    And all the fairest beauties of the court
    Are in her train.
OLD MAN. Bears she such off'rings to Saint Francis' shrine,[1]   10
    So rich, so marvellous rich as rumour says?
    'Twill drain the treasury.
CIT. Since she in all this splendid pomp, returns
    Her publick thanks to the good patron Saint,
    Who from his sick bed hath restor'd her father,
    Thou wouldst not have her go with empty hands?
    She loves magnificence.—
    (*Discovering among the croud* Old Geoffry.)
    Ha! art thou here, old remnant of the wars?
    Thou art not come to see this courtly show,
    Which sets the young agape?   20
GEOF. I came not for the show; and yet, methinks,
    It were a better jest upon me still,
    If thou didst truly know mine errand here.

---

1 Perhaps a shrine to St. Francis of Assisi who was canonized in 1228. Tradition would have it that to free himself from the temptations of the flesh, St. Francis would roll naked in the snow, then throw himself into a thornbush. Where the earth was spotted with his blood, roses would grow.

CIT. I pri'thee say.

GEOF.   What, must I tell it thee?
    As o'er my ev'ning fire I musing sat
    Some few days since, my mind's eye backward turn'd
    Upon the various changes I have pass'd—
    How in my youth with gay attire allur'd,
    And all the grand accoutrements of war,
30   I left my peaceful home: Then my first battles,
    When clashing arms, and sights of blood were new:
    Then all the after chances of the war;
    Ay, and that field, a well-fought field it was,
    When with this arm (I speak not of it oft)
    (*Pointing to his empty sleeve.*)
    Which now thou seest is no arm of mine,
    In a straight pass I stopp'd a thousand foes,
    And turn'd my flying comrades to the charge;
    For which good service, in his tented court,
    My prince bestow'd a mark of favour on me;
40   Whilst his fair consort, seated by his side,
    The fairest lady e'er mine eyes beheld,
    Gave me what more than all besides I priz'd,
    Methinks I see her still! a gracious smile;
    'Twas a heart-kindling smile,—a smile of praise—
    Well, musing thus on all my fortunes past,
    A Neighbour drew the latchet of my door,
    And full of news from town, in many words
    Big with rich names, told of this grand procession.
    E'en as he spoke a fancy seiz'd my soul
50   To see the princess pass, if in her face
    I yet might trace some semblance of her mother.
    This is the simple truth; laugh as thou wilt,
    I came not for the show.

Enter an OFFICER.

OFFICER. (*to* Geof.) Make way, that the procession may have room;
    Stand you aside, and let this man have place.

(*Pushing* Geof. *and endeavouring to put another in his place.*)
GEOF. But that thou art the prince's officer,
　　I'd give thee back thy push with better blows.
OFFICER. What wilt thou not give place? the prince is near,
　　I will complain to him, and have thee caged.
GEOF. Yes do complain, I pray; and when thou dost,　　　　60
　　Say that the private of the tenth brigade,
　　Who sav'd his army on the Danube's bank,
　　And since that time a private hath remain'd,
　　Dares, as a citizen, his right maintain
　　Against thy insolence. Go tell him this,
　　And ask him then what dungeon of his tower
　　He'll have me thrust into?
CIT. (*to* Officer.) This is old Geoffry of the tenth brigade.
OFFI. I knew him not: you should have told me sooner.

[EXIT, *looking much ashamed.*

Martial Musick heard at a distance.
CIT. Hark, this is musick of a warlike kind.　　　　　　70

Enter Second CITIZEN.

(*To* Sec. Cit.) What sounds are these, good friend, which
　　this way bear?
SEC. CIT. The Count of Basil is upon his march,
　　To join the Emp'rour with some chosen troops,
　　And doth through Mantua pass in right of Allies.
GEOF. I have heard a good report of this young soldier.
SEC. CIT. 'Tis said he disciplines his men severely,
　　And acts with them too much the old commander,
　　Which is ungracious in so young a man.
GEOF. I know he loves not ease and revelry;
　　He makes them soldiers at no dearer rate　　　　　　80
　　Than he himself hath paid. What, dost thou think
　　That e'en the very meanest simple craft
　　May not, but with due diligence, be learn'd,
　　And yet the noble art of soldiership

May be attain'd by loit'ring in the sun?
Some men are born to feast, and not to fight;
Whose sluggish minds, e'en in fair honour's field,
Still on their dinner turn—
Let such pot-boiling varlets stay at home,
90 And wield a flesh-hook rather than a sword.
In times of easy service, true it is,
An easy, careless chief, all soldiers love;
But O! how gladly in the day of battle
Would they their jolly bottle-chief desert,
And follow such a leader as Count Basil.
So gath'ring herds, at pressing dangers' call,
Confess the master Deer.
(*Musick is heard again, and nearer. Geoffry walks up and down
with a military triumphant step.*)
CIT. What moves thee thus?
GEOF. I've march'd to this same tune in glorious days.
100 My very limbs catch motion from the sound,
As they were young again.
SEC. CIT.   But here they come.

Enter Count BASIL, *Officers and Soldiers in Procession, with
Colours flying, and martial musick. When they have marched half way
over the Stage, an Officer of the Duke's enters from the opposite side,
and speaks to* Count BASIL, *upon which he gives a sign with his
hand, and the martial musick ceases; soft musick is heard at a little distance, and* VICTORIA, *with a long procession of Ladies, enters from the
opposite side. The General, &c. pay obeisance to her, as she passes; she
stops to return it, and then goes off with her train. After which the military procession moves on, and Exeunt.*

CIT. (*to* Geof.) What thinkst thou of the princess?
GEOF.   She is fair,
But not so fair as her good mother was.   [EXEUNT.

SCENE II.

A Publick Walk on the Ramparts of the Town.

Enter Count ROSINBERG, VALTOMER, *and* FREDERICK.—
VALTOMER *enters by the opposite side of the Stage, and meets them.*

VALT. O! what a jolly town for way-worn soldiers!
Rich steaming pots, and smell of dainty fare,
From every house salute you as you pass:
Light feats and jugglers' tricks attract the eye;
Frolick, and mirth, musick in ev'ry street;
Whilst pretty damsels, in their best attire,
Trip on in wanton groups, then look behind,
To spy the fools a-gazing after them.
FRED. But short will be the season of our ease,
For Basil is of flinty matter made,   10
And cannot be allur'd—
'Faith Rosinberg, I would thou didst command us;
Thou art his kinsman, of a rank as noble,
Some years his elder too; how has it been
That he should be preferr'd? I see not why.
ROS. Ah! but I see it, and allow it well;
He is too much my pride to wake my envy.
FRED. Nay, Count, it is thy foolish admiration
Which raises him to such superiour height;
And truly thou hast so infected us,   20
That I have felt at times an awe before him,
I know not why. 'Tis cursed folly;
Thou art as brave, of as good parts as he.
ROS. Our talents of a diff'rent nature are;
Mine for the daily intercourse of life,
And his for higher things.
FRED. Well, praise him as thou wilt; I see it not;
I'm sure I am as brave a man as he.
ROS. Yes, brave thou art, but 'tis subaltern brav'ry,
And doth respect thyself. Thou'lt bleed as well,   30

Give, and receive as deep an wound as he.
When Basil fights he wields a thousand swords;
For 'tis their trust in his unshaken mind,
O'erwatching all the changes of the field,
Calm and inventive midst the battle's storm,
Which makes his soldiers bold.—
There have been those, in early manhood slain,
Whose great heroick souls did yet inspire
With such a noble zeal their gen'rous troops,
40   That to their latest day of bearing arms,
Their grey-hair'd soldiers would all dangers brave
Of desp'rate service, claim'd with boastful pride,
For having fought beneath them in their youth.
Such men have been; of whom it may be said,
Their spirits conquer'd when their clay was cold.
VALT. Yes, I have seen in the eventful field,
When new occasion mock'd all formed art,
E'en old commanders hold experience cheap,
And look to Basil ere his chin was dark.
50 ROS. One fault he has, I know but only one;
His too great love of military fame
Destroys his thoughts, and makes him oft appear
Unsocial and severe.
FRED. Well, feel I not undaunted in the field?
As much enthusiastick love of glory?
Why am I not as good a man as he?
ROS. He's form'd for great occasions, thou for small.
VALT. But small occasions in the path of life
Lie thickly sown, while great are rarely scatter'd.
60 ROS. By which you would infer that men like Fred'rick,
Should on the whole a better figure make,
Than men of higher parts; but 'tis not so,
For some shew well, and fair applauses gain,
Where want of skill in other men is graceful.
But do not frown, good Fred'rick, no offence;
Thou canst not make a great man of thyself,
Yet wisely deign to use thy native pow'rs,
And prove an honour'd courtly gentleman.
But hush! no more of this, here Basil comes.

Enter BASIL, *who returns their salute without speaking.*

ROS. What thinkst thou, Valtomer, of Mantua's princess?   70
VALT. Fame prais'd her much, but hath not prais'd her more
    Than on a better proof the eye consents to.
    With all that grace and nobleness of mien,
    She might do honour to an Emp'rour's throne;
    She is too noble for a petty court.
    Is it not so, my Lord?—(*To* Basil, *who only bows assent.*)
    Nay, she demeans herself with so much grace,
    Such easy state, such gay magnificence,
    She should be queen of revelry and show.
FRED. She's charming as the goddess of delight.   80
VALT. But after her, she most attracted me
    Who wore the yellow scarf and walk'd the last,
    For tho' Victoria is a lovely woman—
FRED. Nay, it is treason but to call her woman;
    She's a divinity, and should be worshipp'd.
    But on my life, since now we talk of worship,
    She worshipp'd Francis with right noble gifts!
    They sparkled so with gold and precious gems
    Their value must be great; some thousand crowns?
ROS. I would not rate them at a price so mean;   90
    The cup alone, with precious stones beset,
    Would fetch a sum as great. That olive branch
    The princess bore herself, of fretted gold,
    Was exquisitely wrought. I mark'd it more,
    Because she held it in so white a hand.
BASIL. (*in a quick voice.*) Mark'd you her hand? I did not see her hand,
    And yet she wav'd it twice.
ROS. It is a fair one, tho' you mark'd it not.
VALT. I wish some painter's eye had view'd the group,
    As she and all her lovely damsels pass'd;   100
    He would have found wherewith t'enrich his art.
ROS. I wish so too; for oft their fancied beauties
    Have so much cold perfection in their parts,
    'Tis plain they ne'er belong'd to flesh and blood.
    This is not truth, and doth not please so well

As the varieties of lib'ral nature,
Where ev'ry kind of beauty charms the eye;
Large and small featur'd, flat, and prominent,
Ay, by the mass! and snub-nos'd beauties too.
110 'Faith ev'ry woman hath some 'witching charm,
If that she be not proud, or captious.
VALT. Demure, or over-wise, or giv'n to freaks.
ROS. Or giv'n to freaks! hold, hold good Valtomer!
Thou'lt leave no woman handsome under heav'n.
VALT. But I must leave you for an hour or so,
I mean to view the town if aught worth notice.
FRED. I'll go with thee, my friend.
ROS.   And so will I.

[EXEUNT Valt. Fred. *and* Ros.

Re-enter ROSINBERG.

ROS. I have repented me, I will not go;
They will be too long absent.—(*Pauses, and looks at* Basil,
who remains still musing without seeing him.)
120 What mighty thoughts engage my pensive friend?
BAS. O! it is admirable.
ROS. How runs thy fancy? what is admirable?
BAS. Her form, her face, her motion, ev'ry thing!
ROS. The princess? yes, have we not prais'd her much?
BAS. I know you prais'd her, and her off'rings too;
She might have giv'n the treasures of the east
E'er I had known it.
She came again upon my wond'ring sight—
O! didst thou mark her when she first appear'd?
130 Still distant, slowly moving with her train;
Her robe, and tresses floating on the wind,
Like some light figure in a morning cloud?
Then as she onward to the eye became
The more distinct, the lovelier still she grew.
That graceful bearing of her slender form;
Her roundly-spreading breast, her tow'ring neck,

Her face ting'd sweetly with the bloom of youth—
But when on near approach she tow'rds us turn'd,
Kind mercy! what a countenance was there!
And when to our salute she gently bow'd,   140
Didst mark that smile rise from her parting lips?
Soft swell'd her glowing cheek, her eyes smil'd too;
O! how they smil'd! 'twas like the beams of heav'n!
I felt my roused soul within me start,
Like something wak'd from sleep.
ROS. Ah! many a slumb'rer heav'n's beams do wake
To care and misery!
BAS. There's something grave and solemn in your voice
As you pronounce these words. What dost thou mean?
Thou wouldst not sound my knell?   150
ROS. No, not for all beneath the vaulted sky!
But to be plain, thus earnest from your lips
Her praise displeases me. To men like you
If love should come, he proves no easy guest.
BAS. What dost thou think I am beside myself,
And cannot view the fairness of perfection
With that delight which lovely beauty gives,
Without tormenting me with fruitless wishes;
Like the poor child who sees its brighten'd face,
And whimpers for the moon? Thou art not serious?   160
From early youth, war has my mistress been,
And tho' a rugged one, I'll constant prove,
And not forsake her now. There may be joys
Which to the strange o'erwhelming of the soul,
Visit the lover's breast beyond all others;
E'en now, how dearly do I feel there may!
But what of them? they are not made for me—
The hasty flashes of contending steel
Must serve instead of glances from my love,
And for soft breathing sighs the cannon's roar.   170
ROS. (*taking his hand.*) Now am I satisfied. Forgive me Basil.
BAS. I'm glad thou art, we'll talk of her no more.
Why should I vex my friend?
ROS. Thou hast not giv'n orders for the march.

BAS. I'll do it soon; thou need'st not be afraid.
　　To-morrow's sun shall bear us far from hence,
　　Never perhaps to pass these gates again.
ROS. With last night's close did you not curse this town
　　That would one single day your troops retard?
180　And now, methinks, you talk of leaving it,
　　As though it were the place that gave you birth;
　　As tho' you had around these strangers' walls
　　Your infant gambols play'd.
BAS. The sight of what may be but little priz'd,
　　Doth cause a solemn sadness in the mind,
　　When view'd as that we ne'er shall see again.
ROS. No, not a whit to wand'ring men like us,
　　No, not a whit! what custom hath endear'd
　　We part with sadly, tho' we prize it not;
190　But what is new some pow'rful charm must own,
　　Thus to affect the mind.
BAS. (*hastily.*) Yes, what is new, but—No, thou art impatient;
　　We'll let it pass—It hath no consequence.
ROS. I'm not impatient. 'Faith, I only wish
　　Some other route our destin'd march had been,
　　That still thou mightst thy glorious course pursue
　　With an untroubled mind.
BAS. O! wish it, wish it not! bless'd be that route!
　　What we have seen to-day I must remember—[1]
200　I should be brutish if I could forget it.
　　Oft in the watchful post, or weary march,
　　Oft in the nightly silence of my tent,
　　My fixed mind shall gaze upon it still;
　　But it will pass before my fancy's eye,
　　Like some delightful vision of the soul,
　　To soothe, not trouble it.
ROS. What, midst the dangers of eventful war,
　　Still let thy mind be haunted by a woman?
　　Who would, perhaps, hear of thy fall in battle,

1　Cf. Wordsworth, "Preface" to the *Lyrical Ballads*, 266 (Appendix D.1.i) and
　　Coleridge, *Biographia Literaria* (1817), Ch. 13: "the fancy is indeed no other than a
　　mode of memory emancipated from the order of time and space."

As Dutchmen read of earthquakes in Calabria,[1]   210
And never stop to cry alack-a-day!
For me there is but one of all the sex,
Who still shall hold her station in my breast,
Midst all the changes of inconstant fortune;
Because I'm passing sure she loves me well,
And for my sake a sleepless pillow finds
When rumour tells bad tidings of the war;
Because I know her love will never change,
Nor make me prove uneasy jealousy.

BAS. Happy art thou! who is this wond'rous woman?   220
ROS. It is mine own good mother, faith and truth!
BAS. (*smiling.*) Give me thy hand; I love her dearly too.
    Rivals we are not, though our love is one.
ROS. And yet I might be jealous of her love,
    For she bestows too much of it on thee,
    Who hast no claim but to a nephew's share.
BAS. (*going.*) I'll meet thee some time hence. I must to Court.
ROS. A private conf'rence will not stay thee long.
    I'll wait thy coming near the palace gate.
BAS. 'Tis to the publick Court I mean to go.   230
ROS. I thought you had determin'd otherwise.
BAS. Yes, but on farther thought it did appear
    As though it would be failing in respect
    At such a time—That look doth wrong me, Rosinberg!
    For on my life, I had determin'd thus
    Ere I beheld—Before we enter'd Mantua.
    But wilt thou change that soldier's dusty garb,
    And go with me thyself?
ROS.   Yes, I will go.
    (*As they are going* Ros. *stops, and looks at* Basil.)
BAS. Why dost thou stop?
ROS.   'Tis for my wonted caution,
    Which first thou gav'st me, I shall ne'er forget it.   240
    'Twas at Vienna, on a publick day,

---

1   This would appear to be an anachronism. If Baillie is referring to a specific event here, there was, indeed, a major earthquake in the toe of Italy in 1783 which precipitated extensive geological research well into the next century.

Thou but a youth, I then a man full form'd;
Thy stripling's brow grac'd with its first cockade,
Thy mighty bosom swell'd with mighty thoughts;
Thou'rt for the court, dear Rosinberg, quoth thou;
Now pray thee be not caught with some gay dame,
To laugh and ogle, and befool thyself;
It is offensive in the publick eye,
And suits not with a man of thy endowments.
250 So said your serious lordship to me then,
And have on like occasions often since,
In other terms repeated—
But I must go to-day without my caution.
BAS. Nay Rosinberg, I am impatient now.
Did I not say we'd talk of her no more.
ROS. Well, my good friend, God grant we keep our word!

[EXEUNT.

END OF THE FIRST ACT.

ACT II.—SCENE I.

A Room of State. The DUKE OF MANTUA, BASIL, ROSINBERG *and a number of Courtiers, Attendants, &c. The* DUKE *and* BASIL *appear talking together on the front of the Stage.*

DUKE. But our opinions differ widely there;
    From the position of the rival armies,
    I cannot think they'll join in battle soon.
BAS. I am indeed beholden to your highness,
    But tho' unwillingly, we must depart.
    The foes are near, the time is critical;
    A soldier's reputation is too fine
    To be expos'd e'en to the smallest cloud.
DUKE. An untried soldier's is; but yours, my lord,
    Nurs'd with the bloody show'rs of many a field,   10
    And brightest sunshine of successful fortune,
    A plant of such a hardy stem hath grown,
    E'en Envy's sharpest blasts assail it not.
    But after all, by the bless'd holy Cross!
    I feel too warm an interest in the cause
    To stay your progress here a single hour,
    Did I not know your soldiers are fatigu'd,
    And two days' rest would but renew their strength.
BAS. Your highness will be pleas'd to pardon me;
    My troops are not o'ermarch'd, and one day's rest   20
    Is all our needs require.
DUKE.   Ah! hadst thou come
    Unfetter'd with the duties of command,
    I then had well retain'd thee for my guest,
    With claims too strong, too sacred for denial;
    Thy noble sire my fellow-soldier was,
    Together many a rough campaign we serv'd;
    I lov'd him well, and much it pleases me
    A son of his beneath my roof to see.
BAS. Were I indeed free master of myself,   30
    Strong inclination would detain me here;
    No other tie were wanting.

These gracious tokens of your princely favour
I'll treasure with my best rememb'rances;
For he who shews them for my father's sake,
Doth something sacred in his kindness bear,
As tho' he shed a blessing on my head.

DUKE. Well, bear my greetings to the brave Piscaro,[1]
And say how warmly I embrace the cause.

40   Your third day's march will to his presence bring
Your valiant troops: said you not so, my lord?

Enter VICTORIA, *the* Countess of ALBINI, ISABELLA, *and Ladies.*

BAS. (*who changes countenance upon seeing them.*)
Yes, I believe—I think—I know not well—
Yes, please your grace, we march by break of day.

DUKE. Nay, that I know. I ask'd you, noble count,
When you expect th'Imperial force to join.

BAS. When it shall please your grace—I crave your pardon—
I somewhat have mistaken of your words.

DUKE. You are not well? your colour changes, Count,
What is the matter?

BAS. A dizzy mist that swims before my sight—

50   A ringing in mine ears—'tis strange enough—
'Tis slight—'tis nothing worth—'tis gone already.

DUKE. I'm glad it is. Look to your friend, Count Rosinberg,
It may return again.—(*To* Rosinberg, *who stands at a little
distance, looking earnestly at* Basil.—Duke *leaves them, and
joins* Victoria's *party.*)

ROS. Good heavens! Basil, is it thus with thee!
Thy hand shakes too! (*taking his hand*) Would we were far
from hence.

BAS. I'm well again, thou need'st not be afraid.

---

1   The 1851 edition emends this to "Pescara." Fernando Francesco Davolos, Marquis
of Pescara (1489-1525) was born in Naples of Spanish parentage. His father was
killed in a French invasion of Naples when Pescara was a small child. Later, as commander of the Spanish infantry, he was appointed as a lieutenant to Charles V with
orders to repel the French invaders. Pescara was credited historically for his powerful influence over his troops, maintaining the loyalty of his veteran Spanish soldiers
and German mercenaries during the long siege of Pavia.

'Tis like enough my frame is indispos'd
With some slight weakness from our weary march.
Nay, look not on me thus, it is unkindly—
I cannot bear thine eyes. 60

The DUKE, *with* VICTORIA *and her Ladies, advance to the front of
the Stage, to* BASIL.

DUKE. Victoria, welcome here the brave Count Basil.
His kinsman too, the gallant Rosinberg.
May you, and these fair ladies so prevail,
Such gentle suitors cannot plead in vain,
To make them grace my court another day.
I shall not be offended when I see
Your power surpasses mine.
VICT. Our feeble efforts will presumptuous seem
In what your highness fails.
DUKE. There's honour in th'attempt; good success to ye.— 70
(Duke *retires, and mixes with the Courtiers at the bottom of the
Stage.*)
VICT. I fear we incommoded you, my Lord,
With the slow tedious length of our procession.
E'en as I pass'd, against my heart it went
To stop your weary soldiers on their way
So long a time.—
BAS.   Ah! Madam, all too short!
Time never bears such moments on his wing,
But when he flies too swiftly to be mark'd.
VICT. Ah! surely then you make too good amends
By marking now his after-progress well.
To-day must seem a weary length to him 80
Who is so eager to be gone to-morrow.
ROS. They must not linger who would quit these walls;
For if they do, a thousand masked foes,
Some under show of rich luxurious feasts,
Gay, sprightly pastime, and high-zested game;—
Nay, some, my gentle ladies, true it is,
The very worst and fellest of the crew,

In fair alluring shape of beauteous dames,
Do such a barrier form t'oppose their way,
90   As few men may o'ercome.
ISAB. From this last wicked foe should we infer
Yourself have suffer'd much?
ALBIN. No, Isabella, these are common words,
To please you with false notions of your pow'r.[1]
So all men talk of ladies and of love.
VICT. 'Tis even so. If love a tyrant be,
How dare his humble chained votaries,
To tell such rude and wicked tales of him?
BAS. Because they most of lover's ills complain,
100   Who but affect it as a courtly grace,
Whilst he who feels is silent.
ROS. But there you wrong me; I have felt it oft.
Oft has it made me sigh at ladies' feet,
Soft ditties sing, and dismal sonnets scrawl.
ALBIN. In all its strange effects, most worthy Rosinberg,
Has it e'er made thee in a corner sit,
Sad, lonely, moping sit, and hold thy tongue?
ROS. No, faith, it never has.
ALBIN. Ha, ha, ha, ha! then thou hast never lov'd.
110   ROS. Nay, but I have, and felt its bondage too.
VICT. O! it is pedantry to call it bondage!
Love-marring wisdom, reason full of bars,
Deserve, methinks, that appellation more.
Is it not so, my Lord?—(To Basil.)
BAS.   O! surely Madam;
That is not bondage which the soul enthrall'd
So gladly bears, and quits not but with anguish.
Stern honour's laws, the fair report of men,
These are the fetters that enchain the mind,
But such as must not, cannot be unloos'd.
120   VICT. No, not unloos'd, but yet one day relax'd,
To grant a lady's suit, unus'd to sue.
ROS. Your highness deals severely with us now,

---

1 Cf. Wollstonecraft, *Vindication* (Appendix B.2).

And proves indeed our freedom is but small,
Who are constrain'd, when such a lady sues,
To say it cannot be.

VICT. It cannot be! Count Basil says not so.

ROS. For that I am his friend, to save him pain
I take th'ungracious office on myself.

VICT. How ill thy face is suited to thine office!

ROS. (*smiling*.) Would I could suit mine office to my face,   130
If that would please your highness.

VICT. No, you are obstinate and perverse all,
And would not grant it if you had the pow'r.
Albini I'll retire; come Isabella.

BAS. (*aside to* Ros.) Ah! Rosinberg, thou hast too far presum'd;
She is offended with us.

ROS.   No, she is not—
What dost thou fear? be firm and let us go.

VICT. (*pointing to a door leading to other apartments, by which she is
ready to go out.*)
These are apartments strangers love to see;
Some famous paintings do their walls adorn.
It leads you also to the palace court   140
As quickly as the way by which you came.

[EXIT Vict. *led out by* Ros. *and followed by* Isab.

BAS. (*aside, looking after them.*) O! what a fool am I! where fled
my thoughts?
I might as well as he, now by her side
Have held her precious hand enclos'd in mine;
As well as he, who cares not for it neither.
O! damn it, but he does! that were impossible!

ALBIN. You stay behind, my Lord.

BAS. Your pardon Madam; honour me so far—

[EXEUNT, *handing out* Albini.

SCENE II.

A Gallery hung with Pictures. VICTORIA *discovered in conversation with* ROSINBERG, BASIL, ALBINI, *and* ISABELLA.

VICT. (*to* Ros.) It is indeed a work of wond'rous art.
    (*To* Isab.) You call'd Francisco here?
ISAB.   He comes even now.

Enter ATTENDANT.

VICT. (*to* Ros.) He will conduct you to the northern gall'ry;
    Its striking shades will call upon the eye,
    To point its place no guide is wanted there.

[EXEUNT Ros. *and* Attendant.

    (*To* Bas.) Loves not Count Basil too this charming art?
    It is an ancient painting much admir'd.
BAS. Ah! do not banish me these few short moments;
    Too soon they will be gone! for ever gone!
10 VICT. If they are precious to you say not so,
    But add to them another precious day.
    A Lady asks it.
BAS. Ah, Madam! ask the life-blood from my heart!
    Ask all but what a soldier may not give.
VICT. 'Tis ever thus when favours are denied,
    All had been granted but the thing we beg;
    And still some great unlikely substitute,
    Your life, your soul, your all of earthly good,
    Is proffer'd in the room of one small boon.
20 So keep your life-blood, gen'rous, valiant lord,
    And may it long your noble heart enrich,
    Until I wish it shed.
    (Bas. *attempts to speak.*)
    Nay, frame no new excuse; I will not hear it.
    [*She puts out her hand as if she would shut his mouth, but at a distance from it;* Bas. *runs eagerly up to her and presses it to his lips.*]

BAS. Let this sweet hand indeed its threat perform,
And make it heav'n to be for ever dumb!
(VICT. *looks stately and offended—Basil kneels.*)
O! pardon me, I know not what I do.
Frown not, reduce me not to wretchedness,
But only grant—
VICT.   What should I grant to him
Who has so oft my earnest suit deny'd?
BAS. By heav'n I'll grant it! I'll do any thing,   30
Say but thou art no more offended with me.
VICT. (*raising him.*) Well Basil, this good promise is thy pardon.
I will not wait your noble friend's return
Since we shall meet again.—
You will perform your word!
BAS. I will perform it.
VICT. Farewell, my lord.

                    [EXEUNT, *with her Ladies.*

BAS. (*alone.*) "Farewell, my lord,"— O! what delightful
sweetness
The musick of that voice dwells on the ear!
"Farewell, my lord!"—Ay, and then look'd she so—   40
The slightest glance of her bewitching eye,
Those dark blue eyes, command the inmost soul.
Well, there is yet one day of life before me,
And whatsoe'er betides I will enjoy it.
Tho' but a partial sunshine in my lot
I will converse with her, gaze on her still,
If all behind were pain and misery.
Pain! were it not the easing of all pain,
E'en in the dismal gloom of after years,
Such dear rememb'rance on the mind to wear?   50
Like silv'ry moon-beams on the 'nighted deep,
When heav'n's blest sun is gone!
Kind mercy! how my heart within me beat
When she so sweetly pled the cause of love!
Can she have lov'd? why shrink I at the thought?

Why should she not? no, no, it cannot be—
No man on earth is worthy of her love.
Ah! if she could, how blest a man were he!
Where rove my giddy thoughts? it must not be.
60   Yet might she well some gentle kindness bear;
Think of him oft, his absent fate enquire,
And, should he fall in battle, mourn his fall.
Yes, she would mourn—such love might she bestow;
And poor of soul the man who would exchange it
For warmest love of the most loving dame.
But here comes Rosinberg—have I done well?
He will not say I have.

Enter ROSINBERG.

ROS. Where is the princess?
I'm sorry I return'd not ere she went.
BAS. You'll see her still.
70   ROS.   What, comes she forth again?
BAS. She does to-morrow.
ROS.   Thou hast yielded then.
BAS. Come, Rosinberg, I'll tell thee as we go:
It was impossible I should not yield.
ROS. And has the first look[1] of a stranger's face[2]

---

1   It is interesting to note here the extensive imagery of sight and sound throughout
Count Basil. Henry Home, Lord Kames (1692-1782), theorizes in *Elements of Criti-cism* Vol. 1 (1762) that there is a difference in consciousness between the senses of
seeing and hearing and what he calls the organic senses – touching, tasting, and
smelling. The organic senses are "merely corporeal" in nature, while seeing and
hearing really exist within the mind and are considered by Kames to be "more
refined and spiritual." They are the only external senses that are "honoured with
the name of *emotions* or *passions*." They have the intermediary property both to
"revive the spirits when sunk by sensual gratification" and "to restore [the mind's]
usual tone after severe application to study or business …"(1:2,42).
2   In the third edition of *Plays on the Passions* (1800) Baillie eliminated lines 2.2.74-
100. This significant change to the original text was accompanied by the following
explanation:
Note. – My first idea when I wrote this play was to represent Basil as having seen
Victoria for the first time in the procession, that I might show more perfectly the
passion from its first beginning, and also its sudden power over the mind; but I was
induced, from the criticism of one whose judgment I very much respect, to alter it,

So far bewitched thee?

BAS.   A stranger's face!
Long has she been the inmate of my breast!
The smiling angel of my nightly dreams.

ROS. What mean you now? Your mind is raving, Basil.

BAS. I speak in sober earnest. Two years since,
When marching on the confines of this state,   80
We heard the distant musick of the chace,
And trampling horses near, I turn'd to look,
And saw the loveliest sight of woman's form
That ever blest mine eyes. Her fiery steed,
Struck with the strange accoutrements of war,
Became unruly, and despis'd the rein.
I gently led him with his lovely charge
Past all the ranks: she thank'd me courteously;
Then, with the few companions of her sport,
Took to the woods again. I, with my men,   90
Our route pursued, and met with her no more.
————————Her name and state I knew not;
Yet, like a beauteous vision from the blest,
Her form has oft upon my mind return'd;
And tho' this day the sight had ne'er restor'd,
It ne'er had been forgotten. Gentle Rosinberg!
Be not displeas'd! I would have told thee this,
When first to-day we talk'd of Mantua's princess,

and represent him as having formerly seen and loved her. The first Review that
took notice of this work objected to Basil's having seen her before as a defect; and,
as we are all easily determined to follow our own opinion, I have, upon after-con-
sideration, given the play in this edition [*third*], as far as this is concerned, exactly in
its original state. Strong internal evidence of this will be discovered by any one
who will take the trouble of reading attentively the second scenes of the first and
second acts in the present and former editions of this book. Had Basil seen and
loved Victoria before, his first speech, in which he describes her to Rosinberg as
walking in the procession, would not be natural; and there are, I think, other little
things besides, which will show that the circumstance of his former meeting with
her is an interpolation. The blame of this, however, I take entirely upon myself; the
critic, whose opinion I have mentioned, judged of the piece entirely as an unconnected play, and knew nothing of the general plan of this work, which ought to
have been communicated to him. Had it been, indeed, an unconnected play, and
had I put this additional circumstance to it with proper judgment and skill, I am
inclined to think it would have been an improvement.

But thou wert griev'd and jealous of me then,
100   And so I shut my breast and said no more.
ROS. O Basil! thou art weaker than a child.
BAS. Yes, yes, my friend, but 'tis a noble weakness;
        A weakness which hath greater things atchiev'd
        Than all the firm, determin'd strength of reason.
        By heav'n! I feel a new-born pow'r within me
        Shall make me twenty-fold the man I've been
        Before this fated day.
ROS. Fated indeed! but an ill-fated day,
        That makes thee other than thy former self.
110   Yet let it work its will; it cannot change thee
        To ought I shall not love.
BAS. Thanks, Rosinberg! thou art a noble heart!
        I would not be the man thou couldst not love
        For an Imperial Crown.

                            [EXEUNT.

SCENE III.

A Small Apartment in the Palace.

Enter DUKE *and* GAURIECIO.

DUKE. The point is gain'd; my daughter is successful,
        And Basil is detain'd another day.
GAUR. But does the princess know your secret aim?
DUKE. No, that had marr'd the whole: she is a woman;
        Her mind, as suits the sex, too weak and narrow
        To relish deep-laid schemes of policy.
        Besides, so far unlike a child of mine,
        She holds its subtle arts in high derision,
        And will not serve us but with bandag'd eyes,
10   Gauriecio, could I hasty servants find,
        Experienc'd, crafty, close, and unrestrain'd
        By silly superstitious child-learnt fears,
        What might I not effect?

GAUR.   O! any thing;
    The deep and piercing genius of your highness,
    So ably serv'd, might e'en atchieve the empire.
DUKE. No, no, my friend, thou dost o'erprize my parts.
    Yet mighty things might be—deep subtle wits
    In truth are master-spirits in the world.
    The brave man's courage, and the student's lore,
    Are but as tools his secret ends to work,   20
    Who hath the skill to use them.
    This brave Count Basil, dost thou know him well?
    Much have we gain'd but for a single day
    At such a time to hold his troops detain'd;
    When by that secret message of our spy,
    The rival pow'rs are on the brink of action:
    But might we more effect? Know'st thou this Basil?
    Might he be tamper'd with?
GAUR.   That were most dang'rous—
    He is a man, whose sense of right and wrong
    To such a high romantic pitch is wound,   30
    And all so hot and fiery in his nature,
    The slightest hint, as tho' you did suppose
    Baseness and treach'ry in him, so he'll deem it,
    Would be to rouse a flame that might destroy.
DUKE. But int'rest, int'rest; man's all-ruling pow'r,
    Will tame the hottest spirit to your service,
    And skilfully applied, mean service too.
    E'en as there is an element in nature
    Which when subdu'd, will on your hearth fulfil
    The lowest uses of domestick wants.   40
GAUR. Earth-kindled fire, which from a little spark
    On hidden fuel feeds its growing strength,
    Till o'er the lofty fabrick it aspires
    And rages out its pow'r, may be subdu'd,
    And in your base domestick service bound;
    But who would madly in its wild career
    The fire of heav'n arrest to boil his pot?
    No, Basil will not serve your secret schemes,
    Tho' you had all to give ambition strives for.
    We must beware of him.   50

DUKE. His father was my friend, I wish'd to gain him,
    But since fantastick fancies bind him thus,
    The sin be on his head, I stand acquitted,
    And must deceive him, even to his ruin.
GAUR. I have prepar'd Bernardo for your service;
    To-night he will depart for th' Austrian camp,
    And should he find them on the eve of battle,
    I've bid him wait the issue of the field.
    If that our secret friends victorious prove,
60   With th'arrow's speed he will return again;
    But should fair Fortune crown Piscaro's arms,
    Then shall your soothing message greet his ears;
    For till our friends some sound advantage gain,
    Our actions still must wear an Austrian face.
DUKE. Well hast thou school'd him. Did'st thou add withal,
    That 'tis my will he garnish well his speech,
    With honied words of the most dear regard,
    And friendly love I bear him. This is needful;
    And lest my slowness in the promis'd aid
70   Awake suspicion, bid him e'en rehearse
    The many favours on my house bestow'd
    By his Imperial master, as a theme
    On which my gratitude delights to dwell.
GAUR. I have, an' please your highness.
DUKE.   Then 'tis well.
GAUR. But for the yielding up that little fort
    There could be no suspicion.
DUKE. My Governor I have severely punish'd
    As a most daring traitor to my orders.
    He cannot from his darksome dungeon tell,
80   Why then should they suspect?
GAUR. He must not live if Charles should prove victorious.
DUKE. He's done me service, say not so Gauriecio.
GAUR. A traitor's name he will not calmly bear,
    He'll tell his tale aloud—he must not live.
DUKE. Well, if it must—we'll talk of this again.
GAUR. But while with anxious care and crafty wiles,
    You would enlarge the limits of your state,

Your highness must beware lest inward broils
Bring danger near at hand: your northern subjects
E'en now are discontented and unquiet.   90
DUKE. What, dare the ungrateful miscreants thus return
The many favours of my princely grace?
'Tis ever thus indulgence spoils the base,
Raising up pride, and lawless turbulence,
Like noxious vapours from the fulsome marsh
When morning shines upon it—
Did I not lately, with parental care,
When dire invaders their destruction threaten'd,
Provide them all with means of their defence?
Did I not, as a mark of gracious trust,   100
A body of their vagrant youth select
To guard my sacred person? Till that day
An honour never yet allow'd their race.
Did I not suffer them, upon their suit
T'establish manufactures in their towns?
And after all some chosen soldiers spare
To guard the blessings of interiour peace?
GAUR. Nay, please your highness, they do well allow
That when your enemies, in fell revenge,
Your former inroads threaten'd to repay,   110
Their ancient arms you did to them restore,
With kind permission to defend themselves.
That so far have they felt your princely grace
In drafting from their fields their goodliest youth
To be your servants. That you did vouchsafe,
On paying of a large and heavy fine,
Leave to apply the labour of their hands
As best might profit to the country's weal;
And to encourage well their infant trade
Quarter'd your troops upon them—please your grace,   120
All this they do most readily allow.
DUKE. They do allow it then, ungrateful varlets;
What would they have? what would they have, Gauriecio?
GAUR. Some mitigation of their grievous burdens,
Which, like an iron weight around their necks,

Do bend their care-worn faces to the earth,
Like creatures form'd upon its soil to creep,
Not stand erect, and view the sun of heav'n.
DUKE. But they beyond their proper sphere would rise;
130   Let them their lot fulfil as we do ours;
Society of various parts is form'd;
They are its grounds, its mud, its sediment,
And we the mantling top which crowns the whole.
Calm, steady labour is their greatest bliss,
To aim at higher things beseems them not.
To let them work in peace my care shall be,
To slacken labour is to nourish pride.
Methinks thou art a pleader for these fools;
What may this mean Gauriecio?
140 GAUR. They were resolv'd to lay their cause before you,
And would have found some other advocate
Less pleasing to your Grace, had I refus'd.
DUKE. Well, let them know some more convenient season
I'll think of this, and do for them as much
As suits the honour of my princely state;
Their prince's honour should be ever dear
To worthy subjects as their precious lives.
GAUR. I fear, unless you give some special promise,
They will be violent still—
150 DUKE. Then do it, if the wretches are so bold;
We can retract it when the times allow;
'Tis of small consequence. Go see Bernardo,
And come to me again.

[EXIT.[1]

GAUR. (*solus.*) O! happy people! whose indulgent lord
From ev'ry care, with which increasing wealth,
With all its hopes and fears, doth ever move
The human bosom, would most kindly free,
And kindly leave ye nought to do but toil!

---

1 EXEUNT in the 1798 edition.

This creature now, with all his reptile cunning,
Writhing and turning thro' a maze of wiles,   160
Believes his genius form'd to rule mankind,
And calls his sordid wish for territory,
That noblest passion of the soul, ambition:
Born had he been to follow some low trade,
A petty tradesman still he had remain'd,
And us'd the arts with which he rules a state,
To circumvent his brothers of the craft,
Or cheat the buyers of his paltry ware.
And yet he thinks, ha, ha, ha, ha, ha, ha!
I am the tool and servant of his will.   170
Well, let it be; thro' all the maze of trouble
His plots and base oppression must create,
I'll shape myself a way to higher things,
And who will say 'tis wrong?
A sordid being who expects no faith
But as self-interest binds, who would not trust
The strongest ties of nature on the soul,
Deserves no faithful service. Perverse fate!
Were I like him I would despise this dealing;
But being as I am, born low in fortune,   180
Yet with a mind aspiring to be great,
I must not scorn the steps which lead to it:
And if they are not right, no saint am I;
I follow nature's passion in my breast,
Which urges me to rise, in spite of fortune.

[EXIT.

SCENE IV.

An Apartment in the Palace; VICTORIA *and* ISABELLA *are discovered playing at Chess; the* Countess ALBINI *sitting by them, reading to herself.*

VICT. Away with it, I will not play again;
    May men no more look foolish in my presence
    If thou art not a cheat, an errant cheat.
ISAB. To swear that I am false by such an oath,
    Should prove me honest, since its forfeiture
    Would bring your highness gain.
VICT. Thou'rt wrong, my Isabella, simple maid,
    For in the very forfeit of this oath,
    There's death to all the dearest pride of women.
10   May man no more look foolish in my presence!
ISAB. And does your grace, hail'd by applauding crouds,
    In all the graceful eloquence address'd
    Of most accomplish'd, noble, courtly youths,
    Prais'd in the songs of heav'n-inspired bards;
    Those awkward proofs of admiration prize,
    The rustick swain his village fair-one pays?
VICT. O! love will master all the pow'r of art,
    Ay all! and she who never has beheld
    The polish'd courtier, or the tuneful sage,
20   Before the glances of her conq'ring eye,
    A very native simple swain become,
    Has only vulgar charms.
    To make the cunning artless, tame the rude,
    Subdue the haughty, shake th'undaunted Soul;
    Yea, put a bridle in the lion's mouth,
    And lead him forth as a domestick cur,
    These are the triumphs of all-pow'rful beauty!
    Did nought but flatt'ring words and tuneful praise,
    Sighs, tender glances, and obsequious service,
30   Attend her presence, it were nothing worth.
    I'd put a white coif o'er my braided locks,
    And be a plain, good, simple, fire-side dame.

ALB. (*raising her head front her book.*)
      And is, indeed, a plain domestick dame,
      Who fills the duties of an useful state,
      A being of less dignity, than she
      Who vainly on her transient beauty builds
      A little poor ideal tyranny?[1]
ISAB. Ideal too!
ALB.   Yes, most unreal pow'r;
      For she who only finds her self-esteem
      In others' admiration, begs an alms,   40
      Depends on others for her daily food,
      And is the very servant of her slaves;
      Tho' oftentimes, in a fantastick hour,
      O'er men she may a childish pow'r exert,
      Which not ennobles, but degrades her state.[2]
VICT. You are severe, Albini, most severe:
      Were human passions plac'd within the breast
      But to be curb'd, subdu'd, pluck'd by the roots?
      All heav'n's gifts to some good end were giv'n.
ALB. Yes, for a noble, for a gen'rous end.   50
VICT. Am I ungen'rous then?
ALB.   O! most ungen'rous,
      Who for the pleasure of a little pow'r
      Would give most unavailing pain to those
      Whose love you ne'er can recompense again.
      E'en now, to-day, O! was it not ungen'rous
      To fetter Basil with a foolish tie,
      Against his will, perhaps against his duty?
VICT. What, dost thou think against his will, my friend?
ALB. Full sure I am against his reason's will.
VICT. Ah! but indeed thou must excuse me here,   60
      For duller than a shelled crab were she,
      Who could suspect her pow'r in such a mind,
      And calmly leave it doubtful and unprov'd.
      But wherefore dost thou look so gravely on me?
      Ah! well I read those looks! methinks they say,

---

1 Cf. Wollstonecraft, *Vindication* 113 (Appendix B.2).
2 Cf. Wollstonecraft, *Vindication* 147 (Appendix B.2).

Your mother did not so.

ALB. Your highness reads them true, she did not so.
   If foolish vanity e'er soil'd her thoughts
   She kept it low, withheld its aliment;
70   Not pamper'd it with ev'ry motley food,
   From the fond tribute of a noble heart,
   To the lisp'd flatt'ry of a cunning child.

VICT. Nay, speak not thus Albini, speak not thus
   Of little blue-ey'd, sweet, fair-hair'd Mirando.
   He is the orphan of a hapless pair,
   A loving, beautiful, but hapless pair,
   Whose story is so pleasing, and so sad,
   The swains have turn'd it to a plaintive lay,
   And sing it as they tend their mountain sheep.
80   (To Isab.) Besides I am the guardian of his choice,
   When first I saw him dost not thou remember?

ISAB. 'Twas in the publick garden.

VICT.   Even so;
   Perch'd in his nurse's arms, a roughsome quean,[1]
   Ill suited to the lovely charge she bore.
   How steadfastly he fix'd his looks upon me,
   His dark eyes[2] shining thro' forgotten tears!
   Then stretch'd his little arms, and call'd me mam!
   What could I do! I took the bantling home—
   I could not tell the imp he had no mam!

90 ALB. Ah! there my child, thou hast indeed no blame.

VICT. Ay, this is kindly said, thanks sweet Albini!
   Still call me child, and chide me as thou wilt.
   O! would that I were such as thou couldst love!
   Couldst dearly love! as thou didst love my mother.

---

1   An early Middle English term of disparagement for an ill-behaved woman which
    came to mean harlot or strumpet in the sixteenth and seventeenth centuries.
2   The *Critical Review* (September 1798): 17 takes Baillie to task for what appears to
    the critic as an "oversight" in this passage, since Mirando was described previously
    as "blue-ey'd" (2.2.74). Could this seeming contradiction actually be astute obser-
    vation on Baillie's part? Perhaps Baillie accurately distinguishes here between the
    early gray cast of a baby's eyes before they develop pigmentation and the more
    intensely defined colour of a toddler's eyes. Cf. the colour of Victoria's eyes
    (2.2.42).

ALB. (*pressing her to her breast.*)
    And do I not? all perfect as she was,
    I know not that she went so near my heart
    As thou, with all thy faults.
VICT. And sayst thou so? would I had sooner known!
    I had done any thing to give thee pleasure.
ALB. Then do so now, and put away thy faults.   100
VICT. No, say not faults; the freaks of thoughtless youth.
ALB. Nay, very faults they must indeed be call'd.
VICT. O! say but foibles! youthful foibles only!
ALB. Faults, faults, real faults you must confess they are.
VICT. In truth, I cannot do your sense the wrong
    To think so poorly of the one you love.
ALB. I must be gone; thou hast o'ercome me now,
    Another time I will not yield it so.   [EXIT.
ISAB. The Countess is severe, she's too severe;
    She once was young, tho' now advanc'd in years.   110
VICT. No, I deserve it all; she is most worthy.
    Unlike those faded beauties of the court,
    But now the wither'd stems of former flow'rs,
    With all their blossoms shed; her nobler mind
    Procures to her the privilege of man,[1]
    Ne'er to be old till nature's strength decays.
    Some few years hence, if I should live so long,
    I'd be Albini rather than myself.
ISAB. Here comes your little pet.
VICT. I am not in the humour for him now.   120

Enter MIRANDO, *running up to* VICTORIA, *and taking hold of her gown, but she takes no notice of him, while he holds up his mouth to be kissed.*

ISAB. (*to* Mir.) Thou seest the princess can't be troubled with
    thee.
MIR. O! but she will! I'll scramble up her robe,
    As naughty boys do when they climb for apples.

---

1 Cf. Wollstonecraft, *Vindication* 158 (Appendix B.2).

ISAB. Come here, sweet child; I'll kiss thee in her stead.

MIR. Nay, but I will not have a kiss of thee.
Would I were tall! O! were I but so tall!

ISAB. And how tall wouldst thou be?

MIR.   Thou dost not know?
Just tall enough to reach Victoria's lips.

VICT. (*embracing him.*) O! I must bend to this, thou little urchin.

130   Who taught thee all this wit, this childish wit?
Who does Mirando love? (*embraces him again.*)

MIR.   He loves Victoria.

VICT. And wherefore loves he her?

MIR.   Because she's pretty.

ISAB. Hast thou no little prate to-day Mirando?
No tale to earn a sugar-plumb withal?

MIR. Ay, that I have; I know who loves her grace.

VICT. Who is it pray? thou shalt have comfits[1] for it.

MIR. (*looking slily at her.*) It is—it is—it is the count of Maldo.

VICT. Away thou little chit,[2] that tale is old,
And was not worth a sugar-plumb when new.

140 MIR. Well then, I know who loves her highness well.

VICT. Who is it then?

ISAB.   Who is it naughty boy?

MIR. It is the handsome marquis of Carlatzi.

VICT. No, no, Mirando, thou art naughty still;
Thou'st twice had comfits for that tale already.

MIR. Well then, indeed, I know who loves Victoria.

VICT. And who is he?

MIR.   It is Mirando's self.

VICT. Thou little imp! this story is not new,
But thou shalt have thy comfits. Let us go.
Go run before us, Boy.

150 MIR. Nay, but I'll shew you how Count Wolvar did,
When he conducted Isabel from Court.

VICT. How did he do?

MIR. Give me your hand: he held his body thus,
(*putting himself in a ridiculous bowing posture.*)

---

1 Sugar plums; fruits preserved in sugar.
2 A whelp, cub, or kitten.

and then he whisper'd softly; then look'd so;
(*ogling with his eyes affectedly.*)
Then she look'd so, and smil'd to him again.
(*throwing down his eyes affectedly.*)
ISAB. Thou art a little knave, and must be whipp'd.

[EXEUNT. Mirando *leading out* Victoria *affectedly.*

ACT III.—SCENE I.

An Open Street, or Square.

Enter ROSINBERG *and* FREDERICK *by opposite sides of the Stage.*

FRED. So Basil, from the pressing calls of war,
   Another day to rest and pastime gives.
   How is it now? methinks thou art not pleas'd.
ROS. It matters little if I am or not.
FRED. Now pray thee do confess thou art asham'd.
   Thou, who art wisely wont to set at nought
   The noble fire of individual courage,
   And call calm prudence the superiour virtue,
   What sayst thou now, my candid Rosinberg?
10   When thy great captain, in a time like this,
   Denies his weary troops one day of rest
   Before the exertions of approaching battle,
   Yet grants it to a pretty lady's suit?
ROS. Who told thee this? it was no friendly tale,
   And no one else besides a trusty friend,
   Could know his motives. Then thou wrongst me too,
   For I admire, as much as thou dost Fred'rick,
   The fire of valour, e'en rash heedless valour;
   But not like thee do I depreciate
20   That far superiour; yea that god-like talent,
   Which doth direct that fire, because indeed
   It is a talent nature has denied me.
FRED. Well, well, and greatly he may boast his virtue,
   Who risks perhaps th'Imperial army's fate,
   To please a lady's freaks—
ROS.   Go, go, thou'rt prejudic'd:
   A passion, which I do not chuse to name,
   Has warp'd thy judgement.
FRED.   No, by heav'n thou wrongst me!
   I do, with most enthusiastick warmth,
   True valour love; wherever he is found,
30   I love the hero, too; but hate to see

The praises due to him so cheaply earn'd.
ROS. Then mayst thou now these gen'rous feelings prove.
 Behold the man whose short and grizzly hair
 In clust'ring locks, his dark brown face o'ershades;
 Where now the scars of former sabre wounds,
 In hon'rable companionship are seen
 With the deep lines of age; whose piercing eye,
 Beneath its shading eye-brow keenly darts
 Its yet unquenched beams, as tho' in age
 Its youthful fire had been again renew'd,   40
 To be the guardian of its darken'd mate.
 See with what vig'rous steps his upright form
 He onward bears; nay, e'en that vacant sleeve,
 Which droops so sadly by his better side,
 Suits not ungracefully the vet'ran's mien.
 This is the man, whose glorious acts in battle
 We heard to-day related o'er our wine.
 I go to tell the Gen'ral he is come.
 Enjoy the gen'rous feelings of thy breast,
 And make an old man happy.   [EXIT.   50

Enter GEOFFRY.

FRED. Brave soldier, let me profit by the chance
 That led me here; I've heard of thy exploits.
GEOF. Ah! then you have but heard an ancient tale,
 Which has been long forgotten.
FRED. But true it is, and should not be forgotten;
 Tho' Gen'rals, jealous of their soldiers' fame,
 May dash it with neglect.
GEOF. There are, perhaps, who may be so ungen'rous.
FRED. Perhaps, sayst thou? in very truth there are;
 How art thou else rewarded with neglect,   60
 Whilst many a paltry fellow in thy corps
 Has been promoted? it is ever thus.
 Serv'd not Mardini in your company?
 He was, tho' honour'd with a valiant name,
 To those who knew him well, a paltry soldier.

GEOF. Your pardon, Sir, we did esteem him much,
Although inferiour to his gallant friend,
The brave Sebastian.
FRED.   The brave Sebastian!
He was, as I am told, a learned coxcomb,[1]
70   And lov'd a goose-quill better than a sword.
What, dost thou call him brave?
Thou, who dost bear about that war-worn trunk,
Like an old target, hack'd and rough with wounds,
Whilst, after all his mighty battles, he
Was with a smooth skin in his coffin laid,
Unblemish'd with a scar.
GEOF. His duty call'd not to such desp'rate service;
For I have fought where few alive remain'd,
And none unscath'd; where but a few remain'd,
Thus marr'd, and mangl'd. (*Shewing his wounds.*)
80   As belike you've seen,
O'summer nights, around th'evening lamp,
Some wretched moths, wingless, and half-consum'd,
Just feebly crawling o'er their heaps of dead—
In Savoy, on a small, tho' desp'rate post,
Of full three hundred goodly, chosen men,
But twelve were left, and right dear friends were we
Forever after. They are all dead now,
I'm old and lonely—we were valiant hearts—
Fred'rick Dewalter would have stopp'd a breach
90   Against the devil himself. I'm lonely now.
FRED. I'm sorry for thee. Hang ungrateful chiefs!
Why art thou not promoted?
GEOF. After that battle, where my happy fate
Had led me to fulfil a glorious part,
Chaf'd with the gibing insults of a slave,
The worthless fav'rite of a great man's fav'rite,
I rashly did affront; our cautious prince,
With narrow policy dependant made,
Dar'd not, as I am told, promote me then,

---

1 Cf. Iago's contempt for Cassio (*Othello* 1.1.19).

And now he is asham'd, or has forgot it.   100
FRED. Fye, fye upon it! let him be asham'd!
Here is a trifle for thee—(*offering him money.*)
GEOF.   No, good sir,
I have enough to live as poor men do.
When I'm in want I'll thankfully receive
Because I'm poor, but not because I'm brave.
FRED. You're proud, old soldier—
GEOF.   No, I am not proud;
For if I were, methinks I'd be morose,
And willing to depreciate other men.

Enter ROSINBERG.

ROS. (*clapping* Geof. *on the shoulder.*)
How goes it with thee now, my good Field-marshal?
GEOF. The better that I see your honour well,   110
And in the humour to be merry with me.
ROS. 'Faith, by my sword, I've rightly nam'd thee too;
What is a good Field-marshal, but a man
Whose gen'rous courage and undaunted mind,
Doth marshal others on in glory's way?
Thou art not one by princely favour dubb'd,
But one of nature's making.
GEOF. You shew, my lord, such pleasant courtesy,
I know not how—
ROS.   But see, the Gen'ral comes.

Enter BASIL.

ROS. (*pointing to* Geof.) Behold the worthy vet'ran.   120
BAS. (*taking him by the hand.*)
Brave, hon'rable man, your worth I know,
And greet it with a brother-soldier's love.
GEOF. (*taking away his hand in confusion.*)
My Gen'ral, this is too much, too much honour.
BAS. (*taking his hand again.*)
No valiant soldier, I must have it so.

GEOF. My humble state agrees not with such honour.
BAS. Confound thy state! it is no part of thee:
   Let mean souls, highly rank'd, look down on thee;
   As the poor dwarf, perch'd on a pedestal,
   O'erlooks the giant. 'Tis not worth a thought.
130   Art thou not Geoffry of the tenth brigade,
   Whose warlike feats child, maid, and matron know?
   And oft, cross-elbow'd, o'er his nightly bowl,
   The jolly toper[1] to his comrade tells.
   Whose glorious feats of war, by cottage door,
   The ancient soldier tracing in the sand
   The many movements of the varied field,
   In warlike terms to list'ning swains relate;
   Whose bosoms glowing at the wond'rous tale,
   First learn to scorn the hind's inglorious life.
140   Shame seize me if I would not rather be
   The man thou art, than court-created chief,
   Known only by the dates of his promotion.
GEOF. Ah! would I were, would I were young again,
   To fight beneath your standard, noble gen'ral!
   Methinks what I have done were but a jest,
   Ay, but a jest to what I now should do,
   Were I again the man that I have been.
   O! I could fight!
BAS.   And wouldst thou fight for me?
GEOF. Ay, to the death!
150 BAS. Then come brave man, and be my champion still;
   The sight of thee will fire my soldiers' breasts.
   Come, noble vet'ran, thou shalt fight for me.

                              [EXIT *with* Geoffry.

FRED. What does he mean to do?
ROS.   We'll know ere long.
FRED. Our gen'ral bears it with a careless face
   For one so wise.

---

1   Drinking companion or drunkard.

ROS.   A careless face! on what?

FRED. Now feign not ignorance, we know it all.

News which have spread in whispers from the court,

Since last night's messenger arriv'd from Milan.

ROS. As I'm an honest man I know it not!

FRED. 'Tis said the rival armies are so near,   160

A battle must immediately ensue.

ROS. It cannot be. Our gen'ral knows it not.

The Duke is of our side, an ally sworn,

And had such messenger to Mantua come,

He would have been appriz'd upon the instant.

It cannot be, it is some idle tale.

FRED. So may it prove till we have join'd them too,

Then heaven grant they may be nearer still;

For O! my soul for war and danger pants,

As doth the noble lion for his prey.   170

My soul delights in battle.

ROS. Upon my simple word, I'd rather see

A score of friendly fellows shaking hands,

Than all the world in arms. Hast thou no fear?

FRED. What dost thou mean?

ROS.   Hast thou no fear of death?

FRED. Fear is a name for something in the mind,

But what, from inward sense I cannot tell.

I could as little anxious march to battle,

As when a boy to childish games I ran.

ROS. Then as much virtue hast thou in thy valour,   180

As when a child thou hadst in childish play.

The brave man is not he who feels no fear,

For that were stupid and irrational,

But he, whose noble soul its fear subdues,

And bravely dares the danger nature shrinks from.

As for your youth, whom blood and blows delight,

Away with them! there is not in the crew

One valiant spirit.—Ha! what sound is this?

(*shouting is heard without.*)

FRED. The soldiers shout; I'll run and learn the cause.

ROS. But tell me first, how didst thou love the vet'ran?   190

FRED. He is too proud; he was displeas'd with me
Because I offer'd him a little sum.
ROS. What money! O! most gen'rous noble spirit!
Noble rewarder of superiour worth!
A halfpenny for Bellisarius![1]
But hark! they shout again—here comes Valtomer.
(*Shouting heard without.*)

Enter VALTOMER.

What does this shouting mean?
VALT. O! I have seen a sight, a glorious sight!
Thou wouldst have smil'd to see it.
200 ROS. How smile? methinks thine eyes are wet with tears.
VALT. (*passing the back of his hand across his eyes.*)
Faith so they are; well, well, but I smil'd too,
You heard the shouting.
ROS. and FRED. Yes.
VALT.   O! had you seen it!
Drawn out in goodly ranks, there stood our troops;
Here, in the graceful state of manly youth,
His dark face brighten'd with a gen'rous smile,
Which to his eyes such flashing lustre gave,
As tho' his soul, like an unsheathed sword,
Had thro' them gleam'd, our noble gen'ral stood;
And to his soldiers, with heart-moving words,
210   The vet'ran shewing, his brave deeds rehears'd;

---

1   Belisarius (c.505-565) was a Byzantine General under Justinian I who, because of
his many bravely fought battles, was responsible for the great expansion of the East-
ern Empire. Rosinberg's speech alludes to the legendary story of how Belisarius
had to beg in poverty as an old man. Edward Gibbon (1737-94) tells us in *The
Decline and Fall of the Roman Empire* (1776-88) that Belisarius appeared before Justinian on allegations of sedition and his "fortunes were sequestered. From December to July, he was guarded as a prisoner in his own palace. At length his innocence
was acknowledged; his freedom and honours were restored; and death, which
might be hastened by resentment and grief, removed him from the world about
eight months after his deliverance." For a fuller discussion on the possible origins of
the myth dating back to the time of the Macedonian emperor Basil II (963-1025
AD) and to the earliest mention of the myth in the writings of Theophanes (d.817
AD) see Gibbon 659.

Who by his side stood like a storm-scath'd oak,
Beneath the shelter of some noble tree,
In the green honours of its youthful prime.
ROS. How look'd the vet'ran?
VALT.   O! I cannot tell thee!
At first he bore it up with chearful looks,
As one who fain would wear his honours bravely,
And greet the soldiers with a comrade's face;
But when Count Basil, in such moving speech
Told o'er his actions past, and bade his troops
Great deeds to emulate, his count'nance chang'd;   220
High-heav'd his manly breast, as it had been
By inward strong emotion half convuls'd;
Trembled his nether lip; he shed some tears.
The gen'ral paus'd, the soldiers shouted loud;
Then hastily he brush'd the drops away,
And wav'd his hand, and clear'd his tear-chok'd voice,
As tho' he would some grateful answer make;
When back with double force the whelming tide
Of passion came; high o'er his hoary head
His arm be toss'd, and heedless of respect,   230
In Basil's bosom hid his aged face,
Sobbing aloud. From the admiring ranks
A cry arose; still louder shouts resound.
I felt a sudden tightness grasp my throat
As it would strangle me; such as I felt,
I knew it well, some twenty years ago,
When my good father shed his blessing on me.
I hate to weep, and so I came away.
ROS. (*giving* Valt. *his hand.*)
And there, take thou my blessing for the tale.
Hark! how they shout again! 'tis nearer now.   240
This way they march.

Martial Musick heard. Enter Soldiers marching in order, bearing
GEOFFRY *in triumph on their shoulders. After them enter* BASIL; *the*
whole preceded by a band of musick. They cross over the Stage, are
joined by ROS. *&c. and* EXEUNT.

SCENE II.

Enter GAURIECIO *and a* GENTLEMAN, *talking as they enter.*

GAUR. So slight a tie as this we cannot trust.
One day her influence may detain him here,
But love a feeble agent will be found
With the ambitious.

GENT. And so you think this boyish odd conceit
Of bearing home in triumph with his troops
That aged soldier, will your purpose serve?

GAUR. Yes, I will make it serve; for tho' my prince
Is little scrupulous of right and wrong,
10   I have possess'd his mind, as tho' it were
A flagrant insult on his princely state
To honour thus the man he has neglected;
Which makes him relish, with a keener taste,
My purpos'd scheme. Come let us fall to work,
With all their warm heroick feelings rous'd,
We'll spirit up his troops to mutiny,
Which must retard, perhaps undo him quite.
Thanks to his childish love, which has so well
Procur'd us time to tamper with the fools.

20 GENT. Ah! but those feelings he has wak'd within them,
Are gen'rous feelings, and endear himself.

GAUR. It matters not; tho' gen'rous in their nature,
They yet may serve a most ungen'rous end;
And he who teaches men to think, tho' nobly,
Doth raise within their minds a busy judge
To scan his actions. Send thine agents forth,
And sound it in their ears how much Count Basil
Affects all difficult and desp'rate service,
To raise his fortunes by some daring stroke;
30   And to the Emp'rour hath pledg'd his word,
To make his troops all dreadful hazards brave;
For which intent he fills their simple minds
With idle tales of glory and renown;
Using their warm attachment to himself

For most unworthy ends.
This is the busy time, go forth my friend;
Mix with the soldiers now in jolly groups,
Around their ev'ning cups. There, spare no cost,
(*gives him a purse.*)
Observe their words, see how the poison takes,
And then return again.

GENT.   I will, my lord.   40

EXEUNT *severally.*[1]

SCENE III.

A Suite of grand Apartments, with their wide doors thrown open; lighted up with lamps, and filled with company in masks.[2] *Enter several masks, and pass through the first apartment to the other rooms. Then enter* BASIL *in the disguise of a wounded soldier.*

BAS. (*alone.*) Now am I in the region of delight!
Within the blessed compass of these walls
She is; the gay light of those blazing lamps
Doth shine upon her, and this painted floor
Is with her footsteps press'd. E'en now perhaps
Amidst that motley rout she plays her part.
There will I go; she cannot be conceal'd,
For but the flowing of her graceful robe
Will soon betray the lovely form that wears it,
Tho' in a thousand masks. Ye homely weeds,—   10
(*looking at his habit.*)[3]
Which half conceal, and half declare my state,
Beneath your kind disguise, O! let me prosper,
And boldly take the privilege ye give.

---

1   Individually.
2   Popular at court in the sixteenth and early seventeenth centuries, the masquerade
    was a form of entertainment during which guests wearing masks would dance and
    act in character. See Terry Castle's *Masquerade and Civilization* (1986).
3   Outward form or appearance; guise or garb.

Follow her mazy steps, croud by her side;
Thus, near her face my list'ning ear incline,
And feel her soft breath fan my glowing cheek;
Her fair hand seize, yea press it closely too;
May it not be e'en so? by heav'n it shall!
This once, O! serve me well, and ever after
20   Ye shall be treasur'd like a monarch's robes;
Lodg'd in my chamber, near my pillow kept;
And oft with midnight lamp I'll visit ye,
And gazing wistfully, this night recall,
With all its past delights.—But yonder moves
A slender form, dress'd in an azure robe;
It moves not like the rest—it must be she.
(*Goes hastily into another apartment, and mixes with the*
masks.)

Enter ROSINBERG *fantastically dressed, with a willow upon his head,*
and scraps of sonnets, and torn letters fluttering round his neck; pursued
by a group of masks from one of the inner apartments, who hoot at
him, and push him about as he enters.

1ST MASK. Away, thou art a saucy jeering knave,
And fain wouldst make a jest of all true love.
ROS. Nay, gentle ladies, do not buffet me;
30   I am a right true servant of the fair;
And as this woeful chaplet on my brow,
And these tear-blotted sonnets would denote,
A poor abandon'd lover out of place;
With any mistress[1] ready to engage,
Who will enlist me in her loving service.
Of a convenient kind my talents are,
And to all various humours may be shap'd.
2D MASK. What canst thou do?
3D MASK.   Ay, what besides offending?
ROS. O! I can sigh so deeply, look so sad;
40   Pule[2] out a piteous tale on bended knee;

---

1   "lover" in the 1806 edition and "lady" in the 1851 edition.
2   To cry in a thin or weak voice. This appeared as "Pale" in the 1798 edition.

Groan like a ghost, so very wretched be,
As would delight a tender lady's heart
But to behold.
1ST MASK.   Poo, poo, insipid fool!
ROS. But should my lady brisker mettle own,
And tire of all those gentle dear delights,
Such pretty little quarrels I'd invent—
As whether such a fair-one (some dear friend!)
Whose squirrel's tail was pinch'd, or the soft maid,
With fav'rite lap-dog of a surfeit sick,
Have greatest cause of delicate distress: 50
Or whether—
1ST MASK.   Go, thou art too bad indeed!
(aside.) How could he know I quarrell'd with the Count?
2D MASK. Wilt thou do nothing for thy lady's fame?
ROS. Yes, lovely shepherdess, on ev'ry tree,
I'll carve her name, with true-love garlands bound.
Write madrigals upon her roseate cheeks,
Odes to her eye, 'faith ev'ry wart and mole
That spots her snowy skin, shall have its sonnet!
I'll make love-posies for her thimble's edge,[1]
Rather than please her not.   60
3D MASK. But for her sake what dangers wilt thou brave?
ROS. In truth, fair Nun, I stomach dangers less
Than other service, and were something loth
To storm a convent's walls for one dear glance;
But if she'll wisely manage this alone,
As maids have done, come o'er the wall herself,
And meet me fairly on the open plain,
I will engage her tender steps to aid
In all annoyance of rude briar or stone,
Or crossing rill, some half-foot wide, or so,   70
Which that fair lady should unaided pass,
Ye gracious powers forbid! I will defend
Against each hideous fly, whose dreadful buz—
4TH MASK. Such paltry service suits thee best indeed.

---

1   A posy was a short motto or line of poetry inscribed on a knife, within a ring, or
    elsewhere.

What maid of spirit would not spurn thee from her?

ROS. Yes, to recall me soon, sublime Sultana![1]
　　For I can stand the burst of female passion,
　　Each change of humour and affected storm;
　　Be scolded, frown'd upon, to exile sent,
80　Recall'd, caress'd, chid and disgrac'd again;
　　And say what maid of spirit would forego
　　The bliss of one to exercise it thus?
　　O! I can bear ill treatment like a lamb;

4TH MASK. (*beating him.*) Well, bear it then, thou hast deserv'd it
　　well.

ROS. 'Zounds, lady! do not give such heavy blows;
　　I'm not your husband, as belike you guess.

5TH MASK. Come lover, I enlist thee for my swain,
　　Therefore good lady, do forbear your blows,
　　Nor thus assume my rights.

90　ROS. Agreed. Wilt thou a gracious mistress prove?

— 5TH MASK. Such as thou wouldst, such as thy genius suits;
　　For since of universal scope it is
　　All women's humour shalt thou find in me.
　　I'll gently soothe thee with such winning smiles—
　　To nothing sink thee with a scornful frown;
　　Teize thee with peevish and affected fricks,[2]
　　Caress thee, love thee, hate thee, break thy pate;
　　But still between the whiles I'll careful be,
　　In feigned admiration of thy parts,
100　Thy shape, thy manners, or thy graceful mien,
　　To bind thy giddy soul with flatt'ry's charm:
　　For well thou knowst that flatt'ry[3] ever is
　　The tickling spice, the pungent seas'ning,
　　Which makes this motley dish of monstrous scraps
　　So pleasing to the dainty lover's taste.
　　Thou canst not leave, tho' violent in extreme,

1　Wife or concubine of a sultan.
2　Possibly Scots, "fricks" is cited neither in Johnson's *A Dictionary of the English Language* (1755) nor in *Kersey's Dictionarium Anglo-Britannicum* (1708). By 1806 Baillie had changed it to "freaks," defined by Johnson as "a sudden fancy," a whim.
3　Cf. Wollstonecraft, *Vindication* 218 (Appendix B.1).

And most vexatious in her teazing moods,
Thou canst not leave the fond admiring soul
Who did declare, when calmer reason rul'd,
Thou hadst a pretty leg. 110
ROS. Marry, thou hast the better of me there.
5TH MASK. And more, I'll pledge to thee my honest word,
That when your noble swainship shall bestow
More faithful homage on the simple maid,
Who loves you with sincerity and truth,
Than on the changeful and capricious tyrant
Who mocking leads you like a trammell'd ass,
My studied woman's wiles I'll lay aside,
And such a one become.
ROS. Well spoke, brave lady, I will follow thee. 120
(follows her to the corner of the stage.)
Now on my life, these ears of mine I'd give,
To have but one look of that little face,
Where such a biting tongue doth hold its court
To keep the fools in awe. Nay, nay, unmask;[1]
I'm sure thou hast a pair of wicked eyes,
A short and saucy nose; now prithee do.
(unmasking.)
ALB. *(unmasking.)* Well hast thou guess'd me right?
ROS. *(bowing low.)* Wild freedom chang'd to most profound
respect
Doth make an aukward booby of me now.
ALB. I've join'd your frolick with a good intent, 130
For much I wish'd to gain your private ear.
The time is precious, and I must be short.
ROS. On me your slightest word more pow'r will have,
Most honour'd lady, than a conn'd[2] oration.
Thou art the only one of all thy sex,
Who wearst thy years with such a winning grace,
Thou art the more admir'd the more thou fadst.[3]

---

1 Cf. *De Monfort* 2.1.202.
2 Learned or repeated. The OED cites only Baillie's usage of this word in her *Metrical Legends* (Lady G. Baillie, Intro., 42, 1821).
3 Cf. Wollstonecraft, *Vindication* 195 (Appendix B.2).

ALB. I thank your lordship for these courteous words,
But to my purpose. You are Basil's friend;
140　Be friendly to him then, and warn him well
This court to leave, nor be allur'd to stay,
For if he does, there's mischief waits him here
May prove the bane of all his future days.
Remember this, I must no longer stay.
God bless your friend and you; I love you both.

[EXIT.

ROS. (*alone.*) What may this warning mean? I had my fears.
There's something hatching which I know not of.
I've lost all spirit for this masking now.
(*throwing away his papers and his willow.*)
Away ye scraps! I have no need of you.
150　I would I knew what garment Basil wears;
I watch'd him but he did escape my sight;
But I must search again and find him out. 　　　[EXIT.

Enter BASIL *much agitated, with his mask in his hand.*

BAS. In vain I've sought her, follow'd ev'ry form
Where aught appear'd of dignity or grace,
I've listen'd to the tone of ev'ry voice;
I've watch'd the entrance of each female mask;
My flutt'ring heart rous'd like a startled hare,
With the imagin'd rustling of her robes,
At ev'ry dame's approach. Deceitful night,
160　How art thou spent? where are thy promis'd joys?
How much of thee is spent! O! spiteful fate!
And yet within the compass of these walls
Somewhere she is, altho' to me she is not.
Some other eye doth gaze upon her form,
Some other ear doth listen to her voice;
Some happy fav'rite doth enjoy the bliss
My spiteful stars deny.
Disturber of my soul! what veil conceals thee?

What dev'lish spell is o'er this cursed hour?
O! heav'ns and earth, where art thou?

Enter Mask in the dress of a female conjuror.

MASK. Methinks thou art impatient, valiant soldier,
    Thy wound doth gall thee sorely; is it so?
BAS. Away, away, I cannot fool with thee.
MASK. I have some potent drugs may ease thy smart.
    Where is thy wound? is't here?
    (*pointing to the bandage on his arm.*)
BAS.   Poo, poo, begone!
    Thou canst do nought—'tis in my head, my heart—
    'Tis ev'ry where, where med'cine cannot cure.
MASK. If wounded in the heart, it is a wound
    Which some ungrateful fair-one hath inflicted,
    And I may conjure something for thy good.   180
BAS. Ah! if thou couldst! what must I fool with thee?
MASK. Thou must awhile, and be examin'd too.
    What kind of woman did the wicked deed?
BAS. I cannot tell thee. In her presence still
    My mind in such a wild delight hath been,
    I could not pause to picture out her beauty;
    Yet nought of woman e'er was form'd so fair.
MASK. Art thou a soldier, and no weapon bear'st
    To send her wound for wound?
BAS. Alas! she shoots from such a hopeless height,   190
    No dart of mine hath plume to mount so far.
    None but a prince may dare.
MASK. But if thou hast no hope, thou hast no love.
BAS. I love, and yet in truth I had no hope,
    But that she might at least with some good will,
    Some gentle pure regard, some secret kindness,
    Within her dear remembrance give me place.
    This was my all of hope, but it is flown,
    For she regards me not; despises, scorns me;
    Scorns, I must say it too, a noble heart,   200
    That would have bled for her.

(*Mask, discovering*[1] *herself to be* Victoria, *by speaking in her true voice.*)
  O! no, she does not.

           [EXIT *hastily in confusion.*

BAS. (*stands for a moment rivetted to the spot, then holds up both his hands in an extacy.*)
  It is herself! it is her blessed self!
  O! what a fool am I that had no power
  To follow her, and urge th'advantage on.
  Be gone unmanly fears! I must be bold.

           [EXIT *after her.*

      A Dance of Masks.

   Enter DUKE *and* GAURIECIO, *unmasked.*

DUKE. This revelry, methinks, goes gaily on.
  The hour is late, and yet your friend returns not.
GAUR. He will return ere long—nay, there he comes.

      Enter GENTLEMAN.

DUKE. Does all go well? (*going close up to him.*)
GENT.   All as your grace could wish.
210 For now the poison works, and the stung soldiers
  Rage o'er their cups, and with fire-kindled eyes
  Swear vengeance on the chief who would betray them.
  That Frederick too, the discontented man
  Of whom your highness was so lately told,
  Swallows the bait, and does his part most bravely.
  Gauriecio counsel'd well to keep him blind,
  Nor with a bribe attempt him. On my soul!
  He is so fiery he had spurn'd us else,

---

1 Revealing.

And ruin'd all the plot.

DUKE. Speak softly, friend—I'll hear it all in private.   220
A gay and careless face we now assume.

DUKE, GAUR. *and* GEN. *retire into the inner apartment, appearing*
to laugh and talk gaily to the different masks as they pass them.

Re-enter VICTORIA *followed by* BASIL.

VICT. Forbear, my lord, these words offend mine ear.
BAS. Yet let me but this once, this once offend,
Nor thus with thy displeasure punish me;
And if my words against all prudence sin,
O! hear them, as the good of heart do list
To the wild ravings of a soul distraught.
VICT. If I indeed should listen to thy words,
They must not talk of love.
BAS. To be with thee, to speak, to hear thee speak,   230
To claim the soft attention of thine eye,
I'd be content to talk of any thing,
If it were possible to be with thee,
And think of ought but love.
VICT. I fear, my lord, you have too much presum'd,
On those unguarded words, which were in truth
Utter'd at unawares, with little heed,
And urge their meaning far beyond the right.
BAS. I thought, indeed, that they were kindly meant,
As tho' thy gentle breast did kindly feel   240
Some secret pity for my hopeless pain,
And would not pierce with scorn, ungen'rous scorn,
A heart so deeply stricken.
VIC. So far thou'st read it well.
BAS.   Ha! have I well?
Thou dost not hate me then?
VICT.   My father comes;
He were displeas'd if he should see thee thus.
BAS. Thou dost not hate me, then?
VICT. Away, he'll be displeas'd—I cannot say—

BAS. Well, let him come, it is thyself I fear;
250   For did destruction thunder o'er my head,
        By the dread pow'r of heav'n I would not stir
        Till thou hadst answer'd my impatient soul!
        Thou dost not hate me?
VICT. Nay, nay, let go thy hold—I cannot hate thee.
        (*breaks from him and exit.*)
BAS. (*alone.*) Thou canst not hate me! no, thou canst not
        hate me!
        For I love thee so well, so passing well,
        With such o'erflowing heart, so very dearly,
        That it were sinful not to pay me back
        Some small, some kind return.

                Enter MIRANDO, *dressed like Cupid.*

260   MIR. Bless thee, brave soldier.
        BAS. What sayst thou, pretty child? what playful fair
        Has deck'd thee out in this fantastick guise?
        MIR. It was Victoria's self; it was the princess.
        BAS. Thou art her fav'rite then?
        MIR.   They say I am;
        And now, between ourselves, I'll tell thee, soldier,
        I think in very truth she loves me well.
        Such merry little songs she teaches me—
        Sly riddles too, and when I'm laid to rest
        Oft times on tip-toe near my couch she steals,
270   And lifts the cov'ring so, to look upon me.
        And often times I feign as tho' I slept;
        For then her warm lips to my cheek she lays,
        And pats me softly with her fair white hands;
        And then I laugh, and thro' mine eye-lids peep,
        And then she tickles me, and calls me cheat;
        And then we do so laugh, ha, ha, ha, ha!
BAS. What, does she even so, thou happiest child?
        And have those rosy cheeks been press'd so dearly?
        Delicious urchin! I will kiss thee too.
        (*Takes him eagerly up in his arms, and kisses him.*)

MIR. No, let me down, thy kisses are so rough, 280
So furious rough—she doth not kiss me so.
BAS. Sweet boy, where is thy chamber? by Victoria's?
MIR. Hard by her own.
BAS. Then will I come beneath thy window soon,
And, if I could, some pretty song I'd sing
To lull thee to thy rest.
MIR. O! no, thou must not; 'tis a frightful place,
It is the church-yard of the neighb'ring dome.[1]
The princess loves it for the lofty trees,
Whose spreading branches shade her chamber walls; 290
So do not I; for when 'tis dark o'nights
Goblins howl there, and ghosts rise thro' the ground.
I hear them many a time when I'm a bed,
And hide beneath the cloaths my cow'ring head.
O! is it not a frightful thing, my lord,
To sleep alone i' the dark?
BAS. Poor harmless child! thy prate is wondrous sweet.

Enter a group of Masks.

1ST MASK. What dost thou here, thou little truant boy?
Come play thy part with us.

Masks place MIRANDO *in the middle, and range themselves
round him.*

SONG, — A GLEE.[2] 300

Child, with many a childish wile,
Timid look, and blushing smile,
Downy wings to steal thy way,
Gilded bow, and quiver gay,
Who in thy simple mien would trace
The tyrant of the human race?

---

1 Cathedral.
2 A musical composition of English origin for three or more voices, involving little
or no contrapuntal imitation as does a madrigal. Cf. *De Monfort* 3.2.1.

Who is he whose flinty heart
Hath not felt thy flying dart?
Who is he that from the wound
310   Hath not pain and pleasure found?
Who is he that hath not shed
Curse and blessing on thy head?

Ah Love! our weal, our woe, our bliss, our bane,
A restless life have they who wear thy chain!
Ah Love! our weal, our woe, our bliss, our bane,
More hapless still are they who never felt thy pain.

All the masks dance round Cupid. Then enter a band of satyrs, who frighten away Love and his votaries, and conclude the scene, dancing in a grotesque manner.

ACT IV.—SCENE I.

The Street before BASIL's *Lodging.*

Enter ROSINBERG *and two Officers.*

ROS. (*speaking as he enters.*) Unless we find him quickly, all is
    lost.
1ST. OFF. His very guards, methinks, have left their post
    To join the mutiny.
ROS. (*knocking very loud.*) Holla! who's there within? confound
    this door!
    It will not ope. O! for a Giant's strength.
    Holla, holla, within! will no one hear?

Enter a Porter *from the house.*

ROS. (*eagerly to the* Porter.) Is he return'd, is he return'd? not
    yet!
    Thy face doth tell me so.
PORT.   Not yet, my lord.
ROS. Then let him ne'er return—
    Tumult, disgrace, and ruin have their way!   10
    I'll search for him no more.
PORT. He hath been absent all the night, my lord.
ROS. I know he hath.
2D OFF.   And yet 'tis possible
    He may have enter'd by the secret door;
    And now, perhaps, in deepest sleep entranc'd,
    Is dead to ev'ry sound.
    (Ros. *without speaking, rushes into the house, and the rest follow*
    him.)

Enter BASIL.

BAS. The blue air of the morning pinches keenly.
    Beneath her window all the chilly night
    I felt it not. Ah! night has been my day,

And the pale lamp which from her chamber gleam'd,
Has to the breeze a warmer temper lent
20   Than the red burning east.

Re-enter ROSINBERG, *&c. from the house.*

ROS. Himself! himself! He's here, he's here! O! Basil,
   What fiend at such a time could lead thee forth?
BAS. What is the matter which disturbs you thus?
ROS. Matter that would a wiser man disturb.
   Treason's abroad, thy men have mutinied.
BAS. It is not so; thy wits have mutinied,
   And left their sober station in thy brain.
1ST OFF. Indeed, my Lord, he speaks in sober earnest.
30 Some secret enemies have been employ'd
   To fill your troops with strange imaginations;
   As tho' their gen'ral would, for selfish gain,
   Their gen'rous valour urge to desp'rate deeds.
   All to a man, assembled on the ramparts,
   Now threaten vengeance, and refuse to march.
BAS. What! think they vilely of me? threaten too!
   O! most ungen'rous, most unmanly thought!
   Didst thou attempt (*to* Ros.) to reason with their folly?
   Folly it is; baseness it cannot be!
40 ROS. Yes, truly, did I reason's pow'r essay,[1]
   But as well might I reason with the storm,
   And bid it cease to rage————————
   Their eyes look fire on him who questions them;
   The hollow murmurs of their mutter'd wrath
   Sound dreadful thro' the dark extended ranks,
   Like subterraneous grumblings of an earthquake.
   ————————————The vengeful hurricane
   Does not with such fantastick writhings toss
   The wood's green boughs, as does convulsive rage
50   Their forms with frantick gesture agitate.
   Around the chief of hell such legions throng'd,

---

1   Attempt, especially a difficult task.

To bring back curse and discord on creation.

BAS. Nay, they are men, altho' impassion'd ones.
    I'll go to them—

ROS.   And we will stand by thee.
    This sword is thine against ten thousand strong,
    If it should come to this.

BAS.   No, never, never!
    There is no mean. I with my soldiers must
    Or their commander or their victim prove.
    But are my officers all staunch and faithful?

ROS. All but that devil, Fred'rick——   60
    He, disappointed, left his former corps,
    Where he, in truth, had been too long neglected,
    Thinking he should all on the sudden rise,
    From Basil's well-known love of valiant men;
    And now, because it still must be deferr'd,
    He thinks you seek from envy to depress him,
    And burns to be reveng'd.

BAS. Well, well—This grieves me too—But let us go.

[EXEUNT.

SCENE II.

*The ramparts of the Town. The Soldiers are discovered drawn up in
disorderly manner, hollaing and speaking big, and clashing their arms
tumultuously.*

1ST SOL. No, comrade, no, hell gape and swallow me!
    If I do budge for such most dev'lish orders.

2D SOL. Huzza,[1] brave comrades! Who says otherwise?

3D SOL. No one, huzza! confound all treach'rous leaders!
    (*The Soldiers huzza and clash their arms.*)

---

1 An earlier version of "hurrah," this exclamation found in writings of the seventeenth and eighteenth centuries perhaps originated from a sailor's cheer or salute
made when friends came aboard, "Heisau! Hissa!", which was originally a hauling
and hoisting cry. In German, there was also a cry of hunting and pursuit, "Hu'ssa!"

4TH SOL. Heav'n dart its fiery light'ning on his head!
We're men, we're not cattle to be slaughter'd!
2D SOL. They who do long to caper high in air,
Into a thousand bloody fragments blown,
May follow our brave gen'ral.
1ST SOL.   Curse his name!
10   I've fought for him till my strain'd nerves have crack'd!
2D SOL. We will command ourselves; for Milan, comrades.
4TH SOL. Ay, ay, for Milan, valiant hearts, huzza!
(*All the Soldiers cast up their caps in the air, and huzza.*)
2D SOL. Yes, comrades, tempting booty waits us there,
And easy service: keep good hearts, my soldiers!
The gen'ral comes, good hearts! no flinching, boys!
Look bold and fiercely; we're the masters now.
(*They all clash their arms, and put on a fierce threatening aspect
to receive their General, who now enters, followed by* Rosinberg
and Officers. Basil *walks close along the front ranks of the
Soldiers, looking at them very steadfastly; then retires a few paces
back, and raising his arm, speaks with a very full loud voice.*)
BAS. How is it, soldiers, that I see you thus,
Assembled here, unsummon'd by command?
(*A confused murmur is heard amongst the Soldiers; some of them
call out.*)
But we command ourselves; we wait no orders.
(*A confused noise of voices is heard, and one louder than the rest
calls out.*)
20   Must we be butcher'd, for that we are brave?
(*A loud clamour and clashing of arms, then several voices
call out.*)
Damn hidden treach'ry! we defy thy orders.
Fred'rick shall lead us now————
(*Other voices call out.*)
We'll march where'er we list,[1] for Milan march.
(Basil, *waving his hand, and beckoning them to be silent, speaks with
a very loud voice.*) Yes, march where'er ye list, for Milan
march.

---

1   Wish.

SOL. Hear him, hear him!

(*The murmur ceases—a short pause.*)

BAS. Yes, march where'er ye list, for Milan march,
But as banditti, not as soldiers go;
For on this spot of earth I will disband,
And take from you the rank and name of soldiers.

(*A great clamour amongst the ranks——some call out.*)

What wear we arms for?

(*Others call out.*)

              No, he dares not do it.   30

(*One voice very loud.*)

Disband us at thy peril, treach'rous Basil!

(*Several of the Soldiers brandish their arms, and threaten to attack him; the* Officers *gather round* Basil, *and draw their swords to defend him.*)

BAS. Put up your swords,[1] my friends, it must not be.
I thank your zeal, I'll deal with them alone.

ROS. What, shall we calmly stand and see thee butcher'd?

BAS. (*very earnestly.*) Put up, my friends. (Officers *still persist.*)
              What are you rebels too?
Will no one here his gen'ral's voice obey?
I do command you to put up your swords.
Retire, and at a distance wait th' event.
Obey, or henceforth be no friends of mine.

(*Officers retire, very unwillingly.* Basil *waves them off with his hand till they are all gone, then walks up to the front of his Soldiers, who still hold themselves in a threatening posture.*)

Soldiers, we've fought together in the field,   40
And bravely fought; i' the face of horrid death
At honour's call I've led you dauntless on;
Nor do I know the man of all your bands,
That ever poorly from the trial shrunk,
Or yielded to the foe contended space.
Am I the meanest then of all my troops,
That thus ye think, with base unmanly threats,
To move me now? Put up those paltry weapons;

---

1 Cf. *Othello* 1.2.59.

They edgeless are to him who fears them not:
Rocks have been shaken from the solid base;
But what shall move a firm and dauntless mind?
Put up your swords, or dare the threaten'd deed—
Obey, or murder me————————
(*A confused murmur——some of the soldiers call out.*)
March us to Milan, and we will obey thee.
(*Others call out.*)
Ay, march us there, and be our leader still.

BAS. Nay, if I am your leader, I'll command ye;
And where I do command, there shall you go,
But not to Milan. No, nor shall you deviate
E'en half a furlong from your destin'd way,
To seize the golden booty of the east.
Think not to gain, or temporize with me,
For should I this day's mutiny survive,
Much as I've lov'd you, soldiers, ye shall find me
Still more relentless in pursuit of vengeance;
Tremendous, cruel, military vengeance.
There is no mean—a desp'rate game ye play,
Therefore I say, obey, or murder me.
Do as ye will, but do it manfully.
He is a coward who doth threaten me,
The man who slays me, but an angry soldier,
Acting in passion, like the frantick son,
Who struck his sire, and wept.

(*Soldiers call out.*) It was thyself who sought to murder us.

1ST SOL. You have unto the Emp'ror pledg'd your faith,
To lead us foremost in all desp'rate service;
You have agreed to sell your soldiers' blood,
And we have shed our dearest blood for you.

BAS. Hear me, my soldiers————

2D SOL. No, hear him not, he means to cozen[1] you.
Fred'rick will do you right————
(*Endeavouring to stir up noise and confusion amongst them.*)

BAS. What cursed fiend art thou, cast out from hell

---

1 Cheat.

To spirit up rebellion? damned villain!
(*Seizes upon* 2d soldier, *drags him out from the ranks, and
wrests his arms from him; then takes a pistol from his side, and
holds it to his head.*)
Stand there, damn'd, meddling villain, and be silent;
For if thou utt'rest but a single word,
A cough, or hem, to cross me in my speech,
I'll send thy cursed spirit from the earth,
To bellow with the damn'd!
(*The soldiers keep a dead silence*————*after a pause,* Basil
resumes his speech.)
Listen to me, my soldiers————
You say that I am to the Emp'ror pledg'd
To lead you foremost in all desp'rate service,   90
For now you call it not the path of glory,
And if in this I have offended you,
I do indeed repent me of the crime.
But new from battles, where my native troops
So bravely fought; I felt me proud at heart,
And boasted of you, boasted foolishly.
I said fair glory's palm ye would not yield
To e'er the bravest legion train'd to arms.
I swore the meanest man of all my troops
Would never shrink before an armed host,   100
If honour bade him stand. My royal master,
Smil'd at the ardour of my heedless words,
And promis'd, when occasion claim'd our arms,
To put them to the proof.
But ye do peace, and ease, and booty love,
Safe and ignoble service—be it so—
Forgive me that I did mistake you thus,
But do not earn with savage mutiny,
Your own destruction. We'll for Pavia march,
To join the royal army near its walls;   110
And there with blushing forehead will I plead,
That ye are men with warlike service worn,
Requiring ease and rest. Some other chief,
Whose cold blood boils not at the trumpet's sound,

Will in your rearward station head you then,
And so, my friends, we'll part. As for myself,
A volunteer, unheeded in the ranks,
I'll rather fight, with brave men for my fellows,
Than be the leader of a sordid band.
(*A great murmur rises amongst the ranks, soldiers call out.*)
120   We will not part, no, no, we will not part.
(*All call out together.*)
      We will not part, be thou our gen'ral still.
BAS. How can I be your gen'ral? ye obey
As caprice moves you; I must be obey'd
As honest men against themselves perform
A sacred oath.—
Some other chief will more indulgent prove—
You're weary grown—I've been too hard a master.
SOLDIERS. Thyself, and only thee, will we obey.
BAS. But if you follow me, yourselves ye pledge
130   Unto no easy service:—hardships, toils,
The hottest dangers of most dreadful fight,
Will be your portion; and when all is o'er,
Each, like his gen'ral, must contented be
Unbootied to return, a poor brave soldier.
How say ye now? I spread no tempting lure—
A better fate than this, I promise none.
SOLDIERS. We'll follow Basil.
BAS. What token of obedience will ye give?
(*A deep pause.*) Soldiers, lay down your arms.
(*They all lay down their arms.*)
140   If any here are weary of the service,
Now let them quit the ranks, and they shall have
A free discharge, and passport to their homes;
And from my scanty fortune I'll make good
The well-earn'd pay their royal master owes them.
Let those who follow me their arms resume.
(*They all resume their arms.*)
(Basil *holding up his hands.*) High heaven be prais'd!
I had been griev'd to part with you, my soldiers.
Here is a letter from my gracious master,

With offer of preferment in the north,
Most high preferment, which I did refuse,   150
For that I would not leave my gallant troops.
(*Takes out a letter, and throws it amongst them.*)
(*A great commotion amongst the soldiers; many of them quit their
     ranks, and croud about him, calling out.*) Our gallant gen'ral!
(*Others call out.*) We'll spend our heart's blood for thee, noble
     Basil!
BAS. And so you thought me false? this bites to th' quick!
     My soldiers thought me false!
(*They all quit their ranks, and croud eagerly around him. Basil
     waving them off with his hands.*) Away, away, you have
     disgusted me.
(*Soldiers retire to their ranks.*)
'Tis well—retire, and hold yourselves prepar'd
To march upon command; nor meet again
Till you are summon'd by the beat of drum.
Some secret enemy has tamper'd with you,   160
For yet I will not think that in these ranks,
There moves a man who wears a traitor's heart.
(*The soldiers begin to march off, and musick strikes up.*)
(Basil *holding up his hand.*) Cease, cease triumphant sounds,
     Which our brave fathers, men without reproach,
     Rais'd in the hour of triumph; but this hour
     To us no glory brings—
     Then silent be your march—ere that again
     Our steps to glorious strains like these shall move
     A day of battle o'er our heads must pass,
     And blood be shed to wash out this day's stain.   170

[EXEUNT *soldiers, silent and dejected.*

Enter FREDERICK, *who starts back on seeing* BASIL *alone.*

BAS. Advance, lieutenant; wherefore shrink ye back?
     I've ever seen you bear your head erect,
     And front your man, tho' arm'd with frowning death.
     Have you done ought the valiant should not do?

I fear you have.   (Fred. *looks confused.*)
With secret art, and false insinuation,
The simple untaught soldiers to seduce
From their sworn duty, might become the base,
Become the coward well; but oh! what villain
180   Had the curs'd pow'r t'engage thy valiant worth
In such a work as this?

FRED. Is Basil, then, so lavish of his praise
On a neglected pitiful subaltern?
It were a libel on his royal master;
A foul reproach upon fair fortune cast,
To call me valiant:
And surely he has been too much their debtor
To mean them this rebuke.

BAS. Is nature then so sparing of her gifts,
190   That it is wonderful when they are found
Where fortune smiles not?
Thou art by nature brave, and so am I,
But in those distant ranks moves there not one
(*Pointing off the stage.*)
Of high ennobled soul, by nature form'd
A hero and commander, who will, yet,
In his untrophied grave forgotten lie
With meaner men? I dare be sworn there does.

FRED. What need of words? I crave of thee no favour.
I have offended against armed law,
200   And shrink not from my doom.

BAS. I know thee well, I know thou fear'st not death;
On scaffold or in field with dauntless breast
Thou wilt engage him: and if thy proud soul,
In sullen obstinacy scorns all grace
E'en be it so. But if with manly gratitude
Thou truly canst receive a brave man's pardon,
Thou hast it freely.

FRED. It must not be. I've been thine enemy—
I've been unjust to thee—

BAS.   I know thou hast;
210   But thou art brave, and I forgive thee all.

FRED. My lord! my gen'ral! Oh! I cannot speak!
I cannot live and be the wretch I am!
BAS. But thou canst live, and be an honest man
From errour turn'd,—canst live and be my friend.
(*Raising* Fred. *from the ground*.)
Forbear, forbear! see where our friends advance,
They must not think thee suing for a pardon;
That would disgrace us both. Yet, ere they come,
Tell me, if that thou may'st with honour tell,
What did seduce thee from thy loyal faith?
FRED. No cunning traitor did my faith attempt,   220
For then I had withstood him: but of late,
I know not how—a bad and restless spirit
Has work'd within my breast, and made me wretched.
I've lent mine ear to foolish idle tales,
Of very zealous, tho' but new-made friends.
BAS. Softly, our friends approach—of this again.

[EXEUNT.

SCENE III.

An Apartment in BASIL's *lodgings. Enter* BASIL *and* ROSINBERG.

ROS. Thank heaven I am now alone with thee.
Last night I sought thee with an anxious mind,
And curs'd thine ill-tim'd absence—
There's treason in this most deceitful court,
Against thee plotting, and this morning's tumult
Hath been its damn'd effect.
BAS.   Poo, poo, my friend;
The nature of man's mind too well thou know'st,
To judge as vulgar hood-wink'd statesmen do;
Who ever with their own poor wiles misled,
Believe each popular tumult or commotion,   10
Must be the work of deep-laid policy.
Poor, mean, mechanick souls, who little know
A few short words of energetick force,

Some pow'rful passion on the sudden rous'd,
The animating sight of something noble,
Some fond trait of the mem'ry finely wak'd,
A sound, a simple song without design,
In revolutions, tumults, wars, rebellions,
All grand events, have oft effected more
20   Than deepest cunning of their paltry art.
Some drunken soldier, eloquent with wine,
Who loves not fighting, hath harangu'd his mates,
For they in truth some hardships have endur'd.
Wherefore in this should we suspect the court?

ROS. Ah! there is something, friend, in Mantua's court,
Will make the blackest trait of bare-faced treason
Seem fair and guiltless to thy partial eye.

BAS. Nay, 'tis a weakness in thee, Rosinberg,
Which makes thy mind so jealous and distrustful.
30   Why should the duke be false?

ROS. Because he is a double, crafty prince—
Because I've heard it rumour'd secretly,
That he in some dark treaty is engag'd,
E'en with our master's enemy the Frank.[1]

BAS. And so thou think'st—

ROS.   Nay, hear me to the end.
Last night that good and honourable dame,
Noble Albini, with most friendly art,
From the gay clam'rous throng my steps beguil'd,
Unmask'd before me, and with earnest grace,
40   Entreated me, if I were Basil's friend,
To tell him hidden danger waits him here,
And warn him well fair Mantua's court to leave,
She said she lov'd thee much, and hadst thou seen
How anxiously she urg'd—

BAS. (*interrupting him.*) By heav'n and earth,
There is a ray of light breaks thro' thy tale,
And I could leap like madmen in their fricks,
So blessed is the gleam! Ah! no, no, no!

---

1 Frenchman.

It cannot be, alas! it cannot be,
Yet didst thou say she urg'd it earnestly?
She is a woman, who avoids all share   50
In secret politicks; one only charge
Her int'rest claims, Victoria's guardian friend—
And she would have me hence—it must be so.
O! would it were; how saidst thou, gentle Rosinberg?
She urg'd it earnestly—how did she urge it?
Nay, pri'thee, do not stare upon me thus,
But tell me all her words—what said she else?

ROS. O Basil! I could laugh to see thy folly,
But that thy weakness doth provoke me so.
Most admirable, brave, determin'd man!   60
So well, so lately try'd, what art thou now?
A vain deceitful thought transports thee thus.
Thinkst thou———

BAS.   I will not tell thee what I think.

ROS. But I can guess it well, and it deceives thee.
Leave this detested place, this fatal court,
Where damn'd deceitful cunning plots thy ruin.
A soldier's duty calls thee loudly hence.
The time is critical. How wilt thou feel
When they shall tell these tidings in thine ear,
That brave Piscaro, and his royal troops,   70
Our valiant fellows, have the en'my fought,
Whilst we, so near at hand, lay loit'ring here?

BAS. Thou dost disturb thy brain with fancied fears.
Our fortunes rest not on a point so nice
That one short day should be of all this moment;
And yet this one short day will be to me
Worth years of other time.

ROS.   Nay, rather say,
A day to darken all thy days beside,
Confound the fatal beauty of that woman,
Which has bewitch'd thee so!

BAS.   'Tis most ungen'rous   80
To push me thus with rough unsparing hand,
Where but the slightest touch is felt so dearly.

It is unfriendly.

ROS. God knows my heart! I would not give thee pain;
But it disturbs me, Basil, vexes me,
To see thee so enthralled by a woman.
If she is fair, others are fair as she.
Some other face will like emotions raise,
When thou canst better play a lover's part:
90 But for the present, fye upon it, Basil!

BAS. What, is it possible thou hast beheld,
Hast tarried by her too, her converse shar'd,
Yet talkst as tho' she were a common fair-one,
Such as a man may fancy and forget?
Thou art not, sure, so dull and brutish grown;
It is not so, thou dost belie thy thoughts,
And vainly try'st to gain me with the cheat.

ROS. So thinks each lover of the maid he loves,
Yet in their lives some many maidens love.
100 Curse on it! leave this town, and be a soldier!

BAS. Have done, have done! why dost thou bait me thus?
Thy words become disgusting to me, Rosinberg.
What claim hast thou mine actions to controul?
I'll Mantua leave, when it is fit I should.

ROS. Then, 'faith! 'tis fitting thou shouldst leave it now;
Ay, on the instant. Is't not desperation
To stay, and hazard ruin on thy fame,
Tho' yet uncheer'd e'en by that tempting lure,
No lover breathes without? thou hast no hope.

110 BAS. What dost thou mean? curse on the paltry thought.
That I should count and bargain with my heart,
Upon the chances of unstinted favour,
As little souls their base-bred fancies feed?
O! were I conscious that within her breast
I held some portion of her dear regard,
Tho' pent for life within a prison's walls,
Where thro' my grate I yet might sometimes see
E'en but her shadow sporting in the sun;
Tho' plac'd by fate where some obstructing bound,
120 Some deep impassable, between us roll'd,

And I might yet from some high tow'ring cliff,
Perceive her distant mansion from afar,
Or mark its blue smoke rising eve and morn;
Nay, tho' within the circle of the moon
Some spell did fix her, never to return,
And I might wander in the hours of night,
And upward turn mine ever-gazing eye,
Fondly to mark upon its varied disk,
Some little spot that might her dwelling be;
My fond, my fixed heart would still adore   130
And own no other Love. Away, away!
How canst thou say to one who loves like me,
Thou hast no hope?
ROS. But with such hope, my friend, how stand thy fears?
Are they so well refin'd? How wilt thou bear
Ere long to hear that some high, favour'd prince
Has won her heart, her hand, has married her?
Tho' now unshackled, will it always be?
BAS. By heav'n thou dost contrive but to torment!
And hast a pleasure in the pain thou giv'st.   140
There is malignity in what thou say'st.
ROS. No, not malignity, but kindness, Basil,
That fain would save thee from the yawning gulph,
To which blind passion guides thy heedless steps.
BAS. Go, rather save thyself
From the weak passion which has seiz'd thy breast,
T'assume authority with sage-like brow,
And shape my actions by thine own caprice.
I can direct myself—
ROS.   Yes, do thyself,
And let no artful woman do it for thee.   150
BAS. I scorn thy thought: it is beneath my scorn;
It is of meanness sprung—an artful woman!
O! she has all the loveliness of heav'n,
And all its goodness too!
ROS. I mean not to impute dishonest arts.
I mean not to impute—
BAS.   No, 'faith, thou canst not.

ROS. What, can I not? their arts all women have.
But now of this no more; it moves thee greatly.
Yet once again, as a most loving friend,
160   Let me conjure thee, if thou prizest honour,
A soldier's fair repute, a hero's fame,
What noble spirits love; and well I know
Full dearly dost thou prize them, leave this place,
And give thy soldiers orders for the march.
BAS. Nay, since thou must assume it o'er me thus,
Be gen'ral, and command my soldiers too.
ROS. What hath this passion in so short a space,
O! curses on it! so far chang'd thee, Basil?
That thou dost take with such ungentle warmth,
170   The kindly freedom of thine ancient friend.
Methinks the beauty of a thousand maids
Would not have mov'd me thus to treat my friend,
My best, mine earliest friend!
BAS. Say kinsman rather, chance has link'd us so,
Our blood is near, our hearts are sever'd far;
No act of choice did e'er unite our souls.
Men most unlike we are; our thoughts unlike;
My breast disowns thee—thou'rt no friend of mine.
ROS. Ah! have I then so long, so dearly lov'd thee;
180   So often, with an elder brother's care,
Thy childish rambles tended, shar'd thy sports;
Fill'd up by stealth thy weary school-boy's task;
Taught thy young arms thine earliest feats of strength;
With boastful pride thine early rise beheld
In glory's paths, contented then to fill
A second place, so I might serve with thee;
And say'st thou now, I am no friend of thine?
Well, be it so; I am thy kinsman still,
And by that title will I save thy name
190   From danger of disgrace. Indulge thy will:
I'll lay me down and feign that I am sick,
And yet I shall not feign—I shall not feign,
For thy unkindness makes me sick indeed;
It will be said that Basil tarried here

To save his friend, for so they'll call me still;
Nor will dishonour fall upon thy name
For such a kindly deed.—
(Basil *walks up and down in great agitation, then stops, covers
his face with his hands, and seems to be overcome.* Rosinberg
looks at him earnestly.)
ROS.   O! blessed heav'n, he weeps!
(*Runs up to him, and catches him in his arms.*)
O Basil! I have been too hard upon thee.
And is it possible I've mov'd thee thus?
BAS. (*in a convulsed broken voice.*) I will renounce—I'll leave—
ROS.   What says my Basil?   200
BAS. I'll Mantua leave—I'll leave this seat of bliss—
This lovely woman—tear my heart in twain—
Cast off at once my little span of joy—
Be wretched—miserable—whate'er thou wilt—
Dost thou forgive me?
ROS.   O my friend! my friend!
I love thee now more than I ever lov'd thee.
I must be cruel to thee to be kind,[1]
Each pang I see thee feel strikes thro' my heart;
Then spare us both, call up thy noble spirit,
And meet the blow at once—thy troops are ready—   210
Let us depart, nor lose another hour.
(Basil *shrinks from his arms, and looks at him with somewhat of
an upbraiding, at the same time of a sorrowful look.*)
BAS. Nay, put me not to death upon the instant;
I'll see her once again, and then depart.
ROS. See her but once again, and thou art ruin'd.
It must not be—if thou regard'st me—
BAS. Well then, it shall not be. Thou hast no mercy!
ROS. Ah! thou wilt bless me all thine after-life
For what, to thee, seems now so merciless.
BAS. (*sitting down very dejectedly.*)
Mine after life! what is mine after life?
My day is clos'd! the gloom of night is come!   220

---

1 Cf. *Hamlet* 3.4.178.

A hopeless darkness settles o'er my fate.
I've seen the last look of her heav'nly eyes,
I've heard the last sounds of her blessed voice,
I've seen her fair form from my sight depart;
My doom is clos'd!
ROS. (*Hanging over him with pity and affection.*)
Alas! my friend!
BAS. In all her lovely grace she disappear'd,
Ah! little thought I never to return.
ROS. Why so desponding? think of warlike glory.
230   The fields of fair renown are still before thee;
Who would not burn such noble fame to earn?
BAS. What now are arms, or fair renown to me?
Strive for it those who will—and yet a while
Welcome rough war, with all thy scenes of blood,
(*Starting from his seat.*)
Thy roaring thunders, and thy clashing steel,
Welcome once more! what have I now to do
But play the brave man o'er again, and die?

Enter ISABELLA.

240 ISAB. (*to* Bas.) My princess bids me greet you, noble count.
BAS. (*starting.*) What dost thou say?
ROS.   D—n this untimely message!
ISAB. The princess bids me greet you, noble count;
In the cool grove, hard by the southern gate,
She with her train—
BAS.   What, she indeed herself?
ISAB. Herself, my lord, and she requests to see you.
BAS. Thank heav'n for this; I will be there anon.
ROS. (*taking hold of him.*) Stay, stay, and do not be a madman
still.
BAS. Let go thy hold; what, must I be a brute,
A very brute to please thee? no, by heav'n!
(*Breaks from him, and* EXIT.)
ROS. (*striking his forehead.*) All lost again! black curses light upon
her!

(*Turning eagerly to* Isab.) And so thy virtuous mistress sends
thee here
To make appointments, hon'rable dame?   250
ISAB. Not so, my lord, you must not call it so;
The court will hunt to-morrow, and Victoria
Would have your noble gen'ral of her train.
ROS. Confound these women, and their artful snares,
Since men will be such fools!
ISAB. Yes, grumble at our empire[1] as you will—
ROS. What, boast ye of it? empire do ye call it?
It is your shame! a short liv'd tyranny
That ends at last in hatred and contempt.
ISAB. Nay, but some women do so wisely rule,   260
Their subjects never from the yoke escape.
ROS. Some women do, but they are rarely found.
There is not one in all your paltry court
Hath wit enough for the ungen'rous task.
'Faith! of you all, not one, but brave Albini,
And she disdains it.—Good be with you, lady!
(*Going.*)
ISAB. O! would I could but touch that stubborn heart,
How dearly should he pay for this hour's storm!

[EXEUNT *severally.*

---

1 Cf. Appendix B.2 and Wollstonecraft's *Vindication* (168, 171, 212, 229, 322). There is
a tradition to this imagery of dominance between the genders as witnessed in such
works as Laetitia Barbauld's "To a Lady, with some painted flowers" and "Song V,"
Rousseau's *Emile*, and Madame de Staël's *Letters on the Works and Characters of
J.J. Rousseau*. Opposing the notion of a female empire in her *Vindication*, Wollstonecraft uses the word rhetorically. In one instance she proclaims that "It is not
empire, – but equality, that they should contend for" (229) and in another asserts
that "The being who can think justly in one track, will soon extend its intellectual
empire; and she who has sufficient judgment to manage her children, will not submit, right or wrong, to her husband, or patiently to the social laws which make a
nonentity of a wife" (322).

SCENE IV.

A Summer Apartment in the Country, the windows of which look to a forest. Enter VICTORIA *in a hunting dress, followed by* ALBINI *and* ISABELLA, *speaking as they enter.*

VICT. (*to* Alb.) And so you will not share our sport to-day?

ALB. My days of frolick should ere this be o'er,
But thou, my charge, hast kept me youthful still.
I should most gladly go, but since the dawn
A heavy sickness hangs upon my heart,
I cannot hunt to-day.

VICT. I'll stay at home and nurse thee, dear Albini.

ALB. No, no, thou shalt not stay.

VICT.   Nay, but I will.
I cannot follow to the cheerful horn
Whilst thou art sick at home.

10   ALB.   Not very sick.
Rather than thou shouldst stay, my gentle child,
I'll mount my horse, and go e'en as I am.

VICT. Nay, then I'll go, and soon return again.
Meanwhile, do thou be careful of thyself.

ISAB. Hark, hark! the shrill horn calls us to the field,
Your highness hears it?   (*musick without.*)

VICT.   Yes, my Isabella,
I hear it, and methinks e'en at the sound
I vault already on my leathern seat,
And feel the fiery steed beneath me shake

20   His mantled sides, and paw the fretted earth;
Whilst I aloft, with gay equestrian grace,
The low salute of gallant lords return;
Who waiting round with eager watchful eye,
And reined steeds, the happy moment seize.
O! didst thou never hear, my Isabell,
How nobly Basil in the field becomes
His fiery courser's back?

ISAB.   They say most gracefully.

ALB. What, is the valiant count not yet departed?

VICT. You would not have our gallant Basil go
    When I have bade him stay? not so, Albini. 30
ALB. Fye! reigns that spirit still so strong within thee,
    Which vainly covets all men's admiration,
    And is to others cause of cruel pain?
    O! would thou couldst subdue it!
VICT. My gentle friend, thou shouldst not be severe;
    For now in truth I love not admiration
    As I was wont to do; in truth I do not!
    But yet, this once my woman's heart excuse,
    For there is something strange in this man's love,
    I never met before, and I must prove it. 40
ALB. Well, prove it then, be stricter to thyself,
    And bid sweet peace of mind a sad farewell.
VICT. O no! that will not be! 'twill peace restore;
    For after this, all folly of the kind
    Will quite insipid and disgusting be;
    And so I shall become a prudent maid,
    And passing wise at last. (*musick heard without.*)
    Hark, hark! again!
    All good be with you! I'll return ere long.

                    [EXEUNT Victoria *and* Isabella.

ALB. (*solus.*) Ay, go, and ev'ry blessing with thee go, 50
    My most tormenting, and most pleasing charge!
    Like vapour, from the mountain stream art thou,
    Which highly rises on the morning air,
    And shifts its fleeting form with ev'ry breeze,
    For ever varying, and for ever graceful.
    Endearing, gen'rous, bountiful and kind;
    Vain, fanciful, and fond of worthless praise;
    Courteous and gentle, proud and magnificent;
    And yet these adverse qualities in thee,
    No striking contrast, nor dissonance make; 60
    For still thy good and amiable gifts
    The sober dignity of virtue wear not,
    And such a 'witching mien thy follies shew,

They make a very idiot of reproof,
And smile it to disgrace—
What shall I do with thee?—it grieves me much
To hear count Basil is not yet departed.
When from the chace he comes, I'll watch his steps,
And speak to him myself—
70   O! I could hate her for that poor ambition
Which silly adoration only claims,
But that I well remember, in my youth
I felt the like—I did not feel it long;
I tore it soon, indignant from my breast,
As that which did degrade a noble mind. [EXIT.

SCENE V.

A very beautiful Grove in the forest. Musick and horns heard afar off, whilst huntsmen and dogs appear passing over the stage, at a great distance. Enter VICTORIA *and* BASIL, *as if just alighted from their horses.*

VICT. (*speaking to attendants without.*)
    Lead on our horses to the further grove,
    And wait us there—
    (*to* Bas.) This spot so pleasing, and so fragrant is,
    'Twere sacrilege with horses' hoofs to wear
    Its velvet turf, where little elfins dance,
    And fairies sport beneath the summer's moon:
    I love to tread upon it.
BAS. O! I would quit the chariot of a god
    For such delightful footing!
VICT.   I love this spot.
10 BAS. It is a spot where one would live and die.
VICT. See, thro' the twisted boughs of those high elms,
    The sun-beams on the bright'ning foliage play,
    And tinge the scaled bark with ruddy brown.
    Is it not beautiful?
BAS.   'Tis passing beautiful

To see the sun-beams on the foliage play,
(*In a soft voice.*) And tinge the scaled bark with ruddy
brown.

VICT. And here I've stood full often, and admir'd
The graceful bending, o'er that shady pool,
Of yon green willow, whose fair sweepy boughs
So kiss their image on the glassy plain,   20
And bathe their leafy tresses in the stream.

BAS. And I too love to see its drooping boughs
So kiss their image on the glassy plain,
And bathe their leafy tresses in the stream.

VICT. My lord, it is uncivil in you thus
My very words with mock'ry to repeat.

BAS. Nay, pardon me, did I indeed repeat?
I meant it not; but when I hear thee speak,
So sweetly dwells thy voice upon mine ear,
My tongue e'en unawares assumes the tone;   30
As mothers on their lisping infants gaze,
And catch their broken words. I pri'thee pardon!

VICT. But we must leave this grove, the birds fly low,
This should forbode a storm, and yet o'erhead
The sky, bespread with little downy clouds[1]
Of purest white, would seem to promise peace.
How beautiful those pretty snowy clouds!

BAS. Of a most dazzling brightness!

VICT. Nay, nay, a veil that tempers heaven's brightness,
Of softest, purest white.   40

BAS. As tho' an angel, in his upward flight,
Had left his mantle floating in mid-air.

VICT. Still most unlike a garment, small and sever'd,
(*Turning round, and perceiving that he is gazing at her.*)
But thou regard'st them not.

BAS. Ah! what should I regard, where should I gaze?
For in that far-shot glance, so keenly wak'd
That sweetly rising smile of admiration,
Far better do I learn how fair heav'n is,

---

1   Cf. Hamlet's discussion of clouds with Polonius (3.2.367–73).

Than if I gaz'd upon the blue serene.

50 VICT. Remember you have promis'd, gentle count,
No more to vex me with such foolish words.

BAS. Ah! wherefore should my tongue alone be mute?
When every look and every motion tell,
So plainly tell, and will not be forbid,
That I adore thee, love thee, worship thee!
(Victoria *looks haughty and displeased.*)
Ah! pardon me, I know not what I say.
Ah! frown not thus! I cannot see thee frown.
I'll do whate'er thou wilt, I will be silent;
But O! a reined tongue, and bursting heart,
60 Are hard at once to bear! will thou forgive me?

VICT. We'll think no more of it; we'll quit this spot;
I do repent me that I led thee here,
But 'twas the fav'rite path of a dear friend.
Here, many a time we wander'd, arm in arm;
We lov'd this grove, and now that he is absent,
I love to haunt it still.   (Basil *starts.*)

BAS. His fav'rite path—a friend—here arm in arm—
(*Clasping his hands, and raising them to his head.*)
Then there is such an one!
(*Drooping his head, and looking distractedly upon the ground.*)
I dream'd not of it.

VICT. (*pretending not to see him.*) That little lane, with woodbine
all o'ergrown,
70 He lov'd so well!—it is a fragrant path,
Is it not, count?

BAS.   It is a gloomy one!

VICT. I have, my lord, been wont to think it cheerful.

BAS. I thought your highness meant to leave this spot.

VICT. I do, and by this lane we'll take our way;
For here he often walk'd with saunt'ring pace,
And listen'd to the wood-lark's ev'ning song;

BAS. What, must I on his very footsteps go?
Accursed be the ground on which he's trod!

VICT. And is Count Basil so uncourtly grown,
That he would curse my brother to my face?

BAS. Your brother! gracious god! is it your brother?

That dear, that loving friend of whom you spoke,
Is he indeed your brother?
VICT.   He is indeed, my lord.
BAS. Then heav'n bless him! all good angels bless him!
I could weep o'er him now, shed blood for him!
I could—O! What a foolish heart have I!
(*Walks up and down with a hurried step, tossing about his arms*
in transport; then stops short, and runs up to Victoria.) Is it
indeed your brother?
VICT. It is indeed: what thoughts disturb'd thee so?
BAS. I will not tell thee; foolish thoughts they were.
Heav'n bless your brother!
VICT.   Ay, heav'n bless him too!
I have but he; would I had two brave brothers,   90
And thou wert one of them.
BAS. I would fly from thee to earth's utmost bounds,
Were I thy brother—
And yet, methinks, I would I had a sister.[1]
VICT. And wherefore would ye?
BAS.   To place her near thee,
The soft companion of thy hours to prove,
And, when far distant, sometimes talk of me.
Thou couldst not chide a gentle sister's cares.
Perhaps, when rumour from the distant war,   100
Uncertain tales of dreadful slaughter bore,
Thou'dst see the tear hang on her pale wan cheek.
And kindly say, how does it fare with Basil?
VICT. No more of this—indeed there must no more.
A friend's remembrance I will ever bear thee.
But see where Isabella this way comes,
I had a wish to speak with her alone.
Attend us here, for soon will we return,
And then take horse again.   [EXIT.

---

1   Modern literary theorists have more clearly described the theme of sibling incest in
Romantic literature. Three basic relations that recur are erotic ones between a fos-
ter-brother and sister who have been raised as siblings, platonic ones between
remarkably close brothers and sisters who share a common fate, and sexual ones
which are normally considered as incest. Cf. Richardson, "The Dangers of Sympathy" and Thorslev, "Incest as Romantic Symbol."

BAS. (*looking after her for some time.*)

110   See, with what graceful steps she moves along,
Her lovely form in ev'ry action lovely.
If but the wind her ruffl'd garment raise,
It twists it into some light pretty fold,
Which adds new grace. Or should some small mishap,
Some tangling branch, her fair attire derange,
What would in others strange, or awkward seem,
But lends to her some wild bewitching charm.
See, yonder does she raise her lovely arm
To pluck the dangling hedge-flow'r as she goes;
120   And now she turns her head, as tho' she view'd
The distant landscape; now methinks she walks
With doubtful ling'ring steps—will she look back?
Ah no! yon thicket hides her from my sight.
Bless'd are the eyes that may behold her still,
Nor dread that ev'ry look shall be the last!
And yet she said she would remember me.
I will believe it; Ah! I must believe it,
Or be the saddest soul that sees the light!
But lo! a messenger, and from the army;
130   He brings me tidings; grant they may be good!
Till now I never fear'd what man might utter;
I dread his tale, God grant it may be good!

Enter MESSENGER.

    From the army?

MESS.   Yes, my lord.

BAS.   What tidings brings't thou?

MESS. Th' imperial army, under brave Piscaro,
    Have beat the enemy near Pavia's walls.

BAS. Ha! have they fought? and is the battle o'er?

MESS. Yes, conquer'd; ta'en the French king prisoner,
    Who, like a noble, gallant gentleman,
    Fought to the last, nor yielded up his sword
140   Till, being one amidst surrounding foes,
    His arm could do no more.

BAS. What dost thou say? who is made prisoner?
  What king did fight so well?
MESS.   The king of France;
BAS. Thou saidst—thy words do ring so in mine ears,
  I cannot catch their sense—the battle's o'er?
MESS. It is, my lord. Piscaro staid your coming,
  But could no longer stay. His troops were bold,
  Occasion press'd him, and they bravely fought—
  They bravely fought, my lord.
BAS.   I hear, I hear thee.
  Accurs'd am I, that it should wring my heart   150
  To hear they bravely fought.—
  They bravely fought, whilst we lay ling'ring here;
  O! what a fated blow to strike me thus!
  Perdition! shame! disgrace! a damned blow!
MESS. Ten thousand of the enemy are slain;
  We too have lost full many a gallant soul.
  I view'd the closing armies from afar;
  Their close pick'd ranks in goodly order spread,
  Which seem'd alas! when that the fight was o'er,
  Like the wild marshes' crop of stately reeds,   160
  Laid with the passing storm. But woe is me!
  When to the field I came, what dismal sights!
  What waste of life! what heaps of bleeding slain!
BAS. Would I were laid a red, disfigur'd corse,
  Amid those heaps! they fought, and we were absent!
  (*Walks about distractedly, then stops short.*)
  Who sent thee here?
MESS. Piscaro sent me to inform Count Basil
  He needs not now his aid, and gives him leave
  To march his tardy troops to distant quarters.
BAS. He says so, does he? well it shall be so.   170
  (*Tossing his arms distractedly.*)
  I will to quarters, narrow quarters go,
  Where voice of war shall rouse me forth no more.

                                          [EXIT.

MESS. I'll follow after him, he is distracted;
    And yet he looks so wild I dare not do it.

Enter VICTORIA *as if frightened, followed by* ISABELLA.

VICT. (*to* Isab.) Didst thou not mark him as he pass'd thee too?
ISAB. I saw him pass, but with such hasty steps,
    I had no time.
VICT. I met him with a wild disorder'd air,
    In furious haste; he stopp'd distractedly,
180 And gaz'd upon me with a mournful look,
    But pass'd away, and spoke not. Who art thou?
    (*To the* Messenger.)
    I fear thou art a bearer of bad tidings.
MESS. No, rather good as I should deem it, madam,
    Altho' unwelcome tidings to Count Basil.
    Our army hath a glorious battle won;
    Ten thousand French are slain, their monarch captive.
VICT. (*to* Mess.) Ah there it is! he was not in the fight.
    Run after him I pray—nay, do not so—
    Run to his kinsman, good Count Rosinberg,
190 And bid him follow him—I pray thee run!
MESS. Nay, lady, by your leave, you seem not well,
    I will conduct you hence, and then I'll go.
VICT. No, no, I'm well enough, I'm very well,
    Go, hie thee hence, and do thine errand swiftly.

[EXIT Messenger.

    O! what a wretch am I! I am to blame!
    I only am to blame!
ISAB.   Nay, wherefore say so?
    What have you done that others would not do?
VICT. What have I done? I've fool'd a noble heart—
200 I've wreck'd a brave man's honour!

[EXIT, *leaning upon* Isabella.

ACT V.—SCENE I.

A dark night; no moon, but a few stars glimmering; the stage represents (as much as can be discovered for the darkness) a church-yard with part of a chapel, and a wing of the ducal palace adjoining to it. Enter BASIL, *with his hat off, his hair and his dress in disorder, stepping slowly, and stopping several times to listen, as if he was afraid of meeting any one.*

BAS. No sound is here; man is at rest, and I
    May near his habitations venture forth,
    Like some unblessed creature of the night,
    Who dares not meet his face.—Her window's dark;
    No streaming light doth from her chamber beam,
    That I once more may on her dwelling gaze,
    And bless her still. All now is dark for me!
    (*Pauses for some time, and looks upon the graves.*)
    How happy are the dead, who quietly rest
    Beneath these stones! each by his kindred laid,
    Still in a hallow'd neighbourship with those,   10
    Who when alive his social converse shar'd:
    And now, perhaps, some dear surviving friend,
    Doth here at times the grateful visit pay,
    Read with sad eyes his short memorial o'er,
    And bless his mem'ry still!—
    But I, like a vile outcast of my kind,
    In some lone spot must lay my unburied corse,
    To rot above the earth; where, if perchance
    The steps of human wand'rer e'er approach,
    He'll stand aghast, and flee the horrid place,   20
    With dark imaginations frightful made,
    The haunt of damned sprites. O! cursed wretch!
    I' the fair and honour'd field shouldst thou have died,
    Where brave friends, proudly smiling thro' their tears,
    Had pointed out the spot where Basil lay!
    (*A light seen in* VICTORIA's *window.*)
    But ha! the wonted, welcome light[1] appears.

---

1 Cf. *Romeo and Juliet* 2.2.2.

How bright within I see her chamber wall,
Athwart[1] it too, a dark'ning shadow moves,
A slender woman's form; it is herself!
30   What means that motion of its clasped hands?
That drooping head? alas! is she in sorrow?
Alas! thou sweet enchantress of the mind,
Whose voice was gladness, and whose presence bliss,
Art thou unhappy too? I've brought thee woe;
It is for me thou weep'st! Ah! were it so,
Fall'n as I am, I yet could life endure,
In some dark den from human sight conceal'd,
So, that I sometimes from my haunt might steal,
To see and love thee still. No, no, poor wretch!
40   She weeps thy shame, she weeps, and scorns thee too.
She moves again; e'en darkly imag'd thus,
How lovely is that form!
(*Pauses, still looking at the window.*)
To be so near thee, and for ever parted!
For ever lost! what art thou now to me?
Shall the departed gaze on thee again?
Shall I glide past thee in the midnight hour,
Whilst thou perceiv'st it not, and thinkst perhaps
'Tis but the mournful breeze that passes by?
(*Pauses again, and gazes at the window, till the light disappears.*)
'Tis gone, 'tis gone! these eyes have seen their last!
50   The last impression of her heavenly form!
The last sight of those walls wherein she lives,
The last blest ray of light from human dwelling!
I am no more a being of this world,
Farewell! farewell! all now is dark for me!
Come fated deed! come horrour and despair!
Here lies my dreadful way.

             Enter GEOFFRY, *from behind a tomb.*

GEOF. O! stay, my general!

---

1   From side to side.

BAS.   What art thou, from the grave?

GEOF. O! my brave gen'ral! do you know me not?
    I am old Geoffry, the old maimed soldier
    You did so nobly honour.   60

BAS. Then go thy way, for thou art honourable;
    Thou hast no shame, thou needst not seek the dark
    Like fallen, fameless men. I pray thee go!

GEOF. Nay, speak not thus, my noble general!
    Ah! speak not thus! thou'rt brave, thou'rt honour'd still.
    Thy soldier's fame is far too surely rais'd
    To be o'erthrown with one unhappy chance.
    I've heard of thy brave deeds with swelling heart,
    And yet shall live to cast my cap in air
    At glorious tales of thee—   70

BAS. Forbear, forbear! thy words but wring my soul.

GEOF. O! pardon me! I am old maimed Geoffry.
    O! do not go! I've but one hand to hold thee.
    (*Laying hold of* Basil *as he attempts to go away.* Basil *stops, and*
    looks round upon him with softness.)

BAS. Two would not hold so well, old honour'd vet'ran!
    What wouldst thou have me do?

GEOF. Return, my lord, for love of blessed heaven,
    Seek not such desp'rate ways! where would you go?

BAS. Does Geoffry ask? where should a soldier go?
    To hide disgrace? there is no place but one.
    (*Struggling to get free.*)
    Let go thy foolish hold, and force me not   80
    To do some violence to thy hoary head—
    What, wilt thou not? nay, then it must be so:
    (*Breaks violently from him, and* EXIT.)

GEOF. Curs'd, feeble hand! he's gone to seek perdition!
    I cannot run. O! curse that stupid hand,[1]
    He should have met me here! holla, Fernando!

Enter FERNANDO.

---

1 The 1806 and 1851 editions read, "Where is that stupid hind?"

We've lost him, he is gone! he's broke from me!
Did I not bid thee meet me early here,
For that he has been known to haunt this place?
FER. Which way has he gone?
90　GEOF. Towards the forest, if I guess it right;
But do thou run with speed to Rosinberg,
And he will follow him: run swiftly, man!

[EXEUNT.

SCENE II.

*A Wood, wild and savage; an entry to a cave, very much tangled with
brushwood, is seen in the background. The time represents the dawn of
morning.* BASIL *is discovered standing near the front of the stage in a
thoughtful posture, with a couple of pistols laid by him, on a piece of
projecting rock; he pauses for some time.*

BAS. (*alone.*) What shall I be a few short moments hence?
Why ask I now? who from the dead will rise
To tell me of that awful state unknown?
But be it what it may, or bliss, or torment,
Annihilation, dark and endless rest,
Or some dread thing, man's wildest range of thought
Hath never yet conceiv'd, that change I'll dare
Which makes me any thing but what I am.
I can bear scorpions' stings, tread fields of fire,
10　In frozen gulphs of cold eternal lie;
Be toss'd aloft through tracks of endless void,
But cannot live in shame—(*Pauses.*) O! impious thought!
Will the great God of mercy, mercy have
On all but those who are most miserable?
Will he not punish with a pitying hand
The poor fall'n, froward[1] child? (*Pauses.*)
And shall I then against his will offend,

1　Stubborn.

Because he is most good and merciful?
O! horrid baseness! what, what shall I do?
I'll think no more—it turns my dizzy brain—   20
It is too late to think—what must be, must be—
I cannot live, therefore I needs must die.
(*Takes up the pistols, and walks up and down, looking wildly
around him, then discovering the cave's mouth.*)
Here is an entry to some darksome cave,
Where an uncoffin'd corse may rest in peace,
And hide its foul corruption from the earth.
The threshold is unmark'd by mortal foot,
I'll do it here.
(*Enters the cave and* EXIT: *a deep silence; then the report of a
pistol is heard from the cave, and soon after, Enter* Rosinberg,
Valtomer, *two Officers and Soldiers, almost at the same moment,
by different sides of the stage.*)

ROS. This way the sound did come.

VALT. How came ye, soldiers? heard ye that report?

1ST SOL. We heard it, and it seem'd to come from hence,   30
    Which made us this way hie.

ROS. A horrid fancy darts across my mind.
    (*A groan heard from the cave.*)
    (*to* Valt.) Ha! heardst thou that?

VALT. Methinks it is the groan of one in pain.
    (*A second groan.*)

ROS. Ha! there again!

VALT. From this cave's mouth, so dark and choak'd with weeds,
    It seems to come.

ROS.   I'll enter first.

1ST OFF. My Lord, the way is tangled o'er with briers;
    Hard by, a few short paces to the left,
    There is another mouth of easier access;
    I pass'd it even now.   40

ROS.   Then shew the way.   [EXEUNT.

SCENE III.

The Inside of the Cave; BASIL *discovered lying on the ground, with his head raised a little upon a few stones and earth; the pistols lying beside him, and blood upon his breast. Enter* ROSINBERG, VAL-TOMER, *and* OFFICERS. *Rosinberg, upon seeing* Basil, *stops short with horrour, and remains motionless for some time.*

VALT. Great God of heav'n! what a sight is this?
    (Rosinberg *runs to* Basil, *and stoops down by his side.*)
ROS. O Basil! O my friend! what hast thou done?
BAS. (*Covering his face with his hand.*) Why art thou come? I
    thought to die in peace.
ROS. Thou knowst me not—I am thy Rosinberg,
    Thy dearest, truest friend, thy loving kinsman;
    Thou dost not say to me, Why art thou come?
BAS. Shame knows no kindred; I am fall'n, disgrac'd;
    My fame is gone, I cannot look upon thee.
ROS. My Basil, noble spirit! talk not thus!
10   The greatest mind untoward fate may prove:
    Thou art our gen'rous, valiant leader still,
    Fall'n as thou art—and yet thou art not fall'n;
    Who says thou art, must put his harness[1] on,
    And prove his words in blood.
BAS. Ah Rosinberg! this is no time to boast!
    I once had hopes a glorious name to gain;
    Too proud of heart, I did too much aspire;
    The hour of trial came, and found me wanting.
    Talk not of me, but let me be forgotten; —
20   And O! my friend! something upbraids me here,
    (*Laying his hand on his breast.*)
    For that I now remember, how oft-times,
    I have usurp'd it o'er thy better worth,
    Most vainly teaching where I should have learnt;
    But thou wilt pardon me—

---

1 Armour.

ROS. (*Taking* Basil's *hand, and pressing it to his breast.*)
Rend not my heart in twain! O! talk not thus!
I knew thou wert superiour to myself,
And to all men beside: thou wert my pride;
I paid thee def'rence with a willing heart.

BAS. It was delusion, all delusion, Rosinberg!
I feel my weakness now, I own my pride.   30
Give me thy hand, my time is near the close;
Do this for me; thou know'st my love, Victoria—

ROS. O! curse that woman! she it is alone,
She has undone us all!

BAS. It doubles unto me the stroke of death
To hear thee name her thus. O! curse her not!
The fault is mine; she's gentle, good and blameless.—
Thou wilt not then my dying wish fulfil?

ROS. I will! I will! what wouldst thou have me do?

BAS. See her when I am gone; be gentle with her,   40
And tell her that I bless'd her in my death,
E'en in mine agonies I lov'd and bless'd her.
Wilt thou do this?—

ROS.   I'll do what thou desir'st.

BAS. I thank thee Rosinberg; my time draws near.
(*Raising his head a little and perceiving Officers.*)
Is there not some one here? are we alone?

ROS. (*making a sign for the Officers to retire*)
'Tis but a sentry, to prevent intrusion.

BAS. Thou know'st this desp'rate deed from sacred rites[1]
Hath shut me out; I am unbless'd of men,
And what I am in sight of th' awful[2] God,
I dare not think: wilt thou, when I am gone,   50
A good man's prayers to gracious heav'n up send,
For an offending spirit?—Pray for me.
What thinkst thou? altho' an outcast here,
May not some heavenly mercy still be found?

---

1 Final prayers for the dead. Cf. "Introductory Discourse" (p. 107, above) and *Hamlet*
   5.1.241-45.
2 Inspiring reverential awe.

ROS. Thou wilt find mercy—O! my lov'd Basil—
   It cannot be that thou shouldst be rejected.
   I will with bended knee—I will implore—
   It choaks mine utt'rance—I will pray for thee—
BAS. This comforts me—thou art a loving friend.
   (*A noise without.*)
60 ROS. (*to* Off. *without.*) What noise is that?

                    Enter VALTOMER.

VALT. (*to* Ros.) My lord, the soldiers all insist to enter;
   What shall I do? they will not be denied;
   They say that they will see their noble gen'ral.
BAS. Ah, my brave fellows! do they call me so?
ROS. Then let them come.
   (*Enter soldiers, who gather round* Basil, *and look mournfully
   upon him; he holds out his hand to them with a faint smile.*)
BAS. My gen'rous soldiers, this is kindly meant.
   I'm low i'the dust; God bless you all, brave hearts!
1ST SOL. And God bless you, my noble, noble gen'ral!
   We'll never follow such a leader more.
70 2D SOL. Ah! had you staid with us, my noble gen'ral,
   We would have died for you.
   (3d Soldier *endeavours next to speak, but cannot; and kneeling
   down by* Basil, *covers his face with his cloak.* Rosinberg *turns
   his face to the wall and weeps.*)
BAS. (*In a very faint, broken voice.*)
   Where art thou?—do not leave me, Rosinberg—
   Come near to me—these fellows make me weep—
   I have no power to weep—give me thy hand—
   I love to feel thy grasp—my heart beats strangely—
   It beats as tho' its breathings would be few—
   Remember—
ROS.   Is there aught thou wouldst desire?
BAS. Nought but a little earth to cover me,
   And lay the smooth sod even with the ground—
80 Let no stone mark the spot—give no offence
   I fain would say—what can I say to thee?

(*A deep pause; after a feeble struggle,* Basil *expires.*)
1ST SOL. That motion was his last.
2D SOL.   His spirit's fled.
1ST SOL. God grant it peace! it was a noble spirit!
4TH SOL. The trumpet's sound did never rouse a braver.
1ST SOL. Alas! no trumpet e'er shall rouse him more.
      Until the dreadful blast that wakes the dead;
2D SOL. And when that sounds it will not wake a braver.
3D SOL. How pleasantly he shar'd our hardest toil;
      Our coarsest food the daintiest fare he made.
4TH SOL. Ay, many a time i'the cold damp plains has he   90
      With cheerful count'nance cried, good rest my hearts![1]
      Then wrapp'd him in his cloak, and laid him down
      E'en like the meanest soldier in the field.
      (Rosinberg *all this time continues hanging over the body, and*
      gazing upon it. Valtomer *now endeavours to draw him away.*)
VALT. This is too sad, my lord.
ROS. There, seest thou how he lies? so fix'd, so pale?
      Ah! what an end is this! thus lost! thus fall'n!
      To be thus taken in his middle course,
      Where he so nobly strove; till cursed passion
      Came like a sun-stroke on his mid-day toil,
      And cut the strong man down. O Basil! Basil!   100
VALT. Forbear, my friend, we must not sorrow here.
ROS. He was the younger brother of my soul.
VALT. Indeed, my lord, it is too sad a sight.
      Time calls us, let the body be remov'd.
ROS. He was—O! he was like no other man!
VALT. (*Still endeavouring to draw him away.*) Nay now forbear.
ROS.   I lov'd him from his birth!
VALT. Time presses, let the body be remov'd.
ROS. What sayst thou?
VALT.   Shall we not remove him hence?
ROS. He has forbid it, and has charg'd me well
      To leave his grave unknown; for that the church   110
      All sacred rites to the self-slain denies.

---

1   The 1806 and 1851 editions read, "Good rest, my hearts!"

He would not give offence.

1ST SOL. What! shall our gen'ral, like a very wretch,
Be laid unhonour'd in the common ground?
No last salute to bid his soul farewell?
No warlike honours paid? it shall not be.

2D SOL. Laid thus? no, by the blessed light of heav'n!
In the most holy spot in Mantua's walls,
He shall be laid; in face of day be laid;
And tho' black priests should curse us in the teeth,
We will fire o'er him whilst our hands have power
To grasp a musket.

SEVERAL SOLDIERS. Let those who dare forbid it.

ROS. My brave companions, be it as you will.
(*Spreading out his arms as if he would embrace the soldiers.—*
They prepare to remove the body.)

VALT. Nay, stop a while, we will not move it now,
For see a mournful visitor appears,
And must not be denied.

Enter VICTORIA *and* ISABELLA.

VICT. I thought to find him here, where has he fled?
(Rosinberg *points to the body without speaking;* Victoria
shrieks out, and falls into the arms of Isabella.)

ISAB. Ah, my sweet gentle mistress! this will kill thee.

VICT. (*recovering.*) Unloose thy hold, and let me look upon him.
O! horrid, horrid sight! my ruin'd Basil!
Is this the sad reward of all thy love?
O! I have murder'd thee!
(*Kneels down by the body, and bends over it.*)
These wasted streams of life! this bloody wound!
(*Laying her hand upon his heart.*)
Is there no breathing here? all still! all cold!
Open thine eyes, speak, be thyself again,
And I will love thee, serve thee, follow thee,
In spite of all reproach. Alas! alas!
A lifeless corse art thou for ever laid,

And dost not hear my call—   140
ROS. No, madam; now your pity comes too late.
VICT. Dost thou upbraid me? O! I have deserv'd it?
ROS. No, madam, no, I will not now upbraid;
    But woman's grief is like a summer storm,
    Short as it violent is; in gayer scenes,
    Where soon thou shalt in giddy circles blaze,
    And play the airy goddess of the day,
    Thine eye, perchance, amidst the observing crowd,
    Shall mark th' indignant face of Basil's friend,
    And then it will upbraid.   150
VICT. No, never, never? thus it shall not be.
    To the dark, shaded cloister wilt thou go,
    Where sad and lonely, thro' the dismal grate
    Thou'lt spy my wasted form, and then upbraid me.
ROS. Forgive me, heed me not; I'm griev'd at heart;
    I'm fretted, gall'd, all things are hateful to me.
    If thou didst love my friend, I will forgive thee;
    I must forgive thee; with his dying breath
    He bade me tell thee, that his latest thoughts
    Were love to thee; in death he lov'd and blessed thee.   160
    (Victoria *goes to throw herself upon the body, but is prevented by*
    Valtomer *and* Isabella, *who support her in their arms, and*
    endeavour to draw her away from it.)
VICT. Oh! force me not away! by his cold corse
    Let me lie down and weep. O! Basil, Basil!
    The gallant and the brave! how hast thou lov'd me!
    If there is any holy kindness in you
    (*To* Isab. *and* Valt.)
    Tear me not hence.
    For he lov'd me in thoughtless folly lost,
    With all my faults, most worthless of his love;
    And I'll love him in the low bed of death,
    In horrour and decay.—
    Near his lone tomb I'll spend my wretched days   170
    In humble pray'r for his departed spirit:
    Cold as his grave shall be my earthy bed,

As dark my cheerless cell. Force me not hence.
I will not go, for grief hath made me strong.
(*Struggling to get loose.*)
ROS. Do not withhold her, leave her sorrow free.
(*They let her go, and she throws herself upon the body in an
agony of grief.*)
It doth subdue the sternness of my grief
To see her mourn him thus.—Yet I must curse.—
Heav'n's curses light upon her damned father,
Whose crooked policy has wrought this wreck.
180 ISAB. If he has done it, you are well reveng'd,
For his dark plots have been detected all.
Gauriecio, for some int'rest of his own,
His master's secret dealings with the foe
Has to Lanoy[1] betray'd; who straight hath sent,
On the behalf of his imperial lord,
A message full of dreadful threats to Mantua.
His discontented subjects aid him not;
He must submit to the degrading terms
A haughty conq'ring power will now impose.
ROS. And art thou sure of this?
190 ISAB.   I am, my lord.
ROS. Give me thy hand, I'm glad on't, O! I'm glad on't!
It should be so! how like a hateful ape
Detected, grinning 'midst his pilfer'd hoard
A cunning man appears, whose secret frauds
Are open'd to the day! scorn'd, hooted, mock'd!
Scorn'd by the very fools who most admir'd
His worthless art. But when a great mind falls,
The noble nature of man's gen'rous heart
Doth bear him up against the shame of ruin;
200 With gentle censure using but his faults
As modest means to introduce his praise;

---

1   Charles de Lannoy (c. 1482-1527) was a French noblemen and trusted counsellor
of Emperor Charles V. He was appointed Viceroy of Naples in April 1522 and
commanded the forces of the anti-French coalition at the Battle of Pavia. Lannoy
personally escorted Francis I to Spain and negotiated the treaty of Madrid.

For pity like a dewy twilight comes
To close th'oppressive splendour of his day;
And they who but admir'd him in his height,
His alter'd state lament, and love him fall'n.

[EXEUNT.

END OF COUNT BASIL.

THE TRYAL

A COMEDY

PERSONS OF THE DRAMA.

MEN.

MR. WITHRINGTON.
MR. HARWOOD.
SIR LOFTUS PRETTYMAN.
MR. OPAL.
MR. ROYSTON.
HUMPHRY.
JONATHAN.
THOMAS.
SERVANTS, &c.

WOMEN.

AGNES, } *Nieces to* Withrington.
MARIANE, }
Miss ESTON.
Mrs. BETTY, *Maid to* Agnes.

★ ★ *Scene in Bath,*[1] *and in* Mr. WITHRINGTON's *house, in the*
★ *environs of Bath.*

---

1 A city in Somersetshire, England noted since the Roman occupation of England for its curative waters. After two royal visits in 1734 and 1738, Bath became an established centre of English fashion and a favourite setting for eighteenth- and early nineteenth-century writing. Sarah Siddons often acted there, and Elizabeth Inchbald's (1753-1821) *Lovers' Vows* (1798) enjoyed many appreciative audiences. Cf. Samuel Foote's (1720-77) *The Maid of Bath* (1771), Richard Brinsley Sheridan's (1751-1816) *The Rivals* (1775), Frances Burney's *Evelina* (1778), and Jane Austen's (1775-1817) *Persuasion* (1818) and her satire of the city in *Northanger Abbey* (1818).

THE TRYAL

ACT I.—SCENE I.

MR. WITHRINGTON's *house*: *Enter* WITHRINGTON *and his two Nieces hanging upon his arms, coaxing him in a playful manner as they advance towards the front of the Stage.*

WITH. Poo, poo, get along, young gipsies, and don't teaze me any more.

AG. So we will, my good sir, when you have granted our suit.

MAR. Do, dear uncle, it will be so pleasant!

WITH. Get along, get along. Don't think to wheedle me into it. It would be very pleasant, truly, to see an old fellow, with a wig upon his bald pate, making one in a holy-day mummery with a couple of mad caps.[1]

AG. Nay, don't lay the fault upon the wig, good sir, for it is as youthful, and as sly, and as saucy looking as the best head of   10 hair in the county. As for your old wig indeed, there was so much curmudgeon-like austerity about it, that young people fled from before it, as, I dare say, the birds do at present, for I am sure that it is stuck up in some cherry orchard, by this time, to frighten the sparrows.

WITH. You are mistaken, young mistress, it is up stairs in my wig-box.

AG. Well I am glad it is any where but upon your pate, uncle. (*Turning his face towards* Mariane.) Look at him, pray! is he not ten years younger since he wore it? Is there one bit of   20 an old grumbler to be seen about him now?

MAR. He is no more like the man he was than I am like my god-mother. (*Clapping his shoulder.*) You must even do as we have bid you, sir, for this excuse will never bring you off.

---

1   Maniacs; playfully applied to lively and impulsive young women.

WITH. Poo, poo, it is a foolish girl's whimsy: I'll have nothing to do with it.

AG. It is a reasonable woman's desire, gentle guardian, and you must consent to it. For if I am to marry at all, I am resolved to have a respectable man, and a man who is attached to me,[1] and to find out such a one, in my present situation, is impossible. I am provoked beyond all patience with your old greedy lords, and match-making aunts, introducing their poor noodle heirs-apparent to me, like so many dolts dressed out for a race ball.[2] Your ambitious esquires,[3] and proud obsequious baronets[4] are intolerable, and your rakish[5] younger brothers are nauseous: such creatures only surround me, whilst men of sense keep at a distance, and think me as foolish as the company I keep. One would swear I were made of amber, to attract all the dust and chaff of the community.

WITH. There is some truth in this 'faith.

AG. You see how it is with me: so my dear loving good uncle (*Coaxing him.*) do let Mariane take my place for a little while. We are newly come to Bath, no body knows us: we

---

1   Cf. S. T. Coleridge who writes: "But to possess such a power of captivating and enchanting the affections of the other sex! – to be capable of inspiring in a charming and even a virtuous woman, a love so deep, and so entirely personal to *me*! that even my worst vices (if I *were* vicious), even my cruelty and perfidy (if I *were* cruel and perfidious), could not eradicate the passion! to be so loved for my *own self*, that even with a distinct knowledge of my character, she yet died to save me! this, sir, takes hold of two sides of our nature, the better and the worse ... Love *me*, and not my qualities, may be a vicious and an insane wish, but it is not a wish wholly without a meaning" (*Biographia Literaria*, Ch. 23).

2   "Like so many dolts dressed out for a race ball" was deleted in 1806. A race ball is a dance held in conjunction with a horse-race meeting.

3   The holder of the rank directly below a knight.

4   A commoner and holder of a purchased title since their first offering by the British government in 1611.

5   Dissolute; Rake was a seventeenth-century abbreviation of the sixteenth-century term rakehell referring to one who lives a dissolute or dissipated life: a scoundrel or rascal. Even in his satirical *New Bath Guide* (1776), Christopher Anstey (1724-1805) writes, "Brother Simkin's grown a rakehell, — Cards and dances ev'ry day" (131). The rake became a recurring feature of contemporary fiction and the visual arts. Cf. Lord Rake in Sir John Vanbrugh's (1664-1726) *The Relapse, or, Virtue in Danger* (1696) and *The Provoked Wife* (1697) and William Hogarth's series of engravings *The Rake's Progress* (1735).

have been but at one ball, and as I went in plain dress, and Mariane looks so much better than me, she has already been mistaken for the heiress, and I for her portionless[1] cousin: I have told you how we shall manage it, do lend us your assistance!   50

WITH. So in the disguise of a portionless spinster, you are to captivate some man of sense, I suppose.

AG. I would fain have it so.

WITH. Go, go, thou art a fool, Agnes! who will fall in love with a little ordinary girl like thee? why there is not one feature in thy face that a man would give a farthing[2] for.

MAR. You are very saucy, uncle.

AG. I should despair of my beauty to be sure, since I am reckoned so much like you, my dear uncle; yet old nurse told me that a rich lady, a great lady, and the prettiest lady that   60 ever wore silk, fell in love, once on a time, with Mr. Anthony, and would have followed him to the world's end too, if it had not been for an old hunks[3] of a father, who deserved to be drubed for his pains. Don't you think he did, sir?

WITH. (*endeavouring to look angry.*) Old nurse is a fool, and you are an impudent hussy. I'll hear no more of this nonsense. (*Breaks from them and goes towards the door: they run after him, and draw him back again.*)

AG. Nay, good sir, we have not quite done with you yet: grant our request, and then scamper off as you please.

MAR. I'll hold both your arms till you grant it.   70

WITH. (*to Mar.*) And what makes you so eager about it, young lady? you expect, I suppose, to get a husband by the trick. O fy, fy! the poorest girl in England would blush at such a thought, who calls herself an honest one.

AG. And Mariane would reject the richest man in England who could harbour such a suspicion. But give yourself no uneasiness about this, sir, she need not go a husband-hunting, for she is already engaged.— (Mariane *looks frightened,*

---

1 Dowerless; cf. Frances Burney's *Evelina* (1778) and *Cecilia* (1782).
2 A quarter of a penny.
3 A crusty, surly old person; a "bear."

and makes signs to Agnes *over her uncle's shoulder, which she*
answers with a smile of encouragement.)

WITH. Engaged! she is very good, truly, to manage all this mat-
80   ter herself, being afraid to give me any trouble, I suppose.
And pray what fool has she picked out from the herd, to
enter into this precious engagement with!

AG. A foolish enough fellow to be sure, your favourite nephew,
cousin Edward.

WITH. Hang, the silly booby! how could he be such an ideot?
but it can't be, it shan't be,—it is folly to put myself into a
passion about it. (*To* Mariane, *who puts her hand on his shoulder to soothe him.*) Hold off your hands, ma'am. This is news
indeed to amuse me with of a morning.

90   AG. Yes, uncle, and I can tell you more news: for they are not
only engaged, but as soon as he returns from abroad they
are to be married.

WITH. Well, well, let them marry, in the devil's name, and go a
begging if they please.

AG. No, gentle guardian, they need not go a begging; they will
have a good fortune to support them.

WITH. Yes, yes, they will get a prize in the lottery,[1] or find out
the philosopher's stone,[2] and coin their old shoes into
guineas.

100   AG. No, sir, it is not that way the fortune is to come.

WITH. No; he has been following some knight-errant[3] then, I
suppose, and will have an island in the South Sea for his
pains.

AG. No, you have not guessed it yet. (*Stroaking his hand gently.*)
Did you never hear of a good, kind, rich uncle of theirs, the

---

1   *The Loterie Royal* (1776-1836) enjoyed great popularity in France because of its very
    favourable terms. In England, lotteries had existed since 1569 to raise funds for
    specific projects such as harbour repair. Though public concern led to a gradual
    prohibition throughout the eighteenth century, between 1709 and 1824 lotteries
    authorized by acts of parliament raised considerable amounts of money and award-
    ed prizes in the form of annuities. Before 1802 itinerant retailers would sell tickets
    around England over a forty-day period (*Encyclopaedia Britannica* [1911], 17:20-22).

2   Substance believed by alchemists to turn base metals into gold.

3   Don Quixote; Sancho Panza, faithful follower of his knight-errant Quixote,
    becomes a governor of a tropical island despite preferring to rule a portion of the
    sky. See Cervantes' (1547-1615) *Don Quixote* (1604) 2.42-53.

generous Mr. Withrington? he is to settle a handsome provision upon them as soon as they are married, and leave them his fortune at last.

WITH. (*lifting up his hands.*) Well, I must say thou art the impudentest little jade in the kingdom. But did you never hear that this worthy uncle of theirs, having got a new wig, which makes him ten years younger than he was, is resolved to embrace the opportunity, and seek out a wife for himself?

AG. O! that is nothing to the purpose; for what I have said about the fortune must happen, though he should seek out a score of wives.

WITH. Must happen! but I say it shall not happen. Whether should you or I know best?

AG. Why me, to be sure.

WITH. Ha, ha, ha! how so baggage?

AG. (*resting her arm on his shoulder, looking archly in his face.*) You don't know perhaps, that when I went to Scotland last summer, I travelled far, and far, as the tale says, and farther than I can tell, till I came to the Isle of Sky, where every body has the second sight,[1] and has nothing to do but tear a little hole in a tartan plaidy, and peering through it, in this manner, sees every thing past, present, and to come. Now, you must know, I gave an old woman half a crown and a roll of tobacco for a peep or two through her plaid, and what do you think I saw, uncle;

---

1 Many border ballads contain the phrasing "I have dreamed a dreary dream beyond the isle of Skye...." And many tell about the occurrence of "taisgeal" ("report, news, discovery, prognostication; finding of anything that was lost," *Dwelly's Illustrated Gaelic-English Dictionary* 928) on the Isle of Skye, the superstition of "second sight." Martin Martin (c.1660-1719), in his book *A Description of the Western Islands of Scotland* (1703), defines it as the "faculty of discerning objects invisible to other persons" and "foreseeing events and objects." Dr. Johnson was apparently inspired by this book as a child and made his historic trip to the Highlands and Islands in 1773. This interest in second sight seems to have persisted throughout Baillie's life. Margaret Carhart quotes Geraldine Macpherson, who recounted a much earlier meeting with an elderly Baillie. Baillie amused the young girl with "tales of second sight and thrilling ghost stories which she had heard from Sir Walter Scott" (64). Cf. Thomas Pennant's *A Tour in Scotland* (1790), John Aubrey's *Miscellanies* (1721), Anne Ross' *Seers and Second Sight: The Folklore of the Scottish Highlands* (1976), and Derek Cooper's *Skye* (1970).

WITH. The devil dancing a hornpipe,[1] I suppose.

AG. There was somebody dancing to be sure, but it was not the devil though. Who do you think it was now?

WITH. Poo, poo!

AG. It was uncle himself, at Mariane's wedding, leading down the first dance, with the bride. I saw a sheet of parchment in a corner too, signed with his own blessed hand, and a very handsome settlement it was. So he led down the first dance himself, and we all followed after him, as merry as so many hay-makers.

WITH. Thou hast had a sharp sight, faith!

AG. And I took a second peep through the plaidy, and what do you think I saw then, sir?

WITH. Nay, prate on as thou wilt.

AG. A genteel family house, where Edward and Mariane dwelt, and several little brats running up and down in it. Some of them so tall, and so tall, and some of them no taller than this. And there came good uncle amongst them, and they all flocked about him so merrily! every body was so glad to see him, the very scullions from the kitchen were glad; and methought he looked as well pleased himself as any of them. Don't you think he did, sir?

WITH. Have done with thy prating.

AG. I have not done yet, good sir; for I took another peep still, and then I saw a most dismal changed family indeed. There was a melancholy sick bed set out, in the best chamber, every face was sad, and all the children were weeping. There was one dark eyed rogue amongst them, called little Anthony, and he threw away his bread and butter, and roared like a young bull, for woe's me! old uncle was dying. (*Observing* Withrington *affected.*) But old uncle recovered though, and looked as stout as a veteran again. So I gave the old woman her plaidy, and would not look through any more.

WITH. Thou art the wildest little witch in the world, and wilt

---

1 A solitary dance to the accompaniment of a wind instrument, usually associated with sailors.

never be at rest till thou hast got every thing thine own way, I believe.

AG. I thank you, I thank you, dear uncle! (*leaping round his neck.*) it shall be even so, and I shall have my own little boon into the bargain. 170

WITH. I did not say so.

AG. But I know it will be so, and many thanks to you, my dear good uncle! (Mariane *ventures to come from behind,*—Withrington *looks gently to her, she holds out her hand, he hesitates, and* Agnes *joins their hands together, giving them a hearty shake.*)

WITH. Come, come, let me get away from you now: you are a couple of insinuating gipsies.

[EXIT, *hastily.*

MAR. (*embracing* Agnes.) Well, heaven bless thee, my sweet Agnes! thou hast done marvels for me. You gave me a fright though; I thought we were ruined.

AG. O! I knew I should get the better of him some way or other. What a good worthy heart he has! you don't know how dearly I love this old uncle of ours. 180

MAR. I wonder how it is. I used to think him severe and unreasonable, with his fiddle faddle fancies about delicacy and decorum; but since you came amongst us, Agnes, you have so coaxed him, and laughed at him, and played with him, that he has become almost as frolicksome as ourselves.

AG. Let us set about our project immediately. No body knows us here but Lady Fade and Miss Eston: We must let them both into the secret: Lady Fade is confined with bad health, and though Miss Eston, I believe, would rather tell a secret than hold her tongue, yet as long as there are streets and carriages, and balls and ribbons, and parlours and pantries to talk of, there can be no great danger from her. 190

MAR. O! we shall do very well. How I long to frolick it away, in all the rich trappings of heirship, amongst those sneaking wretches the fortune-hunters! They have neglected me as a poor girl, but I will play the deuce[1] amongst them as a rich one.

200 AG. You will acquit yourself very handsomely, I dare say, and find no lack of admirers.

MAR. I have two or three in my eye just now, but of all men living I have set my heart upon humbling Sir Loftus. He insulted a friend of mine last winter, to ingratiate himself with an envious woman of quality, but I will be revenged upon him, O! how I will scorn him, and toss up my nose at him! I hate him like a toad.

AG. That is not the way to be revenged upon him, silly girl! He is haughty and reserved in his manners; and though not 210 altogether without understanding, has never suffered a higher idea to get footing in his noddle than that of appearing a man of consequence and fashion, and though he has no happiness but in being admired as a fine gentleman, and no existence but at an assembly,[2] he appears there with all the haughty gravity, and careless indifference of a person superiour to such paltry amusements. Such a man as this must be laughed at, not scorned, familiarity and contempt must be his portion.

MAR. He shall have it then. And as for his admirer and imitator, 220 Jack Opal, who has for these ten years past, so successfully performed every kind of fine gentlemanship, which every new fool brought into fashion, any kind of bad treatment, I suppose, that happens to come into my head will be good enough for him.

AG. Quite good enough. You have set him down for one of your admirers too?

MAR. Yes, truly, and a great many more besides.

AG. Did you observe in the ball-room last night, a genteel young man, with a dark grey eye, and a sensible counte-230 nance, but with so little of the foppery of the fashion about

---

1 Devil.

2 The assembly is defined by Ephraim Chambers (c.1680-1740) in his *Cyclopaedia; or, An Universal Dictionary of Arts and Sciences* (1751) as "a stated and general meeting of the polite persons of both sexes, for the sake of conversation, gallantry, news, and play." Cf. John Nixon's watercolour *A Genteel Assembly* (1792) and Frances Burney's *Evelina* (1778).

him, that one took him at a distance for a much older man?

MAR. Wore he not a plain brownish coat? and stood he not very near us great part of the evening?

AG. Yes, the very same. Pray endeavour to attract him, Mariane.

MAR. If you are very desirous to see him in my train, I'll try him.

AG. No, not desirous, neither.

MAR. Then wherefore should I try?

AG. Because I would have you try every art to win him, and I would not have him to be won. 240

MAR. O! I comprehend it now! This is the sensible man we are in quest of.

AG. I shall not be sorry if it proves so. I have enquired who he is, as I shall tell you by and by, and what I have learned of him I like. Is not his appearance prepossessing, cousin Mariane?

MAR. I don't know, he is too grave and dignified for such a girl as thou art; I fear we shall waste our labour upon him.

AG. But he does not look always so. He kept very near me, if it did not look vain I should say followed me all the evening, 250 and many a varied expression his countenance assumed. But when I went away arm in arm with my uncle, in our usual good humoured way, I shall never forget the look of pleasant approbation with which he followed me. I had learnt but a little while before the mistake which the company made in regard to us, and at that moment the idea of this project came across my mind like a flash of lightning.

MAR. Very well, gentle cousin; the task you assign me is pleasing to my humour; and the idea of promoting your happiness at the same time will make it delightful. Let me see, how 260 many lovers shall I have, one, two, three. (*Counting on her fingers.*)

AG. I can tell you of one lover more than you wot[1] of.

MAR. Pray who is he?

AG. Our distant cousin the great 'squire, and man of business, from ——shire, he writes to my uncle that he will be in

---

1 Know.

Bath to-day, upon business of the greatest importance, which he explains to him in three pages of close written paper; but whether it is to court me for himself, or for his son, or to solicit a great man, who is here, for a place, no mortal on earth can discover.

MAR. Well, let him come, I shall manage them all. O! if my Edward were here just now, how he would laugh at us!

Enter SERVANT

SER. Miss Eston.

MAR. Let us run out of her way, and say we are not at home. She will sit and talk these two hours.

AG. But you forgot we have something to say to her. (*To the servant.*) Shew her up stairs to my dressing-room.

[EXIT servant.

MAR. Pray let us run up stairs before her, or she will arrest us here with her chat.

[EXEUNT.

MISS ESTON. (*without.*) And it is a very bad thing for all that; I never could abide it. I wonder your master don't stop (*Enters walking straight across the stage, still speaking*) up those nasty chinks, there is such a wind in the hall, 'tis enough to give one a hoarseness. Bye the bye Mrs. Mumblecake is sadly to-day; has your lady sent to enquire for her William? I wonder if her (*EXIT, still talking without*) old coachman has left her; I saw a new face on the, &c. &c.

SCENE II.

The fields before MR. WITHRINGTON's *house. Enter* AGNES, MARIANE, *and* Miss ESTON, *who seems still busy talking, from the house, and passing over the Stage arm in arm, Exeunt. Enter, by the same side by which they went out,* SIR LOFTUS PRETTYMAN, *and* HARWOOD, *who stands looking behind him, as if he followed something with his eyes very eagerly.*

SIR LOFT. (*Advancing to the front of the stage, and speaking to himself.*) How cursedly unlucky this is now! if she had come out but a few moments sooner, I should have passed her walking arm in arm with a British peer. How provokingly these things always happen with me; (*observing* Harwood.) What! is he staring after her too? (*aloud.*) What are you looking at, Harwood? does she walk well?

HAR. I can't tell how she walks, but I could stand and gaze after her till the sun went down upon me.

SIR LOFT. She is a fine woman, I grant you.

HAR. (*vastly pleased.*) I knew she would please, it is impossible she should not! There is something so delightful in the play of her countenance, it would even make a plain woman beautiful.

SIR LOFT. She is a fine woman, and that is no despicable praise from one who is accustomed to the elegance of fashionable beauty.

HAR. I would not compare her to any thing so trifling and insipid.

SIR LOFT. She has one advantage which fashionable beauty seldom possesses.

HAR. What do you mean?

SIR LOFT. A large fortune.

HAR. (*looking disappointed.*) Poo, it is not the heiress I mean.

SIR LOFT. Is it t'other girl you are raving about, she is showy at a distance, I admit, but as awkward as a dairy maid when near you; and her tongue goes as fast as if she were repeating a pater noster.[1]

HAR. What, do you think I am silly enough to be caught with that magpie?

SIR LOFT. Who is it then, Harwood? I see no body with Miss Withrington but Miss Eston, and the poor little creature her cousin.

---

1 The Lord's Prayer.

HAR. Good god! what a contemptible perversion of taste do interest and fashion create! But it is all affectation. (*Looking contemptuously at him.*)

SIR LOFT. (*smiling contemptuously in return.*) Ha, ha, ha! I see how it is with you, Harwood, and I beg pardon too. The lady is very charming, I dare say; upon honour I never once looked in her face. She is a dependant relation of Miss Withrington's, I believe: now I never take notice of such girls, for if you do it once they expect you to do it again. I don't choose that every little creature should say she is acquainted with Sir Loftus Prettyman; I am sparing of my attentions, that she on whom I really bestow them may have the more reason to boast.

HAR. You are right, Prettyman, she who boasts of your attentions should receive them all herself, that nobody else may know how little worth they are.

SIR LOFT. You are severe this morning, Mr. Harwood, but you do not altogether comprehend me, I believe. I know perhaps more of the polite world than a studious templar[1] can be supposed to do, and I assure you, men of fashion,[2] upon this principle, are sparing of their words too, that they may be listened to more attentively when they do speak.

HAR. You are very right still, Sir Loftus, for if they spoke much, I'll be hang'd if they would get any body to listen to them at all.

SIR LOFT. (*haughtily.*) There is another reason why men of fashion are not profuse of their words, inferior people are apt

---

1 A barrister or law student occupying chambers in the Inner or Middle Temple, two of the inns of court.

2 Until as late as the second decade of the nineteenth century, men and women of privilege dressed for display with brightly coloured, expensive fabric, wore wigs, and used excessive amounts of powder and other cosmetics as they moved through fashionable society. Before 1830, a man's concept of masculinity was different, and as Paul Johnson writes in his *The Birth of the Modern*, "this was the last period in history in which men could closely scrutinize the physical beauty of their own sex ... and women could comment on the male form without raising eyebrows" (459). The French Revolution ushered in a simpler sense of fashion. Some members of the French ruling class – "sans culottes" – adopted trousers in the 1790s to demonstrate their solidarity with the working classes, and the English aristocrats and the English notables, such as the Duke of Bedford and Charles James Fox at the

to forget themselves, and despise what is too familiar.

HAR. Don't take so much pains to make me comprehend that   60
the more fools speak the more people will despise them; I
never had a clearer conviction of it in my life.

SIR LOFT. (*haughtily*.) Good morning, sir, I see Lord Saunter in
the other walk, and I must own I prefer the company of
one who knows, at least, the common rules of politeness.

[EXIT.

HAR. (*alone*.) What a contemptible creature it is! He would prefer the most affected ideot, who boasts a little fashion or
consequence, as he calls it, to the most beautiful native
character in the world. Here comes another fool, who has
been gazing too, but I will not once mention her before   70
him.

Enter OPAL.

OP. Good morning, Harwood, I have been fortunate just now!
I have met some fine girls, 'faith!

HAR. I am glad you have met with any thing so agreeable; they
are all equally charming to you, I suppose.

OP. Nay, Harwood, I know how to distinguish. There is a little
animated creature amongst them, all life and spirit, on my
soul I could almost be in love with her.

HAR. Ha! thou hast more discernment than I reckoned upon. If
that goose, Sir Loftus, did not spoil thee, Jack, thou would'st   80
be a very good fellow after all. Why I must tell you, my
good Opal, that lady whom you admire, is the sweetest little gipsey in England.

OP. Is she indeed? I wish I had taken a better look of her face

---

Westminster election of November 1795, took to publicly sporting short hair without powder and simply styled, black clothing to identify more with the rising
wealthy middle class. See Colley Cibber's (1671-1757) Sir Novelty Fashions, hero of
his *Love's Last Shift* (1696), Sir John Vanbrugh's (1664-1726) reworking of Sir Novelty Fashions as Lord Foppington in his *The Relapse, or, Virtue in Danger* (1696), and
Richard Brinsley Sheridan's (1751-1816) *A Trip to Scarborough* (1777).

then; but she wears such a cursed plume of blue feathers
nodding over her nose, there is scarcely one half of it to be
seen.

HAR. (*staring at him with astonishment.*) As I breathe! he has fallen
in love with the magpie!

90   OP. And what is so surprising in this pray? Does not all the
world allow Miss Withrington the heiress to be a fine
woman?

HAR. That is not the heiress, Jack, (*pointing off the stage.*) the tall
lady in the middle is she. But if your Dulcinea[1] could coin
her words into farthings, she would be one of the best
matches in the kingdom.

OP. Pest take it! she was pointed out to me as Miss Withrington. Pest take my stupidity! the girl is well enough, but she
is not altogether—(*Mumbling to himself.*)

100 HAR. So you bestowed all your attention on this blue feathered
lady, and let the other two pass by unnoticed.

OP. No, not unnoticed neither: Miss Withrington is too fine a
figure to be overlooked any where, and for the other poor
little creature, who hung upon her arm so familiarly, I
could not help observing her too, because I wondered Miss
Withrington allowed such a dowdy looking thing to walk
with her in publick. Faith? Prettyman and I locked a vulgar
looking devil up in the stable the other morning, who
insisted upon going with us to the pump-room:[2] men of
110 fashion, you know, are always plagued with paltry fellows
dangling after them.

HAR. Hang your men of fashion! mere paltry fellows are too
good company for them.

OP. Damn it, Harwood! speak more respectfully of that class of
men to whom I have the honour to belong.

HAR. You mistake me, Opal, it was only the men of fashion I

---

1   Mistress of Don Quixote, Dulcinea del Toboso; Don Quixote tells Sancho Panza
    that "nothing in this life makes knights errant more valiant than the knowledge that
    they are favoured by their ladies." See *Don Quixote* Ch. 8-10.

2   A building at a spa where the medicinal water is dispensed for drinking. *The Origi-
    nal Bath Guide* of 1828 described the pumproom as "60 feet long ... In the centre
    on the south side is the pump."

abused, I am too well bred to speak uncivilly in your presence of the other class you mentioned.

OP. I scorn your insinuation, sir; but whatever class of men I belong to, I praise heaven, I have nothing of the sour plodding book-worm about me.

HAR. You do well to praise heaven for the endowments it has bestowed upon you, Opal; if all men were as thankful as you for this blessed gift of ignorance, we could not be said to live in an ungrateful generation.

OP. Talk away, laugh at your own wit as much as you please, I don't mind it. I don't trouble my head to find out bons mots[1] of a morning.

HAR. You are very right, Jack, for it would be to no purpose if you did.

OP. I speak whatever comes readiest to me: I don't study speeches for company, Harwood.

HAR. I hope so, Opal; you would have a laborious life of it indeed, if you could not speak nonsense extempore.

OP. (*Drawing himself up, and walking haughtily to the other side of the stage.*) I had no business to be so familiar with him. Sir Loftus is right; a reserved manner keeps impertinent people at a distance. (*aside—Turns about, makes a very stiff bow to* Harwood, *and* EXIT.]

HAR. (*alone.*) I am glad he is gone. What do I see! (*here* Mariane, Agnes, *and* Miss Eston *walk over the bottom of the stage, attended by* Sir LOFTUS *and* Opal, *and* EXEUNT *by the opposite side.* Har. *looking after them.*) Alas, now! that such impudent fellows should be so successful, whilst I stand gazing at a distance! how lightly she trips! does she not look about to me? by heaven I'll run to her! (*Runs to the bottom of the stage, and stops short.*) Oh no! I cannot do it! but see, her uncle comes this way. He look'd so kindly at her, I could not help loving him; he must be a good man, I'll make up to him, and he perhaps will join the ladies afterwards.

[EXIT.

---

1 Witticisms.

ACT. II—SCENE I.

A Lodging-house. Enter ROYSTON *and* HUMPHRY, *followed by*
JONATHAN, *carrying a portmanteau.*

ROY. What a world of business I have got upon my hands! I
    must set about it immediately. Come here Jonathan; I shall
    send you out in the first place.

JON. Well, sir.

ROY. Take the black trunk, that is left in the hall, upon your
    shoulder, Jonathan, and be sure you don't run against any
    body with it, for that might bring us into trouble. And per-
    haps as you go along, you may chance to meet with some
    of the Duke of Bigwell's servants, or with some body who
    can tell you where his Grace lodges in this town, and you
    may enquire of them, without saying I desired you: you
    understand me, Jonathan?

JON. O yes, your honour!

ROY. But first of all, however, if you see any decent hair-dresser's
    shop in your way, desire them to send some body here for
    my wig; and like enough they may tell you, at the same
    time, where there is an honest Town cryer to be had; I'll
    have Phebe's black whelp cry'd directly; and hark ye,
    Jonathan, you may say as though the dog were your own,
    you understand, they will expect such a devil of a reward
    else; and pri'thee man! step into the corn market,[1] if thou
    can'st find out the way, and enquire the price of oats.

JON. Yes, please your honour, but am I to go trudging about
    to all these places with that great heavy trunk upon my
    shoulder?

ROY. No! numskull! did I not bid you carry it to the Inn, where
    the London stage puts up? by the bye you had better take it
    to the waggon—but first ask the coachman, what he
    charges for the carriage: you can take it to the waggon
    afterwards. I will suffer no man to impose upon me; you

---

1 Grain exchange.

will remember all this distinctly now, as I have told it you Jonathan?

JON. (*counting to himself upon his fingers.*) O yes, your honour! I'll manage it all I warrant!

EXIT.

ROY. What a world of business I have upon my hands, Humphry, I am as busy as a minister of state.

Re-enter JONATHAN, *scratching his head.*

JON. La your honour! I have forgot all about his Grace, and the black whelp.

ROY. Damn your muddle pate; did not I bid you enquire where his Grace lives, and if you happen to see— 40

JON. Ods bodickins![1] I remember it every word now! and the whelp is to be call'd by the Town cryer, just as one would call any thing that is lost.

ROY. Yes yes, go about it speedily (*Exit* JON.) Now in the first place, my good Humphry, I must see after the heiress I told you of, and it is a business, which requires a great deal of management too; for—

Re-enter JONATHAN, *scratching his head.*

Damn that dunder-headed fool! here he is again.

JON. Your honour wont be angry now, but hang me, if I can tell whether I am to take that there trunk, to the coach, or the 50 waggon.

ROY. Take it to the coach—no, no, to the waggon—yes, yes, I should have said—pest take it! carry it where thou wilt, fool, and plague me no more about it. (*Exit* JON.) One might as well give directions to a horse-block. Now, as I was saying, Humphry, this requires a great deal of manage-

---

1 An oath; literally "God's dear body!"

ment; for if the lady don't like me, she may happen to like my son: so I must feel my way a little, before I speak directly to the purpose.

60 HUMPH. Ay, your honour is always feeling your way.

ROY. And as for the Duke, I will ply him as close as I can with solicitations in the mean time, without altogether stating my request; for if I get the lady, George shall have the office, and if he gets the lady, I shall have the office. So we shall have two chances in our favour both ways, my good Humphry.

HUMPH. Belike, sir, if we were to take but one business in hand at a time, we might come better off at the long run.

ROY. O! thou hast no head for business, Humphry: thou hast no
70 genius for business, my good Humphry. (*smiling conceitedly.*)

HUMPH. Why, for certain your honour has a marvellous deal of wit, but I don't know how it is, nothing that we take in hand ever comes to any good; and what provokes me, more than all the rest, is, that the more pains we take about it, the worse it always succeeds.

ROY. Humph, we can't guard against every cross accident.

HUMPH. To be sure sir, cross accidents will happen to every body, but certes! we have more than our own share of them.

80 ROY. Well, don't trouble yourself about it: I have head enough to manage my own affairs, and more than my own too. Why, my lord Slumber can't even grant a new lease, nor imprison a vagabond for poaching, without my advice and direction: did I not manage all Mr. Harebrain's election for him; and, but for one of those cursed accidents or two, had brought him in for his Borough,[1] as neatly as my glove; nay, if his Grace and I get into good understanding together, there is no knowing, but I may have affairs of the nation upon my hands; ha, ha, ha! poor Humphry, thou hast no
90 comprehension of all this: thou think'st me a very wonderful man, dost thou not?

HUMPH. I must own I do sometimes marvel at your honour.

---

1 A constituency which sends elected representatives to Parliament.

Enter Mr. WITHRINGTON.

ROY. Ha! how do you do, my dear cousin! I hope I have the happiness of seeing you in good health; I am heartily rejoiced to see you, my very good sir. (*Shaking him heartily by the hand.*)

WITH. I thank you, sir, you are welcome to Bath, I did not expect the pleasure of seeing you here.

ROY. Why, my dear worthy sir, I am a man of so much business, so toss'd about, so harass'd with a multiplicity of affairs, that I protest, I can't tell myself one day, what part of the world I shall be in the next.   100

WITH. You give yourself a great deal of trouble, Mr. Royston.

ROY. O! hang it! I never spare myself: I must work, to make others work, cousin Withrington; I have got a world of new alterations going on at Royston-hall; if you would take a trip down to see them.

WITH. I am no great traveller, sir.

ROY. I have plough'd up the bowling-green, and cut down the elm-trees; I have built new stables, and fill'd up the horse pond; I have dug up the orchard, and pull'd down the old   110 fruit wall, where that odd little temple used to stand.

WITH. And is the little temple pull'd down too? pray, what has become of your Vicar's sister, Mrs. Mary? we drunk tea with her there, I remember, is she married yet? she was a very modest looking gentlewoman.

ROY. So you remember her too; well I have pull'd down every foot of it, and built a new cart-house with the bricks.—Good commodious stalls for thirty horses, cousin Withrington, they beat Sir John Houndly's all to nothing; it is as clever, a well constructed building as any in the country.   120

WITH. Has Sir John built a new house in the country?

ROY. No, no, the stables I say.

WITH. O you are talking of the stables again.

ROY. But when I get the new addition to the mansion-house finish'd, that will be the grand improvement; the best carpenters' work in the country, my dear sir, all well season'd timber from Norway.

HUMPH. It is part of a disputed wreck, sir, and if the law suit
about the right to it turns out in my master's favour, as it
130   should do, it will be the cheapest built house in the county;
O! let his honour alone for making a bargain.

WITH. So you have got a law suit on your hands, Mr. Royston?
I hope you are not much addicted to this kind of amusement, you will find it a very expensive one.

ROY. Bless you, my good sir, I am the most peaceable creature in
the world, but I will suffer no man to impose upon me.

WITH. (*smiling*.) But you suffer the women sometimes to do so,
do you not?

HUMPH. No, nor the women neither,[1] sir; for it was but t'other
140   day that he prosecuted widow Gibson, for letting her
chickens feed amongst his corn, and it was given in his
honour's favour, as in right it should have been.

WITH. (*archly*.) And who was adjudged to pay the expences of
court, Mr. Humphry?

HUMPH. Ay, to be sure, his honour was obliged to pay that.

WITH. (*archly*.) But the widow paid swingingly[2] for it, I suppose.

HUMPH. Nay 'faith, after all, they but fined her in a sixpence; yet
that always shew'd, you know, that she was in the wrong.

WITH. To be sure, Mr. Humphry, and the sixpence would
150   indemnify your master for the costs of the suit.

HUMPH. Nay, as a body may say, he might as well have let her
alone, for any great matter he made of it that way; but it
was very wrong in her, you know, sir, to let her hens go
amongst his honour's corn, when she knew very well, she
was too poor to make up the loss to his honour.

WITH. Say no more about it, my good Humphry, you have vin-
dicated your master most ably, and I have no doubts at all in
regard to the propriety of his conduct.

HUMPH. (*very well pleased*.) Ay, thank god, I do sometimes make
160   shift in my poor way to edge in a word for his honour.

ROY. (*not so well pleased*.) Thou art strangely given to prating
this morning. (*to* Humph.) By the bye, cousin Withrington, I must consult you about my application to his Grace.

---

1   Cf. *Hamlet* 2.2.305-06.
2   Immensely; a variant of "swinglingly."

HUMPH. (*aside to* Withrington, *pulling him by the sleeve.*) You forget to ask for the lady, sir.

WITH. (*turning round.*) What did you say of his Grace?

ROY. No, no, I should—I meant—did I not say the gracious
young lady your niece; I hope she is well?

WITH. (*smiling.*) She is very well; you shall go home with me,
and visit her.   170

ROY. I am infinitely obliged to you, my worthy good sir, I shall
attend you with the greatest pleasure; some ladies have no
dislike to a good looking gentleman-like man, although he
may be past the bloom of his youth, cousin? however
young men do oftener carry the day, I believe, my son
George is a good likely fellow, I expect him in Bath every
hour, I shall have the honour of following you, my dear sir.
Remember my orders Humphry.

[EXEUNT.

Enter HARWOOD *hastily, looking round as if he sought some one,
and was disappointed.*

HAR. (*alone.*) He is gone, I have miss'd the good uncle of
Agnes—what is the matter with me now, that the sound of   180
an old man's voice should agitate me thus? did I not feel it
was the sound of something which belong'd to her? in
faith! I believe, if her kitten was to mew, I should hasten to
hold some intercourse with it.—I can stay in this cursed
house no longer, and when I do go out, there is but one
way these legs of mine will carry me, the alley which leads
to her dwelling—Well, well, I have been but six times there
to-day already; I may have a chance of seeing her at last—
I'll run after the old gentleman even now—what a delight-
ful witch it is!   190

[EXIT *hastily.*

SCENE II.

WITHRINGTON's *house.* AGNES *and* MARIANE, *discovered,* Mariane *reading a letter, and* Agnes *looking earnestly and gladly in her face.*

AG. My friend Edward is well, I see; pray what does the traveller say for himself?

MAR. (*putting up the letter.*) You shall read it all by and by, every thing that is pleasant and kind.

AG. Heaven prosper you both! you are happier than I am with all my fortune, Mariane, you have a right true lover.

MAR. And so have you, Agnes, my Harwood will bear the trial: I have watch'd him closely, and I will venture my word upon him.

10 AG. (*taking her in her arms.*) Now if thou art not deceiv'd, thou art the dearest sweet cousin on earth! (*Pausing and looking seriously.*) Ah no! it cannot be! I am but an ordinary looking girl, as my uncle says; (*with vivacity;*) I would it were so!

Enter SERVANT.

SER. Sir Loftus Prettyman and Mr. Opal.

MAR. I am at home. (*Exit* SERVANT.) I can't entertain these fools till I have put up my letter: do you receive them, I will soon return   [EXIT.

Enter SIR LOFTUS *and* OPAL *dress'd pretty much alike.* SIR LOFTUS *makes a haughty distant bow to* AGNES, *and* OPAL *makes another very like it.*

AG. Have the goodness to be seated, sir. (*to* Sir Loftus.) Pray, sir, (*to* Opal, *making a courteous motion as if she wish'd them to sit down.*) Miss Withrington will be here immediately. (Sir Loftus *makes a slight bow without speaking;* Opal *does the same, and both saunter about with their hats in their hands.*)

20 AG. I hope you had a pleasant walk after we left you, Sir Loftus?

SIR LOFT. (*Looking affectedly, as if he did not understand her.*) I beg
pardon—O! you were along with Miss Withrington.
(*Mumbling something which is not heard.*)
AG. (*to* Op.) You are fond of that walk, Mr. Opal, I think I have
seen you there frequently.
OP. Ma'am you are very—(*mumbling something which is not heard,
in the same manner with* Sir Loftus, *but still more absurd.*) I do
sometimes walk—(*mumbling again.*)
AG. (*to* Sir Loft.) The country is delightful round Bath.
SIR LOFT. Ma'am!
AG. Don't you think so, Mr. Opal?
OP. 'Pon honour I never attended to it. (*A long pause;* Sir Loftus   30
and Opal *strut about conceitedly. Enter* Mariane, *and both of
them run up to her at once, with great alacrity and satisfaction.*)
SIR LOFT. I hope I see Miss Withrington entirely recovered
from the fatigues of the morning?
MAR. Pretty well, after the fatigue of dressing too, which is a
great deal worse, Sir Loftus. (*carelessly.*)
OP. For the ball, I presume?
SIR LOFT. I am delighted—
MAR. (*addressing herself to* Agnes, *without attending to him.*) Do
you know what a provoking mistake my milliner has
made?
AG. I don't know.   40
SIR LOFT. I hope madam—
MAR. (*to* Ag.) She has made up my whole suit of trimmings
with the colour of all others I dislike.
OP. This is very provoking, indeed I would—
MAR. (*Still speaking to* Ag. *without attending to them.*) And she has
sent home my petticoat all patch'd over with scraps of gold
foil, like a May-day dress for a chimney-sweeper.
SIR LOFT. (*Thrusting in his face near* Mariane, *and endeavouring to
be attended to.*) A very good comparison, ha, ha!
OP. (*Thrusting in his face at the other side of her.*) Very good
indeed, ha, ha, ha!   50
MAR. (*Still speaking to* Agnes, *who winks at her without attending to
them.*) I'll say nothing about it but never employ her again.
SIR LOFT. (*going round to her other ear, and making another attempt.*)

I am delighted, Miss Withrington.

MAR. (*carelessly.*) Are you, Sir Loftus? (*To* Agnes.) I have broken my fan, pray put it by with your own, my dear Agnes! (*Exit* Agnes *into the adjoining room, and* Sir Loftus *gives* Opal *a significant look, upon which he retires to the bottom of the stage, and, after sauntering a little there,* EXIT.)

SIR LOFT. (*seeming a little piqued.*) If you would have done me the honour to hear me, Ma'am, I should have said, I am delighted to see you dress'd, as I hope I may presume from it, you intend going to the ball to-night.

60 MAR. Indeed I am too capricious to know whether I do or not; do you think it will be pleasant?

SIR LOFT. Very pleasant, if the devotions of a thousand admirers can make it so.

MAR. O! the devotions of a thousand admirers, are like the good will of every body, one steady friendship is worth it all.

SIR LOFT. From which may I infer that one faithful adorer, in your eyes, outvalues all the thousand? (*Affecting to be tender.*) Ah! so would I have Miss Withrington to believe! and if that can be any inducement, she will find such a one there, most happy to attend her.

70 MAR. Will she? I wonder who this may be: what kind of man is he pray?

SIR LOFT. (*With a conceited simper, at the same time in a pompous manner.*) Perhaps it will not be boasting too much to say, he is a man of fashion, and of some little consequence in the world.

MAR. Handsome and accomplish'd too, Sir Loftus?

SIR LOFT. I must not presume, ma'am, to boast of my accomplishments.

MAR. (*Affecting a look of disappointment.*) O! lud![1] so it is yourself after all! I have not so much penetration as I thought.
80 (*Yawning twice very wide.*) Bless me! what makes me yawn so? I forgot to visit my old woman, who sells the cakes, this morning; that must be it. (*Yawning again.*) Do you love gingerbread, Sir Loftus? (Sir Loftus *bites his lip, and struts*

---

1   A rushed exclamation of "Lord!"

proudly away to the other side of the stage, whilst Agnes *peeps from the closet,*[1] *and makes signs of encouragement to* Mariane.)

MAR. Well, after all, I believe, it will be pleasant enough to go to the ball, with such an accomplish'd attendant.

SIR LOFT. (*Taking encouragement, and smothering his pride.*) Are you so obliging, Miss Withrington? will you permit me to have the happiness of attending you?

MAR. If you'll promise to make it very agreeable to me; you are fond of dancing, I suppose?   90

SIR LOFT. I'll do any thing you desire me, but why throw away time so precious in the rough familiar exercise of dancing? is there not something more distinguished, more refined, in enjoying the conversation of those we love?

MAR. In the middle of a crowd, Sir Loftus?

SIR LOFT. What is that crowd to us? we have nothing to do but to despise it, whilst they stare upon us with vulgar admiration, we shall talk together, smile together, attend only to each other, like beings of a superiour order.

MAR. O! that will be delightful! but don't you think we may   100
just peep slyly over our shoulder now and then, to see whether they are admiring us? (Sir Loftus *bites his lips again, and struts to the bottom of the stage, whilst* Agnes *peeps out again from the closet, and makes signs to* Mariane.)

MAR. (*Carelessly pulling a small case from her pocket.*) Are not these handsome brilliants, Sir Loftus?

SIR LOFT. (*Very much struck with the sparkling of the diamonds, but pretending not to look at them.*) Upon my word, ma'am, I am no judge of trinkets.

MAR. They are clumsily set, I shall give them to my cousin.

SIR LOFT. (*Forgetting himself.*) Why, ma'am, do you seriously mean—They are of a most incomparable water.[2]

MAR. (*archly.*) I thought you had not attended to them.   110

SIR LOFT. (*tenderly.*) It is impossible in the presence of Miss Withrington, to think of any thing but the cruelty with which she imposes silence on a heart which adores her.

---

1   A small room or private chamber.
2   A standard of transparency for diamonds; *first, second*, and *third* water being the three highest grades.

MAR. Nay, you entirely mistake me, Sir Loftus, I am ready to hear you with the greatest good nature imaginable.

SIR LOFT. It is a theme, perhaps, on which my tongue would too long dwell.

MAR. O! not at all, I have leisure, and a great deal of patience at present, I beg you would by no means hurry yourself.

SIR LOFT. (*After a pause, looking foolish and embarrassed.*) Few
120   words, perhaps, will better suit the energy of passion.

MAR. Just as you please, Sir Loftus, if you chuse to say it in few words I am very well satisfied. (*Another pause. Sir Loftus very much embarrassed.*)

Enter WITHRINGTON *and* HARWOOD, *and* Sir Loftus *seems very much relieved.*

SIR LOFT. (*aside.*) Heaven be praised! they are come.

MAR. (*to* With.) I thought you were to have brought Mr. Royston with you.

WITH. He left us at a shop by the way, to enquire the price of turnip seed; but he will be here by-and-by, if a hundred other things do not prevent him. (*Bows to* Sir Loftus; *then turns to* Harwood, *and speaks as if he resumed a conversation which had just been broken off, whilst* Sir Loftus *and* Mariane *retire to the bottom of the stage.*) I perfectly agree with you,
130   Mr. Harwood, that the study and preparation requisite for your profession is not altogether a dry treasuring up of facts in the memory, as many of your young students conceive: he who pleads the cause of man before fellow-men, must know what is in the heart of man as well as what is in the book of records, and what study is there in nature so noble, so interesting as this?

HAR. But the most pleasing part of our task, my good sir, is not the least difficult. Where application only is wanting I shall not be left behind, for I am not without ambition, though
140   the younger son of a family by no means affluent; and I have a widow mother whose hopes of seeing me respectable, must not be disappointed. I assure you there is nothing—(*Listening.*)

WITH. Go on, Mr. Harwood, I have great pleasure in hearing you.

HAR. I thought I heard a door move.

WITH. It is Agnes in the next room, I dare say, she is always making a noise.

HAR. In the next room!

WITH. But you was going to assure me—Have the goodness to proceed. 150

HAR. I was going to say—I rather think I said—I am sure— (*Listening again.*)

WITH. Poo! there is no body there.

HAR. Well, I said—I think I told you—In faith, my good sir, I will tell you honestly, I have forgot what I meant to say.

WITH. No matter, you will remember it again. Ha, ha, ha! it puts me in mind of a little accident which happened to myself when I was in Lincoln's Inn. Two or three of us met one evening, to be a little cheerful together, and—(*Whilst* Withrington *begins his story,* Agnes *enters softly from the adjoining closet unperceived; but* Harwood *on seeing her, runs eagerly up to her, leaving* Withrington *astonished, in the middle of his discourse.*)

HAR. (*to* Ag.) Ha! after so many false alarms, you steal upon us at last like a little thief. 160

AG. And I steal something very good from you too, if you lose my uncle's story by this interruption; for I know by his face he was telling one.

WITH. Raillery is not always well-timed, Miss Agnes Withrington.

AG. Nay, do not be cross with us, sir. Mr. Harwood knew it was too good to be spent upon one pair of ears, so he calls in another to partake.

WITH. Get along, baggage. 170

AG. So I will, uncle; for I know that only means with you that I should perk myself up by your elbow.

WITH. Well, two or three of us young fellows were met—did I not say—

AG. At Lincoln's Inn. (Withrington *hesitates.*)

HAR. She has named it, sir.

WITH. I know well enough it was there. And if I remember well, George Buckner was one of us. (Agnes *gives a gentle hem to suppress a cough.*)

HAR. (*eagerly.*) You was going to speak, Miss Withrington?

180 AG. No, indeed, I was not.

WITH. Well, George Buckner and two three more of us—We were in a very pleasant humour that night—(Agnes *making a slight motion of her hand to fasten some pin in her dress.*)

HAR. (*eagerly.*) Do you not want something? (*To* Agnes.)

AG. No, I thank you, I want nothing.

WITH. (*Half amused, half peevish.*) Nay, say what you please to one another, for my story is ended.

HAR. My dear sir, we are perfectly attentive.

AG. Now, pray, uncle!

WITH. (*to* Ag.) Now pray hold thy tongue. I forgot, I must con-
190 sult the Court Calendar[1] on Royston's account. (*Goes to a table and takes up a red book, which he turns over.*)

AG. (*to* Har.) How could you do so to my uncle? I would not have interrupted him for the world.

HAR. Ay, chide me well: I dearly love to be chidden.

AG. Do not invite me to it. I am said to have a very good gift that way, and you would soon have too much of it, I believe.

HAR. O no! I would come every hour to be chidden!

AG. And take it meekly too?

HAR. Nay, I would have my revenge: I should call you scolding
200 Agnes, and little Agnes, and my little Agnes.

AG. You forget my dignity, Mr Harwood.

HAR. Oh! you put all dignity out of countenance! The great Mogul[2] himself would forget his own in your presence.

AG. Am I, as the good folks say, such a very humbling sight? But they are going to the garden: I am resolved to be one of the party. (*As she goes to join* Sir Loftus *and* Mariane, *who open a glass door leading to the garden,* Harwood *goes before, walking*

---

1 Court-almanac; an annual handbook of royal courts and their families.

2 Perhaps Kublai Khan (1216-94), founder of the Mongol dynasty. Cf. Coleridge's interest in this warrior and patron of the arts in his poem "Kubla Khan."

backwards, and his face turned to her.) You will break your pate presently, if you walk with that retrograde step, like a dancing-master giving me a lesson. Do you think I shall follow you as if you had the fiddle in your hand? 210

HAR. Ah, Miss Withrington! it is you who have got the fiddle, and I who must follow.

[EXEUNT *into the garden.*

Re-enter Sir LOFTUS *from the Garden, looking about for his hat.*

SIR LOFT. O! here it is.

Enter OPAL.

OP. What, here alone?

SIR LOFT. She is in the garden, I shall join her immediately.

OP. All goes on well, I suppose?

SIR LOFT. Why, I don't know how it is—nobody hears us? (*Looking round.*) I don't know how it is, but she does not seem to comprehend perfectly in what light I am regarded by the world; that is to say, by that part of it which deserves 220 to be called so.

OP. No! that is strange enough.

SIR LOFT. Upon my honour, she treats me with as much careless familiarity as if I were some plain neighbour's son in the country.

OP. 'Pon honour, this is very strange.

SIR LOFT. I am not without hopes of succeeding; but I will confess to you, I wish she would change her manner of behaving to me. On the word of a gentleman, it is shocking! Suppose you were to give her a hint of the consequence I 230 am honoured with in the fashionable circles, that she may just have an idea of the respect which is paid by every well-bred person—You understand me, Opal?

OP. O! perfectly. I shall give her to know that men like us, my dear friend, are accustomed to be looked upon as a class of superiour beings.

SIR LOFT. (*not quite satisfied.*) I don't know—Suppose you were to leave out all mention of yourself—Your own merit could not fail to be inferred.

240 OP. Well, I shall do so.

SIR LOFT. Let us go to the garden.

[EXEUNT.

Enter Miss ESTON, *speaking as she enters.*

EST. I have been all over the town, and here am I at last quite tired to death. How do you?—(*Looking round.*) O la! there is nobody here. Mr. Opal is gone too. I'll wait till their return. (*Takes up a book, then looks at herself in the glass, then takes up the book again. Yawning.*) 'Tis all about the imagination, and the understanding,[1] and I don't know what— I dare say it is good enough to read of a Sunday. (*Yawns, and lays it down.*) O la! I wish they would come.

Enter ROYSTON, *and takes* Miss ESTON *for* Miss WITHRINGTON.

250 ROY. Madam, I have the honour to be your very humble servant. I hoped to have been here sooner, but I have been so overwhelmed with a multiplicity of affairs; and you know, madam, when that is the case—

EST. (*Taking the word out of his mouth.*) One is never master of one's time for a moment. I'm sure I have been all over the town this morning, looking after a hundred things; till my head has been put into such a confusion! La, ma'am! said my millener, do take some lavender drops, you look so pale. Why, says I, I don't much like to take them, Mrs. Trollop,

260 they a'nt always good.

ROY. No more they are, ma'am, you are very right; and if a silly fellow, I know, had taken my advice last year, and bought

---

1 Obviously, Miss Eston is making slow progress through a work of moral philosophy. See introduction.

up the lavender drops, he would have made—

EST. (*Taking the word from him again.*) A very good fortune, I dare say. But people never will take advice, which is very foolish in them, to be sure. Now I always take—

ROY. Be so good as to hear me, ma'am.

EST. Certainly, sir; For I always say if they give me advice it is for my good, and why should not I take it?

ROY. (*Edging in his word as fast as he can.*) And the damn'd foolish   270
fellow too! I once saved him from being cheated in a horse; and—

EST. La! there are such cheats! a friend of mine bought a little lap-dog the other day—

ROY. But the horse, madam, was—

EST. Not worth a guinea, I dare say. Why they had the impudence to palm it on my friend.

Both speaking together.

EST. As a pretty little dog, which had been bred

ROY. It was a good mettled horse, and might

E. up for a lady of quality, and when she had   280

R. have passed as a good purchase at the money,

E. just made a cushion for it at the foot of her

R. but on looking his fore feet—(*Stops short, and lets her go on.*) own bed, she found it was all over mangy. I'm sure I would rather have a plain wholesome cat, than the prettiest mangy dog in the kingdom.

ROY. Certainly, ma'am. And I assure you the horse—for says I to the groom—

Both speaking together.

EST. O! I dare say it was—and who would

ROY. What is the matter with this pastern,[1]   290

E. have suspected that a dog bred up on pur-

R. Thomas? it looks as if it were rubbed—(*Stops short again, and looks at her with astonishment as she goes on talking.*)

E. pose for a lady of quality, should be all over so? nasty creature! It had spots upon its back as large as my watch. (*Tak-*

---

1 A horse's ankle; Samuel Johnson gave this word its own historical notoriety by defining it incorrectly as the knee of the horse in his dictionary.

ing up her watch.) O la! I am half an hour after my time. My mantua-maker[1] is waiting for me. Good morning, sir.

[EXIT, *hastily.*

ROY. (*Looking after her.*) Clack, clack, clack, clack! What a devil of a tongue she has got! 'Faith! George shall have her, and I'll e'en ask the place for myself. (*Looking out.*) But there is company in the garden! I'll go and join them.

[EXIT *to the garden.*

---

1 Dress-maker; "Mantua" is a corruption of "manteau," a loose gown named for the origin of a type of silk worn by women in the seventeenth and eighteenth centuries.

ACT III.—SCENE I.

Mr. WITHRINGTON's *house. A loud laughing without. Enter* ROYSTON, *in a great rage.*

ROY. Ay, ay, laugh away, laugh away, madam, you'll weep by-and-by, mayhap. (*Pauses and listens, laughing still heard.*) What an infernal noise the jade[1] makes. I wish she had a peck of chaff in her mouth, I am sure it is wide enough to hold it.

Enter HUMPHRY.

HUMPH. I have been seeking your honour every where—Lord, sir! I have something to tell you.
ROY. Confound your tales! don't trouble me with a parcel of nonsense.
HUMPH. (*Staring at him, and hearing the laughing without.*) For certain, your honour, there's somebody in this house merrier than you or I. 10
ROY. Damn you, sir! how do you know I am not merry? Go home, and do what I ordered you directly. If that fellow Jonathan is not in the way, I'll horse-whip him within an inch of his life. Begone, I say, why do you stand staring at me, like a madman?

[EXEUNT.

Enter MARIANE *and* AGNES, *by opposite sides.*

MAR. (*holding her sides.*) Oh how my poor sides ach! I shan't be able to laugh again for a month.
AG. You have got rid of one lover who will scarcely attempt you a second time. I have met him hurrying through the hall, and muttering to himself like a madman. It is not your refusal of his son that has so roused him. 20

---

1 A contemptuous name for a horse; occasionally employed in rude references to women.

MAR. No, no, he began his courtship in a doubtful way, as if he would recommend a gay young husband to my choice, but a sly compliment to agreeable men of a middle age, brought him soon to speak plainly for himself.

AG. But how did you provoke him so?

MAR. I will tell you another time. It is later than I thought. (*Looking at her watch.*)

30 AG. Don't go yet. How stands it with you and a certain gentleman I recommended to your notice?

MAR. O! he does not know whether I am tall or short, brown or fair, foolish or sensible, after all the pains I have taken with him: he has eyes, ears, and understanding, for nobody but you, Agnes, and I will attempt him no more. He spoke to me once with animation in his countenance, and I turned round to listen to him eagerly, but it was only to repeat to me something you had just said, which, to deal plainly with you, had not much wit in it neither. I don't

40 know how it is, he seemed to me at first a pleasanter man than he proves to be.

AG. Oh! say not so, Mariane! he proves to be most admirable!

MAR. Well, be it so, he cannot prove better than I wish him to do, and I can make up my list without him. I have a love letter from an Irish baronet in my pocket, and Opal will declare himself presently.—I thought once he meant only to plead for his friend, but I would not let him off so, for I know he is a mercenary creature. I have flattered him a little at the expence of Sir Loftus, and I hope ere long to see

50 him set up for a great man upon his own bottom.

AG. So it was only to repeat to you something that I had been saying?

MAR. Ha! you are thinking of this still, I believe indeed he sets down every turn of your eye in his memory, and acts it all over in secret.

AG. Do you think so? give me your hand, my dear Mariane, you are a very good cousin to me—Marks every turn of mine eye! I am not quite such an ordinary girl as my uncle says—My complexion is as good as your own, Mariane, if it

were not a little sun-burnt. (Mariane *smiles*.) Yes, smile at 60
my vanity as you please, for what makes me vain, makes me
so good humoured too, that I will forgive you. But here
comes uncle. (*Skipping as she goes to meet him*.) O! I am light
as an air-ball! (*Enter* Mr Withrington.) My dear sir, how
long you have been away from us this morning! I am
delighted to see you so pleased and so happy.

WITH. (*with a very sour face*.) You are mistaken, young lady, I am
not so pleased as you think.

AG. O no, sir! you are very good humoured. Isn't he, Mariane?

WITH. But I say I am in very bad humour. Get along with your 70
foolery!

AG. Is it really so? Let me look in your face, uncle? To be sure
your brows are a little knit, and your eyes a little gloomy,
but poo! that is nothing to be called bad humour; if I could
not contrive to look crabbeder than all this comes to, I
would never pretend to be ill humoured in my life. (Mariane *and* Agnes *take him by the hands and begin to play with
him*.)

WITH. No, no, young ladies, I am not in a mood to be played
with. I can't approve of every farce you please to play off in
my family, nor to have my relations affronted, and driven
from my house for your entertainment. 80

MAR. Indeed, sir, I treated Royston better than he deserved, for
he would not let me have time to give a civil denial, but
ran on planning settlements and jointures, and a hundred
things besides; I could just get in my word to stop his
career with a flat refusal, as he was about to provide for our
descendants of the third generation. O! if you had seen his
face then, uncle!

WITH. I know very well how you have treated him.

AG. Don't be angry, sir. What does a man like Royston care for
a refusal? he is only angry that he can't take the law of her 90
for laughing at him.

WITH. Let this be as it may, I don't chuse to have my house in a
perpetual bustle from morning till night, with your plots
and your pastimes. There is no more order nor distinction

kept up in my house, than if it were a cabin in Kamschat-ka,[1] and common to a whole tribe. I can't set my nose into a room of it but I find some visitor, or showman,[2] or mil-lener's apprentice, loitering about: my best books are cast upon footstools and window-seats, and my library is lit-tered over with work-bags: dogs, cats, and kittens, take pos-session of every chair, and refuse to be disturbed: kitchen wenches flaunt up stairs with their new top-knots on, to look at themselves in the pier glasses; and the very beggar children go hopping about my hall, with their half-eaten scraps in their hands, as though it were the entry to a work-house.

AG. (*Clapping his shoulder gently.*) Now don't be impatient, my dear sir, and every thing shall be put into such excellent order as shall delight you to behold. And as for the beggar children, if any of them dare but to set their noses within the door, I'll—What shall I do with them, sir? (*Pauses and looks in his face, which begins to relent.*) I believe we must e'en give them a little pudding after all. (*Both take his hands and coax him.*)

WITH. Come, come, off hands and let me sit down. I am tired of this.

AG. Yes, uncle, and here is one seat, you see, with no cat upon it. (Withrington *sits down, and* Agnes *takes a little stool and sits down at his feet, curling her nose as she looks up to him, and making a good humoured face.*)

WITH. Well, it may be pleasant enough, girls, but allow me to say all this playing, and laughing, and hoidening[3] about is not gentlewomanlike, nay, I might say, is not maidenly. A high bred elegant woman is a creature which man approaches with awe and respect; but nobody would think of accosting you with such impressions, any more than if you were a couple of young female tinkers.

---

1 Kamchatka; a peninsula of north-eastern Siberia, visited by Bering's expedition between 1725 and 1730 and the Krasheninnikov and Steller expeditions between 1733 and 1745.

2 Usually an itinerant exhibitor.

3 Playing the hoyden; behaving in a rude and boisterous manner.

AG. Don't distress yourself about this, sir, we shall get the men to bow to us, and tremble before us too, as well as e'er a hoop-petticoat or long ruffles of them all.

WITH. Tremble before you! ha, ha, ha! (*to* Agnes.) Who would tremble before thee dost thou think?

AG. No despicable man perhaps: What think you of your favourite, Harwood? 130

WITH. Poo, poo, poo! he is pleased with thee as an amusing and good natured creature, and thou thinkest he is in love with thee, forsooth.

AG. A good natured creature! he shall think me a vixen and be pleased with me.

WITH. No, no, not quite so far gone, I believe.

AG. I'll bet you two hundred pounds[1] that it is so. If I win you shall pay it to Mariane for wedding trinkets, and if you win you may build a couple of alms-houses.

WITH. Well, be it so. We shall see, we shall see. 140

MAR. Indeed we shall see you lose your bet, uncle.

WITH. (*to* Mar.) Yes, baggage, I shall have your prayers against me I know.

Enter SERVANT, *and announces* Mr. Opal. *Enter* OPAL.

OP. (*to* Mar.) I hope I have the pleasure of seeing Miss Withrington well this morning. (*Bows distantly to* Withrington, *and still more so to* Agnes, *after the manner of* Sir Loftus.)

WITH. Your servant, sir.

MAR. (*to* Op.) How did you like the ball last night? There was a gay, genteel looking company.

---

1 To understand the dimensions of Agnes' wager beyond her comparison to the cost of two alms-houses, £70 a year in the late eighteenth century would have been considered a comfortable income. In 1776 the state of Maine paid inventor David Bushnell £60 for plans of a submarine that never worked, and in 1780 a Broadwood square piano would have cost £21. William Godwin was paid five guineas by Thomas Hookham in 1783 for his short tale *Damon and Delia*, which he wrote in ten days. In 1806 William Wordsworth's bid for an 18 acre farm in Patterdale fell short by £200, and he accepted a loan which he repaid over three years. Yet, at the other end of the financial spectrum, Joanna Baillie's brother, Dr. Matthew Baillie, considered the most able physician in London before his death in 1823, earned in excess of £10,000 a year.

OP. (*With affected superiority.*) Excepting Lord Saunter, and Lord Poorly, and Sir Loftus, and one or two more of us, I did not know a soul in the room.

WITH. There were some pretty girls there, Mr. Opal?

OP. I am very glad to hear it, 'pon honour. I did not—(*Mumbling.*)

WITH. (*aside.*) Affected puppy, I can't bear to look at him. [EXIT.

MAR. (*Assuming a gayer air as* Withrington *goes out.*) You will soon have a new beau to enrich your circle, Mr. Opal, the handsome and accomplished Colonel Beaumont. He is just returned from abroad, and is now quite the fashion at court. (*To* Agnes.) Don't you think Mr. Opal resembles him?

AG. O! very much indeed.

OP. (*Bowing very graciously.*) Does he not resemble Sir Loftus too? I mean in his air and his manner.

MAR. O! not at all! That haughty coldness of his is quite old fashioned now; so unlike the affable frankness so much admired in the Colonel: you have seen him I presume?

OP. I have never had that honour.

MAR. Then you will not be displeased at the likeness we have traced, when you do.

OP. (*Relaxing from his dignity, and highly pleased.*) The greatest pleasure of my life, ma'am, will be to resemble what pleases you. (Mariane *tips* Agnes *the wink, and she retires to the bottom of the stage.*)

MAR. You flatter me infinitely.

OP. Ah! call it not flattery, charming Miss Withrington! for now I will have the boldness to own to you frankly, I have been, since the first moment I beheld you, your most sincere, your most passionate admirer. Upon hon—(*correcting himself.*) 'faith I have!

MAR. Nothing but my own want of merit can make me doubt of any thing Mr. Opal asserts upon his honour or his faith. (*Turning and walking towards the bottom of the stage, whilst* Opal *follows her stalking in dumb show;*[1] *then* Agnes *joins them, and they all come forward to the front.*)

---

1 Pantomime.

AG. (*to* Mar.) How much that turn of his head puts me mind of the Colonel.

MAR. So it does, my Agnes. (*To* Opal.) Pray have the goodness to hold it so for a moment! There now, it is just the very thing. (Opal *holds his head in a constrained ridiculous posture, and then makes a conceited bow.*) His very manner of bowing too! one would swear it was the Colonel!

AG. Yes, only the Colonel is more familiar, more easy in his carriage.

OP. O! Ma'am! I assure you I have formerly—It is my natural manner to be remarkably easy—But I—(*pauses.*) 190

MAR. Have never condescended to assume any other than your natural manner, I hope.

OP. O! not at all, I detest affectation; there is nothing I detest so much—But upon my soul! I can't tell how it is, I have been graver of late. I am, indeed, sometimes thoughtful.

MAR. O fye upon it! don't be so any more. It is quite old fashioned and ridiculous now. (*To* Agnes, *winking at her.*) Did you see my gloves any where about the room, cousin?

OP. I'll find them. (*Goes to look for them with great briskness.*— 200 Servant *announces* Miss Eston.)

OP. Pest take her! I stared at her once in a mistake, and she has ogled and followed me ever since.

Enter Miss ESTON, *running up to* Mariane *and* Agnes, *and pretending not to see* Opal, *though she cannot help looking askance at him while she speaks.*

EST. O my dear creatures! you can't think how I have longed to see you. Mrs. Thomson kept me so long this morning, and you know she is an intolerable talker. (*Pretending to discover* Opal.) O! how do you do, Mr. Opal? I declare I did not observe you!

OP. (*With a distant haughty bow.*) I am obliged to you, ma'am.

EST. I did see your figure, indeed, but I mistook it for Sir Loftus. 210

OP. (*Correcting himself, and assuming a cheerful frank manner.*) O ma'am! you are very obliging to observe me at all. I believe

Prettyman and I may be nearly of the same height. (*Looking at his watch.*) I am beyond my appointment I see. Excuse me: I must hurry away.   [EXIT, *hastily.*

EST. (*Looking after him with marks of disappointment.*) I am very glad he is gone. He does so haunt me, and stare at me, I am quite tired of it. The first time I ever saw him, you remember how he looked me out of countenance. I was resolved
220   before I came not to take notice of him.

MAR. So you knew you should find him here, then.

EST. O la! one don't know of a morning who one may meet; as likely him as any body else, you know. I really wonder now what crotchet[1] he has taken in his head about me. Do you know, last night, before twilight, I peeped past the blind, and saw him walking with slow pensive steps, under my window.

MAR. Well, what happened then?

EST. I drew in my head, you may be sure; but a little while after,
230   I peeped out again, and, do you know, I saw him come out of the perfumer's shop, just opposite to my dressing-room, where he had been all the while.

MAR. Very well, and what happened next?

EST. La! nothing more. But was it not very odd? What should he be doing all that time in that little paltry shop? The great shop near the Circus[2] is the place where every body buys perfumery.

AG. No, there is nothing very odd in Mr. Opal's buying perfumes at a very paltry shop, where he might see and be
240   seen by a very pretty lady.

EST. (*With her face brightening up.*) Do you think so? O no! you don't?

AG. To be sure I do. But I know what is very strange.

EST. O la! dear creature! What is it?

AG. He bought his perfumes there before you came, when there was no such inducement. Is not that very odd? (Eston *pauses, and looks silly.*)

---

1   A whimsical fancy; hence the notion of someone being crotchety.

2   A circular street of houses. In Bath, the Circus was noted for its excellent view of the city.

Enter Mr. WITHRINGTON, *but upon perceiving* Eston, *bows and retreats again.*

EST. (*Recovering herself.*) Ha! how do you do, Mr. Withrington? I have just seen your friend, Lady Fade. Poor dear soul! she says—

WITH. I am sorry, ma'am, it is not in my power at present—I 250 am in a hurry, I have an appointment. Your servant, ma'am. [EXIT.

EST. Well, now this is very odd! Wherever I go, I find all the men just going out to some appointment. O, I forgot to tell you, Mrs. Thomson has put a new border to her drawing room, just like the one up stairs. Has it not a dark blue ground?[1] (*To* Mariane.)

MAR. I'm sure I cannot tell, let us go up stairs and see. [EXE-UNT.

SCENE II.

Before Mr. WITHRINGTON's *House. Enter* HARWOOD.

HAR. Well here I am again, yet devil take me if I can muster up resolution enough to take the knocker in my hand! What a fool was I to call twice this morning! for with what face can I now visit her again? The old gentleman will look strangely at me; the fine heiress her cousin will stare at me; nay, the very servants begin already to smile with imperti-nent significance, as I enquire with conscious foolishness, if the ladies are at home. Then Agnes herself will look so drolly at me—Ah! but she will look so pleasantly too!— 10 'Faith! I'll e'en go. (*Goes to the door, puts his hand up to the knocker, stops short, and turns from it again. Pauses.*) What a fool am I, to stand thinking about it here! If I were but fairly in the room with her, and the first salutation over, I should not care if the devil himself made faces at me. Oh

---

1 The basic material upon which embroidery is applied.

no! every body is good humoured, every thing is happy that is near her! the kitten who plays by her side takes hold of her gown unchidden. How pleasant it is to love what is so blessed! I would hate the fairest woman on earth if she were not of a sweet temper. Come away, come away, every thing favours me here, but my own foolish fancies.

(*As he goes to the door again, it opens, and enters from the house,* Betty, *crying, with a bundle in her hand.*)

BET. O dear me! O dear me!

HAR. What is the matter with you, my good girl?

BET. I'm sure it was not my fault, and she has abused me worser than a heathen.

HAR. That is hard indeed.

BET. Indeed it is, sir; and all for a little nasty essence bottle, which was little better than a genteel kind of a stink at the best, and I am sure I did but take out the stopper to smell to it, when it came to pieces in my hand like an egg shell; if bottles will break, how can I help it; but la! sir, there is no speaking reason to my mistress, she is as furious and as ill tempered as a dragon.

HAR. Don't distress yourself, Miss Agnes Withrington will make amends to you for the severity of your mistress.

BET. She truly! she is my mistress herself, and she has abused me, O dear me—If it had been Miss Withrington, she would not have said a word to me, but Miss Agnes is so cross, and so ill natured, there is no living in the house with her.

HAR. Girl, you are beside yourself.

BET. No, sir, god be praised! but she is beside herself, I believe. Does she think I am going to live in her service to be call'd names so, and compared to a blackamoor[1] too? if I had been waiting maid to the queen,[2] she would not have compared me to a blackamoor, and will I take such usage

---

1 Literally "black moor"; a term in use since 1581 and mostly out of use by the mid-eighteenth century.

2 Queen Charlotte (1744-1818) was the mother of fifteen children, including Charlotte Augusta Matilda (1766-1828), who married the future king of Würtemberg in 1797, and the infamous George (1762-1830) who was Prince Regent from 1810

from her? what do I care for her cast gowns.

HAR. Well, but she is liberal to you?

BET. She liberal! she'll keep every thing that is worth keeping to herself, I warrant; and lord pity those who are bound to live with her! I'll seek out a new place for myself, and let the devil, if he will, wait upon her next, in the shape of blackamoor; they will be fit company for one another, and if he gets the better of her for scolding, he is a better devil than I take him for: and I am sure, sir, if you were to see her— 50

HAR. Get along! get along! you are too passionate yourself, to be credited.

BET. I know what I know, I don't care what no body says, no more I do; I know who to complain to. [EXIT, *grumbling*.

HAR. (*alone*.) What a malicious toad it is! I dare say now, she has done something very provoking, I cannot bear these pert chamber-maids, the very sight of them is offensive to me. 60

Enter JONATHAN.

JON. Good evening to your honour, can you tell me if Mr. Withrington be at home? for as how, my master has sent me with a message to him.

HAR. (*Impatiently*.) Go to the house and enquire, I know nothing about it. (Jonathan *goes into the house*.)

HAR. (*Alone, after musing some time*.) That girl has put me out of all heart though, with her cursed stories.—No, no, it cannot be—it is impossible! 70

Re-enter JONATHAN *from the house, scratching his head, and looking behind.*

JON. 'Faith there is hot work going on amongst them! thank heaven I am out again!

---

and George IV, King of England, from 1821 to 1830. She was notorious herself for her selfish and irritable behaviour. Cantankerous and miserable from occasional attacks of erysipelas, a skin infection that left her face reddened and swollen to alarming proportions, Queen Charlotte regularly reduced even her daughters to tears.

HAR. What do you mean?

JON. 'Faith! that little lady, in that there house, is the best hand at a scold, saving Mary Macmurrock, my wife's mother, that ever my too blessed eyes looked upon, lord sir! (*going nearer him.*) her tongue goes ting, ting, ting, as shrill as the bell of any pieman, and then, sir, (*going nearer him.*) her two eyes look out of her head, as though they were a couple of glow-worms, and then sir, he, he, he! (*laughing, and going close up to him*) she claps her little hands so, as if—

HAR. Shut your fool's mouth and be damn'd to you!

(*Kicks* Jonathan *off the stage in a violent passion; then leans his back to a tree, and seems thoughtful for some time, and very much troubled.*)

Enter AGNES *from the house, with a stormy look on her face.*

AG. So you are still loitering here, Harwood? you have been very much amused I suppose, with the conversation of those good folks you have talked with.

HAR. No, not much amused, madam, though somewhat astonished, I own; too much astonish'd indeed, to give it any credit.

AG. O! it is true though, I have been very cross with the girl, and very cross with everybody, and if you don't clear up that dismal face of yours, I shall be cross with you too: what could possess you to stay so long under that chesnut-tree a little while ago, always appearing as if you were coming to the house, and always turning back again?

HAR. (*eagerly.*) And is it possible, you were then looking at me, and observing my motions?

AG. Indeed I was just going to open my window and beckon to you, when that creature broke my phial of sweet essence, and put me quite out of temper.

HAR. Hang the stupid jade! I could—

AG. So you are angry too? O! well done! we are fit company for one another, come along with me, come, come, (*impatiently. As she turns to go something catches hold of her gown.*) What at is this? confounded thing! (*Pulls away her gown in a passion, and tears it.*)

HAR. (*aside.*) Witch that she is, she should be beaten for her humours. I will not go with her.

AG. (*Looking behind.*) So you won't go in with me? good evening to you then: we did want a fourth person to make up a party with us, but since you don't like it we shall send to Sir Loftus or Opal, or Sir Ulick O'Grady, or some other good creature; I dare say Sir Loftus will come.

HAR. (*Half aside.*) Cursed Coxcomb! If he sets his snout within the door, I'll pistol him.

AG. (*Overhearing him.*) Ha! well said! you will make the best company in the world, come along, come along, (*he follows her half unwillingly,*) why don't you offer your arm here? don't you see how rough it is? (*He offers his arm.*) Poo, not that arm. (*Offers her the other.*) Poo, not so neither, on t'other side of me.

HAR. What a humoursome¹ creature you are! I have offer'd you two arms, and neither of them will do, do you think I have a third to offer you?

AG. You are a simpleton, or you would have half a dozen at my service.

[EXEUNT *into the house.*

---

1   Peevish or ill-humoured; capricious.

ACT IV.—SCENE I.

HARWOOD's *Lodgings. He is discovered walking about with an irreg-ular disturbed step, his hair and dress all neglected and in disorder; he comes forward to the front of the stage.*

HAR. I have neither had peace nor sleep since I beheld her; O! that I had never known her! or known her only such as my first fond fancy conceived her!—I would my friend were come, I will open my heart to him, he perhaps will speak comfort to me, for surely that temper must be violent indeed, which generous affection cannot subdue; and she must be extravagant beyond all bounds of nature, who would ruin the fond husband who toils for her; no, no, nature makes not such, but when she sets her scowling mark upon them to warn us from our ruin. (*Pauses, walks up and down, then comes forward again.*) Insipid constitutions, good nature is a tiresome thing: passion subdued by reason is worth a score of it—and passion subdued by love?—O! that were better still!— yesterday, as I enter'd her door, I heard her name me to her cousin, with so much gentle softness in her voice, I blest her as she spoke.—Ah! if this were so, all might still be well; who would not struggle with the world, for such a creature as this—Ay, and I must struggle!—O! that this head of mine would give over thinking, but for one half hour! (*Rings the bell.*)

Enter THOMAS.

What brings you here, Thomas?

THOM. Your bell rung, sir.

HAR. Well, well, I did want something but I have forgot it. Bring me a glass of water. (EXIT Thomas. Harwood *sits down by a small writing table, and rests his head upon his hand. Re-enter* Thomas, *with the water.*) You have made good haste, Thomas.

THOM. I did make good haste, sir, lest you should be impatient with me.

HAR. I am sometimes impatient with you, then? I fear indeed I
have been too often so of late; but you must not mind it,   30
Thomas, I mean you no unkindness.
THOM. Lord love you, sir! I know that very well! a young gentleman who takes an old man into his service, because
other gentlemen do not think him quick enough, nor
smart enough for them, as your honour has taken me, can
never mean to show him any unkindness, I know it well
enough; I am only uneasy because I fear you are not so
well of late.
HAR. I thank you, Thomas, I am not very well—I am not ill
neither, I shall be better. (*Pauses.*) I think I have heard you   40
say, you were a soldier in your youth?
THOM. Yes, sir.
HAR. And you had a wife, too, a woman of fiery mettle, to bear
about your napsack?
THOM. Yes, sir, my little stout spirity Jane; she had a devil of a
temper, to be sure.
HAR. Yet you loved her notwithstanding?
THOM. Yes, to be sure, I did, as it were, bear her some kindness.
HAR. I'll be sworn you did!—and you would have been very
sorry to have parted with her.   50
THOM. Why death parts the best of friends, sir: we lived but
four years together.
HAR. And so, your little spirity Jane was taken so soon away
from you?
Give me thy hand, my good Thomas. (*Takes his hand and
presses it.*)
THOM. (*Perceiving tears in his eyes.*) Lord, sir! don't be so distress'd
about it; she did die, to be sure, but truly, between you and
I,[1] although I did make a kind of whimpering at the first, I

---

1 Though retained in 1806, "I" was changed to "me" in the 1851 edition. Grammatical errors were an issue of gender in the eighteenth century. (See Appendix E.3.)
Yet even Sara Coleridge made critical remarks about Baillie's grammar, comment-
ing in a letter that Baillie's poetry was "the worse for a few specks of bad English"
(to Miss E. Trevenen, Hampstead 1833. See Introduction). Baillie was aware of her
grammatical slips, as evidenced in a letter to Samuel Rogers in which she writes:
"Do you remember when I told you, a good while since, of my intention of looking over all my works to correct them for an edition to be published after my

was not ill pleased afterwards to be rid of her; for, truly, sir,
a man who has got an ill tempered wife, has but a dog's life
of it at the best.—Will you have your glass of water, sir?

HAR. (*Looking at him with dissatisfaction.*) No, no, take it away; I
have told you a hundred times not to bring me that chalky
water from the courtyard. (*Turns away from him.*)

Enter Colonel HARDY.—HARWOOD *signs to* Thomas,
and he goes out.

HAR. My dear Colonel, this is kind; I am very glad to see you.
COL. It is so seldom that a young fellow has any inclination for
the company of an old man, that I should feel myself vain
of the summons you have sent me, were I not afraid, from
this dishabille, my dear Harwood, that you are indisposed.
HAR. You are very good; I am not indisposed. I have indeed
been anxious—I rested indifferently last night—I hope I
see you well.
COL. Very well, as you may guess from the speed I have made in
coming to you. These legs do not always carry me so fast;
but you have something particular to say to me.
HAR. I am very sensible of your friendship.—Pray, Colonel, be
seated!— (*They sit down—a long pause.*—Colonel Hardy,
like one expecting to hear something; Harwood, *like one who
knows not how to begin.*)—There are moments in a man's
life, Colonel Hardy, when the advice of a friend is of the

decease, should it be called for, and you giving me a hint never to let a *which* stand
where a *that* might serve the purpose, to prefer the words *while* to *whilst, among* to
amongst, &c.? I acquiesced in all this most readily, throwing as much scorn upon the
rejected expressions as anybody would do, and with all the ease of one who from
natural taste had always avoided them. If you do, you will guess what has been my
surprise and mortification to find through whole pages of even my last dramas,
'whiches,' 'whilsts,' and 'amongsts,' &c., where they need not have been, in abundance. Well; I have profited by your hint, though I was not aware that I needed it at
the time when it was given, and now I thank you for it very sincerely. I cannot
imagine how I came to make this mistake, if it has not been that, in writing songs, I
have often rejected the words in question because they do not sound well in
singing. I have very lately finished my corrections, and now all my literary tasks are
finished. It is time they should, and more serious thoughts fill up their room, or
ought to do" (Hampstead, Friday, 2 February 1832).

greatest value; particularly one, who has also been his 80
father's friend.

COL. My heart very warmly claims both those relations to you,
Harwood; and I shall be happy to advise you, as well as I
am able.

HAR. (*After another pause.*) I am about to commence a laborious
profession.—The mind is naturally anxious.—(*Pauses.*)

COL. But you are too capable of exercising well that profession,
to suffer much uneasiness.

HAR. Many a man, with talents vastly superiour to mine, has
sunk beneath the burden. 90

COL. And many a man, with talents vastly inferiour to yours,
has borne it up with credit.

HAR. Ah! What avails the head with an estranged heart!

COL. You are disgusted, then, with your profession, and have,
perhaps, conceived more favourably of mine? I am sorry
for it: I hoped to see you make a figure at the bar; and your
mother has long set her heart upon it.

HAR. (*With energy.*) O, no! she must not! she shall not be disappointed!—Pardon me, my expressions have gone somewhat wide of my meaning.—I meant to have consulted 100
you in regard to other difficulties.—

COL. And pardon me likewise, for interrupting you; but it
appears to me, that an unlearned soldier is not a person to
be consulted in these matters.

HAR. It was not, altogether, of these matters I meant to speak—
But, perhaps, we had better put it off for the present.

COL. No, no!

HAR. Perhaps, we had better walk out a little way; we may talk
with less restraint as we go.

COL. No, no, there are a thousand impertinent people about. Sit 110
down again, and let me hear every thing you wish to say.

HAR. (*Pausing, hesitating, and much embarrassed.*) There are certain
attachments in which a man's heart may be so deeply interested—I would say so very—or rather I should say so
strangely engaged, that—(*hesitates and pauses.*)

COL. O, here it is! I understand it now. But pray don't be so
foolish about it, Harwood! You are in love?

HAR. (*Appearing relieved.*) I thank your quickness, my dear Colonel, I fear it is somewhat so with me.

120 COL. And whence your fear? Not from the lady's cruelty?

HAR. No, there is another bar in my way, which does, perhaps, too much depress my hopes of happiness.

COL. You have not been prudent enough to fall in love with an heiress?

HAR. No, my dear sir, I have not.

COL. That is a great mistake, to be sure, Harwood; yet many a man has not advanced the less rapidly in his profession, for having a portionless wife to begin the world with. It is a spur to industry.

130 HAR. (*Looking pleased at him.*) Such sentiments are what I expected from Colonel Hardy; and, were it not for female failings, there would be little risk in following them.—I don't know how to express it—I am perhaps too delicate in these matters—We ought not to expect a faultless woman.

COL. No, surely; and, if such a woman were to be found, she would be no fit companion for us.

HAR. (*Getting up, and pressing the* Colonel's *hand between his.*) My dearest friend! your liberality and candour delight me!—I do, indeed, believe that many a man has lived very happily

140 with a woman far from being faultless; and, after all, where is the great injury he sustains, if she should be a little violent and unreasonable?

COL. (*Starting up from his seat.*) Nay, heaven defend us from a violent woman; for that is the devil himself!—(*Seeing Harwood's countenance change.*)—What is the matter with you, Harwood? She is not ill temper'd, I hope?

HAR. (*Hesitating.*) Not—not absolutely so—She is of a very quick and lively disposition, and is apt to be too hasty and unguarded in her emotions.—I do not, perhaps, make

150 myself completely understood.

COL. O! I understand you perfectly,—I have known ladies of this lively disposition, very hasty and unguarded too in their demands upon a man's pocket as well as his patience; but she may be of a prudent and economical turn. Is it so, Harwood?

HAR. (*Throwing himself into a chair very much distress'd.*) I do not say it is, Colonel.

COL. (*Putting his hand kindly upon his shoulder.*) I am sorry to distress you so much, my dear friend, yet it must be so. I see how it is with you: pardon the freedom of friendship, but indeed an expensive and violent temper'd woman is not to be thought of: he who marries such a one forfeits all peace and happiness. Pluck up some noble courage, and renounce this unfortunate connexion.

HAR. (*Starting up.*) Renounce it, Colonel Hardy! Is it from you I receive so hard, so unfeeling a request, who have suffered so much yourself from the remembrance of an early attachment? I thought to have been pitied by you.

COL. I was early chagrined with the want of promotion, and disappointed in my schemes of ambition, which gave my countenance something of a melancholy cast, I believe, and the ladies have been kind enough to attribute it to the effects of hopeless love; but how could you be such a ninny, my dear Harwood?

HAR. I am sorry, sir, we have understood one another so imperfectly.

COL. Nay, nay, my young friend, do not carry yourself so distantly with me. You have sought a love-worn companion, and you have found a plain spoken friend. I am sorry to give you pain; deal more openly with me: when I know who this bewitching creature is, I shall, perhaps, judge more favourably of your passion.

HAR. It is Miss Agnes Withrington.

COL. Cousin to Miss Withrington the heiress?

HAR. Yes it is she. What have I said to amaze you?

COL. You amaze me, indeed!—That little—forgive me if I were almost to say,—plain looking girl! Friendship would sympathize in your feelings; but, pardon me, Harwood, you have lost your wits.

HAR. I believe I have, Colonel, which must plead my pardon, likewise, for expecting this friendship from you.

COL. You distress me.

HAR. I distress myself still more, by suffering so long the pain of this conversation.

COL. Let us end it, then, as soon as you please. When you are in a humour to listen to reason, I shall be happy to have the honour of seeing you.

HAR. When I am in that humour, sir, I will not balk[1] so much as to intrude upon your time.

200 COL. Let me see you, then, when you are not in that humour, and I shall the more frequently have the pleasure of your company. (*Both bow coldly.* EXIT, Colonel Hardy.)

HAR. (*alone.*) What a fool was I to send for this man!—A little plain looking girl! What do the people mean? They will drive me mad amongst them. Why does not the little witch wear high heels to her shoes, and stick a plume of feathers in her cap? Oh! they will drive me distracted!

SCENE II.

Mr. WITHRINGTON's *House.* AGNES *discovered embroidering at a small table,* HARWOOD *standing by her, and hanging fondly over her as she works.*

HAR. How pretty it is! Now you put a little purple on the side of the flower.

AG. Yes, a very little shade.

HAR. And now a little brown upon that.

AG. Even so.

HAR. And thus you work up and down, with that tiny needle of yours, till the whole flower is completed. (*Pauses, still looking at her working.*) Why, Agnes, you little witch! you're doing that leaf wrong.

10 AG. You may pick it out then, and do it better for me. I'm sure you have been idle enough all the morning, it is time you were employed about something.

HAR. And so I will. (*Sitting down by her, and taking hold of the work.*)

AG. (*Covering the flower with her hand.*) O! no, no!

HAR. Take away that little perverse hand, and let me begin.

---

1 Waste.

(*Putting his hand upon hers.*)

AG. What a good for nothing creature you are! you can do nothing yourself, and you will suffer no body else to do any thing. I should have had the whole pattern finished before now, if you had not loitered over my chair so long.

HAR. So you can't work when I look over you? Then I have some influence upon you? O you sly girl! you are caught in your own words at last.

AG. Indeed, Harwood, I wish you would go home again to your law-books and your precedent hunting; you have mispent a great deal of time here already.

HAR. Is it not better to be with you in reality than only in imagination? Ah! Agnes! you little know what my home studies are.—Law, said you! how can I think of law, when your countenance looks upon me from every black lettered page that I turn? When your figure fills the empty seat by my side, and your voice speaks to me in the very mid-day stillness of my chamber? Ah! my sweet Agnes! you will not believe what a foolish fellow I have been since I first saw you.

AG. Nay, Harwood, I am not at all incredulous of the fact, it is only the cause of it which I doubt.

HAR. Saucy girl! I must surely be revenged upon you for all this.

AG. I am tired of this work. (*Getting up.*)

HAR. O! do not give over.—Let me do something for you—Let me thread your needle for you—I can thread one most nobly.

AG. There then. (*Gives him a needle and silk.*)

HAR. (*Pretending to scratch her hand with it.*) So ought you to be punished. (*Threads it awkwardly.*)

AG. Ay, nobly done, indeed! but I shall work no more to-day.

HAR. You must work up my needleful.

AG. I am to work a fool's cap in the corner by-and-by, I shall keep your needleful for that. I am going to walk in the garden.

HAR. And so am I.

AG. You are?

HAR. Yes, I am. Go where you will, Agnes, to the garden or the field, the city or the desert, by sea or by land, I must e'en go too. I will never be where you are not, but when to be where you are is impossible.

AG. O! there will be no getting rid of you at this rate, unless some witch will have pity upon me, and carry me up in the air upon her broomstick.

60 HAR. There, I will not pretend to follow you, but as long as you remain upon the earth, Agnes, hang me! if I can find in my heart to budge an inch from your side.

AG. You are a madman.

HAR. You are a sorceress.

AG. You are an idler.

HAR. You are a little mouse.

AG. Come, come, get your hat then, and let us go. (*Aside, while he goes to the bottom of the stage for his hat.*) Bless me! I have forgot to be ill-humour'd all this time.

[EXIT, *hastily.*

70 HAR. (*Coming forward.*) Gone for her shawl, I suppose. How delightful she is! how pleasant every change of her countenance! How happy must his life be, spent even in cares and toil, where leisure hours are cheer'd with such a creature as this!

AG. (*Without, in an angry voice.*) Don't tell me so: I know very well how it is, and you shall smart for it too, you lazy, careless, impudent fellow! And, besides all this, how dare you use my kitten so?

HAR. (*Who listened with a rueful face.*) Well, now, but this is
80 humanity: she will not have a creature ill used.—I wish she would speak more gently though.

AG. (*Entering.*) Troublesome, provoking, careless fellow.

HAR. It is very provoking in him to use the poor kitten ill.

AG. So it is; but it is more provoking still to mislay my clogs, as he does.

Enter SERVANT, *with clogs.*

SER. Here they are, madam.

AG. Bring them here, I say, (*looks at them.*) These are Miss Withrington's clogs, you blockhead! (*Throws them to the other side
of the stage in a passion.*) I must go without them, I find. (*To
Harwood.*) What are you musing about? If you don't chuse   90
to go with me, good morning.

HAR. (*Sighing deeply.*) Ah, Agnes! you know too well that I cannot stay behind you.   [EXEUNT.

SCENE III.

Miss WITHRINGTON's *Dressing-room. Enter* MARIANE, *who turns
back again towards the door, and calls to* AGNES *without.*

MAR. Agnes, cousin Agnes, where are you going?

AG. (*Without.*) I am returning to Miss Eston, whom I have left
in the parlour, talking to the dog.

MAR. Well, let her talk to the dog a little longer, and let me talk
to you.

Enter AGNES.

I have set Betty to watch at the higher windows to give
notice of Sir Loftus's approach, that we may put ourselves
in order to receive him; for I am resolved to have one bout
more with him, and discharge him for good, I am quite
tired of him now.   10

AG. Do you expect him?

MAR. I am pretty sure he will come about this time, and I must
be prepared for him. I have a good mind to tell him, at
once, I despise him, and that will be a plain easy way of
finishing the business.

AG. No, no, my sweet Mariane! we must send him off with
eclat. You have played your part very well hitherto; keep it

up but for this last time, and let Eston and I go into the closet and enjoy it.

20 MAR. Well then, do so: I shall please you for this once.

Enter BETTY, *in haste.*

BET. (*to* Mar.) Sir Loftus is just coming up the side path, madam, and he'll be at the door immediately.

AG. I'll run and bring Eston directly.   [EXIT.

MAR. (*Looking at the door of the closet.*) Yes, it is very thin: they will hear well, and see through the key hole.

Re-enter AGNES *with* Miss ESTON, *in a great hurry.*

EST. La! I have torn my gown in my haste.

AG. Come along, come along.

EST. It is not so bad a tear though as Mrs. Thomson got the—

30 AG. Come, come, we must not stay here. (*Pushes* Eston *into the closet, and follows.* Mariane *and* Betty *place a table with books, and a chair, near the front of the stage.*)

EST. (*Looking from the closet.*) La! Mariane, how I long to hear you and him begin. I shall be so delighted!

MAR. For heaven sake shut the door! he will be here immediately. (*Shuts the door upon her, and continues to set the room in order.*)

EST. (*Looking out again.*) La! Mariane, do you know how many yards of print Lady Squat has got round her new—(Agnes *from behind, claps her hand on* Eston's *mouth, and draws her into the closet.*—Mariane *seats herself by the table, pretending to read.* EXIT Betty, *and enter* Sir LOFTUS, *a servant announcing him.*)

SIR LOFT. You are very studious this morning, Miss Withrington.

MAR. (*Carelessly.*) Ha! how do you do?

40 SIR LOFT. You have been well amus'd, I hope?

MAR. So, so. I must put in a mark here, and not lose my place. (*Looking on the table.*) There is no paper—O, there is some on the other table: pray do fetch it me! (*Pointing to a table at the bottom of the stage.*) I am very lazy. (*Sits down again indo-lently.*)

SIR LOFT. (*Fetching the paper, and presenting it with a condescending yet self-important air.*) I have the honour to obey you, ma'am.

MAR. I thank you; you are a very serviceable creature, I am sure.

SIR LOFT. (*Drawing himself up proudly, but immediately correcting himself.*) I am always happy to serve Miss Withrington.

MAR. O! I know very well the obliging turn of your disposi-tion. (*Tosses her arm upon the table, and throws down a book.*) I am very stupid this morning. (Sir Loftus *picks up the book, and gives it to her rather sulkily; and she in receiving it drops an ivory ball under the table.*) Bless me! What is the matter with all these things? pray lift it for me, good Sir Loftus! I believe you must creep under the table for it though. (*He stoops under the table with a very bad grace, and she slyly gives it a touch with her foot, which makes it run to the other side of the stage.*) Nay, you must go further off for it now. I am very troublesome.

SIR LOFT. (*Goes after it rather unwillingly, and presenting it to her with still a worse grace.*) Madam, this is more honour than I—(*mumbling.*)

MAR. O, no! Sir Loftus, it is only you that are too good. (*Lolling carelessly in her chair.*) It is so comfortable to have such a good creature by one! your fine fashionable men are admired to be sure, but I don't know how, I feel always restrained in their company. With a good obliging creature like you now, I can be quite at my ease: I can just desire you to do any thing.

SIR LOFT. Upon my honour, madam, you flatter me very much indeed. Upon my honour, I must say, I am rather at a loss to conceive how I have merited these commendations.

MAR. O! Sir Loftus, you are too humble, too diffident of your-self. I know very well the obliging turn of your disposition to every body.

SIR LOFT. (*aside.*) Damn it! is she an ideot? (*aloud.*) Your good opinion, madam, does me a great deal of honour, but I assure you, ma'am, it is more than I deserve. I have great pleasure in serving Miss Withrington;—to be at the service of every body is an extent of benevolence[1] I by no means pretend to.

MAR. Now why are you so diffident, Sir Loftus? Did not old Mrs. Mumblecake tell me the other day, how you ran nine times to the apothecary's to fetch green salve to rub her monkey's tail.

SIR LOFT. She told you a damn'd lie then! (*Biting his lip, and walking up and down with hasty strides.*) Damn it! this is beyond all bearing! I run nine times to the apothecary's to fetch green salve for her monkey's tail! If the cursed hag says so again I'll bury her alive!

MAR. Nay, don't be angry about it. I'm sure I thought it very good in you, and I said so to every body.

SIR LOFT. You have been so obliging as tell all the world too?

MAR. And why should not I have the pleasure of praising you?

SIR LOFT. Hell and the devil! (*Turning on his heel, and striding up and down, and muttering as he goes, whilst she sits carelessly with her arms crossed.*)

MAR. My good Sir Loftus, you will tire yourself. Had you not better be seated?

SIR LOFT. (*Endeavouring to compose himself.*) The influence you have over me, ma'am, gets the better of every thing. I would not have you mistake my character, however; if love engages me in your service you ought to receive it so. I have been less profuse of these attentions to women of the very first rank and fashion; I might therefore have hoped

---

1 Benevolence or the disinterested love of humanity was a primary virtue of the eighteenth century. Fielding (1707-54), for one, ranked benevolence as one of the most exquisite delights amongst friendship and parental and filial affection (Cf. *Tom Jones*, 6.1.), and in his *A Treatise of Human Nature* (1739-40) David Hume (1711-76) contemplates the resulting harm from the lack of it. He writes, that "we may observe in general, that if we can find any quality in a person, which renders him incommodious to those who live and converse with him, we always allow it to be a fault or blemish, without any further examination" (3.3). Throughout the latter part of the century, women such as Hannah More and Elizabeth Fry through their voluntary initiatives with the poor participated in the growth of a benevolent social sensibility. See William Godwin's "Of Self Love and Benevolence" in his 1796 edition of *Political Justice*, and regarding Joanna Baillie's own sense of benevolence, see Introduction.

that you would lend a more favourable ear to my passion.   100

MAR. Indeed you wrong me. You don't know how favourable
my ear may be disposed: sit down here and tell me all about
it. (Sir Loftus *revolts again at her familiarity, but stifles his pride
and sits down by her.*)

SIR LOFT. Permit me to say, madam, that it is time we should
come to an explanation of each other's sentiments.

MAR. Whenever you please, sir.

SIR LOFT. (*Bowing.*) I hope then, I may be allowed to presume,
that my particular attentions to you, pardon me, ma'am,
have not been altogether disagreeable to you.

MAR. O! not at all, Sir Loftus.   110

SIR LOFT. (*Bowing again.*) I will presume then, still farther,
ma'am, and declare to you, that from the very day which
gave birth to my passion, I have not ceased to think of you
with the most ardent tenderness.

MAR. La! Sir Loftus, was it not of a Wednesday?

SIR LOFT. (*Fretted.*) Upon my word I am not so very accurate: it
might be Wednesday, or Friday, or any day.

MAR. Of a Friday, do you think? it runs strangely in my head
that we saw one another first of a Wednesday.

SIR LOFT. (*Very much fretted.*) I say, ma'am, the day which gave   120
birth to my love—

MAR. O! very true! You might see me first of a Wednesday, and
yet not fall in love with me till the Friday. (Sir Loftus *starts
up in a passion, and strides up and down.*—Mariane *rising from
her seat carelessly.*) I wonder where William has put the nuts
I bought for Miss Eston's squirrel. I think I hear a mouse in
the cupboard. (*Goes to the bottom of the room, and opens a
small cupboard in the wall, whilst* Sir Loftus *comes forward to the
front.*)

SIR LOFT. (*aside.*) Damn her freaks![1] I wish the devil had the
wooing of her. (*Pauses.*) I must not lose her for a trifle
though; but when she is once secured, I'll be revenged! I'll
vex her! I'll drive the spirit out of her. (*Aloud, as she comes*   130
forward from the cupboard.) My passion for you, Miss With-

---

1   Cf. *Count Basil*, 3.3.96.

rington, is too generous and disinterested to merit this indifference.

MAR. I'm glad they have not eat[1] the nuts though.

SIR LOFT. (*aside.*) Curse her and her nuts! I'll tame her! (*aloud.*) My sentiments for you, ma'am, are of so delicate and tender a nature, they do indeed deserve your indulgence. Tell me then, can the most disinterested, the most fervent love, make any impression on your heart? I can no longer exist in this state of anxiety! at your feet let me implore you— (*Seems about to kneel, but rather unwilling, as if he wished to be prevented.*)

MAR. Pray, Sir Loftus, don't kneel there! my maid has spilt oil on the floor.

SIR LOFT. Since you will not permit me to have the pleasure of kneeling at—

MAR. Nay, I will not deprive you of the pleasure—There is no oil spilt here. (*Pointing to a part of the floor very near the closet door.*)

SIR LOFT. I see it would be disagreeable to you.

MAR. I see very well you are not inclined to condescend so far.

SIR LOFT. (*Kneeling directly.*) Believe me, madam, the pride, the pleasure of my life, is to be devoted to the most adorable— (*Mariane gives a significant cough, and Agnes and Eston burst from the closet, the door opening on the outside, comes against Sir Loftus as he kneels, and lays him sprawling on the floor.*)

AG. EST. and MAR. (*Speaking together.*) O Sir Loftus! poor Sir Loftus! (*All coming about him, pretending to assist him to get up, but in reality hindering him.*)

SIR LOFT. Damn their bawling! they will bring the whole family here!

Enter Mr. WITHRINGTON *and* OPAL, *and* Sir Loftus, *mad with rage, makes a desperate effort, and gets upon his legs.* Opal *stands laughing at him without any ceremony, whilst he bites his lips, and draws himself up haughtily.*

---

1 Changed to "eaten" in the 1851 edition.

MAR. (*to* Sir Loft.) I'm afraid you have hurt yourself?

SIR LOFT. (*Shortly.*) No, ma'am.

AG. Havn't you rubbed the skin off your shins, Sir Loftus?

SIR LOFT. No, ma'am.

EST. Nor off your toes, Sir Loftus?

SIR LOFT. No, ma'am.

AG. I'm sure he has hurt his poor dear nose, but he is ashamed to own it.

SIR LOFT. Neither toes nor nose! Devil take it!

WITH. Get along, girls, and don't torment this poor man any longer. I am afraid, Sir Loftus, the young gipsies have been making a fool of you.

SIR LOFT. Sir, it is neither in your power nor their's to make a fool of me.

OP. Ha, ha, ha, ha! 'Faith Prettyman you must forgive me! ha, ha, ha, ha! I never thought in my life to have caught you at such low prostrations. But don't be so angry, man! though you do make a confounded silly figure, it must be confess'd. Ha, ha, ha, ha!

SIR LOFT. (*to* Op.) Sir, your impertinence and yourself are equally contemptible: and I desire you would no longer take the trouble of intruding yourself into my company, nor of affronting me, as you have hitherto done, with your awkward imitation of my figure and address.

OP. What the devil do you mean? I imitate your figure and address! I scorn to—I will not deny that I may have insensibly acquired a little of them both for—for—(*Hesitating.*)

AG. For he has observed people laughing at him of late.

SIR LOFT. (*Turning on his heel.*) He is beneath my resentment.

MAR. Be not so angry, good Sir Loftus! let us end this business for the present, and when I am at leisure to hear the remainder of your declarations, which has been so unfortunately interrupted, I'll send and let you know.[1]

SIR LOFT. No, 'faith, madam! you have heard the last words I shall ever say to you upon the subject. A large fortune may make amends for an ordinary person, madam, but not for

---

1 Lines 188 to 196 were deleted in the 1806 edition.

vulgarity and impertinence. Good morning. (*As he is going out enter* Servant.)

SER. Lord Saunter, and Colonel Gorget are coming up stairs, to see how Sir Loftus Prettyman does after his fall.

SIR LOFT. Hell and damnation! I'll go out by the other door.

MAR. That door is locked; you can't go that way.

SIR LOFT. I'll burst it open then. (*Runs to the door: they all get about him to prevent him.*)

SIR LOFT. (*Struggling.*) What, is there no getting out from this den of devils? (*Breaks from them, and* EXIT, *leaving them laughing provokingly behind him.*)

WITH. (*Shaking his head.*) This is too bad, this is too bad, young ladies! I am ashamed to have all this rioting and absurdity going on in my house.

AG. Come away, uncle, and see him go down the back walk, from the parlour windows. I'll warrant you he'll stride it away most nobly. (Withrington *follows, shrugging up his shoulders.*)

[EXEUNT.

ACT V.—SCENE I.

Mr. WITHRINGTON's *Library*. Mr. WITHRINGTON *discovered seated by a table.*

WITH. Who waits there? (*Enter* SERVANT.) Tell Miss Agnes Withrington I wish to see her. [EXIT servant.) What an absurd fellow this Harwood is, to be so completely bewitched with such a girl as Agnes! If she were like the women I remember,[1] there would indeed be some— (Agnes *entering softly behind him, gives him a tap on the shoulder.*)

AG. Well, uncle, what are you grumbling about? Have you lost your wager? Harwood has just left you, I hear.

WITH. I believe you may buy those trinkum, trankum[2] ornaments for Mariane whenever you please.

AG. Pray look not so ungraciously upon the matter! But you can't forgive him, I suppose, for being such a ninny as to fall in love with a little ordinary girl, eh?

WITH. And so he is a ninny, and a fool, and a very silly fellow.

AG. Do tell me what he has been saying to you.

WITH. Why, he confesses thou art ill-tempered, that thou art freakish, that thou art extravagant; and that of all the friends he has spoken with upon the subject, there is not one who will allow thee beauty enough to make a good looking pot-girl.[3]

---

1 Was Baillie thinking of the Rousseauistic ideal of womanhood popular at the time? Maria Edgeworth, a friend of Baillie's since perhaps before 1793 (Carhart 46), certainly endured attempts by her father's friend Thomas Day (Marilyn Butler in Todd, *British Women Writers* 204) to instruct her in the aesthetics of the passive and unintellectual female. See Rousseau's *Emile*. Or was Baillie thinking more about contemporary articles such as one entitled "What a Lady of the Bon Ton should be" in which a writer makes pronouncements more consistent with the character of Withrington as he endures the disorienting deceit and trickery of his spirited nieces: "There is in every age a distinct character for the merit of women. An amiable woman in the days of Queen Elizabeth, would now be an insufferable creature; nor would the beauties in the Courts of Charles II. be able to charm in that of George III" (*The Universal Daily Register*, Thursday, September 14th, 1786).

2 Humorous variations of "trinket" with latinized endings.

3 Barmaid.

20   AG. Did he say so?

WITH. Why, something nearly equivalent to it, Agnes. Yet, notwithstanding all this, there is something about thee so unaccountably delightful to him, that, poor as thou art, he will give up the fair hopes of opulence, and the pleasures of freedom, to watch for thee, drudge for thee, pinch himself for thee, if thou wilt have the condescension, in return, to plague and torment him for life.

AG. Foolish enough indeed, yet heaven bless him for it! What a fortunate woman am I! I sought a disinterested lover, and I
30   have found a most wonderful one.

WITH. I dare say you think yourself very fortunate.

AG. And don't you, likewise, my good sir? but you seem displeased at it.

WITH. You guess rightly enough: I must speak without disguise, Agnes, I am not pleased.

AG. Ah! his want of fortune—

WITH. Poo! you know very well I despise all mercenary balancing of property. It is not that which disturbs me. To be the disinterested choice of a worthy man is what every woman,
40   who means to marry at all, would be ambitious of; and a point in regard to her marriage, which a woman of fortune would be unwilling to leave doubtful. But there are men whose passions are of such a violent over-bearing nature, that love in them, may be considered as a disease of the mind; and the object of it claims no more perfection or pre-eminence amongst women, than chalk, lime, or oatmeal may do amongst dainties, because some diseased stomachs do prefer them to all things. Such men as these, we sometimes see attach themselves even to ugliness and
50   infamy, in defiance of honour and decency. With such men as these, women of sense and refinement can never be happy; nay, to be willingly the object of their love is disrespectable. (*Pauses.*) But you don't care for all this, I suppose? It does well enough for an old uncle to perplex himself with these niceties: it is you yourself the dear man happens to love, and none of those naughty women I have been talking of. So all is very right. (*Pauses, and she seems thoughtful.*)

AG. (*Assuming a grave and more dignified air.*) No, sir, you injure me: prove that his love for me is stronger than his love of virtue, and I will— 60

WITH. What will you do, Agnes?

AG. I will give him up for ever.

WITH. Ay, there spoke a brave girl! you deserve the best husband in Christendom for this.

AG. Nay, my husband-hunting will end here. If Harwood endures not the test, I will indeed renounce him, but no other man shall ever fill his place.

WITH. Well, well, we shall see, we shall see. (*Walks up and down. She is thoughtful.*) You are very thoughtful, Agnes; I fear I have distressed you. 70

AG. You have distressed me, yet I thank you for it. I have been too presumptuous, I have ventured farther than I ought. Since it is so, I will not shrink from the trial. (*Pauses.*) Don't you think he will go through it honourably?

WITH. (*Shaking his head.*) Indeed I know not—I hope he will.

AG. You hope? I thank you for that word, my dear sir! I hope he will too. (*She remains thoughtful: he takes a turn or two cross the stage.*)

WITH. (*Clapping her shoulder affectionately.*) What are you thinking of, niece?

AG. How to set about this business. 80

WITH. And how will you do it?

AG. I will write a letter to Lady Fade, asking pardon for having told some malicious falsehoods of her, to a relation of whom she is dependant upon, and begging she will make up the matter, and forgive me; promising at the same time, most humbly, if she will not expose me for this time, never to offend so any more. Next time he comes I will make him direct the letter himself, that when it falls into his hands again, he may have no doubt of its authenticity. Will this do? 90

WITH. Yes, very well. If he loves you after this, his love is not worth the having.

AG. Ah, uncle! you are very hard hearted! But you are very right: I know you are very right. Pray does not Royston lodge in the same house with Harwood?

WITH. He does.

AG. I wish, by his means, we could conceal ourselves somewhere in his apartments, where we might see Harwood
have the letter put into his hands, and observe his behaviour. I don't know anybody else who can do this for us: do
you think you could put him into good humour again?

WITH. I rather think I can, for he hath still a favour to ask of
me.

AG. We must give him a part to act; do you think he can do it?

WITH. He is a very blundering fellow, but he will be so flattered
with being let into the secret, that I know he will do his
best.

Enter MARIANE.

MAR. What have you been about so long together?

WITH. Hatching a new plot, girl! and we set about it directly
too.

MAR. I am very sure the plot is of your own hatching, then, for
I never saw Agnes with any thing of this kind in her head,
wear such a grave spiritless face upon it before.

WITH. You are mistaken, ma'am, it is of her own contrivance,
but you shall know nothing about it. And I give you warning that this shall be the last of them, if you have got any
more poor devils on your hands to torment, do it quickly;
for I will have an end put to all this foolery. I will have my
family put in order again, and well dressed people to drink
tea with me, as I used to have, instead of all this up and
down irregular kind of living, which I abhor.

MAR. Very well, uncle, I have just been following your advice. I
have discarded Sir Ulick O'Grady, and I have only now
poor Opal to reward for his services. I have got a promise
of marriage from him, in which he forfeits ten thousand
pounds if he draws back, I shall torment him with this a little. It was an extraordinary thing to be sure for an heiress to
demand, but I told him it was the fashion; and now that he
has bound himself so securely, he is quite at heart's ease, and
thinks every thing snug and well settled.

Enter ROYSTON, *a Servant announcing him.*

WITH. Your servant, Mr. Royston, I am very glad to see you. Don't start at seeing the ladies with me, I know my niece, Mariane, and you have had a little misunderstanding, but when I have explained the matter to you, you will be friends with her again, and laugh at it yourself.

ROY. (*coldly.*) I have the honour to wish the ladies good morning.

WITH. Nay, cousin, you don't understand how it is; these girls have been playing tricks upon every man they have met with since they came here; and when that wild creature, (*pointing to* Mariane,) was only laughing at the cheat she had passed upon them all, which I shall explain to you presently, you thought she was laughing at you; shake hands, and be friends with her, cousin; nobody minds what a foolish girl does.

ROY. (*With his face brightening up.*) O! for that matter, I mind these things as little as any body, cousin Withrington. I have too many affairs of importance in my hands, to attend to such little matters as these. I am glad the young lady had a hearty laugh with all my soul; and I shall be happy to see her as merry again whenever she has a mind to it. I mind it! no, no, no!

MAR. I thank you, sir, and I hope we shall be merry again, when you shall have your own share of the joke.

ROY. Yes, yes, we shall be very merry. By the bye, Withrington, I came here to tell you, that I have got my business with the duke put into so good a train,[1] that it can hardly misgive.

WITH. I am happy to hear it.

ROY. You must know I have set very artfully about it, cousin; but I dare say you would guess as much, he, he, he! You know me of old, eh? I have got Mr. Cullyfool to ask it for me on his own account; I have bribed an old housekeeper, who is to interest a great lady in my favour; I have called eleven times on his grace's half cousin, till she has

---

1 Order.

fairly promised to write to my lady dutchess upon the business; I have written to the steward, and promised his son all
my interest at next election, if he has any mind to stand for
our borough, you know, and I have applied by a friend—
No, no, he has applied through the medium of another
friend, or rather, I believe, by that friend's wife, or aunt, or
some way or other, I don't exactly remember, but it is a
very good channel, I know.

WITH. O! I make no doubt of it.

ROY. Nay, my landlady, has engaged her apothecary's wife to
speak to his grace's physician about it; and a medical man,
you know, sometimes asks a favour with great advantage,
when a patient believes that his life is in his hands. The
duke has got a most furious fit of gout, and it has been in
his stomach too, ha, ha, ha, ha!—If we can't succeed without it, I have a friend who will offer a round sum for me, at
last, but I hope this will not be necessary. Pray, do you
know of any other good channel to solicit by?

WITH. 'Faith, Royston! you have found out too many roads to
one place already, I fear you'll lose your way amongst them
all.

ROY. Nay, nay, cousin, I won't be put off so. I have been told this
morning you are acquainted with Mr. Sucksop, the duke's
greatest friend and adviser. Come, come! you must use
your interest for me.

WITH. Well, then, come into the other room, and we shall
speak about it. I have a favour to ask of you too.

ROY. My dear sir, any favour in my power you may absolutely
command at all times. I'll follow you, cousin. (*Goes to the
door with* Withrington *with great alacrity, but, recollecting that
he has forgotten to pay his compliments to the ladies, hurries back
again, and, after making several very profound bows to them, follows* Withrington *into another room.*)

MAR. (*Imitating him.*) Ha, ha, ha, ha!

AG. Softly, Mariane; let us leave this room, if you must laugh, for
he will overhear you.

[EXEUNT.

SCENE II.

Royston's *Lodgings: enter* Royston, *conducting in* Agnes, Mariane, *and* Withrington.

ROY. Now, pray compose yourselves, young ladies, and sit down a little. I'll manage every thing: don't give yourselves any trouble; I'll set the whole plot a going.

WITH. We depend entirely upon you, Royston.

ROY. I know you do, many a one depends upon me, cousin Withrington. I'll shew you how I'll manage it. Jonathan, come here, Jonathan! (*Enter* Jonathan.) Bring me that screen from the other room. (*Exit* Jonathan.) We'll place it here, if you please, cousin, and then you and the ladies can stand as snugly behind it, as kings and queens in a puppet-show, till your time comes to appear. (*Enter* Jonathan *with screen*.) Come hither with it, Jonathan: place it here. (*Pointing*.) No, no, jolter-head,[1] nearer the wall with it. (*Going behind it, and coming out again*.) It will do better a little more to this side, for then it will be farther from the window.

AG. O! it will do very well, sir, you take too much trouble.

ROY. Trouble, my dear ma'am! if it were a hundred times more trouble, I should be happy to serve you. I don't mind trouble, if I can get the thing done cleverly and completely. That's my way of doing things. No, it don't stand to please me yet, it is too near the door now, and the ladies may catch cold, perhaps.

AG. (*Very uneasy*.) Indeed, it stands very well! Harwood will be here before we are ready.

ROY. (*to* Jon.) Blockhead, that thou art! can'st thou not set it up even? Now that will do. (*Getting behind it*.) This will do. (*Coming out again*.) Yes, this will do to a nicety.

MAR. (*Aside*.) Heaven be praised this grand matter is settled at last!

ROY. Now, he'll think it odd, perhaps, that I have a screen in my room; but I have a trick for that, ladies; I'll tell him I mean

---

1 Blockhead.

to purchase lands in Canada,[1] and have been looking over the map of America. (*Agnes* looks *to* Withrington *very uneasy.*)

WITH. Don't do that, Royston, for then he will examine the screen.

ROY. Or, I may say, there is a chink in the wall, and I placed it to keep out the air.

AG. No, no, that won't do. For heaven's sake, sir!

ROY. Then I shall just say, I love to have a screen in my room, for I am used to it at home.

MAR. Bless me, Mr. Royston! can't you just leave it alone, and he'll take no notice of it.

ROY. O ! if he takes no notice of it, that is a different thing, Miss Withrington; but don't be uneasy, I'll manage it all: I'll conduct the whole business.

AG. (*Aside to* Withrington.) O! my good sir! this fool will ruin every thing.

WITH. Be quiet, Agnes, we are in for it now.

ROY. Let me remember my lesson too. Here is the letter for him, with the seal as naturally broken, as if the lady had done it herself. Harwood will wonder, now, how I came to know about all this. 'Faith! I believe, he thinks me a strange diving, penetrating, kind of a genius, already, and he is not far wrong, perhaps. You know me, cousin Withrington: ha, ha, ha, ha! You know me.

AG. O! I wish it were over, and we were out of this house again!

ROY. Don't be uneasy, ma'am, I'll manage every thing. Jonathan, (*Enter* Jonathan,) don't you go and tell Mr. Harwood that I have got company here.

JON. No, no, your honour, I knows better than that; for the ladies are to be behind the screen, sir, and he must know

---

1 Just exactly where in Canada Royston may have planned to purchase land is a matter of speculation. Many English, Scots, and Irish emigrated to Prince Edward Island in the late eighteenth and early nineteenth centuries. Or perhaps Royston's speculative interests led him to land sales in Upper Canada after Britain's modification in 1791 of the Quebec Act of 1774. At this time one-seventh of the province's lands were placed in a reserve. The Church of England, whose role was to tie the colonies more firmly to Britain, received the revenues from the purchase or rental of these lands.

nothing of the matter, to be sure. I'ficken![1] it will be rare sport!

AG. (*Starting.*) I hear a knock at the door.

ROY. It is him, I dare say, run Jonathan.

[EXIT, Jonathan.

AG. Come, come, let us hide ourselves. (*All get behind the screen but* Royston.)

ROY. Ay, ay, it will do very well. (*Looking at the screen.*)

AG. (*Behind.*) Mariane, don't breathe so loud.

MAR. (*Behind.*) I don't breathe loud.

AG. (*Behind.*) Do uncle draw in the edge of your coat.   70

WITH. (*Behind.*) Poo, silly girl! they can't see a bit of it.

Enter Colonel HARDY *and* HARWOOD.

ROY. Ha! your servant, my dear Colonel. How goes it, Harwood? I bid my man tell you I was alone, and very much disposed for your good company; but I am doubly fortunate. (*Bowing to the* Colonel.)

COL. Indeed, Royston, I have been pretty much with him these two days past, and I don't believe he gives me great thanks for my company. I am like an old horse running after a colt, the young devil never fails to turn now and then, and give him a kick for his pains.   80

HAR. Nay, my good friend, I must be an ass's colt, then. I am sure, I mean it not, but I am not happy, and I fear I have been peevish with you.

ROY. (*Attempting to look archly.*) Peevish, and all that, perhaps, the young man is in love, Colonel.

COL. No more, if you please, Royston: we are to speak of this no more.

Enter JONATHAN.

---

1 Could this be a variant of "I reckon"? Though Baillie maintained this expression even in the 1851 edition, it does not appear in standard dictionaries of the day nor in later dictionaries of archaisms and provincialisms.

JON. Did your honour call?

ROY. No, sirrah. (Jonathan *goes, as if he were looking for something, and takes a sly peep behind the screen, to see if they are all there.*) What are you peeping there for? get along, you hound! Does he want to make people believe I keep rary shews[1] behind the wainscot? (EXIT, Jonathan.) But as I was a saying, Colonel, perhaps the young man is in love. He, he, he!

COL. No, no, let us have no more of it.

ROY. But 'faith, I know that he is so! and I know the lady too. She is a cousin of my own, and I am as well acquainted with her, as I am with my own dog.—But you don't ask me what kind of a girl she is. (*To the* Colonel.)

COL. Give over now, Royston: she is a very good girl, I dare say.

ROY. Well, you may think so, but—(*Making significant faces.*) But—I should not say all I know of my own cousin, to be sure, but—

HAR. What are all those cursed grimaces for? Her faults are plain and open as her perfections: these she disdains to conceal, and the others it is impossible.

ROY. Softly, Harwood, don't be in a passion, unless you would imitate your mistress; for she has not the gentlest temper in the world.

HAR. Well, well, I love her the better for it. I can't bear your insipid passionless women: I would as soon live upon sweet curd all my life, as attach myself to one of them.

ROY. She is very extravagant.

HAR. Heaven bless the good folks! would they have a man to give up the woman of his heart, because she likes a bit of lace upon her petticoat.

ROY. Well, but she is—

COL. Devil take you, Royston! can't you hold your tongue about her? you see he can't bear it.

ROY. (*Making signs to the* Colonel.) Let me alone; I know when to speak, and when to hold my tongue, as well as another. Indeed, Harwood, I am your friend; and though the lady is my relation, I must say, I wish you had made a better

---

1 Raree-shews; peep shows.

choice. I have discovered something in regard to her this morning, which shews her to be a very improper one. I cannot say, however, that I have discovered any thing which surprised me, I know her too well.

HAR. (*Vehemently.*) You are imposed upon by some damn'd falsehood.

ROY. But I have proof of what I say; the lady who is injured by her, gave me this letter to shew to Mr. Withrington. (*Taking out the letter.*) 130

HAR. It is some fiend who wants to undermine her, and has forged that scrawl to serve her spiteful purpose.

ROY. I would be glad it were so, my dear friend; but Lady Fade is a woman, whose veracity has never been suspected.

HAR. Is it from Lady Fade? Give it me. (*Snatching the letter.*)

ROY. It is Agnes's hand, is it not?

HAR. It is, at least, a good imitation of it.

ROY. Read the contents, pray!

HAR. Madam, what I have said to the prejudice of your lady-ship's character to your relation, Mr. Worthy, I am heartily 140 sorry for; and I am ready to beg pardon on my knees if you desire it; to acknowledge before Mr. Worthy himself, that it is a falsehood, or make any other reparation, in a private way, that you may desire. Let me, then, conjure your lady-ship not to expose me, and I shall ever remain your most penitent and grateful A. Withrington.

ROY. The lady would not be so easily pacified, though; for she blackened her character, in order to make her best friend upon earth quarrel with her; so she gave me the letter to shew to her uncle. Is it forged, think you? 150

HAR. It is possible!—I will venture to say—Nay, I am sure it is.

ROY. If it is, there is one circumstance which may help to dis-cover the author, it is directed by a different hand on the back. Look at it.

HAR. (*In great perturbation.*) Is it? (*Turns hastily the folds of the letter, but his hand trembles so much, he can't find the back.*)

COL. My dear Harwood! this is the back of the letter; and methinks the writing is somewhat like your own. (*Harwood looks at it; then staggering back, throws himself into a*

  chair, which happens to be behind him, and covers his upper face
  with his hand.)

COL. My dear Harwood!

ROY. See how his lips quiver, and his bosom heaves! Let us
160 unbutton him: I fear he is going into a fit. (Agnes *comes*
  from behind the screen in a fright, and Withrington *pulls her in*
  again.)

COL. (*With great tenderness.*) My dear Harwood!

HAR. (*With a broken voice.*) I'll go to mine own chamber. (*Gets*
  up hastily from his chair, and then falls back again in a faint.)

COL. He's gone off.

ROY. Help, help, here! (*Running about.*) Who has got hartshorn,[1]
  or lavender, or water! help here. (*They all come from behind*
  the screen. Agnes *runs to* Harwood, *and sprinkles him over with*
  lavender, rubbing his temples, &c. whilst Colonel Hardy *stares at*
  them all in amazement.)

AG. Alas! we have carried this too far? Harwood! my dear Harwood!

COL. (*to* Roy.) What is all this?

ROY. I thought we should amaze you. I knew I should manage
170 it.

COL. You have managed finely indeed, to put Harwood into
  such a state, with your mummery.

AG. Will he not come to himself again! get some water, Mariane—See how pale he is. (*He recovers.*) O! he recovers!
  Harwood! do you know me, Harwood?

HAR. (*Looking upon* Agnes, *and shrinking back from her.*) Ha! what
  has brought you here? leave me! leave me! I am wretched
  enough already.

AG. I come to bring you relief, my dear Harwood.

180 HAR. No, madam, it is misery you bring. We must part for ever.

AG. O! uncle! do you hear that? He says we must part for ever.

WITH. (*Taking hold of* Agnes.) Don't be in such a hurry about it.

HAR. (*Rising up.*) How came you here? (*to* Withrington.) and
  these ladies?

ROY. O! it was all my contrivance.

---

1 The hart's horn was the source of ammonia from which its aqueous form, spirit of
  hartshorn (smelling salts), was produced.

WITH. Pray now, Royston, be quiet a little—Mr. Harwood, I will speak to you seriously. I see you are attached to my niece, and I confess she has many faults; but you are a man of sense, and with you she will make a more respectable figure in the world than with any other. I am anxious for her welfare, and if you will marry her I will give her such a fortune as will make it no longer an imprudent step to follow your inclinations.

HAR. No, sir, you shall keep your fortune and your too bewitching niece together. For her sake I would have renounced all ambition, I would have shared with her poverty and neglect, I would have borne with all her faults and weaknesses of nature, I would have toiled, I would have bled for her, but I can never yoke myself with unworthiness.

AG. (*Wiping her eyes, and giving two skips upon the floor.*) O! admirable! admirable! speak to him, uncle! tell him all, my dear uncle! for I can't say a word.

COL. (*Aside to* Royston.) Isn't she a little wrong in the head, Royston?

WITH. Give me your hand, Harwood: you are a noble fellow, and you shall marry this little girl of mine after all. This story of the letter and Lady Fade, was only a concerted one amongst us, to prove what mettle you are made of. Agnes, to try your love, affected to be shrewish and extravagant; and afterwards, at my suggestion, to try your principles, contrived this little plot, which has just now been unravelled: but I do assure you, on the word of an honest man, there is not a better girl in the kingdom. I must own, however, she is a fanciful little toad. (Harwood *runs to* Agnes, *catches her in his arms, and runs two or three times round with her, then takes her hand and kisses it, and then puts his knee to the ground.*)

HAR. My charming, my delightful Agnes! Oh! what a fool have I been! how could I suppose it.

AG. We took some pains upon you, and it would have been hard if we could not have deceived you amongst us all.

HAR. And so thou art a good girl, a very good girl. I know thou art. I'll be hang'd if thou hast one fault in the world.

WITH. No, no, Harwood, not quite so perfect. I can prove her still to be an arrant cheat; for she pretended to be careless of you when she thought of you all the day long, and she pretended to be poor with an hundred thousand pounds, independant of any one, in her possession. She is Miss Withrington the heiress, and this lady, (*pointing to* Mariane) has only been her representative, for a time, for reasons which I shall explain to you by-and-by.

(Harwood *lets go* Agnes's *hand, and steps back some paces with a certain gravity and distance in his air.*)

230 WITH. What is the matter now, Harwood, does this cast a damp upon you?

ROY. It is a weighty distress, truly. Ha, ha, ha, ha!

COL. By heaven! this is good.

AG. (*Going up to* Harwood, *and holding out her hand.*) Do not look so distantly upon me, Harwood. You was[1] willing to marry me as a poor woman; if there is any thing in my fortune which offends you, I scatter it to the winds.

HAR. My admirable girl, it is astonishment, it is something I cannot express, which overcomes, I had almost said dis-
240 tresses me at present. (*Presenting her to the* Colonel.) Colonel Hardy, this is the woman I have raved about, this is the woman I have boasted of, this is my Agnes. And this, Miss Withrington, is Colonel Hardy, my own, and my father's friend.

AG. (*Holding out her hand to the* Colonel.) He shall be mine too. Every friend of your's shall be my friend, Harwood; but the friend of your father my most respected one.

HAR. Do you hear that, Colonel?

COL. I hear it, my heart hears it, I bless you both.

250 HAR. (*to* With.) My dear sir, what shall I say to you for all this goodness?

AG. Tell him he is the dearest good uncle on earth, and we will love him all our lives for it. Yes, indeed, we will, uncle, (*clapping his shoulder,*) very, very dearly.

---

1 Changed to "were" in the 1851 edition.

ROY. Now, good folks, have not I managed it cleverly?

MAR. Pray let me come from the background a little: and since I must quit all the splendour of heiresship, I desire, at least, that I may have some respect paid me for having filled the situation so well, as the old Mayor receives the thanks of the corporation,[1] when the new Mayor—Bless me! here comes Opal! I have not just done with it yet.   260

WITH. Your servant, Mr. Opal.

MAR. (*to* Op.) Are not you surprised to find us all here?

OP. Harwood I know is a very lucky fellow, but I knew you were here. It is impossible, you see, to escape me. But (*half aside to* Mariane.) I wanted to tell you Colonel Beaumont is come to Bath. Now I should like to be introduced to him on his arrival. He will be very much the fashion I dare say, and I should like to have a friendship for him. You understand me? You can procure this for me, I know.   270

WITH. Come, Mr. Opal, you must join in our good humour here, for we have just been making up a match. My niece, Agnes, with a large fortune bestows herself on a worthy man, who would have married her without one; and, Mariane, who for certain reasons has assumed her character of heiress since we came to Bath, leaves all her borrowed state, in hopes that the man who would have married with a fortune, will not now forsake her.

OP. (*Stammering.*) Wh—Wh—What is all this?

ROY. (*Half aside to* Opal.) You seem disturbed, Mr. Opal, you have not been paying your addresses to her, I hope.   280

OP. (*Aside to* Royston.) No, not paying my addresses; that is to say, not absolutely. I have paid her some attention to be sure.

ROY. (*Nodding significantly.*) It is well for you it is no worse.

MAR. (*Turning to* Opal, *who looks very much frightened.*) What is it you say? Don't you think I overheard it? Not paid your addresses to me! O! you false man! can you deny the declarations you have made? the oaths you have sworn? O! you false man!   290

---

1 The civic authorities of a borough.

OP. Upon honour, madam, we men of fashion don't expect to be called to an account for every foolish thing we say.

MAR. What you have written then shall witness against you. Will you deny this promise of marriage in your own hand-writing? (*Taking out a paper.*)

ROY. (*Aside to* Opal.) What, a promise of marriage, Mr. Opal? The devil himself could not have put it into your head to do a worse thing than this.

OP. (*Very frightened, but making a great exertion.*) Don't think, ma'am, to bully me into the match. I can prove that promise to be given to you under the false character of an heiress, therefore your deceit loosens the obligation.

WITH. Take care what you say, sir, (*to* Opal.) I will not see my niece wronged. The law shall do her justice, whatever expence it may cost me.

MAR. Being an heiress or not has nothing to do in the matter, Mr. Opal; for you expressly say in this promise, that my beauty and perfections alone have induced you to engage yourself, and I will take all the men in court to witness, whether I am not as handsome to-day as I was yesterday.

OP. I protest there is not such a word in the paper.

MAR. (*Holding out the paper.*) O base man! will you deny your own writing? (*Opal snatches the paper from her, tears it to pieces.*)

MAR. (*Gathering up the scattered pieces.*) O! I can put them together again. (*Opal, snatching up one of the pieces, crams it into his mouth and chews it.*)

ROY. Chew fast, Opal, she will snatch it out of your mouth else. There is another bit for you. (*Offering him another piece.*)

MAR. (*Bursting into a loud laugh, in which all the company join.*) Is it very nice, Mr. Opal? You munch it up as expeditiously as a bit of plumb-cake.

OP. What the deuce does all this mean?

WITH. This naughty girl, Mr. Opal, has only been amusing her-self with your promise, which she never meant to make any other use of; she is already engaged to a very worthy young man, who will receive with her a fortune by no means contemptible.

OP. Well, well, much good may it do him: what do I care about—(*mumbling to himself.*)

ROY. (*Clapping* Opal's *shoulder.*) Ha, ha, ha! don't look so foolish, man; you did not know a word of all this, now. Ha, ha, ha! how some people do get themselves into scrapes! They have no more notion of managing their affairs than if they were so many sheep. Ha, ha, ha, ha! 330

Enter HUMPHRY.

HUMPH. (*to* Roy.) I would speak a word with your honour. (*Whispers to* Royston.)

ROY. (*In a rage.*) What! given away the place! It is impossible! It is some wicked machination! it is some damn'd trick!

WITH. Be moderate, Royston: what has good Mr. Humphry been telling you?

ROY. O! the devil of a bite! his grace has given away the place to a poor simpleton, who had never a soul to speak for him. 340

WITH. Who told you this, Mr. Humphry?

HUMPH. Truly, sir, I called upon his Grace's gentleman, just to make up a kind of acquaintance with him, as his honour desired me, and he told me it was given away this morning.

ROY. What cursed luck!

HUMPH. Why, says I, I thought my master was to have had it, Mr. Smoothly; and so he would, says he, but one person came to the Duke after another, teazing him about Mr. Royston, till he grew quite impatient; for there was but one of all those friends, says he, winking with his eye so, who did speak at last to the purpose, but then upon Mr. Sucksop's taking up your master's interest, he shrunk back from his word, which offended his grace very much. 350

ROY. Blundering blockhead!

HUMPH. But after all, says he, it might have come round again, if the gout had not stung him so wickedly, when in came the doctor,[1] who has promised to cure him these three weeks,

---

1 The 1806 and 1851 editions deleted any reference to the doctor. They read: "And so he gave away the place directly to poor Mr. Drudgewell, who had no recommendation at all, but fifteen years' hard service in the office."

and only made it so much the worse, and upon his likewise
360 presuming to teaze him about Mr. Royston, he fell into a
violent passion, and gave away the place directly to poor
Mr. Drudgewell, who had no recommendation at all, but
fifteen years hard service in the office.

ROY. Well, now! well, now! you see how the world goes: sim-
pletons and ideots carry every thing before them.

WITH. Nay, Royston, blame yourself too. Did not I tell you,
you had found out too many roads to one place, and would
lose your way amongst them?

ROY. No, no, it is all that cursed perverse fate of mine! By the
370 Lord, half the trouble I have taken for this paltry office,
would have procured some people an archbishoprick.
There is Harwood, now, fortune presses herself upon him,
and makes him, at one stroke, an idle gentleman for life.

HAR. No, sir, an idle gentleman I will never be: my Agnes shall
never be the wife of any thing so contemptible.

AG. I thank you, Harwood; I do, indeed, look for an honourable
distinction in being your wife; you shall still exert your
powers in the profession you have chosen: you shall be the
weak one's stay, the poor man's advocate; you shall gain fair
380 fame in recompense, and that will be our nobility.

WITH. Well said, my children! you have more sense than I
thought you had amongst all these whimsies. Now, let us
take our leave of plots and story-telling, if you please, and
all go to my house to supper. Royston shall drown his disappointment in a can of warm negus,[1] and Mr. Opal shall
have something more palatable than his last spare morsel.

[EXEUNT.

THE END OF THE TRYAL.

---

1 A hot mulled wine made from sherry or port named after its inventor, Colonel
Francis Negus (d. 1732), who served under Marlborough.

DE MONFORT

A TRAGEDY

PERSONS OF THE DRAMA.

MEN.

DE MONFORT.

REZENVELT.

COUNT FREBERG, *Friend to* De Monfort *and* Rezenvelt.

MANUEL, *Servant to* De Monfort.

JEROME, De Monfort's *old Landlord.*

GRIMBALD, *an artful knave.*

BERNARD, *a Monk.*

Monks, Gentlemen, Officers, Page, &c. &c.

WOMEN.

JANE DE MONFORT, *sister to* De Monfort.

COUNTESS FREBERG, *Wife to* Freberg.

THERESA, *Servant to the* Countess.

Abbess, Nuns, *and a* Lay Sister, Ladies, &c.

Scene, a Town in Germany.

"Alone with thee!" (*De Monfort* 5.3.70).
Engraving by N. Schiovonetti. Courtesy University of Chicago Library.

DE MONFORT.

ACT I.—SCENE I.

JEROME's *House. A large old fashioned Chamber.*

JER. (*speaking without.*) This way good masters.

Enter JEROME, *bearing a light, and followed by* Manuel, *and*
Servants *carrying luggage.*

                  Rest your burdens here.
This spacious room will please the Marquis best.
He takes me unawares; but ill prepar'd:
If he had sent, e'en tho' a hasty notice,
I had been glad.
MAN.   Be not disturb'd, good Jerome;
Thy house is in most admirable order;
And they who travel o'cold winter nights
Think homeliest quarters good.
JER. He is not far behind?
MAN.   A little way,
    (*To the servants.*) Go you and wait below till he arrives.   10
JER. (*Shaking* Manuel *by the hand.*)
    Indeed, my friend, I'm glad to see you here,
    Yet marvel wherefore.
MAN. I marvel wherefore too, my honest Jerome:
    But here we are, pri'thee be kind to us.
JER. Most heartily I will. I love your master:
    He is a quiet and a lib'ral man:
    A better inmate[1] never cross'd my door.
MAN. Ah! but he is not now the man he was.
    Lib'ral he will, God grant he may be quiet.
JER. What has befallen him?

---

[1] Lodger.

MAN. I cannot tell thee;
But faith, there is no living with him now.

JER. And yet, methinks, if I remember well,
You were about to quit his service, Manuel,
When last he left this house. You grumbled then.

MAN. I've been upon the eve of leaving him
These ten long years; for many times is he
So difficult, capricious, and distrustful,
He galls my nature—yet, I know not how,
A secret kindness binds me to him still.

JER. Some, who offend from a suspicious nature,
Will afterwards such fair confession make
As turns e'en the offence into a favour.

MAN. Yes, some indeed do so: so will not he;
He'd rather die than such confession make.

JER. Ay, thou art right, for now I call to mind
That once he wrong'd me with unjust suspicion,
When first he came to lodge beneath my roof;
And when it so fell out that I was proved
Most guiltless of the fault, I truly thought

He would have made profession of regret;
But silent, haughty, and ungraciously
He bore himself as one offended still.
Yet shortly after, when unwittingly
I did him some slight service, o' the sudden
He overpower'd me with his grateful thanks;
And would not be restrain'd from pressing on me
A noble recompense. I understood
His o'erstrain'd gratitude and bounty well,
And took it as he meant.

MAN.   'Tis often thus.

I would have left him many years ago,
But that with all his faults there sometimes come
Such bursts of natural goodness from his heart,
As might engage a harder churl than I
To serve him still.—And then his sister too,
A noble dame, who should have been a queen:

The meanest of her hinds,[1] at her command,
Had fought like lions for her, and the poor,
E'en o'er their bread of poverty had bless'd her—
She would have griev'd if I had left my Lord.

JER. Comes she along with him? 60

MAN. No, he departed all unknown to her,
Meaning to keep conceal'd his secret route;
But well I knew it would afflict her much,
And therefore left a little nameless billet,
Which after our departure, as I guess,
Would fall into her hands, and tell her all.
What could I do? O 'tis a noble lady!

JER. All this is strange—something disturbs his mind—
Belike he is in love.

MAN.   No, Jerome, no.
Once on a time I serv'd a noble master, 70
Whose youth was blasted with untoward love,
And he with hope and fear and jealousy
For ever toss'd, led an unquiet life:
Yet, when unruffled by the passing fit,
His pale wan face such gentle sadness wore
As mov'd a kindly heart to pity him;
But Monfort, even in his calmest hour,
Still bears that gloomy sternness in his eye
Which sullenly repells all sympathy.
O no! good Jerome, no, it is not love. 80

JER. Hear I not horses trampling at the gate?
(*Listening.*)
He is arriv'd—stay thou—I had forgot—
A plague upon't! my head is so confus'd—
I will return i'the instant to receive him.

(EXIT *hastily.*)

(*A great bustle without.* EXIT Manuel *with lights, and returns again lighting in* DE MONFORT, *as if just alighted from his journey.*)

---

1 Rustics or servants.

MAN. Your ancient host, my lord, receives you gladly,
And your apartment will be soon prepar'd.
DE MON. 'Tis well.
MAN. Where shall I place the chest you gave in charge?
So please you, say my lord.
90 DE MON. (*Throwing himself into a chair.*) Where-e'er thou wilt.
MAN. I would not move that luggage till you came.
(*Pointing to certain things.*)
DE MON. Move what thou wilt, and trouble me no more.
(Manuel, *with the assistance of other Servants, sets about putting
the things in order, and De Monfort remains sitting in a
thoughtful posture.*)

Enter JEROME, *bearing wine, &c. on a salver. As he approaches* De
Monfort, Manuel *pulls him by the sleeve.*

MAN. (*Aside to* Jerome.) No, do not now; he will not be
disturb'd.
JER. What not to bid him welcome to my house,
And offer some refreshment?
MAN.   No, good Jerome.
Softly, a little while: I pri'thee do.
(Jerome *walks softly on tip-toes, till he gets near* De Monfort,
behind backs, then peeping on one side to see his face.)
JER. (*Aside to* Manuel.) Ah, Manuel, what an alter'd man is
here!
His eyes are hollow, and his cheeks are pale—
He left this house a comely gentleman.
DE MON. Who whispers there?
100 MAN.   'Tis your old landlord, sir:
JER. I joy to see you here—I crave your pardon—
I fear I do intrude.—
DE MON. No, my kind host, I am oblig'd to thee.
JER. How fares it with your honour?
DE MON.   Well enough.
JER. Here is a little of the fav'rite wine
That you were wont to praise. Pray honour me.
(*Fills a glass.*)

DE MON. (*After drinking.*) I thank you, Jerome, 'tis delicious.

JER. Ay, my dear wife did ever make it so.

DE MON. And how does she?

JER.   Alas, my lord! she's dead.

DE MON. Well,[1] then she is at rest.

JER.   How well, my lord?   110

DE MON. Is she not with the dead, the quiet dead,
　　Where all is peace. Not e'en the impious wretch,
　　Who tears the coffin from its earthy vault,
　　And strews the mould'ring ashes to the wind
　　Can break their rest.

JER. Woe's me! I thought you would have griev'd for her.
　　She was a kindly soul! Before she died,
　　When pining sickness bent her cheerless head,
　　She set my house in order—
　　And but the morning ere she breath'd her last,   120
　　Bade me preserve some flaskets of this wine,
　　That should the Lord De Monfort come again
　　His cup might sparkle still.
　　(De Monfort *walks across the stage, and wipes his eyes.*)
　　Indeed I fear I have distress'd you, sir:
　　I surely thought you would be griev'd for her.

DE MON. (*Taking* Jerome's *hand.*) I am, my friend. How long
　　has she been dead?

JER. Two sad long years.

DE MON.   Would she were living still!
　　I was too troublesome, too heedless of her.

JER. O no! she lov'd to serve you.
　　(*Loud knocking without.*)

DE MON. What fool comes here, at such untimely hours,   130
　　To make this cursed noise. (*To* Manuel.) Go to the gate.

[EXIT Manuel.

All sober citizens are gone to bed;
It is some drunkards on their nightly rounds,

1　The initial "well" here indicates a matter for thankfulness and an acceptance of the
　situation.

Who mean it but in sport.

JER. I hear unusual voices—here they come.

Re-enter MANUEL, *shewing in* Count FREBERG *and his* LADY.

FREB. (*Running to embrace* De Monfort.)
 My dearest Monfort! most unlook'd-for pleasure.
 Do I indeed embrace thee here again?
 I saw thy servant standing by the gate,
 His face recall'd, and learnt the joyful tidings.
140 Welcome, thrice welcome here!

DE MON. I thank thee, Freberg, for this friendly visit,
 And this fair Lady too. (*Bowing to the* Lady.)

LADY.   I fear, my Lord,
 We do intrude at an untimely hour:
 But now returning from a midnight mask,
 My husband did insist that we should enter.

FREB. No, say not so; no hour untimely call,
 Which doth together bring long absent friends.
 Dear Monfort, wherefore hast thou play'd so sly,
 To come upon us thus all suddenly?

150 DE MON. O! many varied thoughts do cross our brain,
 Which touch the will, but leave the memory trackless;
 And yet a strange compounded motive[1] make
 Wherefore a man should bend his evening walk
 To th' east or west, the forest or the field.
 Is it not often so?

FREB. I ask no more, happy to see you here
 From any motive. There is one behind,
 Whose presence would have been a double bliss:
 Ah! how is she? The noble Jane de Monfort.[2]

160 DE MON. (*Confused.*) She is—I have—I have left my sister well.

LADY. (*To* Freberg.) My Freberg, you are heedless of respect:

---

1 Writers of the seventeenth and eighteenth centuries spoke of action *on* a motive
 rather than *from* one as we do today.

2 In the Larpent performance version, a treatment of *De Montfort* by John Philip
 Kemble, Rezenvelt's name is mentioned in this dialogue, eliminating Freberg's surprise in 1.1.198. For this and other interesting textual variants see Cox, *Seven Gothic Dramas* 232-313.

You surely meant to say the Lady Jane.

FREB. Respect! No, Madam; Princess, Empress, Queen,
Could not denote a creature so exalted
As this plain native appellation doth,
The noble Jane de Monfort.

LADY. (*Turning from him displeased to* Monfort.)
You are fatigued, my Lord; you want repose;
Say, should we not retire?

FREB.   Ha! is it so?
My friend, your face is pale, have you been ill?

DE MON. No, Freberg, no; I think I have been well.   170

FREB. (*Shaking his head.*) I fear thou hast not, Monfort—Let it
pass.
We'll re-establish thee: we'll banish pain.
I will collect some rare, some cheerful friends,
And we shall spend together glorious hours,
That gods might envy. Little time so spent
Doth far outvalue all our life beside.
This is indeed our life, our waking life,
The rest dull breathing sleep.

DE MON. Thus, it is true, from the sad years of life
We sometimes do short hours, yea minutes strike,   180
Keen, blissful, bright, never to be forgotten;
Which thro' the dreary gloom of time o'erpast
Shine like fair sunny spots[1] on a wild waste.
But few they are, as few the heaven-fir'd souls
Whose magick power creates them. Bless'd art thou,
If in the ample circle of thy friends
Thou canst but boast a few.

FREB. Judge for thyself: in truth I do not boast.
There is amongst my friends, my later friends,
A most accomplish'd stranger. New to Amberg,[2]   190
But just arriv'd; and will ere long depart.
I met him in Franconia[3] two years since.
He is so full of pleasant anecdote,

---

1   Cf. William Wordsworth, *The Prelude* Bk. 12: 208-18.
2   A city approximately 50 km east of Nuremberg.
3   A region of Bavaria.

So rich, so gay, so poignant is his wit,
Time vanishes before him as he speaks,
And ruddy morning thro' the lattice peeps
Ere night seems well begun.

DE MON.   How is he call'd?

FREB. I will surprise thee with a welcome face:
I will not tell thee now.

200 LADY. (*to* Mon.) I have, my Lord, a small request to make,
And must not be denied. I too may boast
Of some good friends, and beauteous countrywomen:
To-morrow night I open wide my doors
To all the fair and gay; beneath my roof
Musick, and dance, and revelry shall reign.
I pray you come and grace it with your presence.

DE MON. You honour me too much to be denied.

LADY. I thank you, Sir; and in return for this,
We shall withdraw, and leave you to repose.

210 FREB. Must it be so? Good night—sweet sleep to thee.
(*To* De Monfort.)

DE MON. (*to* Freb.) Good night. (*To* Lady.)
                        Good-night, fair Lady.

LADY.   Farewel!

[EXEUNT Freberg *and* Lady.]

DE MON. (*to* Jer.) I thought Count Freberg had been now in
France.

JER. He meant to go, as I have been inform'd.

DE MON. Well, well, prepare my bed; I will to rest.

[EXIT Jerome.

DE MON. (*alone.*) I know not how it is, my heart stands back,
And meets not this man's love.—Friends! rarest friends!
Rather than share his undiscerning praise
With every table wit, and book-form'd sage,
And paltry poet puling to the moon,
220 I'd court from him proscription; yea abuse,
And think it proud distinction.   [EXIT.

SCENE II.

A Small Apartment in JEROME's *House: a table and breakfast set out.*
Enter DE MONFORT, *followed by* MANUEL, *and sets himself down*
by the table, with a cheerful face.

DE MON. Manuel, this morning's sun shines pleasantly:
　　These old apartments too are light and cheerful.
　　Our landlord's kindness has reviv'd me much;
　　He serves as though he lov'd me. This pure air
　　Braces the listless nerves, and warms the blood:
　　I feel in freedom here.
　　(*Filling a cup of coffee, and drinking.*)
MAN. 　　　　　　　Ah! sure, my Lord,
　　No air is purer than the air at home.
DE MON. Here can I wander with assured steps,
　　Nor dread, at every winding of the path,
　　Lest an abhorred serpent cross my way,　　　　　　　　10
　　And move—(*Stopping short.*)
MAN. 　　　　　What says your honour?
　　There are no serpents in our pleasant fields.
DE MON. Think'st thou there are no serpents in the world
　　But those who slide along the grassy sod,
　　And sting the luckless foot that presses them?
　　There are who in the path of social life
　　Do bask their spotted skins in Fortune's sun,
　　And sting the soul—Ay, till its healthful frame
　　Is chang'd to secret, fest'ring, sore disease,
　　So deadly is the wound.　　　　　　　　　　　　　　20
MAN. Heaven guard your honour from such horrid skathe:[1]
　　They are but rare, I hope?
DE MON. (*Shaking his head.*) We mark the hollow eye, the
　　wasted frame,
　　The gait disturb'd of wealthy honour'd men,
　　But do not know the cause.
MAN. 'Tis very true. God keep you well, my Lord!

1　A dialectical variant of "scathe"; hurt, harm, or damage, with a potential connec-
　tion to witchcraft.

DE MON. I thank thee, Manuel, I am very well.
  I shall be gay too, by the setting sun.
  I go to revel it with sprightly dames,
30 And drive the night away.
  (*Filling another cup and drinking.*)
MAN. I should be glad to see your honour gay.
DE MON. And thou too shalt be gay. There, honest Manuel,
  Put these broad pieces in thy leathern purse,
  And take at night a cheerful jovial glass.
  Here is one too, for Bremer;[1] he loves wine;
  And one for Jacques: be joyful all together.

Enter SERVANT.

SER. My Lord, I met e'en now, a short way off,
  Your countryman the Marquis Rezenvelt.
DE MON. (*Starting from his seat, and letting the cup fall from his hand.*)
  Who, say'st thou?
SER.   Marquis Rezenvelt, an' please you.
40 DE MON. Thou ly'st—it is not so—it is impossible.
SER. I saw him with these eyes, plain as yourself.
DE MON. Fool! 'tis some passing stranger thou hast seen,
  And with a hideous likeness been deceiv'd.
SER. No other stranger could deceive my sight.
DE MON. (*Dashing his clenched hand violently upon the table, and overturning every thing.*)
  Heaven blast thy sight! it lights on nothing good.
SER. I surely thought no harm to look upon him.
DE MON. What, dost thou still insist? Him must it be?
  Does it so please thee well? (Servant *endeavours to speak.*)
  hold thy damn'd tongue.
  By heaven I'll kill thee. (*Going furiously up to him.*)
MAN. (*In a soothing voice.*)
50 Nay harm him not, my Lord; he speaks the truth;
  I've met his groom, who told me certainly

---

1 Cf. Cox, *Seven Gothic Dramas* 239 n37.

His Lord is here. I should have told you so,
But thought, perhaps, it might displease your honour.
DE MON. (*Becoming all at once calm, and turning sternly to*
Manuel.)
And how dar'st thou to think it would displease me?
What is't to me who leaves or enters Amberg?
But it displeases me, yea ev'n to frenzy,
That every idle fool must hither come
To break my leisure with the paltry tidings
Of all the cursed things he stares upon.
(Servant *attempts to speak*—De Monfort *stamps with*
his foot.)
Take thine ill-favour'd visage from my sight,   60
And speak of it no more.   [EXIT Servant.
DE MON. And go thou too; I choose to be alone.
                                        [EXIT Manuel.
(De Monfort *goes to the door by which they went out; opens it,*
and looks.)
But is he gone indeed? Yes, he is gone.
(*Goes to the opposite door, opens it, and looks: then gives loose to*
all the fury of gesture, and walks up and down in great
agitation.)
It is too much: by heaven it is too much!
He haunts me—stings me—like a devil haunts—
He'll make a raving maniack of me—Villain!
The air wherein thou draw'st thy fulsome breath
Is poison to me—Oceans shall divide! (*Pauses.*)
But no; thou think'st I fear thee, cursed reptile!
And hast a pleasure in the damned thought.   70
Though my heart's blood should curdle at thy sight,
I'll stay and face thee still.
(*Knocking at the chamber door.*)
                    Ha! Who knocks there?
FREBERG. (*Without.*) It is thy friend, De Monfort.
DE MON. (*Opening the door.*) Enter, then.

                    Enter FREBERG.

FREB. (*Taking his hand kindly.*)
  How art thou now? How hast thou past the night?
  Has kindly sleep refresh'd thee?
DE MON. Yes, I have lost an hour or two in sleep,
  And so should be refresh'd
FREB.   And art thou not?
  Thy looks speak not of rest. Thou art disturb'd.
80 DE MON. No, somewhat ruffled from a foolish cause,
  Which soon will pass away.
FREB. (*Shaking his head.*) Ah no, De Monfort! something in thy
  face
  Tells me another tale. Then wrong me not:
  If any secret grief distracts thy soul,
  Here am I all devoted to thy love;
  Open thy heart to me. What troubles thee?
DE MON. I have no grief: distress me not, my friend.
FREB. Nay, do not call me so. Wert thou my friend,
  Would'st thou not open all thine inmost soul,
90 And bid me share its every consciousness?
DE MON. Freberg, thou know'st not man; not nature's man,
  But only him who, in smooth studied works
  Of polish'd sages, shines deceitfully
  In all the splendid foppery of virtue.
  That man was never born whose secret soul
  With all its motley treasure of dark thoughts,
  Foul fantasies, vain musing, and wild dreams,
  Was ever open'd to another's scan.
  Away, away! it is delusion all.
100 FREB. Well, be reserved then: perhaps I'm wrong.
DE MON. How goes the hour?
FREB. 'Tis early: a long day is still before us,
  Let us enjoy it. Come along with me;
  I'll introduce you to my pleasant friend.
DE MON. Your pleasant friend?
FREB.   Yes, he of whom I spake.
  (*Taking his hand.*)
  There is no good I would not share with thee,
  And this man's company, to minds like thine,

Is the best banquet-feast I could bestow.
But I will speak in mystery no more,
It is thy townsman, noble Rezenvelt. 110
(De Mon. *Pulls his hand hastily from* Freberg,
and shrinks back.)
Ha! What is this? Art thou pain-stricken, Monfort?
Nay, on my life, thou rather seem'st offended:
Does it displease thee that I call him friend?
DE MON. No, all men are thy friends.
FREB. No, say not all men. But thou art offended.
I see it well. I thought to do thee pleasure.
But if his presence is not welcome here,
He shall not join our company to-day.
DE MON. What dost thou mean to say? What is't to me
Whether I meet with such a thing as Rezenvelt 120
To-day, to-morrow, every day, or never.
FREB. In truth, I thought you had been well with him.
He prais'd you much.
DE MON. I thank him for his praise—Come, let us move:
This chamber is confin'd and airless grown.
(*Starting.*)
I hear a stranger's voice!
FREB. 'Tis Rezenvelt.
Let him be told that we are gone abroad.[1]
DE MON. (*Proudly.*)
No; let him enter. Who waits there? Ho! Manuel!

Enter MANUEL.

What stranger speaks below?
MAN. The Marquis Rezenvelt.
I have not told him that you are within. 130
DE MON. (*Angrily.*) And wherefore did'st thou not? Let him
ascend.
(*A long pause. De Monfort walking up and down with a quick
pace.*)

---

1 Out of one's house; outdoors.

Enter REZENVELT, *and runs freely up to* De Monfort.

REZ. (*to* De Mon.) My noble Marquis, welcome.

DE MON.   Sir, I thank you.

REZ. (*to* Freb.) My gentle friend, well met. Abroad so early?

FREB. It is indeed an early hour for me.
How sits thy last night's revel on thy spirits?

REZ. O, light as ever. On my way to you
E'en now I learnt De Monfort was arriv'd,
And turn'd my steps aside; so here I am.
(*Bowing gaily to* De Monfort.)

DE MON. I thank you, Sir; you do me too much honour.
(*Proudly.*)

REZ. Nay, say not so; not too much honour, Marquis,
Unless, indeed, 'tis more than pleases you.

DE MON. (*Confused.*) Having no previous notice of your
coming,
I look'd not for it.

REZ. Ay, true indeed; when I approach you next,
I'll send a herald to proclaim my coming,
And make my bow to you by sound of trumpet.

DE MON. (*to* Freb.) (*Turning haughtily from* Rezenvelt *with affected
indifference.*)
How does your cheerful friend, that good old man?

FREB. My cheerful friend? I know not whom you mean.

DE MON. Count Waterlan.

FREB.   I know not one so named.

DE MON. (*Very confused.*) O pardon me—it was at Bâle I knew
him.

FREB. You have not yet enquired for honest Reisdale.
I met him as I came, and mention'd you.
He seem'd amaz'd; and fain he would have learnt
What cause procur'd us so much happiness.
He question'd hard, and hardly would believe
I could not satisfy his strong desire.

REZ. And know you not what brings De Monfort here?

FREB. Truly, I do not.

REZ.   O! 'tis love of me.

I have but two short days in Amberg been,
And here with postman's speed[1] he follows me,
Finding his home so dull and tiresome grown.

FREB. (*to* De Mon.) Is Rezenvelt so sadly miss'd with you?
Your town so chang'd?

DE MON.   Not altogether so:
Some witlings and jest-mongers still remain
For fools to laugh at.

REZ. But he laughs not, and therefore he is wise.
He ever frowns on them with sullen brow
Contemptuous; therefore he is very wise.
Nay, daily frets his most refined soul
With their poor folly, to its inmost core;
Therefore he is most eminently wise.

FREB. Fy, Rezenvelt! You are too early gay;
Such spirits rise but with the ev'ning glass.
They suit not placid morn.
(*To* De Monfort, *who after walking impatiently up and down,
comes close to his ear, and lays hold of his arm.*)
What would you, Monfort?

DE MON. Nothing—Yet, what is't o'clock?
No, no—I had forgot—'tis early still.
(*Turns away again.*)

FREB. (*to* Rez.) Waltser informs me that you have agreed
To read his verses o'er, and tell the truth.
It is a dangerous task.

REZ.   Yet I'll be honest:

---

1   We can imagine the frantic and precarious nature of this speed, particularly in a
mail coach designed for rapid transport. English roads, as Roy Porter describes in
English Society in the Eighteenth Century, were notoriously unpleasant, since "the
bulk goods hauled in huge waggons rutted them, and livestock droves turned them
into ribbon dungheaps" (191). By 1750, however, turnpike roads – a system of toll
highways begun in Stuart times – connected London to other major centres such as
Manchester, Bristol, Birmingham, York, and Dover. At that time, 143 turnpike
trusts controlled 3,400 miles of highway, and by 1770, 500 trusts administered 5,000
miles of roads. Public passenger traffic between Leicester and London began in
1753, loosely servicing the link, as the owner of the service described, "on Monday,
Tuesday, Wednesday *or* Thursday," and by 1765 even a "flying machine" was servicing the link in one day. See Thomas De Quincey's (1785-1859) *The English Mail
Coach* (1849).

180 I can but lose his favour and a feast.
(*Whilst they speak,* De Monfort *walks up and down
impatiently and irresolute; at last pulls the bell violently.*)

Enter SERVANT.

DE MON. (*to* Ser.) What dost thou want?—
SER.   I thought your honour rung.
DE MON. I have forgot—Stay; are my horses saddled?
SER. I thought, my Lord, you would not ride to-day,
    After so long a journey.
DE MON. (*Impatiently.*) Well—'tis good.
    Begone!—I want thee not.   [EXIT Servant.
REZ. (*Smiling significantly.*) I humbly crave your pardon, gentle
    Marquis.
    It grieves me that I cannot stay with you,
    And make my visit of a friendly length.
    I trust your goodness will excuse me now;
190   Another time I shall be less unkind.
    (*To* Freberg.) Will you not go with me?
FREB. Excuse me, Monfort, I'll return again.

                [EXEUNT Rezenvelt *and* Freberg.

DE MON. (*Alone, tossing his arms distractedly.*)
    Hell hath no greater torment for th' accurs'd
    Than this man's presence gives—
    Abhorred fiend! he hath a pleasure too,
    A damned pleasure in the pain he gives!
    Oh! the side glance of that detested eye!
    That conscious smile! that full insulting lip!
    It touches every nerve: it makes me mad.
200   What, does it please thee? Dost thou woo my hate?
    Hate shalt thou have! determin'd, deadly hate,
    Which shall awake no smile. Malignant villain!
    The venom of thy mind is rank and devilish,
    And thin the film that hides it.
    Thy hateful visage ever spoke thy worth:

I loath'd thee when a boy.
That ——[1] should be besotted with him thus!
And Freberg likewise so bewitched is,
That like a hireling flatt'rer, at his heels
He meanly paces, off'ring brutish praise.   210
O! I could curse him too.   [EXIT.

---

1   In the Larpent version the line reads "That all the world should be besotted thus!"
      Cf. Cox, *Seven Gothic Dramas* 249.

ACT II.—SCENE I.

A very splendid apartment in Count FREBERG's *house, fancifully dec-orated. A wide folding door opened, shews another magnificent room lighted up to receive company. Enter through the folding doors the* Count *and* Countess, *richly dressed.*

FREB. (*Looking round.*) In truth, I like those decorations well:
    They suit those lofty walls. And here, my love,
    The gay profusion of a woman's fancy
    Is well display'd. Noble simplicity
    Becomes us less on such a night as this
    Than gaudy show.
LADY. Is it not noble, then? (*He shakes his head.*) I thought it so,
    And as I know you love simplicity,
    I did intend it should be simple too.
10   FREB. Be satisfy'd, I pray; we want to-night
    A cheerful banquet-house, and not a temple.
    How runs the hour?
LADY. It is not late, but soon we shall be rous'd
With the loud entry of our frolick guests.

Enter a PAGE, *richly dressed.*

PAGE. Madam, there is a Lady in your hall,
    Who begs to be admitted to your presence.
LADY. Is it not one of our invited friends?
PAGE. No, far unlike to them; it is a stranger.
LADY. How looks her countenance?
20   PAGE. So queenly, so commanding, and so noble,
    I shrunk at first in awe; but when she smil'd,
    For so she did to see me thus abash'd,
    Methought I could have compass'd sea and land
    To do her bidding.
LADY.   Is she young or old?
PAGE. Neither, if right I guess, but she is fair;
    For time hath laid his hand so gently on her,
    As he too had been aw'd.

LADY.   The foolish stripling!
She has bewitch'd thee. Is she large in stature?
PAGE. So stately and so graceful is her form,
    I thought at first her stature was gigantick,   30
    But on a near approach I found, in truth,
    She scarcely does surpass the middle size.[1]
LADY. What is her garb?
PAGE. I cannot well describe the fashion of it.
    She is not deck'd in any gallant trim,
    But seems to me clad in the usual weeds
    Of high habitual state; for as she moves
    Wide flows her robe in many a waving fold,
    As I have seen unfurled banners play
    With the soft breeze.
LADY.   Thine eyes deceive thee, boy,   40
    It is an apparition thou hast seen.
FREB. (Starting from his seat, where he has been sitting during the
    conversation between the Lady and the Page.)
    It is an apparition he has seen.
    Or it is Jane De Monfort.   [EXIT, hastily.
LADY. (Displeased.) No; such description surely suits not her.
    Did she enquire for me?
PAGE. She ask'd to see the lady of Count Freberg.
LADY. Perhaps it is not she—I fear it is—
    Ha! here they come. He has but guess'd too well.

    Enter FREBERG, leading in JANE DE MONFORT.

FREB. (Presenting her to Lady.) Here, madam, welcome a most
    worthy guest.
LADY. Madam, a thousand welcomes. Pardon me;   50
    I could not guess who honour'd me so far;
    I should not else have waited coldly here.
JANE. I thank you for this welcome, gentle Countess,

---

1 Other descriptive words at this time to denote relative size of one's figure, were
  "fair-," "full-," "great-," and "large-." William MacMichael's *The Gold-Headed Cane*,
  a biography of selected medical acquaintances, describes Joanna Baillie's brother,
  Dr. Matthew Baillie, as being "considerably below the middle size" (156).

But take those kind excuses back again;
I am a bold intruder on this hour,
And am entitled to no ceremony.
I came in quest of a dear truant friend,
But Freberg has inform'd me—
(*To* Freberg.) And he is well you say?

FREB.   Yes, well , but joyless.

60 JANE. It is the usual temper of his mind:
It opens not, but with the thrilling touch
Of some strong heart-string o'the sudden press'd.

FREB. It may be so, I've known him otherwise.
He is suspicious grown.

JANE. Not so, Count Freberg, Monfort is too noble.
Say rather, that he is a man in grief,
Wearing at times a strange and scowling eye;
And thou, less generous than beseems a friend,
Hast thought too hardly of him.

FREB. (*Bowing with great respect.*) So will I say
70 I'll own nor word, nor will, that can offend you.

LADY. De Monfort is engag'd to grace our feast,
Ere long you'll see him here.

JANE. I thank you truly, but this homely dress
Suits not the splendour of such scenes as these.

FREB. (*Pointing to her dress.*) Such artless and majestick elegance,
So exquisitely just, so nobly simple,
Will make the gorgeous blush.

JANE. (*Smiling.*) Nay, nay, be more consistent, courteous knight,
And do not praise a plain and simple guise
80 With such profusion of unsimple words.
I cannot join your company to-night.

LADY. Not stay to see your brother?

JANE. Therefore it is I would not, gentle hostess.
Here he will find all that can woo the heart
To joy and sweet forgetfulness of pain;
The sight of me would wake his feeling mind[1]

---

1 Jane De Monfort alludes here to what was by 1798 the well-ripened tradition of
sentimentality. With Locke, a break was made from the religious notion of the
immateriality of the mind to radical notions that ideas proceed from feelings. Then

To other thoughts. I am no doting mistress,
No fond distracted wife, who must forthwith
Rush to his arms and weep. I am his sister:
The eldest daughter of his father's house: 90
Calm and unwearied is my love for him;
And having found him, patiently I'll wait,
Nor greet him in the hour of social joy,
To dash his mirth with tears.—
The night wears on; permit me to withdraw.

FREB. Nay, do not, do not injure us so far!
Disguise thyself, and join our friendly train.

JANE. You wear not masks to-night?

LADY. We wear not masks, but you may be conceal'd
Behind the double foldings of a veil.   100

JANE. (*After pausing to consider.*) In truth, I feel a little so
inclin'd.
Methinks unknown, I e'en might speak to him,
And gently prove the temper of his mind:
But for the means I must become your debtor.
(*To* Lady.)

LADY. Who waits? (*Enter her* Woman.) Attend this lady to my
wardrobe,
And do what she commands you.

[EXEUNT Jane *and* Waiting-woman.

FREB. (*Looking after* Jane, *as she goes out, with admiration.*)
Oh! what a soul she bears! see how she steps!
Nought but the native dignity of worth
E'er taught the moving form such noble grace.

LADY. Such lofty mien, and high assumed gait
I've seen ere now, and men have call'd it pride.   110

FREB. No, 'faith! thou never did'st, but oft indeed
The paltry imitation thou hast seen.

---

as the understanding of physiology developed, mental life could be traced through
analogies of body processes. Especially before Laurence Sterne's *A Sentimental Journey* (1768) "sentiment" suggested richness in moral reflection. Cf. Locke, Appendix
A; see also Janet Todd's *Sensibility: An Introduction.*

(*Looking at her.*) How hang those trappings on thy motly
gown?
They seem like garlands on a May-day queen,
Which hinds have dress'd in sport.
LADY. I'll doff it, then, since it displeases you.
FREB. (*Softening.*) No, no, thou art lovely still in every garb.
But see the guests assemble.

*Enter groups of well dressed people, who pay their compliments to
Freberg and his* Lady; *and followed by her pass into the
inner apartment, where more company appear assembling,
as if by another entry.*

FREB. (*Who remains on the front of the stage, with a friend or two.*)
120   How loud the hum of this gay meeting croud!
'Tis like a bee-swarm in the noonday sun.
Musick will quell the sound. Who waits without?
Musick strike up.
(*A grand piece of musick is playing, and when it ceases, enter
from the inner apartment* REZENVELT, *with several gentlemen,
all richly dressed.*)
FREB. (*To those just entered.*)
What lively gallants quit the field so soon?
Are there no beauties in that moving crowd
To fix your fancy?
REZ. Ay, marry, are there! men of ev'ry mind
May in that moving croud some fair one find,
To suit their taste, tho' whimsical and strange,
130   As ever fancy own'd.
Beauty of every cast and shade is there,
From the perfection of a faultless form,
Down to the common, brown, unnoted maid,
Who looks but pretty in her Sunday gown.
1ST GENT. There is, indeed, a gay variety.
REZ. And if the liberality of nature
Suffices not, there's store of grafted charms
Blending in one the sweets of many plants
So obstinately, strangely opposite,

As would have well defy'd all other art   140
But female cultivation. Aged youth,
With borrow'd locks in rosy chaplets bound,
Cloaths her dim eye, parch'd lip, and skinny cheek
In most unlovely softness.
And youthful age, with fat round trackless face,
The down-cast look of contemplation deep,
Most pensively assumes.
Is it not even so? The native prude,
With forced laugh, and merriment uncouth,
Plays off the wild coquet's successful charms   150
With most unskilful pains; and the coquet,
In temporary crust of cold reserve,
Fixes her studied looks upon the ground
Forbiddingly demure.
FREB. Fy! thou art too severe.
REZ.   Say, rather, gentle.
I' faith! the very dwarfs attempt to charm
With lofty airs of puny majesty,
Whilst potent damsels, of a portly make,
Totter like nurselings, and demand the aid
Of gentle sympathy.   160
From all those diverse modes of dire assault,
He owns a heart of hardest adamant,
Who shall escape to-night.
FREB. (*To* De Monfort, *who has entered*[1] *during* Rezenvelt's
speech, and heard the greatest part of it.)
                          Ha, ha, ha, ha !
How pleasantly he gives his wit the rein,
Yet guides its wild career!
(De Monfort *is silent.*)
REZ. (*Smiling archly.*)
What, think you, Freberg, the same powerful spell
Of transformation reigns o'er all to-night?
Or that De Monfort is a woman turn'd,
So widely from his native self to swerve,

---

1   In the Larpent version a stage direction indicates this entrance at the end of line
139.

170 As grace my gai'ty with a smile of his?

DE MON. Nay, think not, Rezenvelt, there is no smile
I can bestow on thee. There is a smile,
A smile of nature too, which I can spare,
And yet, perhaps, thou wilt not thank me for it.
(*Smiles contemptuously.*)

REZ. Not thank thee! It were surely most ungrateful
No thanks to pay for nobly giving me
What, well we see, has cost thee so much pain.
For nature hath her smiles, of birth more painful
Than bitt'rest execrations.[1]

180 FREB. These idle words will lead us to disquiet:
Forbear, forbear, my friends. Go, Rezenvelt,
Accept the challange of those lovely dames,
Who thro' the portal comes[2] with bolder steps
To claim your notice.
(*Enter a group of Ladies from the other apartment.* Rezenvelt
shrugs up his shoulders, as if unwilling to go.)

1ST GENT. (*to* Rez.) Behold in sable veil a lady comes,
Whose noble air doth challange fancy's skill
To suit it with a countenance as goodly.
(*Pointing to* Jane De Monfort, *who now enters in a
thick black veil.*)

REZ. Yes, this way lies attraction. (*To* Freberg.) With
permission,
(*Going up to* Jane.)
Fair lady, tho' within that envious shroud
190 Your beauty deigns not to enlighten us,
We bid you welcome, and our beauties here
Will welcome you the more for such concealment.
With the permission of our noble host—
(*Taking her hand, and leading her to the front of the stage.*)

JANE. (*to* Freb.) Pardon me this presumption, courteous sir:
I thus appear, (*pointing to her veil,*) not careless of respect
Unto the gen'rous lady of the feast.
Beneath this veil no beauty shrouded is,

---

1 Curses; expressions of extreme loathing.
2 Changed to "come" in 1806.

That, now, or pain, or pleasure can bestow.
Within the friendly cover of its shade
I only wish unknown, again to see   200
One who, alas!—is heedless of my pain.
DE MON. Yes, it is ever thus. Undo that veil,
    And give thy count'nance to the cheerful light.
    Men now all soft, and female beauty scorn,
    And mock the gentle cares which aim to please.
    It is most damnable! undo thy veil,
    And think of him no more.
JANE. I know it well, even to a proverb grown,
    Is lovers' faith, and I had borne such slight:
    But he who has, alas! forsaken me   210
    Was the companion of my early days,
    My cradle's mate, mine infant play-fellow.
    Within our op'ning minds with riper years
    The love of praise and gen'rous virtue sprung:
    Thro' varied life our pride, our joys, were one;
    At the same tale we wept: he is my brother.
DE MON. And he forsook thee?—No, I dare not curse him:
    My heart upbraids me with a crime like his.
JANE. Ah! do not thus distress a feeling heart.
    All sisters are not to the soul entwin'd   220
    With equal bands; thine has not watch'd for thee,
    Weep'd for thee, cheer'd thee, shar'd thy weal and woe,
    As I have done for him.
DE MON. (*Eagerly.*) Ha! has she not?
    By heaven! the sum of all thy kindly deeds
    Were but as chaff pois'd against the massy gold,
    Compar'd to that which I do owe her love.
    Oh pardon me! I mean not to offend—
    I am too warm—But she of whom I speak
    Is the dear sister of my earliest love;
    In noble virtuous worth to none a second: 230
    And tho' behind those sable folds were hid
    As fair a face as ever woman own'd,
    Still would I say she is as fair as thee.
    How oft amidst the beauty-blazing throng,

I've proudly to th' inquiring stranger told
Her name and lineage! yet within her house,
The virgin mother of an orphan race
Her dying parents left, this noble woman
Did, like a Roman matron, proudly sit,
240   Despising all the blandishments of love;
Whilst many a youth his hopeless love conceal'd,
Or, humbly distant, woo'd her like a queen.
Forgive, I pray you! O forgive this boasting!
In faith! I mean you no discourtesy.

JANE. (*Off her guard, in a soft natural tone of voice.*) Oh no! nor do
me any.

DE MON. What voice speaks now? Withdraw, withdraw this
shade!
For if thy face bear semblance to thy voice,
I'll fall and worship thee. Pray! pray undo!
(*Puts forth his hand eagerly to snatch away the veil, whilst she
shrinks back, and* Rezenvelt *steps between to prevent him.*)

REZ. Stand off: no hand shall lift this sacred veil.

250   DE MON. What, dost thou think De Monfort fall'n so low,
That there may live a man beneath heav'n's roof
Who dares to say he shall not?

REZ. He lives who dares to say—

JANE. (*Throwing back her veil, very much alarmed, and rushing
between them.*)
Forbear, forbear!

(Rezenvelt, *very much struck, steps back respectfully, and makes her a
very low bow. De Monfort stands for a while motionless, gazing upon
her, till she, looking expressively to him, extends her arms, and he, rushing into them, bursts into tears. Freberg seems very much pleased. The
company then gather about them, and the scene closes.*)

SCENE II.

De Monfort's *apartments. Enter* DE MONFORT, *with a disordered
air, and his hand pressed upon his forehead, followed by* JANE.

DE MON. No more, my sister, urge me not again:
    My secret troubles cannot be revealed.
    From all participation of its thoughts
    My heart recoils: I pray thee be contented.
JANE. What, must I, like a distant humble friend,
    Observe thy restless eye, and gait disturb'd,
    In timid silence, whilst with yearning heart
    I turn aside to weep? O no! De Monfort!
    A nobler task thy noble mind will give;
    Thy true intrusted friend I still shall be.   10
DE MON. Ah, Jane, forbear! I cannot e'en to thee.
JANE. Then fy upon it! fy upon it, Monfort!
    There was a time when e'en with murder stain'd,
    Had it been possible that such dire deed
    Could e'er have been the crime of one so piteous,
    Thou would'st have told it me.
DE MON. So would I now—but ask of this no more.
    All other trouble but the one I feel
    I had disclos'd to thee. I pray thee spare me.
    It is the secret weakness of my nature.   20
JANE. Then secret let it be; I urge no farther.
    The eldest of our valiant father's hopes,
    So sadly orphan'd, side by side we stood,
    Like two young trees, whose boughs, in early strength,
    Screen the weak saplings of the rising grove,
    And brave the storm together—
    I have so long, as if by nature's right,
    Thy bosom's inmate and adviser been,
    I thought thro' life I should have so remain'd,
    Nor ever known a change. Forgive me, Monfort,   30
    A humbler station will I take by thee:
    The close attendant of thy wand'ring steps;
    The cheerer of this home, by strangers sought;
    The soother of those griefs I must not know,
    This is mine office now: I ask no more.
DE MON. Oh Jane! thou dost constrain me with thy love!
    Would I could tell it thee!
JANE. Thou shalt not tell me. Nay, I'll stop mine ears,

Nor from the yearnings of affection wring
40   What shrinks from utt'rance. Let it pass, my brother.
I'll stay by thee; I'll cheer thee, comfort thee:
Pursue with thee the study of some art,
Or nobler science,[1] that compels the mind
To steady thought progressive, driving forth
All floating, wild, unhappy fantasies;
Till thou, with brow unclouded, smil'st again,
Like one who from dark visions of the night,
When th' active soul within its lifeless cell
Holds its own world, with dreadful fancy press'd
50   Of some dire, terrible, or murd'rous deed,
Wakes to the dawning morn, and blesses heaven.
DE MON. It will not pass away: 'twill haunt me still.
JANE. Ah! say not so, for I will haunt thee too;
And be to it so close an adversary,
That, tho' I wrestle darkling with the fiend,
I shall o'ercome it.
DE MON.   Thou most gen'rous woman!
Why do I treat thee thus? It should not be—
And yet I cannot—O that cursed villain!
He will not let me be the man I would.
60   JANE. What say'st thou, Monfort? Oh! what words are these?
They have awak'd my soul to dreadful thoughts.
I do beseech thee speak!
(*He shakes his head and turns from her; she following him.*)
By the affection thou didst ever bear me;
By the dear mem'ry of our infant days;
By kindred living ties, ay, and by those
Who sleep i'the tomb, and cannot call to thee,
I do conjure thee speak.
(*He waves her off with his hand, and covers his face with the other, still turning from her.*)
                    Ha! wilt thou not?

---

1   It would appear that Jane de Montfort is aware of contemporary moral thinkers. As
Mary Berry (1763-1852) observed in a letter to her friend Mrs. Cholmley (March
1799), contemporary male authors often made their women characters "clever, captivating, heroic, but never rationally superior…." (see Appendix A).

(*Assuming dignity.*)
Then, if affection, most unwearied love,
Tried early, long, and never wanting found,
O'er gen'rous man hath more authority,   70
More rightful power than crown and sceptre give,
I do command thee.
(*He throws himself into a chair greatly agitated.*)
De Monfort, do not thus resist my love.
Here I entreat thee on my bended knees.
(*Kneeling.*)
Alas! my brother!
(De Monfort *starts up, and, catching her in his arms, raises her
up, then placing her in the chair, kneels at her feet.*)
DE MON. Thus let him kneel who should the abased be,
And at thine honour'd feet confession make.
I'll tell thee all—but oh! thou wilt despise me.
For in my breast a raging passion burns,
To which thy soul no sympathy will own.   80
A passion which hath made my nightly couch
A place of torment; and the light of day,
With the gay intercourse of social man,
Feel like th' oppressive airless pestilence.
O Jane! thou wilt despise me.
JANE.   Say not so:
I never can despise thee, gentle brother.
A lover's jealousy and hopeless pangs
No kindly heart contemns.
DE MON.   A lover, say'st thou?
No, it is hate! black, lasting, deadly hate;
Which thus hath driv'n me forth from kindred peace,   90
From social pleasure, from my native home,
To be a sullen wand'rer on the earth,
Avoiding all men, cursing and accurs'd.
JANE. De Monfort, this is fiend-like, frightful, terrible!
What being, by th' Almighty Father form'd,
Of flesh and blood, created even as thou,
Could in thy breast such horrid tempest wake,
Who art thyself his fellow?

Unknit thy brows, and spread those wrath-clench'd hands:
100   Some sprite accurst within thy bosom mates
To work thy ruin. Strive with it, my brother!
Strive bravely with it; drive it from thy breast:
'Tis the degrader of a noble heart;
Curse it, and bid it part.

DE MON. It will not part. (*His hand on his breast.*) I've lodged it
here too long;
With my first cares I felt its rankling touch,
I loath'd him when a boy.

JANE. Who did'st thou say?

DE MON.   Oh! that detested Rezenvelt!
110   E'en in our early sports, like two young whelps
Of hostile breed, instinctively reverse,
Each 'gainst the other pitch'd his ready pledge,
And frown'd defiance. As we onward pass'd
From youth to man's estate, his narrow art,
And envious gibing malice, poorly veil'd
In the affected carelessness of mirth,
Still more detestable and odious grew.
There is no living being on this earth
Who can conceive the malice of his soul,
120   With all his gay and damned merriment,
To those, by fortune or by merit plac'd
Above his paltry self. When, low in fortune,
He look'd upon the state of prosp'rous men,
As nightly birds, rous'd from their murky holes,
Do scowl and chatter at the light of day,
I could endure it; even as we bear
Th' impotent bite of some half-trodden worm,
I could endure it. But when honours came,
And wealth and new-got titles fed his pride;
130   Whilst flatt'ring knaves did trumpet forth his praise,
And grov'ling idiots grinn'd applauses on him;
Oh! then I could no longer suffer it!
It drove me frantick.—What! what would I give!
What would I give to crush the bloated toad,
So rankly do I loathe him!

JANE. And would thy hatred crush the very man
　　Who gave to thee that life he might have ta'en?
　　That life which thou so rashly did'st expose
　　To aim at his! Oh! this is horrible!
DE MON. Ha! thou hast heard it, then? From all the world,　　140
　　But most of all from thee, I thought it hid.
JANE. I heard a secret whisper, and resolv'd
　　Upon the instant to return to thee.
　　Did'st thou receive my letter?
DE MON. I did! I did! 'twas that which drove me hither.
　　I could not bear to meet thine eye again.
JANE. Alas! that, tempted by a sister's tears,
　　I ever left thy house! these few past months,
　　These absent months, have brought us all this woe.
　　Had I remain'd with thee it had not been.　　150
　　And yet, methinks, it should not move you thus.
　　You dar'd him to the field; both bravely fought;
　　He more adroit disarm'd you; courteously
　　Return'd the forfeit sword,[1] which, so return'd,
　　You did refuse to use against him more;
　　And then, as says report, you parted friends.
DE MON. When he disarm'd this curs'd, this worthless hand
　　Of its most worthless weapon, he but spar'd
　　From dev'lish pride, which now derives a bliss
　　In seeing me thus fetter'd, sham'd, subjected　　160
　　With the vile favour of his poor forbearance;
　　Whilst he securely sits with gibing brow
　　And basely bates me, like a muzzled cur
　　Who cannot turn again.—
　　Until that day, till that accursed day,
　　I knew not half the torment of this hell,
　　Which burns within my breast. Heaven's lightning blast
　　him!
JANE. O this is horrible! Forbear, forbear!
　　Lest heaven's vengeance light upon thy head,
　　For this most impious wish.

1　Another duelling brother, James Harlowe in Samuel Richardson's (1689-1761)
　　Clarissa (1747-48), is disarmed of his sword from "unskilfulness or passion" (1).

DE MON.   Then let it light.
    Torments more fell than I have felt already
    It cannot send. To be annihilated;
    What all men shrink from; to be dust, be nothing,
    Were bliss to me, compar'd to what I am.
JANE. Oh! would'st thou kill me with these dreadful words?
DE MON. (*Raising his arms to heaven.*) Let me but once upon his
    ruin look,
    Then close mine eyes for ever!
    (Jane, *in great distress, staggers back, and supports herself upon*
    the side scene. De Monfort, alarm'd, *runs up to her with a*
    soften'd voice.)
    Ha! how is this? thou'rt ill; thou'rt very pale.
    What have I done to thee? Alas, alas!
    I meant not to distress thee.—O my sister!
JANE. (*Shaking her head.*) I cannot speak to thee.
DE MON.   I have kill'd thee.
    Turn, turn thee not away! look on me still!
    Oh! droop not thus, my life, my pride, my sister!
    Look on me yet again.
JANE.   Thou too, De Monfort,
    In better days, wert wont to be my pride.
DE MON. I am a wretch, most wretched in myself,
    And still more wretched in the pain I give.
    O curse that villain! that detested villain!
    He hath spread mis'ry o'er my fated life:
    He will undo us all.
JANE. I've held my warfare through a troubled world,
    And borne with steady mind my share of ill;
    For then the helpmate of my toil wert thou.
    But now the wane of life comes darkly on,
    And hideous passion tears thee from my heart,
    Blasting thy worth.—I cannot strive with this.
DE MON. (*Affectionately.*) What shall I do?
JANE.   Call up thy noble spirit,
    Rouse all the gen'rous energy of virtue;
    And with the strength of heaven-endued man,
    Repel the hideous foe. Be great; be valiant.

O, if thou could'st! E'en shrouded as thou art
In all the sad infirmities of nature,
What a most noble creature would'st thou be!
DE MON. Ay, if I could: alas! alas! I cannot.
JANE. Thou can'st, thou may'st, thou wilt.
   We shall not part till I have turn'd thy soul.

Enter MANUEL.

DE MON. Ha! some one enters. Wherefore com'st thou here?
MAN. Count Freberg waits your leisure.
DE MON. (*Angrily.*) Be gone, be gone.—I cannot see him now.
                                        [EXIT, Manuel.
JANE. Come to my closet; free from all intrusion,   210
   I'll school thee there; and thou again shalt be
   My willing pupil, and my gen'rous friend;
   The noble Monfort I have lov'd so long,
   And must not, will not lose.
DE MON. Do as thou wilt; I will not grieve thee more.

                                        [EXEUNT.

SCENE III.[1]

Count FREBERG's *House. Enter the* COUNTESS, *followed by the*
PAGE, *and speaking as she enters.*

LADY. Take this and this. (*Giving two packets.*) And tell my
      gentle friend,
   I hope to see her ere the day be done.
PAGE. Is there no message for the Lady Jane?
LADY. No, foolish boy, that would too far extend
   Your morning's route, and keep you absent long.
PAGE. O no, dear Madam! I'll the swifter run.
   The summer's light'ning moves not as I'll move,

---

1   See Cox, *Seven Gothic Dramas* 265 for critical changes to this scene in the Larpent
    version and the 1851 edition.

If you will send me to the Lady Jane.

LADY. No, not so slow, I ween. The summer's light'ning!

10   Thou art a lad of taste and letters grown:

Would'st poetry admire, and ape thy master.

Go, go; my little spaniels are unkempt;

My cards unwritten, and my china broke:

Thou art too learned for a lady's page.

Did I not bid thee call Theresa here?

PAGE. Madam she comes.

Enter THERESA, *carrying a robe over her arm.*

LADY. (*to* Ther.) What has employ'd you all this dreary while?

I've waited long.

THER.   Madam, the robe is finish'd.

LADY. Well, let me see it.

(Theresa *spreads out the robe.*)

(*Impatiently to the* Page.)

20   Boy, hast thou ne'er a hand to lift that fold?

See where it hangs.

(Page *takes the other side of the robe, and spreads it out to its full extent before her, whilst she sits down and looks at it with much dissatisfaction.*)

THER. Does not my lady like this easy form?

LADY. That sleeve is all awry.

THER.   Your pardon, madam;

'Tis but the empty fold that shades it thus.

I took the pattern from a graceful shape;

The Lady Jane De Monfort wears it so.

LADY. Yes, yes, I see 'tis thus with all of you.

Whate'er she wears is elegance and grace,

Whilst ev'ry ornament of mine, forsooth,

30   Must hang like trappings on a May-day queen.

(*Angrily to the* Page, *who is smiling to himself.*)

Youngster be gone. Why do you loiter here?

[EXIT Page.

THER. What would you, madam, chuse to wear to-night?
　One of your newest robes?

LADY. 　　　　　　　　　　　　I hate them all.

THER. Surely, that purple scarf became you well,
　With all those wreaths of richly hanging flowers.
　Did I not overhear them say, last night,
　As from the crouded ball-room ladies past,
　How gay and handsome, in her costly dress,
　The Countess Freberg look'd.

LADY. 　　　　　　　　　　　Did'st thou o'erhear it?

THER. I did, and more than this.

LADY. Well, all are not so greatly prejudic'd;
　All do not think me like a May-day queen,
　Which peasants deck in sport.

THER. 　　　　　　　　　　　And who said this?

LADY. (*Putting her handkerchief to her eyes.*) E'en my good lord,
　Theresa.

THER. He said it but in jest. He loves you well.

LADY. I know as well as thee he loves me well;
　But what of that? he takes no pride in me.
　Elsewhere his praise and admiration go,
　And Jane De Monfort is not mortal woman.

THER. The wond'rous character this lady bears
　For worth and excellence; from early youth
　The friend and mother of her younger sisters
　Now greatly married, as I have been told,
　From her most prudent care, may well excuse
　The admiration of so good a man
　As my good master is. And then, dear madam,
　I must confess, when I myself did hear
　How she was come thro' the rough winter's storm,
　To seek and comfort an unhappy brother,
　My heart beat kindly to her.

LADY. Ay, ay, there is a charm in this I find:
　But wherefore may she not have come as well.
　Through wintry storms to seek a lover too?

THER. No, madam, no, I could not think of this.

LADY. That would reduce her in your eyes, mayhap,

To woman's level.—Now I see my vengeance!
I'll tell it round that she is hither come,
Under pretence of finding out De Monfort,
To meet with Rezenvelt. When Freberg hears it
70   'Twill help, I ween, to break this magick charm.
THER. And say what is not, madam?
LADY. How can'st thou know that I shall say what is not?
    'Tis like enough I shall but speak the truth.
THER. Ah no! there is—
LADY.   Well, hold thy foolish tongue.
    Carry that, robe into my chamber, do:
    I'll try it there myself.   [EXEUNT.

ACT III.—SCENE I.

DE MONFORT *discovered sitting by a table reading. After a little time*
he lays down his book, and continues in a thoughtful posture. Enter to
him JANE DE MONFORT.

JANE. Thanks, gentle brother.—
    (*Pointing to the book.*)
    Thy willing mind has been right well employ'd.
    Did not thy heart warm at the fair display
    Of peace and concord and forgiving love?
DE MON. I know resentment may to love be turn'd;
    Tho' keen and lasting, into love as strong:
    And fiercest rivals in th'ensanguin'd field
    Have cast their brandish'd weapons to the ground,
10   Joining their mailed[1] breasts in close embrace,
    With gen'rous impulse fir'd. I know right well
    The darkest, fellest wrongs have been forgiven
    Seventy times o'er from blessed heavenly love:
    I've heard of things like these; I've heard and wept.
    But what is this to me?
JANE.   All, all, my brother!

---

1   Armoured.

It bids thee too that noble precept learn,
To love thine enemy.

DE MON. Th' uplifted stroke that would a wretch destroy
Gorg'd with my richest spoil, stain'd with my blood,
I would arrest and cry, hold! hold! have mercy:
But when the man most adverse to my nature,   20
Who e'en from childhood hath, with rude malevolence,
Withheld the fair respect all paid beside,
Turning my very praise into derision;
Who galls and presses me where'er I go,
Would claim the gen'rous feelings of my heart,
Nature herself doth lift her voice aloud,
And cries, it is impossible.[1]

JANE. (Shaking her head.)—Ah Monfort, Monfort!

DE MON. I can forgive th' envenom'd reptile's sting,
But hate his loathsome self.

JANE. And canst thou do no more for love of heaven?   30

DE MON. Alas! I cannot now so school my mind
As holy men have taught, nor search it truly:
But this, my Jane, I'll do for love of thee;
And more it is than crowns could win me to,
Or any power but thine. I'll see the man.
Th' indignant risings of abhorrent nature;
The stern contraction of my scowling brows,
That, like the plant,[2] whose closing leaves do shrink

---

1 Cf. Appendix A.4.i.
2 Most likely Mimosa pudica or the "Sensitive plant" whose compound leaves fold
   and collapse when touched. Erasmus Darwin includes the Mimosa in a poetic catalogue personifying plants in the second part of *The Botanic Garden* (1791) entitled
   "The Loves of the Plants," first published alone in 1789. He writes:

> Weak with nice sense, the chaste MIMOSA stands,
> From each rude touch withdraws her timid hands;
> Oft as light clouds o'erpass the Summer-glade,
> Alarm'd she trembles at the moving shade;
> And feels, alive through all her tender form,
> The whisper'd murmurs of the gathering storm;
> Shuts her sweet eye-lids to approaching night;
> And hails with freshen'd charms the rising light.
> Veil'd, with gay decency and modest pride,
> Slow to the mosque she moves, an eastern bride;

At hostile touch, still knit at his approach;
40 The crooked curving lip, by instinct taught,
In imitation of disgustful things
To pout and swell, I strictly will repress;
And meet him with a tamed countenance,
E'en as a townsman, who would live at peace,
And pay him the respect his station claims.
I'll crave his pardon too for all offence
My dark and wayward temper may have done;
Nay more, I will confess myself his debtor
For the forbearance I have curs'd so oft.
50 Life spar'd by him, more horrid than the grave
With all its dark corruption! This I'll do.
Will it suffice thee? More than this I cannot.
JANE. No more than this do I require of thee
In outward act, tho' in thy heart, my friend,
I hop'd a better change, and still will hope.
I told thee Freberg had propos'd a meeting.
DE MON. I know it well.
JANE.   And Rezenvelt consents.
He meets you here; so far he shews respect.
DE MON. Well, let it be; the sooner past the better.
60 JANE. I'm glad to hear you say so, for, in truth,
He has propos'd it for an early hour.
'Tis almost near his time; I came to tell you.
DE MON. What, comes he here so soon? shame on his speed!

There her soft vows unceasing love record,
Queen of the bright seraglio of her Lord.—
So sinks or rises with the changeful hour
The liquid silver in its glassy tower.
So turns the needle to the pole it loves,
With fine vibrations quivering, as it moves.(1.247-61)

In a following note, Darwin likens the plant's collapse after being touched to a deeper sleep "owing to a numbness or paralysis consequent to too violent irritation, like the faintings of animals from pain or fatigue." Interestingly, Margaret Carhart in her *The Life and Work* notes that a production of Mary Berry's *Fashionable Friends* at Strawberry Hill for which Baillie provided the prologue and epilogue was described in a contemporary Dublin review as a "hot-house plant ... of the modish mimosa class" (*Hibernia Magazine*, June 1810) in that it was performed only twice. See Percy Bysshe Shelley's "The Sensitive Plant" (1820).

It is not decent thus to rush upon me.
He loves the secret pleasure he will feel
To see me thus subdued.
JANE. O say not so! he comes with heart sincere.
DE MON. Could we not meet elsewhere? from home—i' the
      fields,
    Where other men—must I alone receive him?
    Where is your agent, Freberg, and his friends,   70
    That I must meet him here?
    (*Walks up and down very much disturbed.*)
    Now did'st thou say?—how goes the hour?—e'en now!
    I would some other friend were first arriv'd.
JANE. See, to thy wish comes Freberg and his dame.
DE MON. His lady too! why comes he not alone?
    Must all the world stare upon our meeting?

        Enter COUNT FREBERG *and his* COUNTESS.

FREB. A happy morrow to my noble marquis
    And his most noble sister.
JANE.   Gen'rous Freberg,
    Your face, methinks, forbodes a happy morn
    Open and cheerful. What of Rezenvelt?   80
FREB. I left him at his home, prepar'd to follow:
    He'll soon appear. (*To* De Monfort.) And now, my worthy
      friend,
    Give me your hand; this happy change delights me.
    (De Monfort *gives him his hand coldly, and they walk to the
    bottom of the stage together, in earnest discourse, whilst* Jane *and
    the* Countess *remain in the front.*)
LADY. My dearest madam, will you pardon me?
    I know Count Freberg's bus'ness with De Monfort,
    And had a strong desire to visit you,
    So much I wish the honour of your friendship.
    For he retains no secret from mine ear.
JANE. (*archly.*) Knowing your prudence.—You are welcome,
      madam,
    So shall Count Freberg's lady ever be.   90

(De Monfort *and* Freberg *returning towards the front of the stage, still engaged in discourse.*)

FREB. He is indeed a man, within whose breast,
    Firm rectitude and honour hold their seat,
    Tho' unadorned with that dignity
    Which were their fittest garb. Now, on my life!
    I know no truer heart than Rezenvelt.

DE MON. Well, Freberg, well,—there needs not all this pains
    To garnish out his worth; let it suffice.
    I am resolv'd I will respect the man,
    As his fair station and repute demand.
100   Methinks I see not at your jolly feasts
    The youthful knight, who sung so pleasantly.

FREB. A pleasant circumstance detains him hence;
    Pleasant to those who love high gen'rous deeds
    Above the middle pitch of common minds;
    And, tho' I have been sworn to secrecy,
    Yet must I tell it thee.
    This knight is near a kin to Rezenvelt
    To whom an old relation, short while dead,
    Bequeath'd a good estate, some leagues distant.
110   But Rezenvelt, now rich in fortune's store,
    Disdain'd the sordid love of further gain,
    And gen'rously the rich bequest resign'd
    To this young man, blood of the same degree
    To the deceas'd, and low in fortune's gifts,
    Who is from hence to take possession of it.
    Was it not nobly done?

DE MON.   'Twas right, and honourable.
    This morning is oppressive, warm, and heavy:
    There hangs a foggy closeness in the air;
    Dost thou not feel it?

120 FREB. O no! to think upon a gen'rous deed
    Expands my soul, and makes me lightly breath.[1]

DE MON. Who gives the feast to night? His name escapes me.
    You say I am invited.

---

1 Changed to "breathe" in 1806.

FREB.   Old Count Waterlan.
  In honour of your townsman's gen'rous gift
  He spreads the board.[1]
DE MON. He is too old to revel with the gay.
FREB. But not too old is he to honour virtue.
  I shall partake of it with open soul;
  For, on my honest faith, of living men
  I know not one, for talents, honour, worth,   130
  That I should rank superiour to Rezenvelt.
DE MON. How virtuous he hath been in three short days!
FREB. Nay, longer, Marquis, but my friendship rests
  Upon the good report of other men;
  And that has told me much.
  (De Monfort *aside, going some steps hastily from* Freberg, *and*
  rending his cloak with agitation as he goes.)
  Would he were come! by heaven I would he were!
  This fool besets me so.
  (*Suddenly correcting himself, and joining the Ladies, who have*
  retired to the bottom of the stage, he speaks to Countess
  Freberg *with affected cheerfulness.*)
  The sprightly dames of Amberg rise by times
  Untarnish'd with the vigils of the night.
LADY. Praise us not rashly, 'tis not always so.   140
DE MON. He does not rashly praise who praises you;
  For he were dull indeed—
  (*Stopping short, as if he heard something.*)
LADY.   How dull indeed?
DE MON. I should have said—It has escap'd me now—
  (*Listening again, as if he heard something.*)
JANE. (*to* De Mon.) What, hear you ought?
DE MON. (*hastily.*)   'Tis nothing.
LADY. (*to* De Mon.) Nay, do not let me lose it so, my lord.
  Some fair one has bewitch'd your memory,
  And robs me of the half-form'd compliment.
JANE. Half-utter'd praise is to the curious mind,
  As to the eye half-veiled beauty is,

---

1 Table.

150   More precious than the whole. Pray pardon him.
       Some one approaches.   (*Listening.*)
   FREB. No, no, it is a servant who ascends;
       He will not come so soon.
   MON. (*Off his guard.*) 'Tis Rezenvelt: I heard his well-known
       foot!
       From the first stair-case, mounting step by step.
   FREB. How quick an ear thou hast for distant sound!
       I heard him not.
       (De Monfort *looks embarrassed, and is silent.*)

             Enter REZENVELT.

       (De Monfort, *recovering himself, goes up to receive* Rezenvelt,
       who meets him with a cheerful countenance.)
   DE MON. (*to* Rez.) I am, my lord, beholden to you greatly.
       This ready visit makes me much your debtor.
160 REZ. Then may such debts between us, noble marquis,
       Be oft incurr'd, and often paid again.
       (*To* Jane.) Madam, I am devoted to your service,
       And ev'ry wish of yours commands my will.
       (*To* Countess.) Lady, good morning. (*To* Freb.) Well, my
       gentle friend,
       You see I have not linger'd long behind.
   FREB. No, thou art sooner than I look'd for thee.
   REZ. A willing heart adds feather to the heel,
       And makes the clown a winged mercury.
   DE MON. Then let me say, that with a grateful mind
170   I do receive these tokens of good will;
       And must regret that, in my wayward moods,
       I have too oft forgot the due regard
       Your rank and talents claim.
   REZ.   No, no, De Monfort,
       You have but rightly curb'd a wanton spirit,
       Which makes me too neglectful of respect.
       Let us be friends, and think of this no more.
   FREB. Ay, let it rest with the departed shades
       Of things which are no more; whilst lovely concord,

Follow'd by friendship sweet, and firm esteem,
Your future days enrich. O heavenly friendship! 180
Thou dost exalt the sluggish souls of men,
By thee conjoin'd, to great and glorious deeds;
As two dark clouds, when mix'd in middle air,
The vivid lightning's flash, and roar sublime.
Talk not of what is past, but future love.
DE MON. (*With dignity.*)
No, Freberg, no, it must not. (*To* Rezenvelt.) No, my lord.
I will not offer you an hand of concord
And poorly hide the motives which constrain me.
I would that, not alone these present friends,
But ev'ry soul in Amberg were assembled, 190
That I, before them all, might here declare
I owe my spared life to your forbearance.
(*Holding out his hand.*) Take this from one who boasts no
feeling warmth,
But never will deceive.
(Jane *smiles upon* De Monfort *with great approbation, and*
Rezenvelt *runs up to him with open arms.*)
REZ. Away with hands! I'll have thee to my breast.
Thou art, upon my faith, a noble spirit!
DE MON. (*Shrinking back from him.*)
Nay, if you please, I am not so prepar'd—
My nature is of temp'rature too cold—
I pray you pardon me. (Jane's *countenance changes.*)
But take this hand, the token of respect; 200
The token of a will inclin'd to concord;
The token of a mind that bears within
A sense impressive of the debt it owes you:
And cursed be its power, unnerv'd its strength,
If e'er again it shall be lifted up
To do you any harm.
REZ. Well, be it so, De Monfort, I'm contented;
I'll take thy hand since I can have no more.
(*Carelessly.*) I take of worthy men whate'er they give.
Their heart I gladly take; if not, their hand: 210
If that too is withheld, a courteous word,

Or the civility of placid looks;
And, if e'en these are too great favours deem'd,
'Faith, I can set me down contentedly
With plain and homely greeting, or, God save ye!
(De Monfort *aside, starting away from him some paces.*)
By the good light, he makes a jest of it!
(Jane *seems greatly distressed, and* Freberg *endeavours to
cheer her.*)

FREB. (*to* Jane.) Cheer up, my noble friend; all will go well;
For friendship is no plant of hasty growth.
Tho' planted in esteem's deep-fixed soil,

220   The gradual culture of kind intercourse
Must bring it to perfection.
(*To the* Countess.) My love, the morning, now, is far
advanced;
Our friends elsewhere expect us; take your leave.

LADY. (*to* Jane.) Farewell! dear madam, till the ev'ning hour.

FREB. (*to* De Mon.) Good day, De Monfort. (*To* Jane.) Most
devoutly yours.

REZ. (*to* Freb.) Go not too fast, for I will follow you.

[EXEUNT Freberg *and his* Lady.

(*To* Jane.) The Lady Jane is yet a stranger here:
She might, perhaps, in the purlieus[1] of Amberg
Find somewhat worth her notice.

230 JANE. I thank you, Marquis, I am much engaged;
I go not out to-day.

REZ. Then fare ye well! I see I cannot now
Be the proud man who shall escort you forth,
And shew to all the world my proudest boast,
The notice and respect of Jane De Monfort.

DE MON. (*Aside, impatiently.*) He says farewell, and goes not!

JANE. (*to* Rez.)   You do me honour.

REZ. Madam, adieu! (*To* Jane.) Good morning, noble marquis.

[EXIT.

---

1   Outskirts; perhaps a scenic forest retreat for riding or walking.

(Jane *and* De Monfort *look expressively to one another, without speaking, and then* EXEUNT, *severally.*)

SCENE II.

A splendid Banquetting Room. DE MONFORT, REZENVELT, FREBERG, MASTER OF THE HOUSE, *and* GUESTS, *are discovered sitting at table, with wine, &c. before them.*

SONG.—A GLEE.

> Pleasant is the mantling bowl,
> And the song of merry soul;
> And the red lamps cheery light,
> And the goblet glancing bright;
> Whilst many a cheerful face, around,
> Listens to the jovial sound.
> Social spirits, join with me;
> Bless the God of jollity.

FREB. (*to* De Mon.) (*Who rises to go away.*)
    Thou wilt not leave us, Monfort? wherefore so?
DE MON. (*Aside to* Freberg.) I pray thee take no notice of me
    now.   10
    Mine ears are stunned with these noisy fools;
    Let me escape.

                              [EXIT, *hastily.*

MASTER OF THE HOUSE. What, is De Monfort gone?
FREB.   Time presses him.
REZ. It seem'd to sit right heavily upon him,
    We must confess.
MASTER. (*to* Freb.) How is your friend? he wears a noble mien,
    But most averse, methinks, from social pleasure.
    Is this his nature?
FREB.   No, I've seen him cheerful,
    And at the board, with soul-enliven'd face,

20 Push the gay goblet round.—But it wears late.
We shall seem topers[1] more than social friends,
If the returning sun surprise us here.
(*To* Mast.) Good rest, my gen'rous host; we will retire.
You wrestle with your age most manfully,
But brave it not too far. Retire to sleep.
MAST. I will, my friend, but do you still remain,
With noble Rezenvelt, and all my guests.
Ye have not fourscore years upon your head;
Do not depart so soon. God save you all!

[EXIT Master, *leaning upon a* Servant.

FREB. (*to the Guests.*) Shall we resume?
30 GUESTS.   The night is too far spent.
FREB. Well then, good rest to you.
REZ. (*to Guests.*) Good rest, my friends.

[EXEUNT *all but* Freberg *and* Rezenvelt.

FREB. Alas! my Rezenvelt!
I vainly hop'd the hand of gentle peace,
From this day's reconciliation sprung,
These rude unseemly jarrings had subdu'd:
But I have mark'd, e'en at the social board,
Such looks, such words, such tones, such untold things,
Too plainly told, 'twixt you and Monfort pass,
That I must now despair.
40 Yet who could think, two minds so much refin'd,
So near in excellence, should be remov'd,
So far remov'd, in gen'rous sympathy.
REZ. Ay, far remov'd indeed.
FREB. And yet, methought, he made a noble effort,
And with a manly plainness bravely told
The galling debt he owes to your forbearance.
REZ. 'Faith! so he did, and so did I receive it;

---

1 Drinking companions; drunkards.

When, with spread arms, and heart e'en mov'd to tears,
I frankly proffer'd him a friend's embrace:
And, I declare, had he as such receiv'd it,   50
I from that very moment had forborne
All opposition, pride-provoking jest,
Contemning carelessness, and all offence;
And had caress'd him as a worthy heart,
From native weakness such indulgence claiming:
But since he proudly thinks that cold respect,
The formal tokens of his lordly favour,
So precious are, that I would sue for them
As fair distinction in the world's eye,
Forgetting former wrongs, I spurn it all;   60
And but that I do bear the noble woman,
His worthy, his incomparable sister,
Such fix'd profound regard, I would expose him;
And as a mighty bull, in senseless rage,
Rous'd at the baiter's will, with wretched rags
Of ire-provoking scarlet, chaffs and bellows,
I'd make him at small cost of paltry wit,
With all his deep and manly faculties,
The scorn and laugh of fools.
FREB. For heaven's sake, my friend! restrain your wrath;   70
For what has Monfort done of wrong to you,
Or you to him, bating one foolish quarrel,
Which you confess from slight occasion rose,
That in your breasts such dark resentment dwells,
So fix'd, so hopeless?
REZ. O! from our youth he has distinguish'd me
With ev'ry'ry mark of hatred and disgust.
For e'en in boyish sports I still oppos'd
His proud pretensions to pre-eminence;
Nor would I to his ripen'd greatness give   80
That fulsome adulation of applause
A senseless croud bestow'd. Tho' poor in fortune,
I still would smile at vain-assuming wealth:
But when unlook'd-for fate on me bestow'd
Riches and splendour equal to his own,

Tho' I, in truth, despise such poor distinction,
Feeling inclin'd to be at peace with him,
And with all men beside, I curb'd my spirit,
And sought to soothe him. Then, with spiteful rage,
90   From small offence he rear'd a quarrel with me,
And dar'd me to the field. The rest you know.
In short, I still have been th' opposing rock,
O'er which the stream of his o'erflowing pride
Hath foam'd and bellow'd. See'st thou how it is?
FREB. Too well I see, and warn thee to beware.
Such streams have oft, by swelling floods surcharg'd,
Borne down with sudden and impetuous force
The yet unshaken stone of opposition,
Which had for ages stopp'd their flowing course.
100   I pray thee, friend, beware.
REZ. Thou canst not mean—he will not murder me?
FREB. What a proud heart, with such dark passion toss'd,
May, in the anguish of its thoughts, conceive,
I will not dare to say.
REZ.   Ha, ha ! thou know'st him not.
Full often have I mark'd it in his youth,
And could have almost lov'd him for the weakness;
He's form'd with such antipathy, by nature,
To all infliction of corporeal pain,
To wounding life, e'en to the sight of blood,
He cannot if he would.
110   FREB.   Then fy upon thee!
It is not gen'rous to provoke him thus.
But let us part; we'll talk of this again.
Something approaches.—We are here too long.
REZ. Well, then, to-morrow I'll attend your call.
Here lies my way. Good night.   [EXIT.

Enter GRIMBALD.

GRIM. Forgive, I pray, my lord, a stranger's boldness.
I have presum'd to wait your leisure here,
Though at so late an hour.

FREB.   But who art thou?

GRIM. My name is Grimbald, sir,
    A humble suitor to your honour's goodness,   120
    Who is the more embolden'd to presume,
    In that the noble Marquis of De Monfort
    Is so much fam'd for good and gen'rous deeds.

FREB. You are mistaken, I am not the man.

GRIM. Then, pardon me; I thought I could not err.
    That mien so dignified, that piercing eye
    Assur'd me it was he.

FREB. My name is not De Monfort, courteous stranger;
    But, if you have a favour to request,
    I may, perhaps, with him befriend your suit.   130

GRIM. I thank your honour, but I have a friend
    Who will commend me to De Monfort's favour:
    The Marquis Rezenvelt has known me long,
    Who, says report, will soon become his brother.

FREB. If thou would'st seek thy ruin from De Monfort,
    The name of Rezenvelt employ, and prosper;
    But, if ought good, use any name but his.

GRIM. How may this be?

FREB.   I cannot now explain.
    Early to-morrow call upon Count Freberg;
    So am I call'd, each burgher knows my house,   140
    And there instruct me how to do you service.
    Good-night.

                                                        [EXIT.

GRIM. (*Alone.*) Well, this mistake may be of service to me;
    And yet my bus'ness I will not unfold
    To this mild, ready, promise-making courtier;
    I've been by such too oft deceiv'd already:
    But if such violent enmity exists
    Between De Monfort and this Rezenvelt,
    He'll prove my advocate by opposition.
    For, if De Monfort would reject my suit,   150
    Being the man whom Rezenvelt esteems,

Being the man he hates, a cord as strong,
Will he not favour me? I'll think of this.

[EXIT.

SCENE III.

A lower Apartment in JEROME'S *House, with a wide folding glass door, looking into a garden, where the trees and shrubs are brown and leafless. Enter* DE MONFORT *with his arms crossed, with a thoughtful frowning aspect, and paces slowly across the stage,* Jerome *following behind him with a timid step. De Monfort hearing him, turns suddenly about.*

DE MON. (*Angrily.*) Who follows me to this sequester'd room?
JER. I have presum'd, my lord. 'Tis somewhat late:
    I am inform'd you eat at home to-night;
    Here is a list of all the dainty fare
    My busy search has found; please to peruse it.
DE MON. Leave me: begone! Put hemlock in thy soup,
    Or deadly night-shade, or rank hellebore,[1]
    And I will mess[2] upon it.
JER.   Heaven forbid!
    Your honour's life is all too precious, sure—
10 DE MON. (*Sternly.*) Did I not say begone?
JER. Pardon, my lord, I'm old, and oft forget.

[EXIT.

DE MON. (*Looking after him, as if his heart smote him.*)
    Why will they thus mistime their foolish zeal,
    That I must be so stern?

---

1   Continuing the botanical allusions in the play, De Monfort speaks of hemlock, the
    powerful medical sedative famous for its role in Socrates' death; night-shade, which
    features highly poisonous black berries; and hellebore, another highly poisonous
    plant used by the Ancients to treat mental disorders.
2   Dine.

O! that I were upon some desert coast!
Where howling tempests and the lashing tide
Would stun me into deep and senseless quiet;
As the storm-beaten trav'ller droops his head,
In heavy, dull, lethargick weariness,
And, midst the roar of jarring elements,
Sleeps to awake no more.   20
What am I grown? All things are hateful to me.

Enter MANUEL.

(*Stamping with his foot.*) Who bids thee break upon my
      privacy?
MAN. Nay, good, my lord! I heard you speak aloud,
      And dreamt not, surely, that you were alone.
DE MON. What, dost thou watch, and pin thine ear to holes,
      To catch those exclamations of the soul,
      Which heaven alone should hear? Who hir'd thee, pray?
      Who basely hir'd thee for a task like this?
MAN. My lord, I cannot hold. For fifteen years,
      Long-troubled years, I have your servant been,   30
      Nor hath the proudest lord in all the realm,
      With firmer, with more honourable faith
      His sov'reign serv'd, than I have served you;
      But, if my honesty is doubted now,
      Let him who is more faithful take my place,
      And serve you better.
DE MON. Well, be it as thou wilt. Away with thee.
      Thy loud-mouth'd boasting is no rule for me
      To judge thy merit by.

Enter JEROME *hastily, and pulls* MANUEL *away.*

JER. Come, Manuel, come away; thou art not wise.   40
      The stranger must depart and come again,
      For now his honour will not be disturb'd.

[EXIT Manuel *sulkily.*

DE MON. A stranger said'st thou.
  (*Drops his handkerchief.*)
JER. I did, good sir, but he shall go away;
  You shall not be disturb'd.
  (*Stooping to lift the handkerchief.*)
                              You have dropp'd somewhat.
DE MON. (*Preventing him.*) Nay, do not stoop, my friend! I pray
  thee not!
  Thou art too old to stoop.—
  I am much indebted to thee.—Take this ring—
  I love thee better than I seem to do.
50 I pray thee do it—thank me not.—What stranger?
JER. A man who does most earnestly entreat
  To see your honour, but I know him not.
DE MON. Then let him enter.   [EXIT Jerome.

A pause. Enter GRIMBALD.

DE MON. You are the stranger who would speak with me?
GRIM. I am so far unfortunate, my lord,
  That, though my fortune on your favour hangs,
  I am to you a stranger.
DE MON. How may this be? What can I do for you?
GRIM. Since thus your lordship does so frankly ask,
60 The tiresome preface of apology
  I will forbear, and tell my tale at once.—
  In plodding drudgery I've spent my youth,
  A careful penman in another's office;
  And now, my master and employer dead,
  They seek to set a stripling o'er my head,
  And leave me on to drudge, e'en to old age,
  Because I have no friend to take my part.
  It is an office in your native town,
  For I am come from thence, and I am told
70 You can procure it for me. Thus, my lord,
  From the repute of goodness which you bear,
  I have presum'd to beg.
DE MON. They have befool'd thee with a false report.

GRIM. Alas! I see it is in vain to plead.
Your mind is pre-possess'd against a wretch,
Who has, unfortunately for his weal,
Offended the revengeful Rezenvelt.
DE MON. What dost thou say?
GRIM. What I, perhaps, had better leave unsaid.
Who will believe my wrongs if I complain? 80
I am a stranger, Rezenvelt my foe,
Who will believe my wrongs?
DE MON. (*Eagerly catching him by the coat.*)
                            I will believe them!
Though they were base as basest, vilest deeds,
In ancient record told, I would believe them.
Let not the smallest atom of unworthiness
That he has put upon thee be conceal'd.
Speak boldly, tell it all; for, by the light!
I'll be thy friend, I'll be thy warmest friend,
If he has done thee wrong.
GRIM. Nay, pardon me, it were not well advis'd, 90
If I should speak so freely of the man,
Who will so soon your nearest kinsman be.
DE MON. What canst thou mean by this?
GRIM.   That Marquis Rezenvelt
Has pledg'd his faith unto your noble sister,
And soon will be the husband of her choice.
So, I am told, and so the world believes.
DE MON. 'Tis false! 'tis basely false!
What wretch could drop from his envenom'd tongue
A tale so damn'd?—It chokes my breath—
(*Stamping with his foot.*) What wretch did tell it thee? 100
GRIM. Nay, every one with whom I have convers'd
Has held the same discourse. I judge it not.
But you, my lord, who with the lady dwell,
You best can tell what her deportment speaks;
Whether her conduct and unguarded words
Belie such rumour.
(De Monfort *pauses, staggers backwards, and sinks into a chair;
then starting up hastily.*)

DE MON. Where am I now? 'midst all the cursed thoughts
      That on my soul like stinging scorpions prey'd,
      This never came before—Oh, if it be!
110   The thought will drive me mad.—Was it for this
      She urged her warm request on bended knee?
      Alas! I wept, and thought of sister's love,
      No damned love like this.
      Fell devil! 'tis hell itself has lent thee aid
      To work such sorcery! (*Pauses.*) I'll not believe it.
      I must have proof[1] clear as the noon-day sun
      For such foul charge as this! Who waits without!
      (*Paces up and down furiously agitated.*)
GRIM. (*Aside.*) What have I done? I've carried this too far.
      I've rous'd a fierce ungovernable madman.

                    Enter JEROME.

DE MON. (*In a loud angry voice.*)
120   Where did she go, at such an early hour,
      And with such slight attendance?
JER. Of whom inquires your honour?
DE MON. Why, of your lady. Said I not my sister?
JER. The Lady Jane, your sister?
DE MON. (*In a faultering voice.*) Yes, I did call her so.
JER. In truth, I cannot tell you where she went.
      E'en now, from the short-beechen walk hard-by,
      I saw her through the garden-gate return.
      The Marquis Rezenvelt, and Freberg's Countess
130   Are in her company. This way they come,
      As being nearer to the back apartments;
      But I shall stop them, if it be your will,
      And bid them enter here.
DE MON. No, stop them not. I will remain unseen,[2]
      And mark them as they pass. Draw back a little.
      (*Grimbald* seems alarm'd, and steals off unnoticed.
      De Monfort *grasps* Jerome *tightly by the hand, and drawing*

---

1   Cf. *Othello* 3.3.160.
2   Cf. *Othello* 4.1.75-151.

back with him two or three steps, not to be seen from the garden,
waits in silence with his eyes fixed on the glass-door.)

DE MON. I hear their footsteps on the grating sand.
How like the croaking of a carrion bird,
That hateful voice sounds to the distant ear!
And now she speaks—her voice sounds cheerly too—
O curse their mirth!—   140
Now, now, they come, keep closer still! keep steady!
(*Taking hold of* Jerome *with both hands.*)

JER. My lord, you tremble much.

DE MON.   What, do I shake?

JER. You do, in truth, and your teeth chatter too.

DE MON. See! see they come! he strutting by her side.
(Jane, Rezenvelt, *and* Countess Freberg *appear through the*
glass-door, pursuing their way up a short walk leading to the
other wing of the house.)
See how he turns his odious face to her's!
Utt'ring with confidence some nauseous jest.
And she endures it too—Oh! this looks vilely!
Ha! mark that courteous motion of his arm—
What does he mean?—He dares not take her hand!
(*Pauses and looks eagerly.*) By heaven and hell he does!   150
(*Letting go his hold of* Jerome, *he throws out his hands*
vehemently, and thereby pushes him against the scene.)

JER. Oh! I am stunn'd! my head is crack'd in twain:
Your honour does forget how old I am.

DE MON. Well, well, the wall is harder than I wist.
Begone! and whine within.

[EXIT Jerome, *with a sad rueful countenance.*

(De Monfort *comes forward to the front of the stage, and makes*
a long pause, expressive of great agony of mind.)
It must be so; each passing circumstance;
Her hasty journey here; her keen distress
Whene'er my soul's abhorrence I express'd;
Ay, and that damned reconciliation,
With tears extorted from me: Oh, too well!

160 All, all too well bespeak the shameful tale.
I should have thought of heav'n and hell conjoin'd,
The morning star[1] mix'd with infernal fire,
Ere I had thought of this—
Hell's blackest magick, in the midnight hour,
With horrid spells and incantation dire,
Such combination opposite, unseemly,
Of fair and loathsome, excellent and base,
Did ne'er produce.—But every thing is possible,
So as it may my misery enhance!
170 Oh! I did love her with such pride of soul!
When other men, in gayest pursuit of love,
Each beauty follow'd, by her side I stay'd;
Far prouder of a brother's station there,
Than all the favours favour'd lovers boast.
We quarrel'd once, and when I could no more
The alter'd coldness of her eye endure,
I slipp'd o' tip-toe to her chamber door;
And when she ask'd who gently knock'd—Oh! oh!
Who could have thought of this?[2]
(*Throws himself into a chair, covers his face with his hand, and bursts into tears. After some time he starts up from his seat furiously.*)
180 Hell's direst torment seize th' infernal villain!
Detested of my soul! I will have vengeance![3]
I'll crush thy swelling pride—I'll still thy vaunting—
I'll do a deed of blood—Why shrink I thus?
If, by some spell or magick sympathy,
Piercing the lifeless figure on that wall
Could pierce his bosom too, would I not cast it?
(*Throwing a dagger against the wall.*)
Shall groans and blood affright me? No, I'll do it.
Tho' gasping life beneath my pressure heav'd,

---

1 Lucifer ('light bringer') is the morning star (Venus). Cf. Isaiah 14 and John Milton's *Paradise Lost* 3.80-135.

2 Cf. note to *Count Basil* 4.5.95 and Richardson, "The Dangers of Sympathy" and Thorslev, "Incest as Romantic Symbol."

3 Cf. *Othello* 3.3.447-62.

And my soul shudder'd at the horrid brink,
I would not flinch.—Fy this recoiling nature!   190
O that his sever'd limbs were strew'd in air,
So as I saw him not!
(*Enter* Rezenvelt *behind, from the glass door.* De Monfort
*turns round, and on seeing him starts back, then drawing his
sword, rushes furiously upon him.*)
Detested robber; now all forms are over:
Now open villany, now open hate!
Defend thy life.

REZ.   De Monfort, thou art mad.

DE MON. Speak not, but draw. Now for thy hated life!
(*They fight:* Rezenvelt *parries his thrusts with great skill, and
at last disarms him.*)
Then take my life, black fiend, for hell assists thee.

REZ. No, Monfort, but I'll take away your sword.
Not as a mark of disrespect to you,
But for your safety. By to-morrow's eve   200
I'll call on you myself and give it back;
And then, if I am charged with any wrong,
I'll justify myself. Farewell, strange man!

[EXIT

(De Monfort *stands for some time quite motionless, like one
stupified. Enter to him a* SERVANT: *he starts.*)

DE MON. Ha! who art thou?

SER.   'Tis I, an' please your honour.

DE MON. (*Staring wildly at him.*) Who art thou?

SER. Your servant Jacques.

DE MON.   Indeed I know thee not.
Leave me, and when Rezenvelt is gone,
Return and let me know.

SER.   He's gone already, sir.

DE MON. How, gone so soon?

SER.   Yes, as his servant told me,
He was in haste to go, for night comes on,   210
And at the ev'ning hour he must take horse,

To visit some old friend whose lonely mansion
Stands a short mile beyond the farther wood;
And, as he loves to wander thro' those wilds
Whilst yet the early moon may light his way,
He sends his horses round the usual road,
And crosses it alone.
I would not walk thro' those wild dens alone
For all his wealth. For there, as I have heard,
Foul murders have been done, and ravens scream;
And things unearthly, stalking thro' the night,
Have scar'd the lonely trav'ller from his wits.
(De Monfort *stands fixed in thought.*)
I've ta'en your mare, an please you, from her field,
And wait your farther orders.
(De Monfort *heeds him not.*)
Her hoofs are sound, and where the saddle gall'd
Begins to mend. What further must be done?
(De Monfort *still heeds him not.*)
His honour heeds me not. Why should I stay?
DE MON. (*Eagerly, as he is going.*) He goes alone saidst thou?
SER. His servant told me so.
DE MON.   And at what hour?
SER. He parts from Amberg by the fall of eve.
Save you, my lord? how chang'd your count'nance is!
Are you not well?
DE MON.   Yes, I am well: begone!
And wait my orders by the city wall:
I'll that way bend, and speak to thee again.

[EXIT, Servant.

(De Monfort *walks rapidly two or three times across the stage;
then siezes his dagger from the wall; looks steadfastly at its point,
and* EXIT, *hastily.*)

ACT IV.—SCENE I.

Moon-light. A wild path in a wood, shaded with trees. Enter DE
MONFORT, *with a strong expression of disquiet, mixed with fear,
upon his face, looking behind him, and bending his ear to the ground,
as if he listened to something.*

DE MON. How hollow groans the earth beneath my tread!
    Is there an echo here? Methinks it sounds
    As tho' some heavy footstep follow'd me.
    I will advance no farther.
    Deep settled shadows rest across the path,
    And thickly-tangled boughs o'er-hang this spot.
    O that a tenfold gloom did cover it!
    That 'midst the murky darkness I might strike;
    As in the wild confusion of a dream,
    Things horrid, bloody, terrible, do pass,   10
    As tho' they pass'd not; nor impress the mind
    With the fix'd clearness of reality.
    (*An owl is heard screaming near him.*)
    (*Starting.*) What sound is that?
    (*Listens, and the owl cries again.*)
                        It is the screech-owl's cry.
    Foul bird of night! what spirit guides thee here?
    Art thou instinctive drawn to scenes of horrour?
    I've heard of this. (*Pauses and listens.*)
    How those fall'n leaves so rustle on the path,
    With whisp'ring noise, as tho' the earth around me
    Did utter secret things!
    The distant river, too bears to mine ear   20
    A dismal wailing. O mysterious night!
    Thou art not silent; many tongues hast thou.
    A distant gath'ring blast sounds thro' the wood,
    And dark clouds fleetly hasten o'er the sky:
    O! that a storm would rise, a raging storm;
    Amidst the roar of warring elements;
    I'd lift my hand and strike: but this pale light,

The calm distinctness of each stilly[1] thing,
Is terrible. (*Starting*.) Footsteps are near—
30   He comes, he comes! I'll watch him farther on—
I cannot do it here.

[EXIT.

Enter REZENVELT, *and continues his way slowly across the stage, but just as he is going off the owl screams, he stops and listens, and the owl screams again.*

REZ. Ha! does the night-bird greet me on my way?
How much his hooting is in harmony
With such a scene as this! I like it well.
Oft when a boy,[2] at the still twilight hour,
I've leant my back against some knotted oak,
And loudly mimick'd him, till to my call
He answer would return, and thro' the gloom
We friendly converse held.
40   Between me and the star-bespangl'd sky
Those aged oaks their crossing branches wave,
And thro' them looks the pale and placid moon.
How like a crocodile, or winged snake,
Yon sailing cloud bears on its dusky length!
And now transformed by the passing wind,
Methinks it seems a flying Pegasus.
Ay, but a shapeless band of blacker hue
Come swiftly after.—
A hollow murm'ring wind comes thro' the trees;
50   I hear it from afar; this bodes a storm.
I must not linger here—
(*A bell heard at some distance.*)
                                   What bell is this?
It sends a solemn sound upon the breeze.
Now, to a fearful superstitious mind,

---

1   Characterized by stillness; secret.
2   Cf. Wordsworth, *Lyrical Ballads* vol. 2 and *The Prelude* 5.364-425 (Appendix D.2).

In such a scene, 'twould like a death-knell come:
For me it tells but of a shelter near,
And so I bid it welcome.

[EXIT.

SCENE II.

The inside of a Convent Chapel, of old Gothick architecture, almost dark; two torches only are seen at a distance, burning over a new-made grave.[1] The noise of loud wind, beating upon the windows and roof, is heard. Enter two MONKS.

1ST MONK. The storm increases: hark how dismally
    It howls along the cloisters. How goes time?
2D MONK. It is the hour: I hear them near at hand;
    And when the solemn requiem has been sung
    For the departed sister, we'll retire.
    Yet, should this tempest still more violent grow,
    We'll beg a friendly shelter till the morn.
1ST MONK. See, the procession enters: let us join.

(The organ strikes up a solemn prelude. Enter a procession of Nuns, *with the* Abbess, *bearing torches. After compassing the grave twice, and remaining there some time, whilst the organ plays a grand dirge, they advance to the front of the stage.)*

SONG, BY THE NUNS.

Departed soul, whose poor remains
This hallow'd lowly grave contains;   10
Whose passing storm of life is o'er,

---

1 In the revised fourth edition (1802) and fifth edition (1806) Baillie provided the following note to this stage direction: "I have put above *newly-covered* instead of *new-made* grave, as it stands in the former editions, because I wish not to give the idea of a funeral procession, but merely that of a hymn or requiem sung over the grave of a person who has been recently buried."

Whose pains and sorrows are no more!
Bless'd be thou with the bless'd above!
Where all is joy, and purity, and love.

Let him, in might and mercy dread,
Lord of the living and the dead;
In whom the stars of heav'n rejoice,
To whom the ocean lifts his voice,
Thy spirit purified to glory raise,
To sing with holy saints his everlasting praise.

Departed soul, who in this earthly scene
Hast our lowly sister been.
Swift be thy way to where the blessed dwell!
Until we meet thee there, farewell! farewell!

Enter a LAY SISTER, *with a wild terrified look, her hair and dress all
scattered, and rushes forward amongst them.*

ABB. Why com'st thou here, with such disorder'd looks,
    To break upon our sad solemnity?
SIST. Oh! I did hear, thro' the receding blast,
    Such horrid cries! it made my blood run chill.
ABB. 'Tis but the varied voices of the storm,
    Which many times will sound like distant screams:
    It has deceiv'd thee.
IST SIST. O no, for twice it call'd, so loudly call'd,
    With horrid strength, beyond the pitch of nature.
    And murder! murder! was the dreadful cry.
    A third time it return'd with feeble strength,
    But o' the sudden ceas'd, as tho' the words
    Were rudely smother'd in the grasped throat;
    And all was still again, save the wild blast
    Which at a distance growl'd—
    Oh! it will never from my mind depart!
    That dreadful cry all I' the instant still'd,
    For then, so near, some horrid deed was done,
    And none to rescue.

ABB. Where didst thou hear it?

SIST.   In the higher cells,
   As now a window, open'd by the storm,
   I did attempt to close.

1ST MONK. I wish our brother Bernard were arriv'd;
   He is upon his way.

ABB. Be not alarm'd; it still may be deception.
   'Tis meet we finish our solemnity,   50
   Nor shew neglect unto the honour'd dead.
   (*Gives a sign, and the organ plays again: just as it ceases a loud knocking is heard without.*)

ABB. Ha! who may this be? hush!
   (*Knocking heard again.*)

2D MONK. It is the knock of one in furious haste,
   Hush, hush! What footsteps come? Ha! brother Bernard.

Enter BERNARD *bearing a lantern.*

1ST MONK. See, what a look he wears of stiffen'd fear!
   Where hast thou been, good brother?

BERN. I've seen a horrid sight!
   (*All gathering round him and speaking at once.*)
                             What hast thou seen?

BERN. As on I hasten'd, bearing thus my light,
   Across the path, not fifty paces off,
   I saw a murther'd corse stretch'd on its back,   60
   Smear'd with new blood, as tho' but freshly slain.

ABB. A man or woman?

BERN.   A man, a man!

ABB. Did'st thou examine if within its breast
   There yet is lodg'd some small remains of life?
   Was it quite dead?

BERN.   Nought in the grave is deader.
   I look'd but once, yet life did never lodge
   In any form so laid.—
   A chilly horrour seiz'd me, and I fled.

1ST MONK. And does the face seem all unknown to thee?

BERN. The face! I would not on the face have look'd   70

For e'en a kingdom's wealth, for all the world.
O no! the bloody neck, the bloody neck!
(*Shaking his head, and shuddering with horrour. Loud knocking heard without.*)

SIST. Good mercy! who comes next?

BERN.   Not far behind
I left our brother Thomas on the road;
But then he did repent him as he went,
And threaten'd to return.

2D MONK.   See, here he comes.

Enter brother THOMAS, *with a wild terrified look.*

1ST MONK. How wild he looks!

BERN. (*Going up to him eagerly.*) What, hast thou seen it too?

THOM. Yes, yes! it glar'd upon me as it pass'd.

80   BERN. What glar'd upon thee?
(*All gathering round* Thomas *and speaking at once.*)
                            O! what hast thou seen?

THOM. As, striving with the blast, I onward came,
Turning my feeble lantern from the wind,
Its light upon a dreadful visage gleam'd,
Which paus'd, and look'd upon me as it pass'd.
But such a look, such wildness of despair,
Such horrour-strain'd features never yet
Did earthly visage show. I shrunk and shudder'd.
If damned spirits may to earth return
I've seen it.

BERN.   Was there blood upon it?

90   THOM. Nay, as it pass'd, I did not see its form;
Nought but the horrid face.

BERN. It is the murderer.

1ST MONK.   What way went it?

THOM. I durst not look till I had pass'd it far,
Then turning round, upon the rising bank,
I saw, between me and the paly sky,
A dusky form, tossing and agitated.
I stopp'd to mark it, but, in truth, I found

'Twas but a sapling bending to the wind,
And so I onward hied,[1] and look'd no more.
IST MONK. But we must look to't; we must follow it: 100
     Our duty so commands. (*To* 2d Monk.) Will you go,
     brother?
     (*To* Bernard.) And you, good Bernard?
BERN.   If I needs must go.
IST MONK. Come, we must all go.
ABB.   Heaven be with you, then!

                                [EXEUNT *Monks.*

SIST. Amen, amen! Good heaven be with us all!
     O what a dreadful night!
ABB. Daughters retire; peace to the peaceful dead!
     Our solemn ceremony now is finish'd.

SCENE III.

A large room in the Convent, very dark. Enter the ABBESS, *Lay
Sister bearing a light, and several* Nuns. *Sister sets down the light on
a table at the bottom of the stage, so that the room is still very gloomy.*

ABB. They have been longer absent than I thought;
     I fear he has escap'd them.
IST NUN.   Heaven forbid!
SIST. No no, found out foul murder ever is,
     And the foul murd'rer too.
2D NUN. The good Saint Francis will direct their search;
     The blood so near his holy convent shed
     For threefold vengeance calls.
ABB. I hear a noise within the inner court,
     They are return'd; (*listening.*) and Bernard's voice I hear:
     They are return'd.
SIST.   Why do I tremble so?   10

---

1 Sped.

It is not I who ought to tremble thus.

2D NUN. I hear them at the door.

BERN. (*Without.*) Open the door, I pray thee, brother Thomas;
 I cannot now unhand the prisoner.

(*All speak together, shrinking back from the door, and staring upon one another.*)
 He is with them.

 (*A folding door at the bottom of the stage is opened, and enter
 Bernard, Thomas, and the other two Monks, carrying lanterns
 in their hands, and bringing in* De Monfort. *They are likewise
 followed by other Monks. As they lead forward* De Monfort *the
 light is turned away, so that he is seen obscurely; but when they
 come to the front of the stage they all turn the light side of their
 lanterns on him at once, and his face is seen in all the
 strengthened horrour of despair, with his hands and cloaths
 bloody.*)

(Abbess *and* Nuns *speak at once, and starting back.*) Holy saints be
 with us!

BERN. (*to* Abb.) Behold the man of blood!

ABB. Of misery too; I cannot look upon him.

BERN. (*to* Nuns.) Nay, holy sisters, turn not thus away.
 Speak to him, if, perchance, he will regard you:
 For from his mouth we have no utt'rance heard,
 Save one deep and smother'd exclamation,
 When first we seiz'd him.

ABB. (*to* De Mon.) Most miserable man, how art thou thus?
 (*Pauses.*)
 Thy tongue is silent, but those bloody hands
 Do witness horrid things. What is thy name?

DE MON. (*Roused; looks steadfastly at the* Abbess *for some time, then
 speaking in a short hurried voice.*) I have no name.

ABB. (*to* Bern.) Do it thyself: I'll speak to him no more.

SIST. O holy saints! that this should be the man,
 Who did against his fellow lift the stroke,
 Whilst he so loudly call'd.—
 Still in mine ear it sounds: O murder! murder!

DE MON. (*Starting.*) He calls again!

SIST. No, he did call, but now his voice is still'd.

'Tis past.

DE MON. (*In great anguish.*) 'Tis past!

SIST. Yes it is past, art thou not he who did it?

(De Monfort *utters a deep groan, and is supported from falling by the Monks. A noise is heard without.*)

ABB. What noise is this of heavy lumb'ring steps,
Like men who with a weighty burden come?

BERN. It is the body: I have orders given
That here it should be laid.

(*Enter men bearing the body of* Rezenvelt, *covered with a white cloth, and set it down in the middle of the room: they then uncover it.* De Monfort *stands fixed and motionless with horrour, only that a sudden shivering seems to pass over him when they uncover the corps. The* Abbess *and* Nuns *shrink back and retire to some distance; all the rest fixing their eyes steadfastly upon* De Monfort. *A long pause.*)

BERN. (*to* De Mon.) See'st thou that lifeless corps, those bloody wounds, 40
See how he lies, who but so shortly since
A living creature was, with all the powers
Of sense, and motion, and humanity?
Oh! what a heart had he who did this deed!

1ST MONK. (*Looking at the body.*) How hard those teeth against the lips are press'd,
As tho' he struggled still!

2D MONK. The hands, too, clench'd: the last efforts of nature.

(De Monfort *still stands motionless. Brother* Thomas *then goes to the body, and raising up the head a little, turns it towards* De Monfort.)

THOM. Know'st thou this gastly face?

DE MON. (*Putting his hands before his face in violent perturbation.*)
Oh do not! do not! veil it from my sight!
Put me to any agony but this! 50

THOM. Ha! dost thou then confess the dreadful deed?
Hast thou against the laws of awful heav'n
Such horrid murder done? What fiend could tempt thee?

(*Pauses and looks steadfastly at* De Monfort.)

DE MON. I hear thy words but do not hear their sense—

Hast thou not cover'd it?

BERN. (*to* Thom.) Forbear, my brother, for thou see'st right well
    He is not in a state to answer thee.
    Let us retire and leave him for a while.
    These windows are with iron grated o'er;
60   He cannot 'scape, and other duty calls.

THOM. Then let it be.

BERN. (*to* Monks, &c.) Come, let us all depart.

(EXEUNT Abbess *and* Nuns, *followed by the* Monks. *One* Monk
lingering a little behind.)

DE MON. All gone! (*Perceiving, the* Monk.)
          O stay thou here!

MONK.   It must not be.

DE MON. I'll give thee gold; I'll make thee rich in gold,
    If thou wilt stay e'en but a little while.

MONK. I must not, must not stay.

DE MON.   I do conjure thee!

MONK. I dare not stay with thee.   (*Going.*)

DE MON.   And wilt thou go?
    (*Catching hold of him eagerly.*)
    O! throw thy cloak upon this grizly form!
    The unclos'd eyes do stare upon me still.
    O do not leave me thus!

                  [Monk *covers the body, and* EXIT.

DE MON. (*Alone, looking at the covered body, but at a distance.*)
70   Alone with thee! but thou art nothing now,
    'Tis done, 'tis number'd with the things o'erpast,
    Would! would it were to come!
    What fated end, what darkly gath'ring cloud
    Will close on all this horrour?
    O that dire madness would unloose my thoughts,[1]
    And fill my mind with wildest fantasies,

---

1 See Appendix A.5.iii.

Dark, restless, terrible! ought, ought but this!
(*Pauses and shudders.*)
How with convulsive life he heav'd beneath me,
E'en with the death's wound gor'd. O horrid, horrid!
Methinks I feel him still.—What sound is that?   80
I heard a smother'd groan.—It is impossible!
(*Looking steadfastly at the body.*)
It moves! it moves! the cloth doth heave and swell.
It moves again.—I cannot suffer this—
Whate'er it be I will uncover it.
(*Runs to the corps and tears off the cloth in despair.*)
All still beneath.
Nought is there here but fix'd and grizly death.
How sternly fixed! Oh! those glazed eyes!
They look me still.
(*Shrinks back with horrour.*)
Come, madness! come unto me senseless death!
I cannot suffer this! Here, rocky wall,   90
Scatter these brains, or dull them.
(*Runs furiously, and, dashing his head against the wall, falls
upon the floor.*)

Enter two MONKS, *hastily.*

1ST MONK. See; wretched man, he hath destroy'd himself.
2D MONK. He does but faint. Let us remove him hence.
1ST MONK. We did not well to leave him here alone.
2D MONK. Come, let us bear him to the open air.

[EXEUNT, *bearing out* De Monfort.

Before the gates of the Convent. Enter JANE DE MONFORT, FREBERG *and* MANUEL. *As they are proceeding towards the gate,* JANE *stops short and shrinks back.*

FREB. Ha! wherefore? has a sudden illness seiz'd thee?

JANE. No, no, my friend.—And yet I am very faint—
   I dread to enter here!

MAN.   Ay! so I thought:
   For, when between the trees, that abbey tower
   First shew'd its top, I saw your count'nance change.
   But breathe a little here; I'll go before,
   And make enquiry at the nearest gate.

FREB. Do so, good Manuel.
   (Manuel *goes and knocks at the gate.*)
   Courage, dear madam: all may yet be well.

10 Rezenvelt's servant, frighten'd with the storm,
   And seeing that his master join'd him not,
   As by appointment, at the forest's edge,
   Might be alarm'd, and give too ready ear
   To an unfounded rumour.
   He saw it not; he came not here himself.

JANE. (*Looking eagerly to the gate, where* Manuel *talks with the* Porter.)
   Ha! see, he talks with some one earnestly.
   And sees't thou not that motion of his hands?
   He stands like one who hears a horrid tale.
   Almighty God!
   (Manuel *goes into the convent.*)
                    He comes not back; he enters.

20 FREB. Bear up, my noble friend.

JANE. I will, I will! But this suspence is dreadful.
   (*A long pause.* Manuel *re-enters from the convent, and comes forward slowly, with a sad countenance.*)
   Is this the pace[1] of one who bears good tidings?

---

1 "pace" in Larpent version; "face" in 1806 and 1851 editions.

O God! his face doth tell the horrid fact;
There is nought doubtful here.
FREB.   How is it, Manuel?
MAN. I've seen him through a crevice in his door:
    It is indeed my master.
    (*Bursting into tears.*)
    (Jane *faints, and is supported by* Freberg.—*Enter* ABBESS *and*
    several NUNS *from the convent who gather about her, and apply*
    remedies. She recovers.)
1ST NUN. The life returns again.
2D NUN.   Yes, she revives.
ABB. (*to* Freb.) Let me entreat this noble lady's leave
    To lead her in. She seems in great distress: 30
    We would with holy kindness soothe her woe,
    And do by her the deeds of christian love.
FREB. Madam, your goodness has my grateful thanks.

           [EXEUNT, *supporting* Jane *into the convent.*

SCENE II.

De Monfort *is discovered sitting in a thoughtful posture. He remains*
so for some time. His face afterwards begins to appear agitated, like one
whose mind is harrowed with the severest thoughts; then, starting from
his seat, he clasps his hands together, and holds them up to heaven.

DE MON. O that I had ne'er known the light of day!
    That filmy darkness on mine eyes had hung,
    And clos'd me out from the fair face of nature!
    O that my mind, in mental darkness pent,
    Had no perception, no distinction known,
    Of fair or foul, perfection nor defect;
    Nor thought conceiv'd of proud pre-eminence!
    O that it had! O that I had been form'd
    An idiot from the birth! a senseless changeling,
    Who eats his glutton's meal with greedy haste,   10
    Nor knows the hand who feeds him.—

(*Pauses; then, in a calmer sorrowful voice.*)
What am I now? how ends the day of life?
For end it must; and terrible this gloom,
The storm of horrours that surround its close.
This little term of nature's agony
Will soon be o'er, and what is past is past:
But shall I then, on the dark lap of earth
Lay me to rest, in still unconsciousness,
Like senseless clod that doth no pressure feel
20   From wearing foot of daily passenger;
Like steeped rock o'er which the breaking waves
Bellow and foam unheard? O would I could!

Enter MANUEL, *who springs forward to his master, but is checked
upon perceiving* De Monfort *draw back and look sternly at him.*

MAN. My lord, my master! O my dearest master!
    (De Monfort *still looks at him without speaking.*)
    Nay, do not thus regard me; good my lord!
    Speak to me: am I not your faithful Manuel?
DE MON. (*In a hasty broken voice.*) Art thou alone?
MAN. No, Sir, the lady Jane is on her way;
    She is not far behind.
DE MON. (*Tossing his arm over his head in an agony.*)
    This is too much! All I can bear but this!
30   It must not be.—Run and prevent her coming.
    Say, he who is detain'd a pris'ner here
    Is one to her unknown. I now am nothing.
    I am a man, of holy claims bereft;
    Out from the pale of social kindred cast;
    Nameless and horrible.—
    Tell her De Monfort far from hence is gone
    Into a desolate, and distant land,
    Ne'er to return again. Fly, tell her this;
    For we must meet no more.

Enter JANE DE MONFORT, *bursting into the chamber, and followed
by* FREBERG, ABBESS, *and several* NUNS.

JANE. We must! we must! My brother, O my brother!   40
    (De Monfort *turns away his head and hides his face with his*
    arm. Jane *stops short, and, making a great effort, turns to*
    Freberg, *and the others who followed her; and with an air of*
    dignity stretches out her hand, beckoning them to retire. All retire
    but Freberg, *who seems to hesitate.*)
And thou too, Freberg: call it not unkind.

            [EXIT Freberg, Jane *and* De Monfort *only remain.*

JANE. My hapless Monfort!
    (De Monfort *turns round and looks sorrowfully upon her; she*
    opens her arms to him, and he, rushing into them, hides his face
    upon her breast and weeps.)
JANE. Ay, give thy sorrow vent: here may'st thou weep.
DE MON. (*In broken accents.*) Oh! this, my sister, makes me feel
    again
    The kindness of affection.
    My mind has in a dreadful storm been tost;
    Horrid and dark.—I thought to weep no more.—
    I've done a deed—But I am human still.
JANE. I know thy suff'rings: leave thy sorrow free:
    Thou art with one who never did upbraid;   50
    Who mourns, who loves thee still.
DE MON. Ah! sayst thou so? no, no; it should not be.
    (*Shrinking from her.*) I am a foul and bloody murderer,
    For such embrace unmeet. O leave me! leave me!
    Disgrace and publick shame abide me now;
    And all, alas! who do my kindred own
    The direful portion share.—Away, away!
    Shall a disgrac'd and publick criminal
    Degrade thy name, and claim affinity
    To noble worth like thine?—I have no name—   60
    I am nothing, now, not e'en to thee; depart.
    (*She takes his hand, and grasping it firmly, speaks with a*
    determined voice.)
JANE. De Monfort, hand in hand we have enjoy'd
    The playful term of infancy together;

And in the rougher path of ripen'd years
We've been each other's stay. Dark lowers our fate,
And terrible the storm that gathers over us;
But nothing, till that latest agony
Which severs thee from nature, shall unloose
This fix'd and sacred hold. In thy dark prison-house;
In the terrifick face of armed law;
Yea, on the scaffold, if it needs must be,
I never will forsake thee.

DE MON. (*Looking at her with admiration.*)
Heav'n bless thy gen'rous soul, my noble Jane!
I thought to sink beneath this load of ill,
Depress'd with infamy and open shame;
I thought to sink in abject wretchedness:
But for thy sake I'll rouse my manhood up,
And meet it bravely; no unseemly weakness,
I feel my rising strength, shall blot my end,
To clothe thy cheek with shame.

JANE. Yes, thou art noble still.

DE MON. With thee I am; who were not so with thee?
But, ah, my sister! short will be the term:
Death's stroke will come, and in that state beyond,
Where things unutterable wait the soul,
New from its earthly tenement discharg'd,
We shall be sever'd far.
Far as the spotless purity of virtue
Is from the murd'rer's guilt, far shall we be.
This is the gulf of dread uncertainty
From which the soul recoils.

JANE. The God who made thee is a God of mercy;
Think upon this.

DE MON. (*Shaking his head.*) No, no! this blood! this blood!

JANE. Yea, e'en the sin of blood may be forgiv'n,
When humble penitence hath once aton'd.

DE MON. (*Eagerly.*) What, after terms of lengthen'd misery,
Imprison'd anguish of tormented spirits,
Shall I again, a renovated soul,
Into the blessed family of the good

Admittance have? Think'st thou that this may be? 100
Speak if thou canst: O speak me comfort here!
For dreadful fancies, like an armed host,
Have push'd me to despair. It is most horrible—
O speak of hope! if any hope there be.
(Jane *is silent and looks sorrowfully upon him; then clasping her*
hands, and turning her eyes to heaven, seems to mutter a prayer.)
DE MON. Ha! dost thou pray for me? heav'n hear thy prayer!
I fain would kneel—Alas! I dare not do it.
JANE. Not so; all by th' Almighty Father form'd
May in their deepest mis'ry call on him.
Come kneel with me, my brother.
(*She kneels and prays to herself; he kneels by her, and clasps his*
hands fervently, but speaks not. A noise of chains clanking is
heard without, and they both rise.)
DE MON. Hear'st thou that noise? They come to interrupt us. 110
JANE. (*Moving towards a side door.*) Then let us enter here.
DE MON. (*Catching hold of her with a look of horrour.*) Not
there—not there—the corps—the bloody corps.
JANE. What, lies he there?—Unhappy Rezenvelt!
DE MON. A sudden thought has come across my mind;
How came it not before? Unhappy Rezenvelt!
Say'st thou but this?
JANE. What should I say? he was an honest man;[1]
I still have thought him such, as such lament him.
(De Monfort *utters a deep groan.*)
What means this heavy groan?
DE MON.   It hath a meaning.

Enter ABBESS *and* MONKS, *with two* OFFICERS *of justice carrying*
fetters in their hands to put upon DE MONFORT.

JANE. (*Starting.*) What men are these? 120
1ST OFF. Lady, we are the servants of the law,
And bear with us a power, which doth constrain
To bind with fetters this our prisoner.

---

1 Between lines 118 and 119 the Larpent version includes the line: "Spite of the levi-
ties which misbecame him"; cf. Cox, *Seven Gothic Dramas* 304.

(*Pointing to* De Monfort.)

JANE. A stranger uncondemn'd? this cannot be.

1ST OFF. As yet, indeed, he is by law unjudg'd,
But is so far condemn'd by circumstance,
That law, or custom sacred held as law,
Doth fully warrant us, and it must be.

JANE. Nay, say not so; he has no power to escape:
130   Distress hath bound him with a heavy chain;
There is no need of yours.

1ST OFF. We must perform our office.

JANE. O! do not offer this indignity!

1ST OFF. Is it indignity in sacred[1] law
To bind a murderer? (*To* 2d Officer.) Come, do thy work.

JANE. Harsh are thy words, and stern thy harden'd brow;
Dark is thine eye; but all some pity have
Unto the last extreme of misery.
I do beseech thee! if thou art a man—
(*Kneeling to him.*)
(De Monfort *roused at this, runs up to* Jane, *and raises her
hastily from the ground; then stretches himself up proudly.*)

140 DE MON. (*to* Jane.) Stand thou erect in native dignity;
And bend to none on earth the suppliant knee,
Though cloath'd in power imperial. To my heart
It gives a feller gripe than many irons.
(*Holding out his hands.*)
Here, officers of law, bind on those shackles,
And if they are too light bring heavier chains.
Add iron to iron, load, crush me to the ground;
Nay, heap ten thousand weight upon my breast,
For that were best of all.
(*A long pause, whilst they put irons upon him. After they are on,*
Jane *looks at him sorrowfully, and lets her head sink on her
breast.* De Monfort *stretches out his hands, looks at them, and
then at* Jane; *crosses them over his breast, and endeavours to
suppress his feelings.*[2])

---

1 "equal" in Larpent version; cf. Cox, *Seven Gothic Dramas* 305.

2 Later editions also include this note: "Should this play ever again be acted, perhaps
it would be better that the curtain should drop here; since here the story may be

1ST OFF. I have it, too, in charge to move you hence,
    (*To* De Monfort.)
    Into another chamber, more secure. 150
DE MON. Well, I am ready, sir.
    (*Approaching* Jane, *whom the* Abbess *is endeavouring to comfort, but to no purpose.*)
    Ah! wherefore thus! most honour'd and most dear?
    Shrink not at the accoutrements of ill,
    Daring the thing itself.
    (*Endeavouring to look cheerful.*)
    Wilt thou permit me with a gyved[1] hand?
    (*She gives him her hand, which he raises to his lips.*)
    This was my proudest office.

        [EXEUNT, De Monfort *leading out* Jane.

SCENE III.

A long narrow gallery in the convent, with the doors of the cells on each side. The stage darkened. A Nun *is discovered at a distance listening. Enter another* Nun *at the front of the stage, and starts back.*

1ST NUN. Ha! who is this not yet retir'd to rest?
    My sister, is it you?
    (*To the other who advances.*)
2D NUN. Returning from the sister Nina's cell,
    Passing yon door where the poor pris'ner lies,
    The sound of one who struggl'd with despair
    Struck on me as I went: I stopp'd and listen'd;
    O God! such piteous groans!
1ST NUN. Yes, since the ev'ning sun it hath been so.
    The voice of mis'ry oft hath reach'd mine ear,
    E'en in the cell above.
2D NUN.   How is it thus? 10

---

    considered as completed, and what comes after, prolongs the piece too much when our interest for the fate of De Monfort is at an end."
1   Shackled.

Methought he brav'd it with a manly spirit,
And led, with shackl'd hands, his sister forth,
Like one resolv'd to bear misfortune boldly.

IST NUN. Yes, with heroick courage, for a while
He seem'd inspir'd; but, soon depress'd again,
Remorse and dark despair o'erwhelm'd his soul,
And so he hath remain'd.

Enter Father BERNARD, *advancing from the further end of the*
gallery, bearing a crucifix.

IST NUN. How goes it, father, with your penitent?
We've heard his heavy groans.

20 BERN. Retire, my daughters; many a bed of death,
With all its pangs and horrour I have seen,
But never ought like this.

2D NUN. He's dying, then?

BERN.   Yes, death is dealing with him.
From violent agitation of the mind,
Some stream of life within his breast has burst;
For many times, within a little space,
The ruddy-tide has rush'd into his mouth.
God, grant his pains be short!

IST NUN.   Amen, amen!

2D NUN. How does the lady?

30 BERN. She sits and bears his head upon her lap;
And like a heaven-inspir'd angel, speaks
The word of comfort to his troubled soul:
Then does she wipe the cold drops from his brow,
With such a look of tender wretchedness,
It wrings the heart to see her.

IST NUN. Ha! hear ye nothing?

2D NUN. (*Alarmed.*)   Yes, I heard a noise.

IST NUN. And see'st thou nothing?
(*Creeping close to her sister.*)

BERN.   'Tis a nun in white.

Enter LAY SISTER *in her night cloaths, advancing from the dark end of the gallery.*

(*To* Sister.) Wherefore, my daughter, hast thou left thy cell?
It is not meet at this untimely hour.
SIST. I cannot rest. I hear such dismal sounds,   40
Such wailings in the air, such shrilly shrieks,
As though the cry of murder rose again
From the deep gloom of night. I cannot rest:
I pray you let me stay with you, good sisters!
(*Bell tolls.*)
NUNS. (*Starting.*) What bell is that?
BERN.   It is the bell of death.
A holy sister was upon the watch
To give this notice. (*Bell tolls again.*) Hark! another knell!
The wretched struggler hath his warfare clos'd;[1]
May heaven have mercy on him.
(*Bell tolls again.*)
Retire, my daughters; let us all retire,   50
For scenes like this to meditation call.

                    [EXEUNT, *bell tolling again.*

SCENE IV.

A hall or large room in the convent. The bodies of DE MONFORT *and* REZENVELT *are discovered laid out upon a low table or platform, covered with black.* FREBERG, BERNARD, ABBESS, MONKS, *and* NUNS *attending.*

ABB. (*to* Freb.) Here must they lie, my lord, until we know
Respecting this the order of the law.

---

1   Though the 1851 edition does not retain them, on the 7th of December 1815, Baillie wrote in a letter of making changes to De Monfort's death. She wrote: "Did I not tell you in a former letter that I have altered *De Monfort* and made the ending more dramatic by killing De Mon. on the stage? and I really think it a great improvement and Mr. Lamb and Lord Byron I am told think so too." (Quoted in Donkin, 220 n39. National Library of Scotland, MS 3886.)

FREB. And you have wisely done, my rev'rend mother.
  (*Goes to the table, and looks at the bodies, but without uncovering them.*)
  Unhappy men! ye, both in nature rich,
  With talents and with virtues were endu'd.
  Ye should have lov'd, yet deadly rancour came,
  And in the prime and manhood of your days
  Ye sleep in horrid death. O direful hate!
  What shame and wretchedness his portion is,
  Who, for a secret inmate, harbours thee!
  And who shall call him blameless who excites,
  Ungen'rously excites, with careless scorn,
  Such baleful passion in a brother's breast,
  Whom heav'n commands to love. Low are ye laid:
  Still all contention now.—Low are ye laid.
  I lov'd you both, and mourn your hapless fall.
ABB. They were your friends, my lord?
FREB. I lov'd them both. How does the Lady Jane?
ABB. She bears misfortune with intrepid soul.
  I never saw in woman bow'd with grief
  Such moving dignity.
FREB.   Ay, still the same.
  I've known her long; of worth most excellent;
  But, in the day of woe, she ever rose
  Upon the mind with added majesty,
  As the dark mountain more sublimely tow'rs
  Mantled in clouds and storm.

                    Enter MANUEL *and* JEROME.

MAN. (*Pointing.*) Here, my good Jerome, there's a piteous sight.
JER. A piteous sight! yet I will look upon him:
  I'll see his face in death. Alas, alas!
  I've seen him move a noble gentleman;
  And when with vexing passion undisturb'd,
  He look'd most graciously.
  (*Lifts up in mistake the cloth from the body of* Rezenvelt, *and starts back with horrour.*)

Oh! this was bloody work! Oh, oh! oh, oh!
That human hands could do it!
(*Drops the cloth again.*)

MAN. That is the murder'd corps; here lies De Monfort.
(*Going to uncover the other body.*)

JER. (*Turning away his head.*) No, no! I cannot look upon him
now.

MAN. Didst thou not come to see him?

JER. Fy! cover him—inter him in the dark—
Let no one look upon him.

BERN. (*to* Jer.) Well dost thou show the abhorrence nature feels   40
For deeds of blood, and I commend thee well.
In the most ruthless heart compassion wakes
For one who, from the hand of fellow man,
Hath felt such cruelty.
(*Uncovering the body of* Rezenvelt.)
This is the murder'd corse,
(*Uncovering the body of* De Monfort.)
                                        But see, I pray!
Here lies the murderer. What think'st thou here?
Look on those features, thou hast seen them oft,
With the last dreadful conflict of despair,
So fix'd in horrid strength.
See those knit brows, those hollow sun'ken eyes;   50
The sharpen'd nose, with nostrils all distent;
That writhed mouth, where yet the teeth appear,
In agony, to gnash the nether lip.
Think'st thou, less painful than the murd'rer's knife
Was such a death as this?
Ay, and how changed too those matted locks!

JER. Merciful heaven! his hair is grisly grown,
Chang'd to white age,[1] what was, but two days since,
Black as the raven's plume. How may this be?

---

1 Folklore had it that hair, which retained a natural sympathetic connection to the
body, was the seat of one's soul. Byron writes in the opening lines of "The Prisoner
of Chillon":

> My hair is grey, but not with years,
> Nor grew it white

60 BERN. Such change, from violent conflict of the mind,
     Will sometimes come.
   JER.   Alas, alas! most wretched!
     Thou wert too good to do a cruel deed,
     And so it kill'd thee. Thou hast suffer'd for it.
     God rest thy soul! I needs must touch thy hand,
     And bid thee long farewell.
     (*Laying his hand on* De Monfort.)
   BERN. Draw back, draw back! see where the lady comes.

Enter JANE DE MONFORT. FREBERG, *who has been for sometime*
retired by himself to the bottom of the stage, now steps forward to lead
her in, but checks himself on seeing the fixed sorrow of her
countenance, and draws back respectfully. JANE *advances to the table,*
and looks attentively at the covered bodies. MANUEL *points out the*
body of DE MONFORT, *and she gives a gentle inclination of the*
head, to signify that she understands him. She then bends tenderly
over it, without speaking.

   MAN. (*To* Jane, *as she raises her head.*) Oh, madam! my good
     lord.
   JANE. Well says thy love, my good and faithful Manuel;
     But we must mourn in silence.
70 MAN. Alas! the times that I have follow'd him!
   JANE. Forbear, my faithful Manuel. For this love
     Thou hast my grateful thanks; and here's my hand:
     Thou hast lov'd him, and I'll remember thee:
     Where'er I am; in whate'er spot of earth
     I linger out the remnant of my days,
     I'll remember thee.

                    In a single night,
               As men's have grown from sudden fears....

Ernest Hartley Coleridge comments in a note to these lines in his 1901 edition of
The Works of Lord Byron (4.13) that "it has been said that the Queen's [Marie
Antoinette] hair turned grey during the return from Varennes to Paris; but Carlyle
(*French Revolution*, 1839, I.182) notes that as early as May 4, 1789, on the occasion of
the assembly of the States-General, 'Her hair is already grey with many cares and
crosses'" (13).

MAN. Nay, by the living God! where'er you are,
  There will I be. I'll prove a trusty servant:
  I'll follow you, e'en to the world's end.
  My master's gone, and I, indeed, am mean,   80
  Yet will I show the strength of nobler men,
  Should any dare upon your honour'd worth
  To put the slightest wrong. Leave you, dear lady!
  Kill me, but say not this!
  (*Throwing himself at her feet.*)
JANE. (*Raising him.*) Well, then! be thou my servant, and my
  friend.
  Art thou, good Jerome, too, in kindness come?
  I see thou art. How goes it with thine age?
JER. Ah, madam! woe and weakness dwell with age:
  Would I could serve you with a young man's strength!
  I'd spend my life for you.
JANE.   Thanks, worthy Jerome.   90
  O! who hath said, the wretched have no friends![1]
FREB. In every sensible and gen'rous breast
  Affliction finds a friend; but unto thee,
  Thou most exalted and most honourable,
  The heart in warmest adoration bows,
  And even a worship pays.
JANE. Nay, Freberg, Freberg! grieve me not, my friend.
  He to whose ear my praise most welcome was,
  Hears it no more; and, oh our piteous lot!
  What tongue will talk of him? Alas, alas!   100
  This more than all will bow me to the earth;
  I feel my misery here.
  The voice of praise was wont to name us both:
  I had no greater pride.
  (*Covers her face with her hands, and bursts into tears. Here they
  all hang about her:* Freberg *supporting her tenderly;* Manuel
  embracing her knees, and old Jerome *catching hold of her robe
  affectionately.* Bernard, Abbess, Monks, *and* Nuns, *likewise,
  gather round her, with looks of sympathy.*)

---

1 Cf. Dryden, *All for Love* 3.1.83.

Enter Two OFFICERS *of law.*

1ST OFF.   Where is the prisoner?
       Into our hands he straight must be consign'd.
BERN. He is not subject now to human laws;
       The prison that awaits him is the grave.
1ST OFF. Ha! sayst thou so? there is foul play in this.
MAN. (*to* Off.) Hold thy unrighteous tongue, or hie thee
       hence,
110   Nor, in the presence of this honour'd dame,
       Utter the slightest meaning of reproach.
1ST OFF. I am an officer on duty call'd,
       And have authority to say, how died?
       (*Here* Jane *shakes off the weakness of grief, and repressing*
       Manuel, *who is about to reply to the* Officer, *steps forward with*
       dignity.)
JANE. Tell them by whose authority you come,
       He died that death which best becomes a man
       Who is with keenest sense of conscious ill
       And deep remorse assail'd, a wounded spirit.
       A death that kills the noble and the brave,
       And only them. He had no other wound.
1ST OFF. And shall I trust to this.
120   JANE.   Do as thou wilt:
       To one who can suspect my simple word
       I have no more reply. Fulfill thine office.
1ST OFF. No, lady, I believe your honour'd word,
       And will no farther search.
JANE. I thank your courtesy: thanks, thanks to all!
       My rev'rend mother, and ye honour'd maids;
       Ye holy men; and you, my faithful friends,
       The blessing of the afflicted rest with you:
       And he, who to the wretched is most piteous,
130   Will recompense you.—Freberg, thou art good,
       Remove the body of the friend you lov'd,
       'Tis Rezenvelt I mean. Take thou this charge:
       'Tis meet that, with his noble ancestors,
       He lie entomb'd in honourable state.

And now, I have a sad request to make,
Nor will these holy sisters scorn my boon;
That I, within these sacred cloister walls
May raise a humble, nameless tomb to him,
Who, but for one dark passion, one dire deed,
Had claim'd a record of as noble worth,   140
As e'er enrich'd the sculptur'd pedestal.[1]

[EXEUNT.

FINIS.

---

1   [Baillie's note from the later editions] The last three lines of the last speech are not
    intended to give the reader a true character of *De Monfort*, whom I have endeav-
    oured to represent throughout the play as, notwithstanding his other good qualities,
    proud, suspicious, and susceptible of envy, but only to express the partial sentiments
    of an affectionate sister, naturally more inclined to praise him from the misfortune
    into which he had fallen.
    [Second Baillie note] The Tragedy of *De Monfort* has been brought out at Drury-
    Lane Theatre, adapted to the stage by *Mr. Kemble*. I am infinitely obliged to that
    gentleman for the excellent powers he has exerted, assisted by the incomparable tal-
    ents of his sister, *Mrs. Siddons*, in endeavouring to obtain for it that public favour,
    which I sincerely wish it had been found more worthy of receiving.

Appendix A: The Moral Writers

1. John Locke, *An Essay Concerning Human Understanding* (1690)

i. Chapter 20: *Of Modes of Pleasure and Pain*

Pleasure and *Pain*, and that which causes them, Good and Evil, are the hinges on which our *Passions* turn: and if we reflect on our selves, and observe how these, under various Considerations, operate in us; what Modifications or Tempers of Mind, what internal Sensations, (if I may so call them,) they produce in us, we may thence form to our selves the *Ideas* of our *Passions*.

Thus any one reflecting upon the thought he has of the Delight, which any present, or absent thing is apt to produce in him, has the *Idea* we call *Love*. For when a Man declares in Autumn, when he is eating them, or in Spring, when there are none, that he *loves* Grapes, it is no more, but that the taste of Grapes delights him; let an alteration of Health or Constitution destroy the delight of their Taste, and he then can be said to *love* Grapes no longer.

On the contrary, the Thought of the Pain, which any thing present or absent is apt to produce in us, is what we call Hatred. Were it my business here, to enquire any farther, than into the bare *Ideas* of our *Passions*, as they depend on different Modifications of Pleasure and Pain, I should remark, that our *Love* and *Hatred* of inanimate insensible Beings, is commonly founded on that Pleasure and Pain which we receive from their use and application any way to our Senses, though with their Destruction: But *Hatred* or *Love*, to Beings capable of Happiness or Misery, is often the Uneasiness or Delight, which we find in our selves arising from a consideration of their very Being, or Happiness. Thus the Being and Welfare of a Man's Children or Friends, producing constant Delight in him, he is said constantly to *love* them. But it suffices to note, that our *Ideas* of *Love* and *Hatred*, are but the Dispositions of the Mind, in respect of Pleasure and Pain in general, however caused in us.

The uneasiness a Man finds in himself upon the absence of any thing, whose present enjoyment carries the *Idea* of Delight with it, is that we call *Desire*, which is greater or less, as that uneasiness is more or less vehement. Where by the bye it may perhaps be of some use to remark, that the chief if not only spur to humane Industry and Action is uneasiness....

Joy is a delight of the Mind, from the consideration of the present or assured approaching possession of a Good; and we are then possessed of any Good, when we have it so in our power, that we can use it when we please. Thus a Man almost starved, has *Joy* at the arrival of Relief, even before he has the pleasure of using it: and a Father, in whom the very well-being of his Children causes delight, is always, as long as his Children are in such a State, in the possession of that Good; for he needs but to reflect on it to have that pleasure.

Sorrow is uneasiness in the Mind, upon the thought of a Good lost, which might have been enjoy'd longer; or the sense of a present Evil.

Hope is that pleasure in the Mind, which every one finds in himself, upon the thought of a probable future enjoyment of a thing, which is apt to delight him.

Fear is an uneasiness of the Mind, upon the thought of future Evil likely to befal us.

Despair is the thought of the unattainableness of any Good, which works differently in Men's Minds, sometimes producing uneasiness or pain, sometimes rest and indolency.

Anger is uneasiness or discomposure of the Mind, upon the receit of any Injury, with a present purpose of Revenge.

Envy is an uneasiness of Mind, caused by the consideration of a Good we desire, obtained by one, we think should not have had it before us.

These two last, *Envy* and *Anger*, not being caused by Pain and Pleasure simply in themselves, but having in them some mixed Considerations of our selves and others, are not therefore to be found in all Men, because those other parts of valuing their Merits, or intending Revenge, is wanting in them: But all the rest terminated purely in Pain and Pleasure, are, I think, to be found in all Men. For we *love, desire, rejoice,* and *hope,* only in respect of Pleasure; we *hate, fear*, and *grieve* only in respect of Pain ultimately: In fine all these Passions are moved by things, only as they appear to be the Causes of Pleasure and Pain, or to have Pleasure or Pain some way or other annexed to them. Thus we extend our Hatred usually to the subject, (at least if a sensible or voluntary Agent,) which has produced Pain in us, because the fear it leaves is a constant pain: But we do not so constantly love what has done us good; because Pleasure operates not so strongly on us, as Pain; and because we are not so ready to have hope, it will do so again. But this by the bye.

2. David Hume, *A Treatise of Human Nature* (1739-40)

i. Book 2 Part 2 Section 9

In order to cause a transition of passions, there is required a double relation of impressions and ideas; nor is one relation sufficient to produce this effect. But that we may understand the full force of this double relation, we must consider, that it is not the present sensation alone or momentary pain or pleasure which determines the character of any passion, but the whole bent or tendency of it from the beginning to the end. One impression may be related to another, not only when their sensations are resembling, as we have all along supposed in the preceding cases, but also when their impulses or directions are similar and correspondent. This cannot take place with regard to pride and humility, because these are only pure sensations, without any direction or tendency to action. We are, therefore, to look for instances of this peculiar relation of impressions only in such affections as are attended with a certain appetite or desire, such as those of love and hatred.

Benevolence, or the appetite which attends love, is a desire of the happiness of the person beloved, and an aversion to his misery, as anger, or the appetite which attends hatred, is a desire of the misery of the person hated, and an aversion to his happiness. A desire, therefore, of the happiness of another, and aversion to his misery, are similar to benevolence; and a desire of his misery and aversion to his happiness, are correspondent to anger. Now, pity is a desire of happiness to another, and aversion to his misery, as malice is the contrary appetite. Pity, then, is related to benevolence, and malice to anger; and as benevolence has been already found to be connected with love, by a natural and original quality, and anger with hatred, it is by this chain the passions of pity and malice are connected with love and hatred.

This hypothesis is founded on sufficient experience. A man, who, from any motives, has entertained a resolution of performing an action, naturally runs into every other view or motive which may fortify that resolution, and give it authority and influence on the mind. To confirm us in any design, we search for motives drawn from interest, from honour, from duty. What wonder, then, that pity and benevolence, malice and anger, being the same desires arising from different principles, should so totally mix together as to be undistinguishable: As to the connection betwixt benevolence and love, anger and hatred, being original and primary, it admits of no difficulty.

ii. Book 2 Part 2 Section 10

I have supposed all along that the passions of love and pride, and those of humility and hatred, are similar in their sensations, and that the two former are always agreeable, and that the two latter painful. But though this be universally true, it is observable, that the two agreeable as well as the two painful passions have some differences, and even contrarieties, which distinguish them. Nothing invigorates and exalts the mind equally with pride and vanity; though at the same time love or tenderness is rather found to weaken and enfeeble it. The same difference is observable betwixt the uneasy passions. Anger and hatred bestow a new force on all our thoughts and actions; while humility and shame deject and discourage us. Of these qualities of the passions, it will be necessary to form a distinct idea. Let us remember that pride and hatred invigorate the soul, and love and humility enfeeble it.

It is a remarkable property of human nature, that any emotion which attends a passion is easily converted into it, though in their natures they be originally different from, and even contrary to, each other. It is true, in order to make a perfect union among the passions, there is always required a double relation of impressions and ideas; nor is one relation sufficient for that purpose. But though this be confirmed by undoubted experience, we must understand it with its proper limitations, and must regard the double relation as requisite only to make one passion produce another. When two passions are already produced by their separate causes, and are both present in the mind, they readily mingle and unite, though they have but one relation, and sometimes without any. The predominant passion swallows up the inferior, and converts it into itself. The spirits, when once excited, easily receive a change in their direction; and it is natural to imagine this change will come from the prevailing affection. The connection is in many respects closer betwixt any two passions, than betwixt any passion and indifference.

When a person is once heartily in love, the little faults and caprice of his mistress, the jealousies and quarrels to which that commerce is so subject, however unpleasant, and related to anger and hatred, are yet found to give additional force to the prevailing passion. It is a common artifice of politicians, when they would affect any person very much by a matter of fact, of which they intend to inform him, first to excite his curiosity, delay as long as possible the satisfying it, and by that means raise his anxiety and impatience to the utmost, before they give him a full insight into the business. They know that his curiosity will precipitate him into the passion they design to raise, and assist the object in its influence on the mind. A soldier advancing to the battle is naturally inspired with courage and confidence, when he thinks on his friends and fellow-soldiers; and is struck with fear and terror when he reflects on the enemy. Whatever new emotion, therefore, proceeds from the former, naturally increases the courage; as the same emotion, proceeding from the latter, augments the fear, by the relation of ideas, and the conversion of the inferior emotion into the predominate. Hence it is, that in martial discipline, the uniformity and lustre of our habit, the regularity of our figures and motions, with all the pomp and majesty of war, encourage ourselves and allies; while the same objects in the enemy strike terror into us, though agreeable and beautiful in themselves.

Since passions, however independent, are naturally transfused into each other, if they are both present at the same time, it follows, that when good or evil is placed in such a situation as to cause any particular emotion besides its direct passion of desire or aversion, that latter passion must acquire new force and violence.

This happens, among other cases, whenever any object excites contrary passions. For it is observable that an opposition of passions commonly causes a new emotion in the spirits, and produces more disorder than the concurrence of any two affections of equal force. This new emotion is easily converted into the predominant passion, and increases its violence beyond the pitch it would have arrived at had it met with no opposition....

3. Edmund Burke, *A Philosophical Enquiry into the Origin of our Ideas of the Sublime and Beautiful* (1757)

i. Part 1 Section 13: *Sympathy*

It is by the first of these passions that we enter into the concerns of others; that we are moved as they are moved, and are never suffered to be indifferent spectators of almost any thing which men can do or suffer. For sympathy must be considered as a sort of substitution, by which we are put into the place of another man, and affected in many respects as he is affected; so that this passion may either partake of the nature of those which regard self-preservation, and turning upon pain may be a source of the sublime; or it may turn upon ideas of pleasure; and then, whatever has been said of the social affections, whether they regard society in general, or only some particular modes of it, may be applicable here. It is by this principle chiefly that poetry, painting, and other affecting arts, transfuse their passions from one breast to another, and are often capable of grafting a delight on wretchedness, misery, and death itself. It is a common observation, that objects which in the reality would shock, are in tragical, and such like representations, the source of a very high species of pleasure. This taken as a fact, has been the cause of much reasoning. The satisfaction has been commonly attributed, first, to the comfort we receive in considering that so melancholy a story is no more than a fiction; and next, to the contemplation of our own freedom from the evils which we see represented. I am afraid it is a practice much too common in inquiries of this nature, to attribute the cause of feelings which merely arise from the mechanical structure of our bodies, or from the natural frame and constitution of our minds, to certain conclusions of the reasoning faculty on the objects presented to us; for I should imagine, that the influence of reason in producing our passions is nothing near so extensive as it is commonly believed.

ii. Part I Section 14: *The effects of sympathy in the distresses of others*

To examine this point concerning the effect of tragedy in a proper manner, we must previously consider, how we are affected by the feelings of our fellow creatures in circumstances of real distress. I am convinced we have a degree of delight, and that no small one, in the real misfortunes and pains of others; for let the affection be what it will in appearance, if it does not make us shun such objects, if on the contrary it induces us to approach them, if it makes us dwell upon them, in this case I conceive we must have a delight or pleasure of some species or other in contemplating objects of this kind. Do we not read the authentic histories of scenes of this nature with as much pleasure as romances or poems, where the incidents are ficti-tious? The prosperity of no empire, nor the grandeur of no king, can so agreeably affect in the reading, as the ruin of the state of Macedon,[1] and the distress of its unhappy prince. Such

---

1 Macedon was a northern Greek kingdom, important from the fourth to the second century BC. Perseus's defeat by the Romans in the Third Macedonian War led to the partitioning of his kingdom into four separate republics.

a catastrophe touches us in history as much as the destruction of Troy does in fable! Our delight in cases of this kind, is very greatly heightened, if the sufferer be some excellent person who sinks under an unworthy fortune. Scipio and Cato[1] are both virtuous characters; but we are more deeply affected by the violent death of the one, and the ruin of the great cause he adhered to, than with the deserved triumphs and uninterrupted prosperity of the other; for terror is a passion which always produces delight when it does not press too close, and pity is a passion accompanied with pleasure, because it arises from love and social affection. Whenever we are formed by nature to any active purpose, the passion which animates us to it, is attended with delight, or a pleasure of some kind, let the subject matter be what it will; and as our Creator has designed we should be united by the bond of sympathy, he has strengthened that bond by a proportionable delight; and there most where our sympathy is most wanted, in the distresses of others. If this passion was simply painful, we would shun with the greatest care all persons and places that could excite such a passion; as, some who are so far gone in indolence as not to endure any strong impression actually do. But the case is widely different with the greater part of mankind; there is no spectacle we so eagerly pursue, as that of some uncommon and grievous calamity; so that whether the misfortune is before our eyes, or whether they are turned back to it in history, it always touches with delight. This is not an unmixed delight, but blended with no small uneasiness. The delight we have in such things, hinders us from shunning scenes of misery; and the pain we feel, prompts us to relieve ourselves in relieving those who suffer; and all this antecedent to any reasoning, by an instinct that works us to its own purposes, without our concurrence.

---

1 Publius Cornelius Scipio Africanus (236?-184 BC), a Roman soldier, and M. Porcius Cato, "The Censor," (234-149 BC), a renowned conservative and isolationist Roman politician, both served with distinction against Hannibal in Italy. After a long-standing rivalry, Cato drove Scipio into exile in 184 BC.

It is thus in real calamities. In imitated distresses the only difference is the pleasure resulting from the effects of imitation; for it is never so perfect, but we can perceive it is an imitation, and on that principle are somewhat pleased with it. And indeed in some cases we derive as much or more pleasure from that source than from the thing itself. But then I imagine we shall be much mistaken if we attribute any considerable part of our satisfaction in tragedy to a consideration that tragedy is a deceit, and its representations no realities. The nearer it approaches the reality, and the further it removes us from all idea of fiction, the more perfect is its power. But be its power of what kind it will, it never approaches to what it represents. Chuse a day on which to represent the most sublime and affecting tragedy we have; appoint the most favourite actors; spare no cost upon the scenes and decorations; unite the greatest efforts of poetry, painting and music; and when you have collected your audience, just at the moment when their minds are erect with expectation, let it be reported that a state criminal of high rank is on the point of being executed in the adjoining square; in a moment the emptiness of the theatre would demonstrate the comparative weakness of the imitative arts, and proclaim the triumph of the real sympathy. I believe that this notion of our having a simple pain in the reality, yet a delight in the representation, arises from hence, that we do not sufficiently distinguish what we would by no means chuse to do, from what we should be eager enough to see if it was once done. We delight in seeing things, which so far from doing, our heartiest wishes would be to see redressed. This noble capital, the pride of England and of Europe, I believe no man is so strangely wicked as to desire to see destroyed by a conflagration or an earthquake, though he should be removed himself to the greatest distance from the danger. But suppose such a fatal accident to have happened, what numbers from all parts would croud to behold the ruins, and amongst them many who would have been content never to have seen London in its glory? Nor is it either in real or fictitious distresses, our immunity from them which produces our delight; in my own mind I can discover nothing like it. I apprehend that this mistake is owing to a sort of sophism, by which we are frequently imposed upon; it arises from our not distinguishing between what is indeed a necessary condition to our doing or suffering any thing in general, and what is the cause of some particular act. If a man kills me with a sword, it is a necessary condition to this that we should have been both of us alive before the fact; and yet it would be absurd to say, that our being both living creatures was the cause of his crime and of my death. So it is certain, that it is absolutely necessary my life should be out of any imminent hazard before I can take a delight in the sufferings of others, real or imaginary, or indeed in any thing else from any cause whatsoever. But then it is a sophism to argue from thence, that this immunity is the cause of my delight either on these or on any occasions. No one can distinguish such a cause of satisfaction in his own mind I believe; nay when we do not suffer any very acute pain, nor are exposed to any imminent danger of our lives, we can feel for others, whilst we suffer ourselves; and often then most when we are softened by affliction; we see with pity even distresses which we would accept in the place of our own.

4. Adam Smith, *The Theory of Moral Sentiments* (1759)

i. Part 1 Section 2 Chapter 1: *Of Sympathy*

How selfish soever man may be supposed, there are evidently some principles in his nature, which interest him in the fortune of others, and render their happiness necessary to him, though he derives nothing from it except the pleasure of seeing it. Of this kind is pity or compassion, the emotion which we feel for the misery of others, when we either see it, or are made to conceive it in a very lively manner. That we often derive sorrow from the sorrow of others, is a matter of fact too obvious to require any instances to prove it; for this sentiment, like all the other original passions of human nature, is by no means confined to the virtuous and humane, though they perhaps may feel it with the most exquisite sensibility. The greatest ruffian, the most hardened violator of the laws of society, is not altogether without it.

As we have no immediate experience of what other men feel, we can form no idea of the manner in which they are affected, but by conceiving what we ourselves should feel in the like situation. Though our brother is upon the rack, as long as we ourselves are at our ease, our senses will never inform us of what he suffers. They never did, and never can, carry us beyond our own person, and it is by the imagination only that we can form any conception of what are his sensations. Neither can that faculty help us to this any other way, than by representing to us what would be our own, if we were in his case. It is the impressions of our own senses only, not those of his, which our imaginations copy. By the imagination we place ourselves in his situation, we conceive ourselves enduring all the same torments, we enter as it were into his body, and become in some measure the same person with him, and thence form some idea of his sensations, and even feel something which, though weaker in degree, is not altogether unlike them. His agonies, when they are thus brought home to ourselves, when we have thus adopted and made them our own, begin at last to affect us, and we then tremble and shudder at the thought of what he feels. For as to be in pain or distress of any kind excites the most excessive sorrow, so to conceive or to imagine that we are in it, excites some degree of the same emotion, in proportion to the vivacity or dulness of the conception....

Pity and compassion are words appropriated to signify our fellow-feeling with the sorrow of others. Sympathy, though its meaning was, perhaps, originally the same, may now, however, without much impropriety, be made use of to denote our fellow-feeling with any passion whatever.

Upon some occasions sympathy may seem to arise merely from the view of a certain emotion in another person. The passions, upon some occasions, may seem to be transfused from one man to another, instantaneously, and antecedent to any knowledge of what excited them in the person principally concerned. Grief and joy, for example, strongly expressed in the look and gestures of any one, at once affect the spectator with some degree of a like painful or agreeable emotion. A smiling face is, to every body that sees it, a cheerful object; as a sorrowful countenance, on the other hand, is a melancholy one.

This, however, does not hold universally, or with regard to every passion. There are some passions of which the expressions excite no sort of sympathy, but before we are acquainted with what gave occasion to them, serve rather to disgust and provoke us against them. The furious behaviour of an angry man is more likely to exasperate us against himself than against his enemies. As we are unacquainted with his provocation, we cannot bring his case home to ourselves, nor conceive any thing like the passions which it excites. But we plainly see what is the situation of those with whom he is angry, and to what violence they may be exposed from so enraged an adversary. We readily, therefore, sympathize with their fear or resentment, and are immediately disposed to take part against the man from whom they appear to be in so much danger....

Even our sympathy with the grief or joy of another, before we are informed of the cause of either, is always extremely imperfect. General lamentations, which express nothing but the anguish of the sufferer, create rather a curiosity to inquire into his situation, along with some disposition to sympathize with him, than any actual sympathy that is very sensible. The first question which we ask is, What has befallen you? Till this be answered, though we are uneasy both from the vague idea of his misfortune, and still more from torturing ourselves with conjectures about what it may be, yet our fellow-feeling is not very considerable....

ii. Part 1 Section 2 Chapter 2: *Of those Passions which take their origin from a particular turn or habit of the Imagination*

EVEN of the passions derived from the imagination, those which take their origin from a peculiar turn or habit it has acquired, though they may be acknowledged to be perfectly natural, are, however, but little sympathized with. The imaginations of mankind, not having acquired that particular turn, cannot enter into them; and such passions, though they may be allowed to be almost unavoidable in some part of life, are always, in some measure, ridiculous. This is the case with that strong attachment which naturally grows up between two persons of different sexes, who have long fixed their thoughts upon one another. Our imagination not having run in the same channel with that of the lover, we cannot enter into the eagerness of his emotions. If our friend has been injured, we readily sympathize with his resentment, and grow angry with the very person with whom he is angry. If he has received a benefit, we readily enter into his gratitude, and have a very high sense of the merit of his benefactor. But if he is in love, though we may think his passion just as reasonable as any of the kind, yet we never think ourselves bound to conceive a passion of the same kind, and for the same person for whom he has conceived it. The passion appears to every body, but the man who feels it, entirely disproportioned to the value of the object; and love, though it is pardoned in a certain age because we know it is natural, is always laughed at, because we can not enter into it. All serious and strong expressions of it appear ridiculous to a third person; and though a lover may be good company to his mistress, he is so to nobody else. He himself is sensible of this; and as long as he continues in his sober senses, endeavours to treat his own passion with raillery and ridicule. It is the only style in which we care to hear of it; because it is the only style in which we ourselves are disposed to talk of it....

Of all the passions, however, which are so extravagantly disproportioned to the value of their objects, love is the only one that appears, even to the weakest minds, to have any thing in it that is either graceful or agreeable. In itself, first of all, though it may be ridiculous, it is not naturally odious; and though its consequences are often fatal and dreadful, its intentions are seldom mischievous. And then, though there is little propriety in the passion itself, there is a good deal in some of those which always accompany it. There is in love a strong mixture of humanity, generosity, kindness, friendship, esteem; passions with which, of all others, for reasons which shall be explained immediately, we have the greatest propensity to sympathize, even notwithstanding we are sensible that they are, in some measure, excessive. The sympathy which we feel with them, renders the passion which they accompany less disagreeable, and supports it in our imagination, notwithstanding all the vices which commonly go along with it; though in the one sex it necessarily leads to the last ruin and infamy; and though in the other, where it is apprehended to be least fatal, it is almost always attended with an incapacity for labour, a neglect of duty, a contempt of fame, and even of common reputation. Notwithstanding all this, the degree of sensibility and generosity with which it is supposed to be accompanied, renders it to many the object of vanity; and they are fond of appearing capable of feeling what would do them no honour if they had really felt it....

iii. Part 1 Section 2 Chapter 3: *Of the unsocial Passions*

THERE is another set of passions, which, though derived from the imagination, yet before we can enter into them, or regard them as graceful or becoming, must always be brought down to a pitch much lower than that to which undisciplined nature would raise them. These are, hatred and resentment, with all their different modifications. With regard to all such passions, our sympathy is divided between the person who feels them and the person who is the object of them. The interests of these two are directly opposite. What our sympathy with the person who feels them would prompt us to wish for, our fellow-feeling with the other would lead us to fear. As they are both men, we are concerned for both, and our fear for what the one may suffer, damps our resentment for what the other has suffered. Our sympathy, therefore, with the man who has received the provocation, necessarily falls short of the passion which naturally animates him, not only upon account of those general causes which render all sympathetic passions inferior to the original ones, but upon account of that particular cause which is peculiar to itself, our opposite sympathy with another person. Before resentment, therefore, can become graceful and agreeable, it must be more humbled and brought down below that pitch to which it would naturally rise, than almost any other passion.

Mankind, at the same time, have a very strong sense of the injuries that are done to another. The villain, in a tragedy or romance, is as much the object of our indignation, as the hero is that of our sympathy and affection. We detest Iago as much as we esteem Othello; and delight as much in the punishment of the one, as we are grieved at the distress of the other. But though mankind have so strong a fellow-feeling with the injuries that are done to their brethren, they do not always resent them the more that the sufferer appears to resent them. Upon most occasions, the greater his patience, his mildness, his humanity, provided it does not appear that he wants spirit, or that fear was the motive of his forbearance, the higher their resentment against the person who injured him. The amiableness of the character exasperates their sense of the atrocity of the injury.

Those passions, however, are regarded as necessary parts of the character of human nature. A person becomes contemptible who tamely sits still, and submits to insults, without attempting either to repel or to revenge them. We cannot enter into his indifference and insensibility: we call his behaviour mean-spiritedness, and are as really provoked by it as by the insolence of his adversary. Even the mob are enraged to see any man submit patiently to affronts and ill usage. They desire to see this insolence resented, and resented by the person who suffers from it. They cry to him with fury, to defend, or to revenge himself. If his indignation rouses at last, they heartily applaud, and sympathize with it. It enlivens their own indignation against his enemy, whom they rejoice to see him attack in his turn, and are as really gratified by his revenge, provided it is not immoderate, as if the injury had been done to themselves.

But though the utility of those passions to the individual, by rendering it dangerous to insult or injure him, be acknowledged; and though their utility to the public, as the guardians of justice, and of the equality of its administration, be not less considerable, as shall be shewn hereafter; yet there is still something disagreeable in the passions themselves, which makes the appearance of them in other men the natural object of our aversion. The expression of anger towards any body present, if it exceeds a bare intimation that we are sensible of his ill usage, is regarded not only as an insult to that particular person, but as a rudeness to the whole company. Respect for them ought to have restrained us from giving way to so boisterous and offensive an emotion. It is the remote effects of these passions which are agreeable; the immediate effects are mischief to the person against whom they are directed. But it is the immediate, and not the remote effects of objects which render them agreeable or disagreeable to the imagination. A prison is certainly more useful to the public than a palace; and the person who founds the one is generally directed by a much juster spirit of patriotism, than he who builds the other. But the immediate effects of a prison, the confinement of the wretches shut up in it, are disagreeable; and the imagination either does not take time to trace out the remote ones, or sees them at too great a distance to be much affected by them. A prison, therefore, will always be a disagreeable object; and the fitter it is for the purpose for which it was intended, it will be the more so. A palace, on the contrary, will always be agreeable; yet its remote effects may often be inconvenient to the public. It may serve to promote luxury, and set the example of the dissolution of manners. Its immediate effects, however, the conveniency, the pleasure, and the gaiety of the people who live in it, being all agreeable, and suggesting to the imagination a thousand agreeable ideas, that faculty generally rests upon them, and seldom goes further in tracing its more distant consequences....

... Hatred and anger are the greatest poison to the happiness of a good mind. There is, in the very feeling of those passions, something harsh, jarring, and convulsive, something that tears and distracts the breast, and is altogether destructive of that composure and tranquillity of mind which is so necessary to happiness, and which is best promoted by the contrary passions of gratitude and love. It is not the value of what they lose by the perfidy and ingratitude of those they live with, which the generous and humane are most apt to regret. Whatever they may have lost, they can generally be very happy without it. What most disturbs them is the idea of perfidy and ingratitude exercised towards themselves; and the discordant and disagreeable passions which this excites, constitute, in their own opinion, the chief part of the injury which they suffer.

How many things are requisite to render the gratification of resentment completely agreeable, and to make the spectator thoroughly sympathize with our revenge? The provocation must first of all be such that we should become contemptible, and be exposed to perpetual insults, if we did not, in some measure, resent it. Smaller offences are always better neglected; nor is there any thing more despicable than that froward and captious humour which takes fire upon every slight occasion of quarrel. We should resent more from a sense of the propriety of resentment, from a sense that mankind expect and require it of us, than because we feel in ourselves the furies of that disagreeable passion. There is no passion, of which the human mind is capable, concerning whose justness we ought to be so doubtful, concerning whose indulgence we ought so carefully to consult our natural sense of propriety, or so diligently to consider what will be the sentiments of the cool and impartial spectator. Magnanimity, or a regard to maintain our own rank and dignity in society, is the only motive which can ennoble the expressions of this disagreeable passion. This motive must characterize our whole stile and deportment. These must be plain, open, and direct; determined without positiveness, and elevated without insolence; not only free from petulance and low scurrility, but generous, candid, and full of all proper regards, even for the person who has offended us. It must appear in short, from our whole manner, without our labouring affectedly to express it, that passion has not extinguished our humanity; and that if we yield to the dictates of revenge, it is with reluctance, from necessity, and in consequence of great and repeated provocations. When resentment is guarded and qualified in this manner, it may be admitted to be even generous and noble.

iv. Part 1 Section 2 Chapter 3: *Of the social Passions*

The sentiment of love is, in itself, agreeable to the person who feels it. It sooths and composes the breast, seems to favour the vital motions, and to promote the healthful state of the human constitution; and it is rendered still more delightful by the consciousness of the gratitude and satisfaction which it must excite in him who is the object of it. Their mutual regard renders them happy in one another, and sympathy, with this mutual regard, makes them agreeable to every other person. With what pleasure do we look upon a family, through the whole of which reign mutual love and esteem, where the parents and children are companions for one another, without any other difference than what is made by respectful affection on the one side, and kind indulgence on the other; where freedom and fondness, mutual raillery and mutual kindness, show that no opposition of interest divides the brothers, nor any rivalship of favour sets the sisters at variance, and where every thing presents us with the idea of peace, cheerfulness, harmony, and contentment? On the contrary, how uneasy are we made when we go into a house in which jarring contention sets one half of those who dwell in it against the other; where amidst affected smoothness and complaisance, suspicious looks and sudden starts of passion betray the mutual jealousies which burn within them, and which are every moment ready to burst out through all the restraints which the presence of the company imposes?

Those amiable passions, even when they are acknowledged to be excessive, are never regarded with aversion. There is something agreeable even in the weakness of friendship and humanity. The too tender mother, the too indulgent father, the too generous and affectionate friend, may sometimes, perhaps, on account of the softness of their natures, be looked upon with a species of pity, in which, however, there is a mixture of love, but can never be regarded with hatred and aversion, nor even with contempt, unless by the most brutal and worthless of mankind. It is always with concern, with sympathy and kindness, that we blame them for the extravagance of their attachment. There is a helplessness in the character of extreme humanity which more than any thing interests our pity. There is nothing in itself which renders it either ungraceful or disagreeable. We only regret that it is unfit for the world, because the world is unworthy of it, and because it must expose the person who is endowed with it, as a prey to the perfidy and ingratitude of insinuating falsehood, and to a thousand pains and uneasinesses, which, of all men, he the least deserves to feel, and which generally too he is, of all men, the least capable of supporting. It is quite otherwise with hatred and resentment. Too violent a propensity to those detestable passions, renders a person the object of universal dread and abhorrence, who, like a wild beast, ought, we think, to be hunted out of all civil society.

5. Dugald Stewart, *Elements of the Philosophy of the Human Mind* (1792)

[In her preface to *The Martyr*, first published alone in 1826 and later included in her three volumes of twelve plays entitled *Dramas* in 1836, Baillie reveals her familiarity with Dugald Stewart's work. She refers to him as a "great philosophical writer," citing his discussion on superstition in *Elements of the Philosophy of the Human Mind*, Vol. 1, 368.

In her preface to the third volume of *Plays on the Passion*, she writes that "… I have attempted to trace a natural connection from association of ideas, by which one thing produces another, or is insinuated to have done so from beginning to end" (*Works* 230).]

i. Chapter 5 Part 1 Section 1: *Of the Association of Ideas*

THAT one thought is often suggested to the mind by another; and that the sight of an external object often recalls former occurrences, and revives former feelings, are facts which are perfectly familiar, even to those who are the least disposed to speculate concerning the principles of their nature. In passing along a road which we have formerly travelled in the company of a friend, the particulars of the conversation in which we were then engaged, are frequently suggested to us by the objects we meet with. In such a scene, we recollect that a particular subject was started; and, in passing the different houses, and plantations, and rivers, the arguments we were discussing when we last saw them, recur spontaneously to the memory. The connexion which is formed in the mind between the words of a language and the ideas they denote; the connexion which is formed between the different words of a discourse we have committed to memory; the connexion between the different notes of a piece of music in the mind of the musician, are all obvious instances of the same general law of our nature.

THE influence of perceptible objects in reviving former thoughts and former feelings, is more particularly remarkable. After time has, in some degree, reconciled us to the death of a friend, how wonderfully are we affected the first time we enter the house where he lived! Every thing we see; the apartment where he studied; the chair upon which he sat, recal to us the happiness we have enjoyed together; and we should feel it a sort of violation of that respect we owe to his memory, to engage in any light or indifferent discourse when such objects are before us. In the case, too, of those remarkable scenes which interest the curiosity, from the memorable persons or transactions which we have been accustomed to connect with them in the course of our studies, the fancy is more awakened by the actual perception of the scene itself, than by the mere conception or imagination of it. Hence the pleasure we enjoy in visiting classical ground; in beholding the retreats which inspired the genius of our favourite authors, or the fields which have been dignified by exertions of heroic virtue....

ii. Chapter 7 Part 1 Section 5: *On the benefits of fictitious narratives*

I would not, however, be understood to disapprove entirely of fictitious narratives, or of pathetic compositions. On the contrary, I think that the perusal of them may be attended with advantage, when the effects which I have mentioned are corrected by habits of real business. They soothe the mind when ruffled by the rude intercourse of society, and stealing the attention insensibly from our own cares, substitute, instead of discontent and distress, a tender and pleasing melancholy. By exhibitions of characters a little elevated above the common standard, they have a tendency to cultivate the taste in life; to quicken our disgust at what is mean or offensive, and to form the mind insensibly to elegance and dignity. Their tendency to cultivate the powers of moral perception has never been disputed; and when the influence of such perceptions is powerfully felt, and is united with an active and manly temper, they render the character not only more amiable, but more happy in itself, and more useful to others; for although a rectitude of judgment with respect to conduct, and strong moral feelings, do, by no means, alone constitute virtue; yet they are frequently necessary to direct our behaviour in the more critical situations of life; and they increase the interest we take in the general prosperity of virtue in the world. I believe, likewise, that, by means of fictitious history, displays of character may be most successfully given, and the various weaknesses of the heart exposed. I only meant to insinuate, that a taste for them may be carried too far; that the sensibility which terminates in imagination, is but a refined and selfish luxury; and that nothing can effectually advance our moral improvement, but an attention to the active duties which belong to our stations.

iii. Chapter 7 Part 1 Section 5: *Inconveniences resulting from an ill-regulated Imagination*

It was undoubtedly the intention of Nature, that the objects of perception should produce much stronger impressions on the mind than its own operations. And, accordingly, they always do so, when proper care has been taken in early life, to exercise the different principles of our constitution. But it is possible, by long habits of solitary reflection, to reverse this order of things, and to weaken the attention to sensible objects to so great a degree, as to leave the conduct almost wholly under the influence of imagination. Removed to a distance from society, and from the pursuits of life, when we have been long accustomed to converse with our own thoughts, and have found our activity gratified by intellectual exertions, which afford scope to all our powers and affections, without exposing us to the inconveniences resulting from the bustle of the world, we are apt to contract an unnatural predilection for meditation, and to lose all interest in external occurrences. In such a situation too, the mind gradually loses that command which education, when properly conducted, gives it over the train of its ideas; till at length the most extravagant dreams of imagination acquire as powerful an influence in exciting all its passions, as if they were realities. A wild and mountainous country, which presents but a limited variety of objects, and these only of such a sort as "awake to solemn thought," has a remarkable effect in cherishing this enthusiasm.

When such disorders of the imagination have been long confirmed by habit, the evil may perhaps be beyond a remedy; but in their inferior degrees, much may be expected from our own efforts; in particular, from mingling gradually in the business and amusements of the world; or, if we have sufficient force of mind for the exertion, from resolutely plunging into those active and interesting and hazardous scenes, which, by compelling us to attend to external circumstances, may weaken the impressions of imagination, and strengthen those produced by realities.

Appendix B: Mary Wollstonecraft, A Vindication of the Rights of Woman (1792)

1. [On soldiers, professions, and masculine corruption]: 122-24

It is impossible for any man, when the most favourable circumstances concur, to acquire sufficient knowledge and strength of mind to discharge the duties of a king, entrusted with uncontrouled power; how then must they be violated when his very elevation is an insuperable bar to the attainment of either wisdom or virtue; when all the feelings of a man are stifled by flattery, and reflection shut out by pleasure! Surely it is madness to make the fate of thousands depend on the caprice of a weak fellow creature, whose very station sinks him necessarily below the meanest of his subjects! But one power should not be thrown down to exalt another—for all power inebriates weak man; and its abuse proves that the more equality there is established among men, the more virtue and happiness will reign in society. But this and any similar maxim deduced from simple reason, raises an outcry—the church or the state is in danger, if faith in the wisdom of antiquity is not implicit; and they who, roused by the sight of human calamity, dare to attack human authority, are reviled as despisers of God, and enemies of man. These are bitter calumnies, yet they reached one of the best of men, whose ashes still preach peace, and whose memory demands a respectful pause, when subjects are discussed that lay so near his heart.

After attacking the sacred majesty of Kings, I shall scarcely excite surprise by adding my firm persuasion that every profession, in which great subordination of rank constitutes its power, is highly injurious to morality.

A standing army,[1] for instance, is incompatible with freedom; because subordination and rigour are the very sinews of military discipline; and despotism is necessary to give vigour to

---

1 A permanent army of professional soldiers. Before the seventeenth century, Britain's armies were raised for special occasions and later disbanded.

enterprizes that one will directs. A spirit inspired by romantic notions of honour, a kind of morality founded on the fashion of the age, can only be felt by a few officers, whilst the main body must be moved by command, like the waves of the sea; for the strong wind of authority pushes the crowd of subalterns forward, they scarcely know or care why, with headlong fury.

Besides, nothing can be so prejudicial to the morals of the inhabitants of country towns as the occasional residence of a set of idle superficial young men, whose only occupation is gallantry, and whose polished manners render vice more dangerous, by concealing its deformity under gay ornamental drapery. An air of fashion, which is but a badge of slavery, and proves that the soul has not a strong individual character, awes simple country people into an imitation of the vices, when they cannot catch the slippery graces, of politeness. Every corps is a chain of despots, who, submitting and tyrannizing without exercising their reason become dead weights of vice and folly on the community. A man of rank or fortune, sure of rising by interest, has nothing to do but to pursue some extravagant freak; whilst the needy gentleman, who is to rise, as the phrase turns, by his merit, becomes a servile parasite or vile pander....

2. [*On the tyranny of the sexes*]: 130–33

... Many are the causes that, in the present corrupt state of society, contribute to enslave women by cramping their understandings and sharpening their senses. One, perhaps, that silently does more mischief than all the rest, is their disregard of order. To do every thing in an orderly manner, is a most important precept, which women, who, generally speaking, receive only a disorderly kind of education, seldom attend to with that degree of exactness that men, who from their infancy are broken into method, observe. This negligent kind of guess-work, for what other epithet can be used to point out the random exertions of a sort of instinctive common sense, never brought to the test of reason? prevents their generalizing matters of fact—so they do to-day, what they did yesterday, merely because they did it yesterday.

This contempt of the understanding in early life has more baneful consequences than is commonly supposed; for the little knowledge which women of strong minds attain, is, from various circumstances, of a more desultory kind than the knowledge of men, and it is acquired more by sheer observations on real life, than from comparing what has been individually observed with the results of experience generalized by speculation. Led by their dependent situation and domestic employments more into society, what they learn is rather by snatches; and as learning is with them, in general, only a secondary thing, they do not pursue any one branch with that persevering ardour necessary to give vigour to the faculties, and clearness to the judgment. In the present state of society, a little learning is required to support the character of a gentleman; and boys are obliged to submit to a few years of discipline. But in the education of women, the cultivation of the understanding is always subordinate to the acquirement of some corporeal accomplishment; even while enervated by confinement and false notions of modesty, the body is prevented from attaining that grace and beauty which relaxed half-formed limbs never exhibit. Besides, in youth their faculties are not brought forward by emulation; and having no serious scientific study, if they have natural sagacity it is turned too soon on life and manners. They dwell on effects, and modifications, without tracing them back to causes; and complicated rules to adjust behaviour are a weak substitute for simple principles.

As a proof that education gives this appearance of weakness to females, we may instance the example of military men, who are, like them, sent into the world before their minds have been stored with knowledge or fortified by principles. The consequences are similar; soldiers acquire a little superficial knowledge, snatched from the muddy current of conversation, and, from continually mixing with society, they gain, what is termed a knowledge of the world; and this acquaintance with manners and customs has frequently been confounded with a knowledge of the human heart. But can the crude fruit of casual observation, never brought to the test of judgment, formed by comparing speculation and experience, deserve such a distinction? Soldiers, as well as women, practise the minor virtues with punctilious politeness. Where is then the sexual difference, when the education has been the same? All the difference that I can discern, arises from the superior advantage of liberty, which enables the former to see more of life.

It is wandering from my present subject, perhaps, to make a political remark; but, as it was produced naturally by the train of my reflections, I shall not pass it silently over.

Standing armies can never consist of resolute, robust men; they may be well disciplined machines, but they will seldom contain men under the influence of strong passions, or with very vigorous faculties. And as for any depth of understanding, I will venture to affirm, that it is as rarely to be found in the army as amongst women; and the cause, I maintain, is the same. It may be further observed, that officers are also particularly attentive to their persons, fond of dancing, crowded rooms, adventures, and ridicule. Like the fair sex, the business of their lives is gallantry.—They were taught to please, and they only live to please. Yet they do not lose their rank in the distinction of sexes, for they are still reckoned superior to women, though in what their superiority consists, beyond what I have just mentioned, it is difficult to discover.

The great misfortune is this, that they both acquire manners before morals, and a knowledge of life before they have, from reflection, any acquaintance with the grand ideal outline of human nature. The consequence is natural; satisfied with common nature, they become a prey to prejudices, and taking all their opinions on credit, they blindly submit to authority. So that, if they have any sense, it is a kind of instinctive glance, that catches proportions, and decides with respect to manners; but falls when arguments are to be pursued below the surface, or opinions analyzed.

May not the same remark be applied to women? Nay, the argument may be carried still further, for they are both thrown out of a useful station by the unnatural distinctions established in civilized life. Riches and hereditary honours have made cyphers of women to give consequence to the numerical figure; and idleness has produced a mixture of gallantry and despotism into society, which leads the very men who are the slaves of their mistresses to tyrannize over their sisters, wives, and daughters. This is only keeping them in rank and file, it is true. Strengthen the female mind by enlarging it, and there will be an end to blind obedience; but, as blind obedience is ever sought for by power, tyrants and sensualists are in the right when they endeavour to keep women in the dark, because the former only want slaves, and the latter a play-thing. The sensualist, indeed, has been the most dangerous of tyrants, and women have been duped by their lovers, as princes by their ministers, whilst dreaming that they reigned over them....

Appendix C: *Prologue and Epilogue to the Tragedy of* De Montfort *from the Larpent Version*

[The manuscripts in the Larpent collection at the Huntington Library were those submitted to John Larpent (1741-1824), Examiner of Plays from 1778 to 1824, in accordance with a British law passed in 1737. These manuscripts, which were in his possession at the time of his death, were sold to a private collector in 1832. The Huntington Library purchased them in 1917. See Dougald Macmillan, *Catalogue of the Larpent Plays in the Huntington Library*. San Marino: Huntington Library, 1939.]

Theatre Royal Drury Lane April 26th 1800

Prologue

By Hon. F. North

Too long has fancy led her fairy Dance,
Thro' all the various mazes of Romance;
On classic ground her motley standard rear'd
While honest nature blush'd, and disappear'd—
    O, Shame!—Why borrow from a foreign store?
As if the rich should pilfer from the poor.—
We who have forc'd th' astonish'd world to yield,
Led by immortal Shakspeare to the Field;—
Whose lines? have felt all tender Otway's woe,
Have glow'd with Dryden, & have wept with Rowe.—
And we, their sons, now dull & senseless grown,
When all the realm of Comedy's our own?
Congreve and Vanbrugh? boast eternal Fame,
And living Authors, we forbear to name.
    Should you approve, on this auspicious day
The British Drama reassumes her sway.
    Ye men, be candid to a virgin muse,—

To move you more,—Perhaps a woman sues:[1]
Let her Dramatic saplin[2] 'scape your rage,
And spare this tender scyon[3] of the Stage—
Support the infant Tree, ye pitying fair
Protect its blossoms from the blighting air,—
So may its leaves move gently with your sighs,
Its branches flourish water'd by your Eyes.—

Epilogue

By Duchess of Devonshire

Ere yet affections Tears have ceas'd to flow
I come to cherish, not forget my woe
No kindred heart will bid me check the tear
A sister's love may claim protection here.
Dire is the passion that our scenes unfold
And foreign to each heart of British mould
For Britons Sons their generous code maintain
Prompt to defend & slow in giving pain.
Warm in the Battle, yet the contest o'er
They deem to vanquish'd to be foes no more.
Sure with compassion then this night they'll view
De Montfort's fate, it's ruthless court pursue,
And mourn a nature once by honour grac'd
By one foul deed's attrocious guilt defac'd.
To court your smiles & win your hop'd applause
Ah! let me proudly boast my Sex's cause
A Female Muse triumphant has design'd
A paragon indeed of woman kind!
Has in this fair majestic portrait wove
Commanding wisdom, & devoted Love
And bade e'en strength & tenderness agree
In maiden meditation—fancy free.

---

1   To pursue or woo.
2   Perhaps a variant of sapling.
3   A shoot or twig, also heir or descendant.

Yet tho' she fail'd a Brother to controul
And soothe the frantic troubles of his soul
Will be the Lesson of tonight imprest
To wake the judgement & to calm the breast
To check by strong example's potent spell
And each advance of subtle passion quell.
E'en in these happier times where restless rage
Nor dark revenge, no fatal conflicts wage
Where mild reflection heals the transient strife
And smoothy flows the tranquil course of life:—
Yet may our Muse with timely voice impart
Some wholsome Lesson to the erring heart
May check fell vengeance for a past offence
And from the suff'ring mind remove suspense.
Thus turn not heedless from the scene tho' pass'd
Nor view in vain distructive passion's blast,
But cherish ties, for which 'tis life to live
Enjoy the good your Love & kindness give
Banish from Friendship each offending fear
And from confiding Love the doubtful tear
Such the bright picture which the contrast shews
Such the reverse of hatred's deadly woes
Thus let us bid the scenes dread horror cease
And hail the blessing of Domestic peace.

Appendix D: William Wordsworth

1. "Preface" to *Lyrical Ballads* (1800)

i. Paragraphs 6-9

The principal object then which I proposed to myself in these Poems was to make the incidents of common life interesting by tracing in them, truly though not ostentatiously, the primary laws of our nature: chiefly as far as regards the manner in which we associate ideas in a state of excitement. Low and rustic life was generally chosen because in that situation the essential passions of the heart find a better soil in which they can attain their maturity, are less under restraint, and speak a plainer and more emphatic language; because in that situation our elementary feelings exist in a state of greater simplicity and consequently may be more accurately contemplated and more forcibly communicated; because the manners of rural life germinate from those elementary feelings; and from the necessary character of rural occupations are more easily comprehended; and are more durable; and lastly, because in that situation the passions of men are incorporated with the beautiful and permanent forms of nature. The language too of these men is adopted (purified indeed from what appear to be its real defects, from all lasting and rational causes of dislike or disgust) because such men hourly communicate with the best objects from which the best part of language is originally derived; and because, from their rank in society and the sameness and narrow circle of their intercourse, being less under the action of social vanity they convey their feelings and notions in simple and unelaborated expressions. Accordingly such a language arising out of repeated experience and regular feelings is a more permanent and a far more philosophical language than that which is frequently substituted for it by Poets, who think that they are conferring honour upon themselves and their art in proportion as they separate themselves from the sympathies of men, and indulge in arbitrary and capricious habits of expression in order to furnish food for fickle tastes and fickle appetites of their own creation.

I cannot be insensible of the present outcry against the triviality and meanness both of thought and language, which some of my contemporaries have occasionally introduced into their metrical compositions; and I acknowledge that this defect where it exists, is more dishonorable to the Writer's own character than false refinement or arbitrary innovation, though I should contend at the same time that it is far less pernicious in the sum of its consequences. From such verses the Poems in these volumes will be found distinguished at least by one mark of difference, that each of them has a worthy *purpose*. Not that I mean to say, that I always began to write with a distinct purpose formally conceived; but I believe that my habits of meditation have so formed my feelings, as that my descriptions of such objects as strongly excite those feelings, will be found to carry along with them a *purpose*. If in this opinion I am mistaken I can have little right to the name of a Poet. For all good poetry is the spontaneous overflow of powerful feelings; but though this be true, Poems to which any value can be attached, were never produced on any variety of subjects but by a man who being possessed of more than usual organic sensibility had also thought long and deeply. For our continued influxes of feeling are modified and directed by our thoughts, which are indeed the representatives of all our past feelings; and as by contemplating the relation of these general representatives to each other, we discover what is really important to men, so by the repetition and continuance of this act feelings connected with important subjects will be nourished, till at length, if we be originally possessed of much organic sensibility, such habits of mind will be produced that by obeying blindly and mechanically the impulses of those habits we shall describe objects and utter sentiments of such a nature and in such connection with each other, that the understanding of the being to whom we address ourselves, if he be in a healthful state of association, must necessarily be in some degree enlightened, his taste exalted, and his affections ameliorated.

I have said that each of these poems has a purpose. I have also informed my Reader what this purpose will be found principally to be: namely to illustrate the manner in which our feelings and ideas are associated in a state of excitement. But speaking in less general language, it is to follow the fluxes and refluxes of the mind when agitated by the great and simple affections of our nature. This object I have endeavoured in these short essays to attain by various means; by tracing the maternal passion through many of its more subtle windings, as in the poems of the IDIOT BOY and the MAD MOTHER; by accompanying the last struggles of a human being at the approach of death, cleaving in solitude to life and society, as in the Poem of the FORSAKEN INDIAN; by shewing, as in the Stanzas entitled WE ARE SEVEN, the perplexity and obscurity which in childhood attend our notion of death, or rather our utter inability to admit that notion; or by displaying the strength of fraternal, or to speak more philosophically, of moral attachment when early associated with the great and beautiful objects of nature, as in THE BROTHERS; or, as in the Incident of SIMON LEE, by placing my Reader in the way of receiving from ordinary moral sensations another and more salutary impression than we are accustomed to receive from them. It has also been part of my general purpose to attempt to sketch characters under the influence of less impassioned feelings, as in the OLD MAN TRAVELLING, THE TWO THIEVES, &c. characters of which the elements are simple, belonging rather to nature than to manners, such as exist now and will probably always exist, and which from their constitution may be distinctly and profitably contemplated. I will not abuse the indulgence of my Reader by dwelling longer upon this subject; but it is proper that I should mention one other circumstance which distinguishes these Poems from the popular Poetry of the day; it is this, that the feeling therein developed gives importance to the action and situation and not the action and situation to the feeling. My meaning will be rendered perfectly intelligible by referring my Reader to the Poems entitled POOR SUSAN and the CHILDLESS FATHER, particularly to the last Stanza of the latter Poem.

ii. Paragraph 10

Having dwelt thus long on the subjects and aim of these Poems, I shall request the Reader's permission to apprize him of a few circumstances relating to their *style*, in order, among other reasons, that I may not be censured for not having performed what I never attempted. Except in a very few instances the Reader will find no personifications of abstract ideas in these volumes, not that I mean to censure such personifications: they may be well fitted for certain sorts of composition, but in these Poems I propose to myself to imitate, and, as far as possible, to adopt the very language of men, and I do not find that such personifications make any regular or natural part of that language. I wish to keep my Reader in the company of flesh and blood, persuaded that by so doing I shall interest him. Not but that I believe that others who pursue a different track may interest him likewise: I do not interfere with their claim, I only wish to prefer a different claim of my own. There will also be found in these volumes little of what is usually called poetic diction; I have taken as much pains to avoid it as others ordinarily take to produce it; this I have done for the reason already alleged, to bring my language near to the language of men, and further, because the pleasure which I have proposed to myself to impart is of a kind very different from that which is supposed by many persons to be the proper object of poetry. I do not know how without being culpably particular I can give my Reader a more exact notion of the style in which I wished these poems to be written than by informing him that I have at all times endeavoured to look steadily at my subject, consequently I hope it will be found that there is in these Poems little falsehood of description, and that my ideas are expressed in language fitted to their respective importance. Something I must have gained by this practice, as it is friendly to one property of all good poetry, namely good sense; but it has necessarily cut me off from a large portion of phrases and figures of speech which from father to son have long been regarded as the common inheritance of Poets. I have also thought it expedient to restrict myself still further, having abstained from the use of many expressions, in themselves proper and beautiful, but which have been foolishly repeated by bad Poets till such feelings of disgust are connected with them as it is scarcely possible by any art of association to overpower.

2. From *Lyrical Ballads* Vol. 2 (1800)

[Cf. *De Monfort: A Tragedy* 4.1.32-39.]

There was a Boy, ye knew him well, ye Cliffs
And Islands of Winander! many a time,
At evening, when the stars had just begun
To move along the edges of the hills,
Rising or setting, would he stand alone,
Beneath the trees, or by the glimmering lake,
And there, with fingers interwoven, both hands
Press'd closely palm to palm and to his mouth
Uplifted, he, as through an instrument,
Blew mimic hootings to the silent owls
That they might answer him. And they would shout
Across the wat'ry vale and shout again
Responsive to his call, with quivering peals,
And long halloos, and screams, and echoes loud
Redoubled and redoubled, a wild scene
Of mirth and jocund din. And, when it chanced
That pauses of deep silence mock'd his skill,
Then, sometimes, in that silence, while he hung
Listening, a gentle shock of mild surprize
Has carried far into his heart the voice
Of mountain torrents, or the visible scene
Would enter unawares into his mind
With all its solemn imagery, its rocks,
Its woods, and that uncertain heaven, receiv'd
Into the bosom of the steady lake.

Fair are the woods, and beauteous is the spot,
The vale where he was born: the Church-yard hangs
Upon a slope above the village school,
And there along that bank when I have pass'd
At evening, I believe, that near his grave
A full half-hour together I have stood,
Mute—for he died when he was ten years old.

Appendix E: Contemporary Reviews

1. *Literary Leisure* 1 (Jan. 1800): 221-34

No. 19: Thursday, January 30, 1800

A PERFECT tragedy has been deemed the noblest triumph of human intellect; and indeed, when one considers the nice discrimination of character, the knowledge of the heart of man, the power of arresting attention and exciting interest, that is required in a writer of tragedy, one cannot so much wonder that so many have failed, as that any have at all succeeded. An epic poet, when he has once arranged his plan, can supply by narrative or description the blanks in character and sentiment. He can call in the aid of super-natural machinery—nay, it is even a part of his business so to do, in order to facilitate events sufficiently out of the common way, to excite wonder by their grandeur, and curiosity about their termination. It is much easier to make a man act than think—it is much easier to develop the workings of his mind in a series of lines in the author's own person ... than to put into the mouth of each character those very words which display the feelings themselves, and not only the feelings and passions themselves, but with that peculiar discrimination which marks the individual.

There is, perhaps, a regular progress common to all great passions; but it is marked by very distinct shades in the breasts of every different person. No two people would perhaps express emotion in the same manner, or be guided by similar feeling to similar conduct. To mark these variations of character with all their delicate traits of diversity, is more peculiarly the province of the dramatic writer. The aim of tragedy is in general to surprise, to elevate the mind, to affect the feelings, and interest the curiosity of the spectator. For this purpose a grand and uncommon incident is usually selected, distinguished personages are made the victims of misfortune, and exalted sentiments are clothed in poetical imagery. There are undoubtedly many of them fine poems;—whether they are peculiarly entitled to the term *dramatic*, I do not mean to enquire; but they are certainly less calculated to interest the heart, than those ruder structures, built by the hands of our immortal Shakespeare, where probability is frequently violated in the incidents, and disregarded in the conclusion—where poetical imagery is perpetually sacrificed to the jingle of words, and the most sublime sentiments too often debased by an irresistible conceit; but where individual truth of character is inviolably preserved.

Some dramatic writers, conscious of the want of interest in the more regular tragedies, have daringly overleaped all bounds, and imitated Shakespeare in his transgressions of the rules alone. But, however the man who wishes to write a drama, feels inclined to complain of the difficulties imposed on him by the arbitrary laws of critics, he may rest assured, that it is much easier to compress an incident into a given portion of time, and to contract it into a certain space, than to make the characters speak at once the language of nature and of passion....

... however it may be the business of dramatic writings to elevate the mind, and interest the feelings, they have a higher task to perform, to which the others bear only the proportionable value of being the best means to promote the more desirable end. It is surely their business to inculcate right sentiments, and promote the diffusion of virtue; and what mode of writing is so well adapted to convey right impressions with such powerful and general effect? This is a point, however, which, for a considerable time, has never seemed to occur to any author. Writers have rather considered their own powers, than the beneficial effect their labours might produce. Shakespeare himself, so capable of tracing the spring and progress of passion, of marking the almost insensible motives which operate to produce a deviation from virtue, has been far from making it the settled principle of his plays. He wrote from the impulse of the moment, and the desultory and vague style of his plots sufficiently proves that, however those master-strokes of nature might occur to him in the unfolding of the incidents, the incidents were by no means imagined with a view to produce those undeniable proofs of his exquisite researches into the human heart. Had Shakespeare formed such a plan, how might the world have benefited! It remained, however, for the present age to produce a genius capable of conceiving such an idea, and hardy enough to attempt its execution with no inadequate pen. My readers will instantly see that I allude to "A Series of Plays." The specimen already before the Public gives the most glowing promise of the success of the whole; the preliminary dissertation exhibits a depth of reasoning, an acuteness of penetration, an accuracy of observation, not often to be met with.

In reading that excellent essay, one is tempted to regret, that so much beautiful imagery, and glowing colouring should be thrown away on a prose discourse. Poetical beauties are scattered over it with a profusion which would have enriched a long poem, and which the author, with unsparing hand, uses to illustrate a disquisition, whose intrinsic merit would have been a sufficient recommendation. No one can doubt the ability of the writer for the self-imposed task—no one can imagine a clearer eye to distinguish those small beginnings of passion, which "are as when a man letteth out water."[1] The remarks on the eagerness with which people of all descriptions watch indications of character, and symptoms of agitation, must come home to the heart of every individual; and with what beautiful, what affecting solemnity, and what exquisite precision are described the effects on the mind of the observer, of the discovery of such tumultuous passions existing in the breast of a fellow-creature!

... this so interesting research into the heart of man, is performed with a clearness and precision that undeniably award to dramatic writings the preference in this difficult, though most engaging task. To the dramatist it alone belongs to represent man—Novelists, poets, historians, may describe him,—but he describes himself in a well-executed drama. The impulses of passion mark themselves by words too minute to become the subject of observation to the historian; and though sometimes seized by the Novelist, the general fear that they should escape the attention of the reader, causes them to be beat and ham-

---

1 Proverbs 17:14.

mered out till they cover an incalculable surface of paper.
When a minute indication of nature is thus displayed with artifice and ostentation, you may remember the eloquence of the
writer, but interest is excited no longer.

When, in the swellings of his heart over the lost Cordelia,
Lear interrupts the moanings of the father with the abrupt
request to an attendant,—"Pray you undo this button!" what
bosom of feeling does not throb in sympathy with the venera-
ble King's? What description could so forcibly have excited the
consciousness of that bursting agony, that at length mastered
the powers of life.

This ingenious and reflecting writer justly observes that
tragedians have in general selected "strong outlines of character,
bold features of passion, and striking dramatic situations,"—
thus neglecting "those smaller touches of nature, which so well
develop the mind;"—and after shewing how much more interest is to be excited, and how much more good produced by
"unveiling the mind under the dominion of those strong and
fixed passions which, seemingly unprovoked by outward circumstance, will from small beginnings brood within the breast,
till all the better dispositions, all the fair gifts of nature are
borne down before them,"—proceeds to an investigation of
the different species of comic dramas. The remarks here are
equally judicious and acute, and produce a similar conviction in
the mind of the reader, of the power possessed by the author of
this dissertation to form a new era in dramatic poetry, and rescue the stage from the unmeaning ribaldry and high-flown
heroics which too often disgrace it. The unfolding of the plan,
of which the three plays now before the public, form but a
small part, strikes the mind as grand, noble, and highly laudable;
nor can a doubt arise of the capability of the author to execute
a project which none but a superior genius could have been
capable of forming, which does honour to the present age, and
will sufficiently clear it from the imputation, equally disgraceful, of frivolous levity, or metaphysical absurdity.

At a period, when many people are prostituting splendid talents in the pursuit of wild and pernicious chimeras, involving
themselves in the bewildering clouds of modern philosophy,

and broaching speculations and opinions which threaten to overturn all moral relations and all social order—when others (perhaps a subordinate link in the same great chain of modern sophistry) endeavour to debase the public taste to spectacles of mere show and pageantry, substituting the puerility of fairy tales, and the exploded horrors of romance, for delineations of human nature, and bold pictures of character,—it is some comfort to advocate for the dignity of the species, to find an individual arise, who can calmly look down on the frivolous or pernicious pursuits of the literary world, and, with a firm and vigorous pencil, can at once form a bold outline, and fill it up with truth and correctness.

From the Blue Beards, the Pizarros, the Castle Spectres of the English stage,[1] from the wild ravings of the German drama, and the lax morality thence incorporated with our theatrical exhibitions, from the mummery of pageantry, and the cant-words of comedy, it is a welcome relief to turn to the page where the powers of the mind find real exercise—where the feeling heart subscribes to the truth of the portrait—where the powers of a Siddons[2] and a Jordan[3] will find adequate employment—and where the embellishments of poetry are made subservient to the noblest purposes.

It must be the sincere wish of every lover of literary merit, that the author of these admirable performances would emerge from retirement, and lest the world know whither to address the applause they have excited; but it is to be hoped that it will not be long ere conscious merit will boldly face the day....

---

1   Blue Beard is the villain of Charles Perrault's 1697 tale "Barbe-bleue" upon which numerous burlesques and dramatizations were based, such as George Colman the Younger's (1762-1836) *Bluebeard* (1798). *Pizarro* (1799), a tragedy based on a German play by August Friedrich Ferdinand von Kotzebue (1761-1819) about the Spanish conqueror of Peru, Francisco Pizarro (1478-1541), was the most popular of Richard Brinsley Sheridan's (1751-1816) later plays. *The Castle Spectre* is Matthew Lewis's (1775-1818) highly successful gothic drama, first performed at Drury Lane Theatre on December 14, 1797.

2   Sarah Siddons (1755-1831), sister of John Philip Kemble, was a leading actor of her day.

3   Dorothy Jordan (1761-1816) was a popular comic actor.

2. *Edinburgh Review* 4 (July 1803): 269-86

[This review by Francis Jeffrey appeared as the lead article.]

THESE plays require a double criticism; first, as to the merit of the peculiar plan upon which they are composed; and, secondly, as to their own intrinsic excellence.

To such peculiar plans, in general, we confess that we are far from being partial; they necessarily exclude many beauties, and ensure nothing but constraint: the only plan of a dramatic writer should be, to please and to interest as much as possible; but when, in addition to this, he resolves to write upon nothing but scriptural subjects, or to imitate the style of Shakespeare, or to have a siege, or the history of a passion in every one of his pieces, he evidently cuts himself off from some of the means of success, puts fetters upon the freedom of his own genius, and multiplies the difficulties of a very arduous undertaking.

The writer of the pieces before us, has espoused the patronage of what she has been pleased to call *characteristic truth*, as the great charm of dramatic composition; and, in order to magnify its importance, has degraded all the other requisites of a perfect drama to the rank of very weak and unprofitable auxiliaries. With a partiality not at all unusual in the advocates of a peculiar system, she admits, indeed, that a play may have qualities that give nearly as much pleasure; but maintains, that this is altogether owing to the *folly* of mankind, and that if we were constituted as we ought to be, we should care very little for any thing but the just representation of character in our dramatic performances this sentiment, we think, is pretty clearly expressed, in the following passage of the "Introductory Discourse," prefixed to the former volume.

> Our love of the grand, the beautiful, the novel, and above all of the marvellous, is very strong; and if we are richly fed with what we have a good relish for, we may be weaned to forget our native and favourite aliment: yet we can never so far forget it, but that we shall cling to, and acknowledge it again, whenever it is presented before us.

In a work abounding with the marvellous and unnatural, if the author has any how stumbled upon an unsophisticated genuine stroke of nature, we will immediately perceive and be delighted with it, though we are *foolish enough*, at the same time, to admire all the nonsense with which it is surrounded.

Now, we really cannot perceive why the admiration of novelty and grandeur should be considered as more foolish, than the admiration of just sentiments, or consistent character. The same power that gave us a relish for the one, formed us to be delighted with the other; and the wisdom that guides us, to the gratification of the first propensity can scarcely condemn our indulgence in the second. Where the object is to give pleasure, nothing that pleases can be foolish; and a striking trait of characters, or of nature, will only please the more, when it occurs in a performance, which has already delighted us with its grandeur, its novelty, and its beauty. The skilful delineation of character, is no doubt among the highest objects of the drama, but this has been so generally admitted, that it was the less necessary to undervalue all the rest. The true object of the drama, is to interest and delight; and this it can frequently accomplish, by incident, as effectually as by character. There are innumerable *situations* that excite our sympathy in the strongest degree, though the character of those who are placed in them be left almost entirely to be filled up from our general conceptions of human nature. Mothers bereaved of their children; lovers separated or restored to each other; the young and valiant cut off by untimely death; tyrants precipitated from their thrones; and many other occurrences or representations, are capable of awakening the highest interest, and the most anxious curiosity, although the character should be drawn only with these vague and undistinguishing features that fancy has associated with the situation.

But, even if we could agree with Miss Baillie that the striking delineation of character was the cardinal excellence of the drama, we should find great difficulty in admitting that her plan was the most likely to ensure its attainment. The peculiarity of that plan consists in limiting the interest of the piece, in a great degree, to the developement of some one great passion in the principal character, and in exhibiting this passion in all the successive stages of its progress, from its origin to its final catastrophe. It does not appear to us that either of these observances is well calculated to increase the effect of any dramatic production.

If any thing more is meant by limiting the interest of the piece to the consequences of a single passion, than is implied in the vulgar rules for preserving unity of character and of action, we are inclined to think, that something more is meant than can very easily be justified. The old maxims evidently require the predominancy of certain motives in the minds of the leading characters, and a certain consistency in the sympathies that are excited by their fortunes. To carry these restrictions still farther, and to confine the whole interest of the story to the developement of a single passion, seems to us to be altogether impracticable, and could not even be attempted, in a very imperfect degree, without violating that unity of action by which the general effect of the piece would be very materially impaired. To confine the attention, and tie down the sympathies to the observance of one master passion through a whole play, is plainly impossible; first, because that passion, in order to prove its strength, must have some other passion to encounter and overcome in the bosom where it is at last to reign; and, secondly, because a certain portion of our sympathy must necessarily be reserved for the fate and the feelings of those who are the objects and the victims of this ruling passion in the hero. The first partition of our sympathy is altogether unavoidable; and Miss Baillie herself has accordingly been forced to submit to it. *Count Basil* is distracted between love and a passion for military glory; and the interest and sympathy excited by the whole story, may be referred to the one passion, just as properly as to the other. *De Montfort* is represented as struggling between a high sense of honour, and a frantic and disgraceful antipathy; nor could the latter have been made interesting in any degree, unless our sympathy had first been very powerfully engaged for the former.... The second division of interest that is claimed by those who inspire or oppose the domineering passion of the chief personage, is scarcely less necessary. We cannot easily sympathise with a lover, unless we take some concern in the object of his attachment; and are seldom much offended by the oppressions of a tyrant, when we do not enter very warmly into the feelings of those whom he oppresses. The only way in which the interest we take in the story can be in any degree engrossed by the hero, is to provide him with a succession of inferior patients and observers, through whom he moves in the grand career of his passion, and who are successively forgotten for the sake of those who replace them. By this contrivance, which is but seldom practicable, it is very obvious, however, that the interest of the piece is impaired and dissipated, and the unity of the action entirely broken....

The peculiarity of Miss Baillie's plan, however, does not consist so much in reducing any play to the exhibition of a single passion, as in attempting to comprehend within it a complete view of the origin, growth, and consummation of this passion, under all its aspects of progress and maturity. The plan seems to us almost as unpoetical as that of the bard who began the tale of the Trojan war from the egg of Leda;[1] and really does not appear very well calculated for a species of composition, in which the time of the action represented has usually been more circumscribed than in any other. Miss Baillie, however, is of opinion, that it will turn out to be a very valuable discovery; and insists much upon the advantage that will be gained by adhering to it, both in the developement of character, the increase of interest, and the promotion of moral improvement. We are afraid that these expectations are more sanguine than reasonable.

To delineate a man's character, by tracing the progress of his ruling passion, is like describing his person by the yearly admeasurement of his foot, or rather by a termly report of the increase of a wen, by which his health and his beauty are ultimately destroyed. A ruling passion distorts and deforms the character; and its growth, instead of developing that character more fully, constantly withdraws more and more of it from our

---

1 In Greek mythology, Zeus appeared to Leda, wife of Tyndareus, as a swan. Two eggs were the product of their union, from which came Castor, Clytemnestra, Polydeuces, and Helen.

view. The growth of the passion is not the growth of the mind; and its progress and symptoms are pretty conform, in whatever subject it may have originated. *Amor omnibus idem,*[1] at least, says, the poet; and it may fairly be admitted, that men become assimilated, by their common subjection to some master passion, who had previously been distinguished by very opposite characters. To delineate character, therefore, by the progress of such a passion, is like following a cloud of smoke, in order to discriminate more clearly the objects that it envelopes.

These considerations are so very obvious, that though Miss Baillie has certainly talked a great deal about tracing a passion from its origin, we are persuaded that she really did not expect much assistance from this maxim in the delineation of character. She has built, in general, upon a truer ground; and seems to have perceived very clearly the method of employing a predominating passion, so as to give brilliancy and effect to characteristic representation. This method, which, however, is by no means new, consists principally in the occasional introduction of the passion, or peculiar turn of mind, in transactions of inferior moment, and in circumstances where it does not serve at all to help forward the action of the piece. By this apparently accidental disclosure of consistency, a stamp of nature and reality is given to the whole delineation; and the glimpses that are thus caught of the hero, in the course of his ordinary deportment, serve, in a manner, to confirm those impressions that had been excited by his more studied and imposing appearances. In private life, and on trifling occasions, the splendid drapery of the passions is usually laid aside; and, if we are permitted to look in upon them in this situation, we fancy that we recognise their genuine features with less uncertainty. If care be taken, therefore, to relieve the glare and pomp of the main action, by the insertion of a few such casual incidents, we seem to be let into the interior of the character, and attain a certain familiarity with the chief personages, that renders our conception of their whole character much more lively, entire, and impressive. It is upon this principle, that the effect of most of the fine strokes of nature and of character, which occur in

---

1   "Love in all things the same."

the writings of the poets, will be found to depend; and it is a principle, that has been quite familiar to criticism, ever since it was illustrated by the ancient commentators of Homer.[1]

But, though Miss Baillie has not overlooked this powerful instrument, for the developement of characteristic effect, there is another, of still greater importance, which appears to be, in a good measure, excluded by her doctrine of the unity of passion. The art to which we now allude, is that by which all appearance of individual reality is communicated to an ideal personage, and the functions of a dramatic hero assigned to a living being, with the whole of whose capacities and dispositions we are made to feel that we are acquainted. This poetical deception, however, can never be accomplished by the display of a single passion, and cannot even take place, we should imagine, where such a display is made the chief object of our attention. It is to be effected, indeed, only by an occasional neglect and intermission of the principal action, and of the passions by which that action is forwarded, by the introduction of arbitrary and inconsiderable occurrences, and slight and transient indications of habits, sentiments, and failings that could not have been inferred from the conduct or emotions of the chief characters in the greater incidents of the piece. It is by these, and by these alone, that a definite object can be created for our sympathies to attach upon, and the true image of a living man be presented to our imagination. There is no man alive, of whose whole character we could judge merely from his conduct or expressions in some important transaction; and our sympathies are always, but feebly excited for those with whose internal feelings we are so imperfectly acquainted. It is not enough, therefore,

---

1 In his *Ancilla to Classical Readers* (New York: Columbia University Press, 1954), Moses Hadas notes: "Like Dante and Shakespeare, Homer belongs to the ages, and in his pages various epochs have realized their own aspirations. Alexander the Great declared Homer to be the best and most reliable source of military science (Plutarch, *Alexander* 8); Horace found in him a moralist plainer and better than Chrysippus and Crantor (*Epistles* 1.2); in the 3rd century AD Porphyry saw in the Odyssean cave of the nymphs a Neoplatonic allegory (On the Cave of the Nymphs in the *Odyssey*); Montaigne finds all knowledge in him (2.36) ... Pope felt that the fire which is discerned in Vergil, flashes in Lucan and Statius, glows in Milton and surprises us in Shakespeare, is found at its best only in Homer, 'in him only it burns everywhere clearly and everywhere irresistibly'" (Preface to *Iliad*).

that the qualities bestowed upon our heroes be suitable to the conduct which is assigned them, or consistent with each other. A naked combination of the qualities necessary to account for the action, will never make up the idea of a real and entire man. There must be a delineation of those, also, that are of no use at the moment, and are not necessarily implied by the presence of the leading features. Without these, an action, indeed, may be represented; but the actors will be utterly unknown, and all impression of reality, along with every emotion of individual sympathy, will be utterly excluded. A play, which discriminates its characters only by the great and leading passions that are essential to the parts they have to sustain, must be as deficient in interest and effect, therefore, as a picture which shows no more of the figures than is necessary to explain its subject; that displays the hand of the murderer, and the bleeding bosom of his victim, but omits all representation of the countenance and gestures of either or of those circumstances in the surrounding scenery which may suggest aggravations or apologies for the crime. By the plan of Miss Baillie, however, these subordinate and arbitrary traits of character appear to be in a great measure excluded. Her heroes are to be mere personifications of single passions; and the growth and varied condition of one grand feature is to be incessantly held out to our observation, while all impenetrable shade is to be spread upon all the rest of the physiognomy. Among the debasements of modern tragedy, against which Miss Baillie declaims with so much animation, there is none, perhaps, so material as this, which her doctrine has so evident a tendency to sanction; nor is there any thing by which the writings of Shakespeare, and Beaumont and Fletcher,[1] are so remarkably distinguished from those of the latter dramatists, as by the individual truth and completeness of their representations of character. They are all drawn with the full lineaments, and just proportions of real men; and, while the qualities, by which their conduct is to be determined, are marked with sufficient boldness and vivacity, the subordinate attributes are not forgotten, by which we recognise them to be

---

1 Francis Beaumont (c. 1584-1616) and John Fletcher (1579-1625) were English dramatists and occasional collaborators.

creatures like ourselves, and are enabled to attach our feelings upon some definite and tangible object.

As to the *moral* effect of the drama, conducted upon this or upon any other plan, we confess that we are disposed to be very sceptical. Those plays are the best, we believe, that have done the least harm. The display of great passions is apt to excite an admiration which is not always extinguished by a fictitious view of their tragical effects; and the exhibition of interesting occurrence may sometimes beget a disgust and contempt for the insipidity of ordinary life. There is something of cant, how-ever, in this also. Plays have, for the most part, no moral effect at all; and they are seen or read for amusement and curiosity only; and the study of them forms so small a part of the occupation of any individual, that it is really altogether fantastical to ascribe to them any sensible effect in the formation of his character.

But even if the case were otherwise, and we were to believe all the pretty things that have been delivered by our essayists as to the moral effects of the stage, we really do not perceive that Miss Baillie's plan of composition is at all likely to forward that great and salutary object. It is her persuasion, it seems, that, 'looking back to the first rise, and tracing the progress of pas-sion, points out to us those stages, in the approach of the enemy, where he might have been combated most successfully, and where the suffering him to pass, may be considered as occasioning all the misery that ensues.' Now, though this obser-vation sounds tolerably well when taken in the abstract, it unfortunately fails altogether in the application. The greater part of the passions that are made use of in the drama, are laud-able in themselves, and only become vicious in their excess; while, at the same time, their progress is so gradual, that it is fre-quently almost impossible to say where they ought to have been arrested. To look back to the first rise of such a passion, therefore, will be of no use to us in any case; since it is not till long after that period, that it can become an object of jealousy or alarm; and since the occasions and stages of its increase are so complicated and multiplied, that it must often be impracticable to settle where the vicious series begins. The passion itself, too, may often be confirmed, before it indicates any tendency to evil; and the warning of the drama must either come too late, or lead us to repress some of the noblest and most generous propensities of our nature. The love of Count Basil, for instance, for an accomplished and virtuous princess, has nothing in it that should lead the readers of that tragedy to stifle such an honourable and successful passion in their own bosoms, or to shut the avenues of their hearts to the approaches of beauty and merit....

In all such cases, the shades, by which a passion graduates into criminality, are so fine, and the temptations and apologies by which its seductions are made effectual, so variously and nicely adapted to the circumstances of the imaginary character, that it is impossible to suppose, for a moment, that any one can be taught to guard against them by the peculiar incidents of one dramatic representation. Every one knows, that violent passions are apt to hurry men into crimes and improprieties; and this vulgar lesson, which surely stands in no need of illustration, can scarcely be brought more home to our feelings by a drama, which can never accommodate its fable to the particular character and situation of individuals.

If there be any passions to which Miss Baillie's dramatic warnings can be applicable, they can only be those therefore, that are intrinsically and fundamentally vicious, and against the remotest approaches of which we ought to be continually on our guard. Hatred, jealousy, envy, and some others, are in this class; and it may be conceived, that, to trace these to their origin, may contribute to the preservation of our morality, by enabling us to detect them in their rudiments, and to resist them in their infancy. It has happened, however, that Miss B., by a very singular infelicity in the execution of her plan, has been at the trouble to trace the origin and progress of love and ambition with great care and exactness, while she has only given us a view of hatred in its matured and confirmed state. She has taught us, in this way, how to distinguish and resist the first symptoms of those passions, which, in their beginning, are neither criminal nor dangerous; and has left us altogether without any instructions for combating or discovering those other passions that are never for a moment either innocent or satisfactory, and against the first dawnings of which our conscientious vigilance should have been directed. Basil and Ethwald are made to run their whole career of love and ambition before us, while it is almost impossible to say at what period their passions become criminal; while De Montfort presents himself, in the very first scene, the victim of a confirmed and inveterate hatred. If Miss B. really believed that her readers would be better able to resist the influence of bad passions, by studying their natural history and early symptoms, in her plays, she ought certainly to have traced this of hatred to its origin, more carefully than any other, since there is none of which it would be so desirable to cut off the shoots, or extirpate the seeds, at the beginning....

Upon the whole, then, we are pretty decidedly of opinion, that Miss Baillie's plan of composing separate plays upon the passions, is, in so far as it is at all new or original, in all respects extremely injudicious; and we have been induced to express this opinion more fully and strongly, from the anxiety that we feel to deliver her pleasing and powerful genius from the trammels that have been imposed upon it by this unfortunate system. It is paying no great compliment, perhaps, to her talents, to say, that they are superior to those of any of her contemporaries among the English writers of tragedy; and that, with proper management, they bid fair to produce something that posterity will not allow to be forgotten. Without perplexing herself with the observances of an arbitrary system, she will find that all tragical subjects imply the agency of the greater passions: and that she will have occasion for all her skill, in the delineation of character, and all her knowledge of the human heart, although she should only aim (as Shakespeare and Otway[1] have done before her) at the excitation of virtuous sympathy, and the production of a high pathetic effect. Her readers, and her critics, will then discover those moral lessons, which she is now a little too eager to obtrude upon their notice; and will admire, more freely, the productions of a

---

1   Thomas Otway (1652-85), English dramatist, was best known for his tragedy *Venice Preserved* (1682).

genius, that seems less incumbered with its task, and less conscious of its exertions....

Upon the whole, we think there is no want of genius in this book, although there are many errors of judgement; and are persuaded, that if Miss Baillie will relinquish her plan of producing twin dramas on each of the passions, and consent to write tragedies without any deeper design than that of interesting her readers, we shall soon have the satisfaction of addressing her with more unqualified praise, than we have yet bestowed upon any poetical adventurer.

3. *Imperial Review* 1 (March 1804): 335-44

... The sex of the author is a consideration which must enhance our estimate of the measure and the force of her genius. A female writer has many impediments to surmount before she can rise to a given height in literature. These should be allowed to bespeak for her an equal share of encouraging partiality with an author of the other sex, whose circumstances had precluded him from the benefit of early instruction. We are far from thinking that either man or woman should be trained with a view to prompt and determine them to future authorship; but the different mode of education which is adopted to prepare them for the separate duties in life, should choice or accident afterwards lead them into the walks of literature, is wholly in favour of the former, and enables him to start from vantage ground. His youth is devoted to the study of the ancient masters and models of composition: he is regularly exercised in style, and apprenticed to the mechanism of versification: his mind is enriched, and its powers are kept in action, by scientific views of the nature of man and the world which he inhabits; and all those stores are liberally replenished, from which the illustrations of the philosopher, or the imagery of the poet, may afterwards be drawn. But these advantages a female must fabricate for herself; and, if she has either perseverance and resolution to do so, or if her genius burst forth without them, its flight is to be hailed with all that cheering indulgence, which, on account of the hindrances that opposed their outset, we are ready to yield to a Burns,[1] or (*maximo intervallo fecundus*)[2] a Bloomfield.[3] Here, however, where no such indulgence is required, we must transfer all we should have given in this way as an additional tribute to our admiration of that native strength, which, without the usual aids, could soar to so lofty an elevation....

If our author's plan were less stiff and perceptive it would perhaps be more effectual even for instruction. We should therefore rejoice to see her relieved from its rules: for though we perceive no constraint arising from it in her past productions, this only tempts us to exclaim, 'if she can move thus in trammels, how will she appear when at large!' Under the control of principle so excellent, and so sweetly seasoned with the spirit of that religion for which, even in a Play, her veneration appears, she may, with perfect security, trust her genius to range at will through every subject, and through every careless and unstudied variety of plan. A mind so prepared has only to charm, and it must instruct.

We derive a more particular satisfaction from so rare a combination of splendid talent and virtuous principle, at a time when the public have been insulted with effusions of female sentiment, creating an abhorrence and alarm, but partially relieved by the impotence and inferiority of genius which they evince.

We shall now offer a few remarks on each play in their order.

The first exhibits the domineering sway and impetuous operation of love, in a mind of masculine and heroic strength, but altogether unaccustomed to such feelings, and unguarded by experience against their fatal effects. We see it rush into the soul with sudden and resistless fury; destroying the tone and balance of its faculties; overwhelming every consideration of duty; and bending, for a time, even the master passion before it. We see this passion resume its power, with a recoil propor-

---

1   Scottish farmer and poet, Robert Burns (1759-96).
2   "Fruitful after a great interval."
3   English shoemaker's apprentice and versifier, Robert Bloomfield (1766-1823).

tioned to its forcible suppression; and in the shock which it occasions, the catastrophe is rapidly, but naturally, produced. The plot is simple and one; and the interest, unless where we felt it languish, in the conference between the duke and his minister, strong and progressive through the whole. The author has, perhaps, succeeded best in those scenes where the hero, forgetting his new passion, is made to act in the original greatness of his character. We, at least, were powerfully affected by the suppression of the mutiny; and we envy little all the enjoyments of that mind which could remain unagitated by the scenes that close the piece. With respect to the characters, we were, on a hasty perusal of this play, struck with the same objection, which we see, from a note to the first act, had been successfully pressed upon the author by a friend. We thought the instantaneous rise of so ardent a passion inconsistent with the dignity and wisdom of the hero's character: and, though easily conceivable in some "unfledged ensign," who ogled the fair spectators as he carried his colours into country quarters, we thought it a hard exertion of faith to believe, that a Wolfe[1] or an Abercromby,[2] under all the counteracting influence of high responsible situation, should be so unhinged by a window-glance, as to suspend the march of an army when every thing depended on its advance. We now, however, retract this objection, and congratulate the author on returning to her original idea, which she had surrendered, in her second edition, to that of her friend; but which proceeds, in our more matured opinion, from a profound and penetrating acquaintance with the human heart. Love makes ever the most violent ravages, and puts on the most foolish and doting appearances in minds the least accustomed to it; in the bashful old bachelor, or the literary recluse, who have not been in the early habit of a companionable and easy intercourse with women. A soft look, at some unlucky moment, suddenly awakens a belief, the proudest which the heart of man is formed to cherish, that they

---

1   James Wolfe (1727-59), who had risen rapidly from the rank of ensign to major-general, died engaging Montcalm on the Plains of Abraham.

2   Most likely Sir Ralph Abercromby (1734-1801), who led the British forces in Ireland in 1797 and died commanding an expedition to the Mediterranean.

are objects of a tender regard: strange, but delicious agitations, coming with the greater welcome as they come late, betray them into a situation which is new and perplexing, and which destroys all sense of prudence and propriety. To such a class of characters, Basil, who is represented as a soldier even to pedantry, evidently belongs. "To men like you," his friend observes, "if love should come, he comes no easy guest:" and his mistress says, "There is something strange in this man's love I never met before." From such a peculiarity, we may account in the most natural manner for his sudden captivation; for the absurdity of disclosing the state of his heart to a supposed stranger in a mask; for the repetition of his mistress's words, which is, however, carried somewhat beyond probability; and for his ridiculous terror at giving her offence; which, had he been as well versed in women as in war, he would have known was never caused by extravagant admiration. Of the other characters, the duke and Gauriecio rank, perhaps, too nearly with the common-place villains who are always at hand to help on a dramatic plot: and we could have wished that the heroine had not been so deeply tinctured with coquetry, which, if it add to her idea something of airy elegance, takes in proportion from the soft and tender interest she inspires. The language possesses pathos, variety, and vigour. We regret that the author thought it necessary to measure out the whole in lines of ten syllables; for, where the dialogue is colloquial or playful, it is impossible to maintain the dignity of English blank verse; and as, in reading, these passages must be converted into prose, they should, perhaps, have been so in writing also. Obsolete phraseology, and modes of eking out a verse, borrowed from the age of Shakespear, occasionally offend us. We find "no tale to earn a sugar plum *withal:*" "*for that* (because) I am his friend:" "passing sure;" "soul distraught;" with awkward expletives, lame lines, and words arbitrarily accented. Perishable writers may be suffered, without danger of doing harm, to trick themselves out in "antique ruff and bonnet:" but the anxiety we feel for the progressive refinement of our language and versification, obliges us to warn an author, whose works posterity will read, if posterity partake of human nature, against giving up, as of no value, any ground which the genius and judgment of two centuries have laboured to gain.

The next play, a Comedy on Love, we read with more amusement than admiration. We were amused, as we should be by the hoyden waggeries of holiday misses; or, by a caricature of follies, to which we had seen some faint resemblance in real life. The dialogue has more liveliness than elegance; and the manners, though diverting, are deficient in delicacy. We have abundance of the Wrongheads and Foppingtons, but look in vain for a Clarinda or Lady Townly.[1] The behaviour of the misses, with a view to mortify the selfish coxcombs, appears too rude and impudent; and the mutual sarcasms of the gentlemen too coarse for modern customs to admit. Neither are we quite satisfied with the character of the hero. He is represented as a young man bred up in London, and on a companionable footing with fops of fashion; yet he falls in love as instantaneously as his counterpart in the tragedy, with a girl, whose appearance is by no means seducing. On her part the attachment is equally sudden; and, before their acquaintance is two days old, we find them as familiar as if they had been playmates from the cradle. In the course of the hero's probation, where he appears almost a Patient Grizzel[2] in breeches, we see his passion surmount the evidence of ill temper and selfish extravagance in his mistress, yet subdued in a moment by a single instance of calumny. We own ourselves at some loss to perceive so rapidly the line of distinction between these vices. Calumny is a breach of truth and justice; but ill temper naturally betrays us into expressions which are false and unjust; and from the latter, when matured by indulgence, the former may justly be dreaded. We do not complain that probability is violated, because Harwood stops short on the detection of wickedness in his

---

1 Characters from contemporary plays: Sir Francis Wronghead from Colley Cibber's (1671-1757) *The Provoked Husband* (1728); Lord Foppington from Sir John Vanbrugh's (1664-1726) *The Relapse* (1696); Clarinda from Benjamin Hoadly's (1706-57) *The Suspicious Husband* (1747); and Lady Townly from *The Provoked Husband* (1728).

2 *The Pleasant Comedy of Patient Grissel* (1603), a play based on Chaucer's *The Clerk's Tale*, was written by Thomas Dekker (c. 1570-1632) in collaboration with Henry Chettle (c. 1560-c. 1607) and William Haughton.

mistress; but because the same moral delicacy does not lead him to pause, at least, on his conviction of her fury, meanness, and extravagance, which are the legitimate parents of wicked conduct. A grammatical inaccuracy has escaped the author, where she says, "Let Eston and I (me) go into the closet." This, though not unfrequent in female conversation, yet, being put into the mouth of one of the heroines, who is not characterised by similar slips, we presume was not intended. In spite of these objections, however, we read this play with continued interest.

We come now to the tragedy on Hatred; and gladly re-enter the native element of the author. Here we have powerful conception of character, and masterly expression of passion. We have simple sublimity of language, towering generosity of sentiment, and all the pathos of keen and clinging attachment. A picture is given, severely true to nature, of a wretched man, who labours under a species of that partial and incipient mania so exquisitely described by Professor Stewart,[1] in his chapter on an ill-regulated imagination. A rooted loathing, and resentful disgust, contracted in youth for one of his companions, which "grows with his growth, and strengthens with his strength,"[2] at last takes such exclusive possession of his mind, as to mingle with every thought, and master every action. Continually agonized by this baneful passion, he draws its nourishment from the slightest incidents, and dwells with excruciating ingenuity on every idea which can sharpen its exacerbations, and augment its force. His busy and distempered fancy spins a web of gloomy thought around him, where, shut out from the cheerful light of day, and rejecting every comfort Providence has bestowed, he broods in misery of his own creating, till, exasperated by mortifications he had himself provoked, and stung with doubts he trembles to probe, he is driven to a deed of complicated horror, and an agony of remorse snaps the lacerated thread of his existence.

A sort of dread disastrous light is skilfully spread around this piece. The characters are strongly and distinctly marked. They come forward to the eye as we read. We insensibly "body forth

---

1   Scottish philosopher Dugald Stewart (1753-1828). See introduction.
2   Alexander Pope, *Essay on Man* 2.135.

their form and pressure,"[1] and see them move before us, as on a darkened stage, while we shudder at every step, with the horrid anticipation of some unholy deed. To impose a frame of mind so suited to her purpose attests the magic power of the poet.

In this drama a lesson of high utility is taught. It warns, with an awful voice, the votaries of gloomy sensibility not to suffer any single idea of an unpleasing nature to rest too long in their minds. It warns them to resist its first approaches, and, by forcing themselves to partake the comforts and the duties of life, to vary the paths of reflection, and preserve all the chords of the soul in unison....

Our objections to this play are few, and we hazard them with hesitation. We find some difficulty in reconciling the different parts of the hero's character. In the account which he gives of the origin and growth of his antipathy, we perceive it founded on a puerile lust after universal estimation, and a spiteful envy of his antagonist; "who, even from childhood, withheld the fair respect all paid besides." He is a Haman, who can enjoy no peace while a single Mordecai refuses his homage. With that low and little passion perpetually working at the bottom of his mind, which could hardly fail to meet with mortifications from more quarters than one, and to influence his actions in various ways, how are we to account for the correct and dignified conduct he has maintained to the middle period of life, and for the uniform esteem and approbation of all who knew him, and chiefly of his penetrating sister? In all the character of Rezenvell [sic], too, we apprehend some incongruity may be discovered. From the generosity of his behaviour on different occasions, from his eagerness to embrace his rival, in the reconciliation scene, and from the profound admiration he entertains for Jane, we should not have expected the taunting pleasantries and pestering visits with which he teases and inflames the mind

---

1   Most likely the reviewer is loosely quoting Hamlet's advice to his actors: "Be not too tame neither, but let your own discretion be your tutor: suit the action to the word, the word to the action; with this special observance, that you o'er-step not the modesty of nature: for any thing so overdone is from the purpose of playing, whose end, both at the first and now, was and is, to hold, as't were, the mirror up to nature; to show virtue her own feature, scorn her own image, and the very age and body of the time his form and pressure" (3.2.18-26).

of Monfort. What had passed between them should, in a disposition that was really desirous to avoid a renewal of the scene, have dictated a guarded and forbearing respect. If it be urged, that his former manner was continued with a generous design to persuade his antagonist that all past offences were forgotten, and to conceal their quarrel from the world, the plea will not suffice, as he could not fail to observe the indignation and disgust his levity excited in the mind of Monfort. The picture of Jane is admirably executed, and we tremble to touch it. Yet why is she represented as verging into autumnal virginity? "Time" is said "to have laid his hand on her, though lightly;" and she herself exclaims, "but now the wane of life comes darkly on." Her beauty is frequently vaunted; but a defect in youth is a defect in beauty…. We are not quite convinced that we should have been so industriously prohibited from imaging Jane of a more lovely age; which would have added probability to the suspicion her brother conceives of an attachment between her and Rezenvell. The proofs of such an attachment are abundantly slight to weigh even with a mind so maddened as that of Monfort. On this point, however, we strongly suspect ourselves of error, and doubt not but many may consider the very circumstance we have questioned as throwing a rich and mellow lustre of grace, and majesty, and interest, around this exquisite picture.

We must again object to moulding such conversation, as that of a footman taking furnished lodgings, into blank verse:

> "The house is in most admirable order.
> —Go you, and wait below till he arrives.
> Indeed, my friend, I'm glad to see you here,"

This, however, is made up for by another servant, who describes the appearance of the heroine in language rather too poetical:

> "As she moves,
> White flows her robe in many a waving fold,
> As I have seen unfurled banners play
> With the soft breeze."

Is not some poverty of invention betrayed, by introducing a second duel, with the very same circumstances which accompanied the first? And is not the author open to a more serious charge, for teaching that a man, though harbouring the most abominable passion, may live in the enjoyment of universal veneration and esteem, only to be interrupted by a concurrence of untoward accidents, which few have reason to dread? This, and the example in Basil of a self-destroyer who falls with dignity, and is entombed with honour, we regard, notwithstanding the explanation contained in the preface, as important defects. The young and enthusiastic, whose minds receive the deepest impression from plays, are seldom the readers of prefaces....

4. *Dramatic Censor* (April–May 1800): 112–64

[Thomas Dutton (b. 1767?) wrote the following eight reviews of the Drury Lane theatre's performances of *De Monfort* between April 29 and May 9, 1800 in the *Dramatic Censor, or, Weekly Theatrical Report*. They form a comprehensive and interesting narrative of a serious play's struggle on the late eighteenth-century British stage. The play was adapted for performance by J. P. Kemble (1757-1823); he also played the title role. Amongst letters and other items of interest of Baillie's housed at the Royal College of Surgeons of England is the plot summary from this series of reviews (Slagle 1:80).]

DRURY-LANE, TUESDAY, April 29, 1800.

The sanction of KEMBLE's *fosterage* to a Tragedy, which had already acquired no inconsiderable degree of celebrity among the fashionable circles, in its *pristine* state, by the circumstances (involving an air of mystery) under which it was originally produced, naturally wound up public expectation to its highest pitch, and rendered the Lovers of the Drama eager to witness the result of this combination of talent, on the part of the writer, and the adapter of the Play.

The literary reader scarcely need to be informed, that the *printed* Tragedy, on which Mr. KEMBLE has employed his practical skill in scenic representation, is one of a series of Plays, illustrative of the passions, published without the name of the author, but tacitly acknowledged to be the production of a female writer, and generally attributed to the pen of Mrs. HUNTER, the widow of the late celebrated anatomist. This report has recently been contradicted, and the Play in question is now referred to Miss BAILEY, sister to the physician of that name; Mrs. HUNTER, who originally suffered herself to act as a screen to her friend, generously disdaining, after the success the Play experienced in the closet, to imitate the *jack-daw*[1] in the fable, by placing to her own account the merit due to another.

Hence it appears, that to appreciate the merits of the new Tragedy, as a dramatic composition, and to award a righteous verdict on the respective claims of both parties concerned in its production, it is essentially necessary to compare the Play, as now *acted* (with Mr. KEMBLE's alterations) at Drury-Lane, with the original, as *written* by Miss BAILEY. With this view, we have endeavoured to procure the printed copy, but have not been successful in our attempt, the Play, it seems, being out of print. We hope, however, in the course of the ensuing week to obviate this difficulty, and to be enabled to bring the Tragedy to the test of fair criticism, with respect to the individual merit or demerit of the author and the adapter; and shall, therefore, postpone till next week that thorough investigation and *analysis*, which, but for the reasons already assigned, we should now enter upon.... Mean while, we shall content ourselves with generally observing, that the success of the Play depends more, in our humble opinion, in the exquisite acting of Mr. KEMBLE and Mrs. SIDDONS, than on its own intrinsic merit. The language is, indeed, chaste and elegant; the diction elevated and impressive, without becoming turgid, vapid, and bombastic; and the sentiments are delicate and natural. But the Piece wants interest—it wants variety—it wants activity—it is too barren of incident—and very little art has been employed in the conduct of the plot. It is, likewise, independant of these negative dis-

---

1 Crow. Probably a reference to the fable of the jackdaw decked out in peacock's feathers.

qualifications, liable to stronger objections, in a moral and dramatic light, than any Theatrical production we have of late witnessed. These objections, we fear, are inherent, constitutionally inherent to the Piece, and therefore irremediable. This consideration causes us more deeply to regret, that men with Mr. KEMBLE's powers, should employ their talents upon improving the crude conceptions of others, instead of trusting to the resources of their own minds, and drawing upon the stable bank of their own genius. It is not in the nature of things for discordant elements to assimilate: a drama, constructed on this principle of *participation*, seldom exhibits the appearance of a perfect *whole*: it seldom discovers unity of design or execution; but, with very few exceptions, betrays its *double* parentage.

N.B. Our remarks on the performers are, together with our *Analysis* of the New Tragedy, reserved for next week.

DRURY-LANE, WEDNESDAY, April 30, 1800.

The new Tragedy experienced considerable curtailment on the second representation, the leading features of which we shall detail in our next. We were particularly pleased with the omission of the scene which ushered in the fourth act, in which a new performer, under the title of a *screech-owl*, bore a principal part. But the piece is still much too long, and would receive great additional improvement by totally rescinding the part of *Conrad*, who is only an incumbrance to the Play. Various other alterations are necessary to take off the heaviness of the Tragedy, by shortening the term of its duration.

DRURY-LANE, FRIDAY, May 2, 1800.

When we last week deferred our strictures on this Play, we were in hopes of obtaining an opportunity of balancing the respective claims of the Author and the Adapter, by comparing the printed *original* with the *representation*. In this hope, however, we have been disappointed, the Tragedy being out of print, and either lent out to read, or not composing a part of the catalogue of the different circulating libraries to which we have applied. We have, therefore, no alternative left, but to proceed upon the same principle on which we have acted in similar cases, and which we laid down in our remarks on Mrs. INCH-BALD's *Wise Man of the East*[1]—See the satirical Poem, entitled *The Apparition of Zoroaster, to the Theatrical Midwife of Leicester Fields*, page 73—

> "*Be this a truth to all Play-mongers known,*
> "*Whatever they adopt, becomes their own.*"

Applying this principle, therefore, in its most unlimited extent, to Mr. KEMBLE, we must hold that gentleman equally responsible for what he *retains*, as for what he *adds*. Vested with full power of *rejection* or *admission*—holding, as it were, the keys to *lock out*, or *let in*—he must equally participate in the *censure*, or the *praise*, due to the work to which he lends his sanction, and his fosterage.

We shall not enlarge upon the plot, which, as we have already observed in our last, is barren of incident, and, therefore, unworthy of minute detail. The language, likewise, has been sufficiently animadverted upon. It exhibits many specimens of a refined and classical style; but this is a recommendation ill calculated to compensate, especially with an English audience, who delight in bustle and intricacy of situation, for the want of interest and variety. In this respect, the new Tragedy partakes of the characteristic features of the French Drama, where declamation supplies the place of incident, and complicate developement of plot.

The *characters*, then, will form the leading topic of our disquisitions in the present instance; and, in this point of view, we are sorry to say, we never saw a Tragedy more woefully deficient, more culpably ill-conducted. *De Montfort*, the hero of the piece, is a systematic villain, without one *foil* to his vices. His

---

1 Elizabeth Inchbald (1753-1821) translated Kotzebue's (1761-1819) *The Wise Man of the East* (1799). Thomas Dutton, editor of the *Dramatic Censor*, wrote *The Wise Men of the East, or the Apparition of Zoroaster, the Son of Oromases, to the Theatrical Midwife of Leicester Fields*, a satirical poem on Mrs. Inchbald.

hatred towards *Rasenfeld* is not the passion of a great and generous soul: it originates in a mean sordid jealousy; he challenges
his rival to personal combat, and owes his forfeit life to the forbearance of his adversary. Yet this magnanimity, on the part of
Rasenfeld, has no effect on the impenetrable feelings of *De
Montfort*: his hatred now grows more fierce and implacable; yet,
strange to tell! black and deadly as the Author represents that
hate, it is almost instantly soothed and appeased by the
intreaties, not of a mistress, but a sister. A reconciliation next
takes place, through that sister's intervention—with what sincerity, on the part of *De Montfort*, we leave our readers to
judge—when, at the very moment that he professes friendship,
he refuses to ratify those professions by a friend's embrace. A
few hours after this event, this magnanimous man, this reconciled enemy, suffers himself to be wrought up to such a parox-
ysm of rage and revenge, by a forged and clumsy tale (to which
he lends an eager ear with a degree of credulity, bordering
upon weakness, that tends to render his character still more
despicable), that, forgetful of oaths, protestations, and every tie
which honour and duty can impose, he challenges his rival
under his own roof; and, when the latter nobly declines the
contest with a mad-man, displays himself not only a villain, but
a rank coward, and resolves upon assassination. He perpetrates
the murder—not in the moment of passion, but cooly, deliber-
ately, and by plan—and now, instead of being held up to detes-
tation, he is extolled as a paragon of virtue, and a long harangue
made on his noble qualities, not one of which he demonstrates
by his actions. Instead of incurring the punishment of his
crime, and being made an example to society, he is relieved
from ignominy, dies of a broken heart, and is pompously
lamented, instead of being execrated and despised. So much for
the *morality* of the Drama; not to mention the absurdity and
absolute contradiction, in attributing such fine feelings to a
man who could descend to such meanness, such cowardice,
such base and infamous villainy.

Rasenfeld possesses some *traits* of nobleness and magnanimity; but his character is unnecessarily degraded, and lessened in
esteem, by the petulance of his disposition. He, likewise, betrays

a want of caution, incompatible with just delineation of character, in exposing himself to the danger of assassination, after the emphatic warning given him by *Count Albert*, and which so perfectly corresponds with the behaviour of *De Montfort*, that *Rasenfeld* instinctively exclaims—"Sure, he will not *murder* me!"—to which *Albert* makes reply, by observing, that he will not be answerable for the consequences; at the same time plainly intimating his suspicions of foul play.

Jane De Montfort is a true romance-heroine, who deals in sentiment by wholesale, and makes a long preachment to palliate murder, and depicts an assassin like a saint!

The rest of the characters are mere *cyphers* in the account. In fact, the Tragedy of *De Montfort* is a true *family*[1] Play, the avowed aim of which seems to have been the exhibiting of the ★KEMBLES to advantage, by putting an *extinguisher*[2] on all the rest of the Performers.

As for the Play itself, it is difficult to ascertain to what class of the Drama it properly belongs. The bills of the Theatre announce it under the title of a Tragedy; but, baiting the heaviness and dull solemnity of the piece, it seems to be a heterogeneous compound of Tragedy, Comedy, Farce, Opera, Pantomime, and Puppet-Shew; in which dancing, feasting, revelry, *drunken songs*, screech-owls, murders, funeral processions, music and lamentations, are promiscuously jumbled together. It has all the dullness of the *Laureat's*[3] late production, without half its merit.

---

1   Sarah Siddons (1755-1831) and John Philip Kemble (1757-1823), both renowned tragic actors, were brother and sister, children of Roger Kemble (1721-1802), a travelling theatrical manager. Sarah's success on the stage gave John his first opportunity to act, and on September 30, 1783 he played Hamlet at the Drury Lane Theatre. Most noted for his bulk, their brother Stephen Kemble (1758-1822) was able to play Falstaff without any stuffing, and their other brother, Charles (1775-1854), distinguished himself in comedy and later was appointed Examiner of Plays (censor). The family would soon grow larger. Maria Theresa de Camp (1773-1838) later married Charles, and they had two children, Frances Anne (1809-93), an actor, and Adelaide Sartoris, a singer.

2   To appreciate the full impact of the metaphor here, we must realize that extinguishers in the eighteenth century were the commonplace conical caps used to extinguish candles or lamps.

3   Henry James Pye (1745-1813), poet laureate just prior to Robert Southey (1774-1843), was not highly respected as a writer.

Among the Perfomers, Mr. KEMBLE takes the undisputed lead. His acting is the chief recommendation the Play possesses. Mr. TALBOT[1] has the next best *male* part, in which he acquits himself with address; and would succeed still better, if he did not, by an affectation of ease, degenerate into slovenliness. His pronunciation is distinct, but rather too flippant.

Mrs. SIDDONS, as *Jane de Montfort*, has ample scope for her powers; but she is apt to fall at times into *rant* and exaggerated declamation. We must, likewise, notice an impropriety in her dress, which destroys the illusion of the scene. She is very anxious to have an interview with her brother, without being known to him; and for this purpose asks the *Countess Albert*, whether *masks* will be worn at the entertainment, where she proposes to meet him? The *Countess* replies in the negative, but recommends to her to conceal her face in the *double* foldings of a veil: a proposal in which Lady Jane cheerfully acquiesces. She makes her appearance, however, soon after, with no other concealment than a *single* veil, of so *thin* a texture, that all her features are recognized; nor does she even attempt to disguise her voice. Yet this clumsy stratagem imposes on *De Montfort*, and prevents him from knowing his sister.

DOWTON's[2] character of *Jerome*, is a palpable copy of *Adam* in the *Iron Chest*,[3] and the performer overacts his part in a manner, which completely turns into farce. BARRYMORE[4] has little

---

1 Born in Boston, Montague Talbot (1774-1831) forfeited a substantial inheritance from his uncle by choosing a life on the British stage. He made his first recorded Drury Lane appearance on April 27, 1799. However, his "trifling air" and "girlish form," as described by John Wilson Croker in 1804, disqualified him from competing with John Philip Kemble as an actor of tragedy. After his performance in *De Monfort* as Rezenvelt, unable to maintain his position on the London stage, he moved to Dublin, where he directed various theatre companies and became popular as a comic actor.

2 William Dowton's (1764-1851) 36-year career at the Drury Lane Theatre began as Sheva in Richard Cumberland's (1732-1811) comedy, *The Jew* (1794), on October 11, 1796. Dowton was considered to be a versatile actor who excelled as Malvolio.

3 George Colman the Younger (1762-1836) wrote this dramatization of William Godwin's *Things as They Are; or, The Adventures of Caleb Williams* in 1796 at the request of Richard Brinsley Sheridan. It was first performed at Drury Lane Theatre on 12 March 1796.

4 William Barrymore (1759-1830) played Count Albert. He first appeared at Drury Lane Theatre on October 3, 1782 where he performed for most of his life. His

or nothing to do, but to strut upon the stage; and CAULFIELD's[1] part, as *Conrad*, is an absolute excrescence, which not only requires the pruning knife, but ought to be totally lopped off.

Miss HEARD[2] appears in a very grand and elegant dress, as the *Countess Albert*; but has a very insignificant part to sustain. She seems, in fact, like the rest of the performers, unconnected with the KEMBLES, to be introduced for the express purpose of serving as a foil to the *family*. This Actress has, latterly, laboured very assiduously, and almost constantly, in the dramatic vineyard, her name, with very few exceptions, being in every bill, either in the Play or Entertainment, and not unfrequently in both. It is to be hoped, that the Proprietors do not confine their notice of her *usefulness* to the imposition of additional labour, without having due respect to the well-known aphorism—"*the labourer is worthy of proportionate hire!*"[3]

The scenery to the new Tragedy reflects great credit on the artists. The interior perspective of the convent, in particular, ranks among the grandest scenes the stage can boast. We have only to regret, that the piece is not more worthy of the embellishments bestowed upon it.

*The part of Rasenfeld was originally intended for Mr. C. KEMBLE; but that gentleman being prevented from acting by indisposition, the character devolved upon its present representation, Mr. TALBOT.

---

most effective role was Osmond in Matthew Lewis's (1775-1818) *The Castle Spectre* (1798).

1   Thomas Caulfield's (1766-1815) acting seldom rose above journeyman performances. Though popular for his comic roles, he may have fallen into contemporary obscurity had it not been for his much publicized, lengthy affair with Maria Teresa Bland (1770-1838), a singer of considerable reputation. Caulfield later found more appreciation for his acting in the United States.

2   Elizabeth Heard (c. 1775- ?) was the daughter of poet and dramatist William Heard, who abandoned his training in medicine to write. He only wrote two weak plays: *The Snuff Box; or, A Trip to Bath* (1775), a comedy, and *Valentine's Day*, a musical drama performed at Drury Lane on March 22, 1776. Elizabeth Heard was considered a reliable and natural actor, but she was mysteriously dismissed from Drury Lane after the 1800-01 season.

3   Luke 10.7.

DRURY-LANE, SATURDAY, May 3, 1800.

It may justly be considered as a bad omen of the success of the new Tragedy, when it is found necessary to call in the aid of such a vile *farrago*[1] of folly and absurdity, as the Entertainment of this evening. The crowded houses, and unbounded applause, with which *De Montfort* continues to be received, are unhappily confined to the *Play-bills*. The *Theatre* exhibits "a beggarly account of empty boxes!"

Mrs. SIDDONS fatigued herself so much with her exertions, in the character of *Jane De Montfort*, that she was unable to speak the *Epilogue*. An apology was accordingly made for its omission, and very favourably received by a drowsy audience, who were happy to find the Tragedy had reached its conclusion.

DRURY-LANE, MONDAY, May 5, 1800.

If Mrs. Siddons, who took her benefit this evening, placed her hopes of success on the attractions of the new Tragedy, she was woefully deceived in her appreciation of its merit. She was honoured with a fashionable, but not a numerous house.

DRURY-LANE, TUESDAY, May 6, 1800.

[No specific comments on the performance.]

DRURY-LANE, WEDNESDAY, May 7, 1800.

To judge from symptoms, which grow more prominent and alarming every night, the new Tragedy has not much longer to linger out a miserable existence.

DRURY-LANE, FRIDAY, May 9, 1800.

We have been favoured with the loan of the *original* of the

---

1 A confused mixture or hotchpotch.

Tragedy, by a kind friend, whose urbanity blends the scholar with the gentleman, and to whom Dramatic Literature, in particular, is under the greatest obligations. We profited of this opportunity to compare the play, as *printed*, with the *representation*, and find, that all the objections, which we pointed out in our last Number, are imputable to the *author*—are inherent to the *original*. This remark is not meant to exculpate Mr. KEMBLE from that share of censure which attaches to him, as the *adapter*, from that obloquy, which he voluntarily inherits and entails upon himself, by his *adoption* of a faulty offspring. It were to be wished, that he had allowed himself greater latitude and scope in the exercise of his own judgement, and made freer use of his critical prerogative. With very few exceptions, he has confined his amendments to the rectification of occasional *grammatical errors*; among which, *here* instead of *hither*; *there* for *thither*; the confounding of the *preterite* and *participle*; with various other inaccuracies ... called particularly for his correcting hand. All the heterogeneous ingredients in this dramatic compound; the spurious leaven of farce, opera, pantomine, and puppet-shew, so copiously kneaded into the dough of Tragedy, are furnished by the author; who, in the *introductory discourse* to the *series of plays*, of which *De Montfort* forms a part, expressly lays it down as a rule, that show, sing-song, battles, screech-owls, banquets and processions, are the *legitimate* and *necessary* substitutes for *plot* and *incident*; adding withal, in compliment to the good sense and understanding of the audience, that these are things from which *children* receive great pleasure and edification!

The principal, or at least the most characteristic alteration, which Mr. KEMBLE appears to have introduced, respects the last scene in the Third Act, where *De Montfort*, under the impression of *Conrad's* tale, that *Rezenvelt* has gained the affections of his sister, challenges that nobleman to personal combat. In the original, *Rezenvelt* accepts the challenge, and a second time disarms his adversary, whose life he spares, but refuses to return his forfeit sword.

> ———————"I'll take away your sword;
> "Not as a mark of *disrespect* to you,

"But for your *safety*——By to-morrow's eve
"I'll call on you myself, and give it back;
"And then, if I am charged with any wrong,
"I'll justify myself.——Farewell, strange man!"

Mr. KEMBLE makes *Rezenvelt* decline the challenge. He tells
De Montfort to find out some free, some untried arm; some
adversary, against whom he had not that very morning sworn
never more to raise his arm in anger. "To such a one," he says,
"you may again be a trifling life in debt!—again acknowledge,
and again forget!—I'll not be guilty of your perjuries."—This
conduct, on the part of *Rezenvelt*, undoubtedly displays a
dignified and manly mind; and possibly many of our readers
will agree with us, that his refusal to fight *De Montfort*, together
with the taunts which accompanied that refusal, must have a
greater tendency to inflame *De Montfort's* hatred, and prompt
the assassination of the man, who denied him the means of *open*
revenge, than had he a second time been the debtor of *Rezenvelt's* generosity—had he a second time owed his forfeit life to
his forbearance.

The Glee in the Third Act is the composition of Mr. Shaw,[1]
and is worthy of that gentleman's professional celebrity. It
receives due credit and effect from the manly voice of Mr.
SEDGEWICK.[2] As the *Glee* is not printed for the accommoda-
tion of those who wish to hear the *words* as well as the *notes* of
a Song, we subjoin a copy——

"Pleasant is the mantling bowl,
And the song of merry soul;
And the red lamps' cheery light;
And the goblets glancing bright;

---

1 Thomas Shaw (d. 1830), violinist, conductor, and composer, began his career at
Drury Lane, composing music for some of its extravaganzas. Later he became the
theatre's orchestra leader and part proprietor. Though prominent enough to be visited by Haydn in 1791, he experienced financial difficulties in 1798 because Sheridan failed to pay him regularly. He ended his life in obscurity as a music teacher in
Paris.

2 Thomas Sedgwick (d. 1803), actor and singer, debuted at Drury Lane Theatre on
October 25, 1789 in a song with Michael Kelly and Anna Maria Crouch.

Whilst many a cheerful face around
Listens to the jovial sound.
Social spirits, join with me;
Bless the god of jollity."

Mr. KELLY[1] furnishes the music to the *Dirge*, or *Requiem*, in the Fourth Act, which is entitled to considerable praise for richness of harmony, and appropriate solemnity.—The following is a copy of the words—

"Departed soul! whose poor remains
This hallowed lowly grave contains;
Whose passing storm of life is o'er,
Whose pains and sorrows are no more!
Bless'd be thou with the blest above,
Where all is joy, and purity, and love!

Let him, in might and mercy dread!
Lord of the living and the dead!
In whom the stars of heaven rejoice,
To whom the ocean lifts his voice,
Thy spirit purified to glory raise,
To sing with holy saints his everlasting praise.

Departed soul! who in this earthly scene
Hast our lowly sister been,
Swift be thy flight to where the blessed dwell!
Until we meet thee there—farewell! farewell!"

The Prologue to *De Montfort*, if we are rightly informed, is the production of the Honourable FRANCIS NORTH.—The Epilogue is attributed to the elegant pen of the DUCHESS OF DEVONSHIRE.

---

1   Michael Kelly (1764?-1826), Irish actor, singer, and composer, trained with Gluck and Mozart. He first appeared at Drury Lane on April 20, 1787 where he later held the position of musical director, setting to music such works as Sheridan's *Pizarro* (1799). He was a constant presence in English opera until 1808.

Works Cited/Recommended Reading

Baillie, Joanna. *A view of the General Tenour of the New Testament Regarding the Nature and Dignity of Jesus Christ.* London: Longman, 1831.

———. *The Dramatic and Poetical Works.* 1851. Hildesheim and New York: Georg Olms Verlag, 1976. Facsimile edition.

———. *Joanna Baillie: A Series of Plays.* 3 vols. 1798, 1802, 1812. Ed. Donald H. Reiman. New York and London: Garland Press, 1977.

———. *A Series of Plays.* Ed. Jonathan Wordsworth. Oxford and New York: Woodstock Books, 1990.

Baillie, Matthew. *The Morbid Anatomy of Some of the Most Important Parts of the Human Body.* 1793. Albany, N.Y.: Barber & Southwick, 1795.

———. *The Works of Matthew Baillie, M.D., to Which is Prefixed an Account of His Life, Collected from Authentic Sources.* 2 vols. Ed. James Wardrop. London: Longman, Hurst, Rees, Orme, Brown and Green, 1825.

Bennett, Susan. "Genre Trouble: Joanna Baillie, Elizabeth Polack—Tragic Subjects, Melodramatic Subjects." Ed. Tracy C. Davis and Ellen Donkin. *Women and Playwriting in Nineteenth-Century Britain.* Cambridge: Cambridge UP, 1999. 215-32.

Berry, Mary and Agnes. *The Berry Papers.* Ed. Lewis Melville. London: John Lane, 1914.

Bevis, Richard W. *The Laughing Tradition: Stage Comedy in Garrick's Day.* Athens: The U of Georgia P, 1980.

———. *English Drama: Restoration and Eighteenth Century, 1660-1789.* London: Longman, 1988.

Bishop of Salisbury. *Remarks on the General Tenour of the New Testament, Regarding the Nature and Dignity of Jesus Christ: Addressed to Mrs. Joanna Baillie.* Salisbury: W.B. Brodie, 1831.

Boswell, James. *Boswell's Life of Johnson.* Ed. R.W. Chapman. Oxford: Oxford UP, 1976.

Braudy, Leo. *The Frenzy of Renown: Fame and Its History.* New York and Oxford: Oxford UP, 1986.

Brewer, William D. "Joanna Baillie and Lord Byron." *Keats-Shelley Journal* 44 (1995): 165-81.

———. "The Prefaces of Joanna Baillie and William Wordsworth." *The Friend: Comments on Romanticism* 1.2 (1991): 34-47.

Bryson, Gladys. *Man and Society: The Scottish Inquiry of the Eighteenth Century.* New York: Augustus M. Kelley, 1968.

Burke, Edmund. *A Philosophical Enquiry into the Origin of our Ideas of the Sublime and Beautiful.* 1757. Ed. Adam Phillips. Oxford: Oxford UP, 1990.

Burney, Fanny. *Evelina: Or the History of a Young Lady's Entrance into the World.* Ed. Edward A. Bloom. Oxford: Oxford UP, 1982.

Burroughs, Catherine B. "English Romantic Women Writers and Theatre Theory: Joanna Baillie's Prefaces to the *Plays on the Passions.*" *Re-Visioning Romanticism: British Women Writers, 1776-1837.* Ed. Carol Shiner Wilson and Joel Haefner. Philadelphia: U of Pennsylvania P, 1994. 174-96.

———. "The English Romantic Closet: Women Theatre Artists, Joanna Baillie, and 'Basil.'" *Nineteenth-Century Contexts* 19:2 (1995): 125-49.

———. "'Out of the Pale of Social Kindred Cast': Conflicted Performance Styles in Joanna Baillie's *De Monfort.*" *Romantic Women Writers: Voices and Counter Voices.* Ed. Paula R. Feldman and Theresa M. Kelley. Hanover, NH: U of New England P, 1995. 223-35.

———. "'A Reasonable Woman's Desire': The Private Theatrical and Joanna Baillie's *The Tryal.*" *Texas Studies in Literature and Language* 38-3/4 (Fall/Winter 1996): 265-84.

———. *Closet Stages.* Philadelphia: U of Pennsylvania P, 1997.

———. "Joanna Baillie's Poetic Aesthetic: Passion and 'the Plain Order of Things.'" *Approaches to Teaching British Women Poets of the Romantic Period.* Ed. Stephen C. Behrendt and Harriet Kramer Linkin. New York: Modern Language Association of America, 1997. 135-40.

Campbell, T.D. "Francis Hutcheson: 'Father' of the Scottish Enlightenment." *The Origins and Nature of the Scottish Enlightenment.* Ed. R.H. Campbell and Andrew S. Skinner. Edinburgh: John Donald Publishers, 1982. 167-85.

Carhart, Margaret S. *The Life and Work of Joanna Baillie*. 1923. North Haven: Archon Books, 1970.

Carlson, Marvin. *Theories of the Theatre: A Historical and Critical Survey, from the Greeks to the Present*. Ithaca: Cornell UP, 1984.

Carswell, Donald. "Joanna Baillie." *Scott and His Circle*. Garden City, NY: Doubleday, Doran, 1930. 171-96.

Cassirer, Ernst. *The Philosophy of the Enlightenment*. Trans. Fritz C.A. Koelln and James P. Pettegrove. Boston: Beacon Press, 1951.

Castle, Terry. *Masquerade and Civilization: The Carnivalesque in 18th-Century English Culture and Fiction*. Stanford: Stanford UP, 1986.

Chitnis, Anand C. *The Scottish Enlightenment: A Social History*. London: Croom Helm, 1976.

Clayden, P.W. *Rogers and His Contemporaries*. London: Smith, Elder, 1889.

Coleridge, Sara. *Memoir and Letters of Sara Coleridge*. Ed. Edith Coleridge. London: Henry S. King, 1873.

Cox, Jeffrey N., ed. *Seven Gothic Dramas 1789-1825*. Athens: Ohio UP, 1992.

Curran, Stuart. "The I Altered." *Romanticism and Feminism*. Ed. Anne K. Mellor. Bloomington and Indianapolis: Indiana UP, 1988. 185-207.

Dibdin, Charles. *A Complete History of the Stage*. 1800. New York: Garland Press, 1970.

Donkin, Ellen. *Getting Into The Act: Women Playwrights in London, 1776-1829*. London: Routledge, 1995.

Dorr, Priscilla. "Joanna Baillie." *An Encyclopedia of British Women Writers*. Ed. Paul and June Schlueter. New York: Garland Press, 1988. 15-21.

Douglas, David, ed. *Familiar Letters of Sir Walter Scott*. Vols 1 and 2. Edinburgh: D. Douglas, 1894.

Dussinger, John A. *The Discourse of the Mind in Eighteenth-Century Fiction*. The Hague: Mouton, 1974.

Edgeworth, Maria. *Letters from England: 1813-1844*. Ed. Christina Colvin. Oxford: Clarendon Press, 1871.

Evans, Bertram. *Gothic Drama from Walpole to Shelley*. Berkeley and Los Angeles: U of California P, 1947.

Foote, Samuel. *A Treatise on the Passions.* 1747. New York: Benjamin Blom, 1971. Facsimile.

Fox, Christopher, ed. *Psychology and Literature in the Eighteenth Century.* New York: AMS Press, 1987.

Friedman-Romell, Beth H. "Duelling Citizenships: Scottish Patriotism v. British Nationalism in Joanna Baillie's 'The Family Legend.'" *Nineteenth-Century Theatre* 26 (1998): 24-49.

———. "Staging the State: Johanna Baillie's 'Constantine Paleologus.'" Ed. Tracy C. Davis and Ellen Donkin. *Women and Playwriting in Nineteenth-Century Britain.* Cambridge: Cambridge UP, 1999. 151-73.

Fritz, Paul and David Williams, eds. *City & Society in the 18th Century.* Toronto: Hakkert, 1973.

Gamer, Michael. "National Supernaturalism: Joanna Baillie, Germany, and the Gothic Drama." *Theatre Survey: The Journal of the American Society for Theatre Research* 38:2 (1997): 49-88.

Genest, John, ed. *Some Account of the English Stage.* 1832. New York: Burt Franklin, 1965.

Gibbon, Edward. *The Decline and Fall of the Roman Empire Vol. II.* New York: The Modern Library, nd.

Gilroy, Amanda. "From Here to Alterity: The Geography of Femininity in the Poetry of Joanna Baillie." Ed. Douglas Gifford and Dorothy McMillan. *A History of Scottish Women's Writing.* Edinburgh: Edinburgh UP, 1997. 143-57.

Gross, Gloria Sybil. *This Invisible Riot of the Mind: Samuel Johnson's Psychological Theory.* Philadelphia: U of Pennsylvania P, 1992.

Hamilton, Catherine Jane. "Joanna Baillie." *Women Writers: Their Works and Ways.* Vol. 1. London and New York: Ward, Lock, Bowden, 1892-93. 110-31.

Hartley, David. *Observations on Man, His Frame, His Duty, And His Expectations.* 1749. Ed. Theodore L. Huguelet. Gainesville: Scholars' Facsimiles & Reprints, 1966.

Henderson, Andrea. "Passion and fashion in Joanna Baillie's 'Introductory Discourse.'" *PMLA* 112 (1997): 198-213.

Home, Henry, Lord Kames. *Elements of Criticism: In Three*

Volumes. 1762. Intro. Robert Voitle. Hildesheim: Georg
Olms Verlag, 1970.

———. *Essays on the Principles of Morality and Natural Religion.*
1758. Hildesheim: Georg Olms Verlag, 1976.

Hume, David. *A Treatise of Human Nature: Being an attempt to
introduce the experimental method of reasoning into moral
subjects.* 1739, 1740. Garden City: Doubleday, 1961.

Hutcheson, Francis. *An Essay on the Nature and Conduct of the
Passions and Affections.* 1728. New York: Garland Press,
1971.

Insch, A.G. "Joanna Baillie's *De Monfort* in Relation to her
Theory of Tragedy." *The Durham University Journal* 23
(June 1962): 114-20.

Jameson, Fredric. *The Political Unconscious: Narrative as a Socially
Symbolic Act.* Ithaca: Cornell UP, 1981.

Johnson, Samuel. *Samuel Johnson Selected Writings.* Ed. R.T.
Davies. London: Faber and Faber, 1965.

Keay, John and Julia, eds. *Collins Encyclopedia of Scotland.*
London: Harper Collins, 1994.

Kuritz, Paul. *The Making of Theatre History.* Englewood Cliffs:
Prentice Hall, 1988.

Lebrun, Charles. *A Method to learn to Design the Passions.* 1734.
Intro. Alan T. McKenzie. Los Angeles: U of California P,
1980.

Leech, Clifford and T.W. Craik, eds. *The Revels History of
Drama in English.* vol 6. London: Methuen, 1975.

Lindsay, Maurice. *History of Scottish Literature.* London: Robert
Hale, 1977.

Locke, John. *An Essay Concerning Human Understanding.* 4th ed.
1700. Ed. Peter H. Nidditch. Oxford: Clarendon Press,
1975.

Lonsdale, Roger, ed. *Eighteenth-Century Women Poets: An
Oxford Anthology.* Oxford: Oxford UP, 1989.

Marshall, Peter H. *William Godwin.* New Haven and London:
Yale UP, 1984.

MacMichael, William. *The Gold-Headed Cane.* 1827. London:
The Royal College of Physicians, 1968.

Mathur, Om Prakash. *The Closet Drama of the Romantic Revival.*

Salzburg: Universität Salzburg, 1978.

MacCunn, Florence. *Sir Walter Scott's Friends*. Edinburgh and London: William Blackwood, 1909.

McGann, Jerome J. *The Romantic Ideology: A Critical Investigation*. Chicago: U of Chicago P, 1983.

McKerrow, Mary. "Joanna Baillie and Mary Brunton: Women of the Manse." *Living by the Pen: Early British Women Writers*. Ed. Dale Spender. New York: Teachers College Press, 1992. 160–74.

McMillan, Dorothy. "'Dr.' Baillie." *1798: The Year of the Lyrical Ballads*. Ed. Richard Cronin. Romanticism in Perspective. 8. New York and Houndsmill: Macmillan–St. Martin's, 1998. 68–92.

Mellor, Anne K. "Joanna Baillie and the Counter-Public Sphere." *Studies in Romanticism* 33 (1994): 559–67.

Meynell, Alice. *The Second Person Singular and Other Essays*. London: Oxford UP, 1922.

Mudge, Bradford Keyes. *Sara Coleridge, A Victorian Daughter*. New Haven: Yale UP, 1989.

Murphy, Arthur. *The Life of David Garrick, Esq*. Vol. 1. London: J. Wright, 1801.

Nagler, A.M. *A Source Book in Theatrical History* (1952). New York: Dover Publications, 1959.

Nettleton, Henry George. *English Drama of the Restoration and Eighteenth Century: 1642-1780*. New York: Macmillan, 1914.

Nicoll, Allardyce. *The English Theatre: A Short History*. London: Thomas Nelson, 1936.

———. *British Drama*. London: Harrap, 1978.

Noble, Aloma E. *Joanna Baillie as a Dramatic Artist*. Ann Arbor: UMI, 1983.

Norton, M. "The Plays of Joanna Baillie." *Review of English Studies* 23 (1947): 131–43.

Norton, Rictor. *Mistress of Udolpho: The Life of Ann Radcliffe*. London: Leicester UP, 1999.

Page, Judith W. *Wordsworth and the Cultivation of Women*. Berkeley: U of California P, 1994.

Postman, Neil. *Amusing Ourselves To Death: Public Discourse in the Age of Show Business*. Harmondsworth: Penguin, 1986.

Purinton, Marjean D. *Romantic Ideologies Unmasked: The*

Mentally Constructed Tyrannies in Dramas of William Wordsworth, Lord Byron, Percy Shelley, and Joanna Baillie. Newark: U of Delaware P, 1994.

Rannie, David Watson. *Wordsworth and His Circle.* London: Methuen, 1907.

Reiman, Donald H. "Introduction." *Miscellaneous Plays by Joanna Baillie.* 3 vols. New York: Garland Press, 1977. 1: v-viii.

Richardson, Alan. "The Dangers of Sympathy: Sibling Incest in English Romantic Poetry." *SEL* 25 (1985): 737-54.

Richardson, Samuel. *Clarissa.* Ed. George Sherburn. Boston: Houghton Mifflin Company, 1962.

Roberts, R. Ellis. *Samuel Rogers and His Circle.* New York: E.P. Dutton and Company, 1910.

Rodin, Alvin E. *The Influence of Matthew Baillie's Morbid Anatomy.* Springfield, Ill.: Charles C. Thomas, 1973.

Rousseau, Jean-Jacques. *La Nouvelle Héloïse.* Trans. Judith H. McDowell. Pennsylvania: Pennsylvania State UP, 1968.

Sadler, Thomas. *A Sermon, Preached at Hampstead, on Sunday, March 9, 1851 on the Occasion of the Death of Mrs. Joanna Baillie.* London: Edward T. Whitfield, 1851.

Schiller, Friedrick. *The Poems of Schiller.* Trans. Edgar A. Bowring. New York: R. Worthington, 1851.

Scott, Sir Walter. *Marmion.* London: W & R Chambers, 1910.

———. *The Private Letter-books of Sir Walter Scott.* Ed. Wilfred Partington. London: Hodder and Stoughton, 1930.

———. *The Letters of Sir Walter Scott.* Ed. H.J.C. Grierson. London: Constable, 1932.

———. *The Journal of Sir Walter Scott.* Ed. W.E.K. Anderson. Oxford: Clarendon Press, 1972.

Scullion, Adrienne. "Some Women of the Nineteenth-Century Scottish Theatre: Joanna Baillie, Francis Wright and Helen MacGregor." Ed. Douglas Gifford and Dorothy McMillan. *A History of Scottish Women's Writing.* Edinburgh: Edinburgh UP, 1997. 158-78.

Shelley, Mary. *The Journals of Mary Shelley: 1814-1844.* Ed. Paula R. Feldman and Diana Scott-Kilvert. Oxford: Clarendon Press, 1987.

Simmons, James R. Jr. "'Small, Prim, and Quaker-Like':

Reinventing Joanna Baillie as Jane Eyre. *Brontë Society Transactions* 21:4 (1994): 149-51.

Slagle, Judith Bailey. *The Collected Letters of Joanna Baillie.* 2 vols. Madison: Fairleigh Dickinson UP, 1998.

Smith, Adam. *The Theory of Moral Sentiments.* 1759. Indianapolis: Liberty Fund, 1984.

Smith, Janet Adam. "Some Eighteenth-Century Ideas of Scotland." *Scotland in the Age of Improvement.* Ed. N.T. Phillipson and Rosalind Mitchison. Edinburgh: Edinburgh UP, 1970.

Smith, George Barnett. "Joanna Baillie." *The Dictionary of National Biography.* 22 vols. Oxford: Oxford UP, 1921. 1: 885-89.

Sotheby, William, Esq. "To Joanna Baillie." *Literary Souvenir; and Cabinet of Poetry and Romance.* Ed. Alaric A. Watts. London: Longman, Rees, Orme, Brown, Green and John Andrews, 1827. 96.

Stafford, Barbara Maria. *Body Criticism: Imaging the Unseen in Enlightenment Art and Medicine.* Cambridge: MIT Press, 1997.

Stewart, Dugald. *Elements of the Philosophy of the Human Mind.* 1792. New York: Garland Press, 1971.

Thorndike, Ashley H. *English Comedy.* 1929. New York: Cooper Square Publishers, 1965.

Thorne, J.O. and T.C. Collocott. *Chambers Biographical Dictionary.* Edinburgh: W & R Chambers, 1990.

Thorslev, Peter L. "Incest as Romantic Symbol." *Comparative Literature Studies* 2 (1965): 41-58.

Tobin, Terence. *Plays by Scots 1660-1800.* Iowa City: U of Iowa P, 1974.

Todd, Janet. *Sensibility: An Introduction.* London: Methuen, 1986.

————, ed. *British Women Writers.* New York: Continuum, 1989.

Tryon, Thomas. *A Discourse of the Causes, Natures and Cure of Phrensie, Madness or Distraction.* 1689. Intro. Michael V. DePorte. Los Angeles: The Augustan Reprint Society, 1973.

Wardrop, James, Esq. *The Life of Matthew Baillie, M.D.* London:

A. and R. Spottiswoode, 1825.

Watkins, Daniel P. "Class, Gender, and Social Motion in
Joanna Baillie's *De Monfort*." *The Wordsworth Circle* 23-2
(Spring 1992): 109-17.

Willey, Basil. *The English Moralists*. London: Chatto & Windus,
1964.

Williams, Raymond. "David Hume: Reasoning and
Experience." *Writing in Society*. London: Verso, 1983.

Wollstonecraft, Mary. *A Vindication of the Rights of Men and A
Vindication of the Rights of Woman*. Ed. D.L. Macdonald
and Kathleen Scherf. Peterborough: Broadview Press,
1997.

Wordsworth, William. *The Prelude: Selected Poems and Sonnets*.
Ed. Carlos Baker. New York: Holt, Rinehart and
Winston, 1954.

Wordsworth, William and Samuel Taylor Coleridge. *Lyrical
Ballads*. 1798, 1800. Ed. R.L. Brett and A.R. Jones.
London: Methuen, 1963.

Wordsworth, William and Dorothy. *The Letters of William and
Dorothy Wordsworth*. Ed. Alan G. Hill. 2nd ed. 8 vols.
Oxford: Clarendon Press, 1993.

Yudin, Mary. "Joanna Baillie's Introductory Discourse as a
Precursor to Wordsworth's 'Preface' to *Lyrical Ballads*."
*Compar(a)ison: An International Journal of Comparative
Literature* 1 (1994): 101-12.

Zall, P.M. "The Cool World of Samuel Taylor Coleridge: The
Question of Joanna Baillie." *The Wordsworth Circle* 13
(Winter 1982): 17-20.

Contemporary Reviews

Analytical Review 27 (May 1798): 524-28.
Annual Review 1 (1802): 680-85.
British Critic 13 (Mar. 1799): 284-90.
British Critic 20 (Aug. 1802): 184-94.
British Critic 40 (Dec. 1812): 554-59.
British Review 3 (Mar. 1812): 172-90.
Critical Review ns 24 (Sept. 1798): 13-22.
Critical Review ns 37 (Feb. 1803): 200-12.

Critical Review s4 1 (May 1812): 449-62.
Eclectic Review 10 (July 1813): 21-32; (Aug. 1813): 167-86.
Edinburgh Magazine (Scots Magazine) ns 2 (June 1818): 517-20.
Edinburgh Review 2 (July 1803): 269-86.
Edinburgh Review 19 (Feb. 1812): 261-90.
European Magazine 42 (Aug. 1802): 126.
Imperial Review 1 (Mar. 1804), 335-44; 2 (May 1804): 89-97.
Lady's Monthly Museum 13 (Aug. 1804): 126-27.
Literary Journal 5 (Jan. 1805): 49-64.
Literary Leisure 1 (Jan. 1800): 221-34.
Monthly Magazine Suppl. v5 (July 15, 1798): 507-08.
Monthly Magazine Suppl. v14 (Jan. 25, 1803): 600.
Monthly Mirror 11 (Feb. 1801): 112-14.
Monthly Mirror 14 (Oct. 1802): 258-59.
Monthly Review ns v27 (Sept. 1798): 66-69.
Monthly Review ns v43 (Jan. 1804): 31-39.
Monthly Review ns v69 (Dec. 1812): 382-93.
New Annual Register 23 (1802): [319].
New London Review 1 (Jan. 1799): 72-74.
Poetical Register 2 (1802): 449-50.

Internet Sources

Bugajski, Ken A. "Joanna Baillie: An Annotated Bibliography."
    Online. *Romanticism On the Net.* Internet. October 1999.
    Available: users.ox.ac.uk/~scato385/bwpbaillie.html.
Carlson, Julie A. Rev. of *Closet Stages: Joanna Baillie and the
    Theater Theory of British Romantic Women Writers.* Online.
    Romantic Circles. Internet. Jan. 1999.
    Available: http://www.otal.umd.edu/rc/reviews/
    burroughs.html.
Hume, David. "Essays on Suicide and the Immortality of the
    Soul." 1783. *The Writings of David Hume.* Ed. James Fieser
    (Internet Release 1995). *Five Dissertations.* National
    Library of Scotland. Online. Internet. May 1999.
    Available: jfieser@utm.edu.
Johnson, Samuel. "Review of Soame Jenyns, 'A Free Enquiry
    into the Nature and Origin of Evil.'" 1757. *The Works of*

Samuel Johnson. 1825. Online. Internet. October 1999.
Available: andromeda.rutgers.edu/~jlynch/Texts/jenyns.
html.